The Development of Russian
Evangelical Spirituality

The Development of Russian Evangelical Spirituality

A Study of Ivan V. Kargel (1849–1937)

GREGORY L. NICHOLS

◆PICKWICK *Publications* · Eugene, Oregon

THE DEVELOPMENT OF RUSSIAN EVANGELICAL SPIRITUALITY
A Study of Ivan V. Kargel (1849–1937)

Copyright © 2011 Gregory L. Nichols. All rights reserved. Except for brief quotations in critical publications or reviews, no part of this book may be reproduced in any manner without prior written permission from the publisher. Write: Permissions, Wipf and Stock Publishers, 199 W. 8th Ave., Suite 3, Eugene, OR 97401.

Pickwick Publications
An Imprint of Wipf and Stock Publishers
199 W. 8th Ave., Suite 3
Eugene, OR 97401

www.wipfandstock.com

ISBN 13: 978-1-61097-160-7

Cataloguing-in-Publication data:

Nichols, Gregory L.

The development of Russian evangelical spirituality : a study of Ivan V. Kargel (1849–1937) / Gregory L. Nichols.

xiv + 382 pp. ; 23 cm. Includes bibliographical references and index.

ISBN 13: 978-1-61097-160-7

1. Kargel, Ivan Veniaminovich. 2. Baptists—Russia—History—19th century. 3. Baptists—Russia—History—20th century. 4. Baptists—Soviet Union—History. 5. Russia—Church history—19th century. 6. Russia—Church history—20th century. I. Title.

BX6310.R8 N56 2011

Manufactured in the U.S.A.

Contents

Foreword • vii

Preface • ix

Acknowledgments • xi

Abbreviations • xiii

1 Introduction: Johann Kargel and the Evangelical World • 1

2 The Shaping of a Baptist Leader (1849–1874) • 21

3 First Saint Petersburg Period: Exposed to Evangelicalism (1875–1880) • 47

4 Bulgarian Period: Released from Spiritual Narrowness (1880–1884) • 80

5 Second Saint Petersburg Period: Part of the Pashkovite Circle (1884–1887) • 105

6 Reaching the Russian Empire (1887–1898) • 139

7 Third Saint Petersburg Period: Evangelical Christian Endeavors (1898–1909) • 178

8 Teaching on the Sanctified Life • 218

9 Kargel as a Spiritual Guide • 253

10 Conclusion • 294

Appendix 1: 1913 Confession of Faith by Ivan V. Kargel • 309

Appendix 2: Timeline • 315

Appendix 3: Map of German Baptist Churches in Eastern Volhynia • 329

Appendix 4: Kargel's Map of his Trip to Siberia in 1890 from *Zwischen den Ended der Erde* • 330

Appendix 5: Map of the Caucasus Region • 331

Appendix 6: Map of the Provinces of Western (European) Russia, c. 1900 • 332

Appendix 7: Map of the Historic Russian Provinces in Modern-day Ukraine • 333

Appendix 8: Photograph of Ivan Kargel • 334

Appendix 9: Sketching of Ivan Kargel • 335

Bibliography • 337

Index • 359

Foreword

I CONSIDER THAT THIS book marks a significant new phase in academic studies of the history of evangelical Christianity in Russia. A limited number of such studies have been undertaken, but this work by Gregory Nichols probes at more depth than has been done before, the nature of the evangelical spirituality that emerged in Russia in the later nineteenth century and the early twentieth century. This is done by an examination of the life, the influence and the varied contributions of Johann (Ivan) Kargel (1849-1937). The story of evangelicalism in the English-speaking world has been very well told and perceptively analyzed by a number of historians in recent years. The main figures and the defining features in that story are well known. However, readers of such histories are unlikely to know much, if anything, about Ivan Kargel. Yet he is a figure of enormous significance in the Russian context.

One of the strengths of this study is that it makes clear the varied, and at times complex, connections between Kargel and streams of evangelical spirituality in Germany and in England. This is done through an examination of crucial sources in three languages—Russian, German, and English. Of particular importance is the use made of the Pashkov Papers, originally available at the University of Birmingham. Now, thanks to efforts by Gregory Nichols, a copy of this very important and extensive archive of material relating to major Russian evangelical developments is available at the International Baptist Theological Seminary, Prague. From the analysis of correspondence in particular, the inner as well as the outer experiences of these evangelical communities is brought to life in this book in a new and vivid way.

The research into Ivan Kargel and Russian evangelical spirituality and the fruit of that research to be found here will be of great interest to those who want to understand more about the richness of evangelical history in Russia. Over several decades Kargel was a central and shaping figure in this wider story. The specific nature of holiness thinking in Russia is also illuminated by this book in a way that has not been done in any other academic work. The way in which Kargel absorbed Keswick and Brethren thinking and adapted them to the Russian setting as he pursued and promoted his own spiritual and ecclesial aspirations is particularly revealing.

Baptists in Russia look back to Kargel as one of their most revered spiritual leaders. Gregory Nichols has calculated that nearly 25 percent of the all the issues of the main Russian Baptist periodical *Bratsky Vestnik* [The Fraternal Herald] published between its beginnings in 1945 and the year 1988 contained an article from or a reference to Ivan Kargel. Volumes of his works have been re-published in recent years. Thus this book provides invaluable insights into what was at one time the largest Baptist community in Europe. Also, because of Kargel's prolific evangelistic travels and links with Baptists in other countries, this study ranges widely across Eastern European countries, and all those who are engaged in work on religion in Eastern Europe will find themselves greatly indebted to Gregory Nichols for the way he has coupled painstaking original research and a compelling presentation.

Ian M. Randall
Senior Research Fellow
International Baptist Theological Seminary
Prague

Preface

THIS BOOK FOCUSES ON the way in which the life and ministry of Johann G. Kargel (1849–1937), also known as Ivan Veniaminovich Kargel, contributed to the formation of the identity of Russian-speaking evangelicals, particularly as it relates to their understanding of Christian spirituality. The focus is on Kargel's personal development and ministry, first within the German Baptist context as a German Baptist minister in Saint Petersburg and as a Baptist pioneer in Bulgaria, and then later as a major leader among Russian evangelicals. He had an enormous influence within the Russian evangelical milieu of his time, particularly through his approach to spirituality. The book shows how Kargel related to the different streams of evangelical life in Russia.

In the early days of the Free Church movements in the Russian Empire, there were three distinct starting points: southern Russia, which produced the Mennonite Brethren and Stundists, Tiflis which produced the Russian Baptist Union, and Saint Petersburg which produced the Evangelical Christian Union. Kargel was connected, in varying degrees, with each of these groups, and had considerable influence as a leader within the Evangelical Christian movement. A crucial connection for Kargel was with Colonel Vasily Pashkov, a wealthy and aristocratic figure in Saint Petersburg. From the 1880s onwards Kargel committed himself to the non-denominational evangelical approach of Pashkov and also attempted to promote a form of evangelical spirituality derived from the holiness movements that affected evangelicalism from the 1870s onwards. Kargel was especially drawn to the spirituality of the Keswick Convention.

The book has been organized mainly as a chronological study, since there are clear phases in Kargel's spiritual development. The first chapters show how he was shaped initially by German Baptist thinking, but then felt that this approach to church life and spiritual experience was too narrow. As part of the Pashkovite circle Kargel had many opportunities to reach out across the Russian Empire, and his activities in this area are examined as part of the analysis of his spiritual development. The last two chapters of the book give particular attention to the final decades of Kargel's life and in particular to his contribution as one who commended the teaching of the inner life and who acted as a spiritual guide.

In this study I have relied heavily upon primary sources, most notable the large number of personal letters between Pashkov and the Kargels (both Ivan and his wife Anna). This source has not previously been used in this way. From these sources, the book offers a new understanding of the shaping of Russian-speaking evangelicalism and in particular of its spirituality. Kargel was uniquely influential in this process of development and his writings continue to affect evangelical Christians in several countries in Eastern Europe.

Acknowledgments

I am deeply indebted to many people who have encouraged me in various ways during the research and writing of this book. Dr. Ian Randall's guidance, encouragement, questions, and suggestions have proven invaluable as I have made my way through this project. In addition to being an excellent formal supervisor he has proved to be a challenging conversation partner and personal mentor. I must also thank Sergei V. Sannikov who provided early guidance, directing me to Ivan Kargel and the tremendous benefit that would result from an in-depth examination of his influence on Russian evangelicals. I give a deep heart-felt thank you to Albert Wardin, who has spent many hours with me in correspondence, in conferences, and in his home. He has been a priceless source of information, accurate details, and inspiration. I am also indebted to Marina S. Karetnikova for her relentless efforts to gather and publish Kargel's Russian material. My research would not have been possible without her work.

I am thankful to the International Baptist Theological Seminary (IBTS) whose community has shown itself to be matchless in regards to research in this area. The academic standards, when matched with a broad range of experience and placed within a diverse cultural community, have been of great benefit. I am thankful for the challenge and opportunity that Keith Jones, the IBTS Rector, and Parush Parushev, the Academic Dean, provided for me in learning the discipline of presenting papers and participating in the outstanding conferences held on the Prague campus, where I was exposed to scholars from around the world. As a result of their encouragement, some of this material has been published in *Eastern European Baptist History: New Perspectives* and *Baptistic Theologies*. I am also grateful for the excellent library of IBTS and for Katharina Penner who went beyond standard expectations in her assistance to me. I must also extend a thank you to Philippa Bassett, archivist for the University of Birmingham, England, and for their permission to use the Pashkov Papers in this work, as well as for their assistance in ensuring that a copy of this vital archive is available in continental Europe at the International Baptist Theological Seminary.

I am also thankful to David Malone, former classmate and Head of Wheaton College Archives and Special Collections, for his painstaking care of some unique sources that have been beneficial to this work. Thanks are given to Bill Sumner and the Southern Baptist Historical Library and Archives in Nashville, Tennessee, for the time they provided me during my visit. Likewise, my thanks go to Alf Redekopp and Lawrence Klippenstein and the Mennonite Heritage Centre in Winnipeg, Manitoba, for the hours they gave me in my research. Johannes Dyck must also be acknowledged for his crucial assistance with documents, his helpful insights, and his willingness to share his knowledge on the various topics in which we are involved together in research. Jerry Frank is to be thanked for his research and creation of four maps, which are included as appendices. These will be especially useful as he has identified and listed the various names of many of the locations mentioned in this book. My appreciation also goes to Tony DiLeonardi for quiet hours of writing afforded me in his family's cabin. The language has been improved at various stages by Phil Alexander, Janice Randall, and Mary Raber for which I am truly thankful.

Finally, this would not have been possible without the assistance of Deborah Nichols, my wife. Her willingness to spend countless hours with me in the translation and interpretation of the German sources has added a depth to this work that it otherwise would not have possessed. In addition, Debby willingly took on extra responsibility at home and in ministry, which provided me with the time and peace to complete this project.

Abbreviations

AUCEC-B	All Union Council of Evangelical Christians-Baptists
BWA	Baptist World Alliance
ECU	Evangelical Christian Union
HEC-B	History of Evangelical Christians-Baptist in the USSR
MB	Mennonite Brethren
n.d.	No date listed
n.p.	No publisher, no place of publication listed
o.s.	Old Style (Julian calendar)
SESER	Society for the Encouragement of Spiritual and Ethical Reading

1

Introduction

Johann Kargel and the Evangelical World

JOHANN G. KARGEL[1] (1849–1937) was one of the most formative leaders in the Russian-speaking evangelical world, where he is known as Ivan Veniaminovich Kargel. He wrote and taught in German and Russian, using either of the above names depending on the language in which he was working.[2] His writings and teaching in the later nineteenth- and early twentieth-century period helped to shape the Russian evangelical movement and Russian Baptist expressions of evangelical spirituality. His influence was not limited to the Russian Empire but spread to other countries that bordered on the Empire. There are evangelical movements in several countries that claim Ivan Kargel as a major contributor to their formation.[3]

When Johann Kargel is examined in the light of contemporary understandings of Christian spirituality, he is clearly to be identified with the evangelical Holiness stream of spirituality within Protestant life.[4] The evangelical spirituality that took shape in the eighteenth-century English-speaking world was to spread and significantly

---

1. Johann Kargel often used the letter "G" to represent a second name when signing his works. It is not known what "G" represents. His descendents have suggested that it possibly stands for "Gustav," which is a name the family still uses.

2. Throughout this work, I will use the name Johann when Kargel was working primarily in German or in a German-speaking context and the name Ivan when, later on, he was working primarily in a Russian environment.

3. Such groups include the Evangelical Christian Union, the Baptist Union, and the Union of Christians of Evangelical Faith-Pentecostals, all in the Russian-speaking world; the Baptists of Germany, Bulgaria, and Estonia; and the Russian-speaking evangelicals of Finland.

4. See Randall, *What a Friend We Have in Jesus*.

impact Christianity in other countries.[5] Kargel was shaped by a view of spirituality that was not only generally evangelical, but was also particular to the Holiness stream. His writings exhibit traits similar to the Holiness spirituality of the English Keswick Convention.[6] Kargel developed a particular perspective on Christian spirituality: he called people to personal trust in Jesus Christ for both justification and sanctification; focused in his teaching on "abiding in Christ" in order to live a life of victory; stressed the power of the Holy Spirit; and saw the life of discipleship as involving following Christ on the pathway of suffering. This book will examine the various influences on Kargel's life and seek to show how he developed a unique expression of evangelical spirituality in the Russian setting.

JOHANN KARGEL AND THE RUSSIAN BAPTIST CONTEXT

Four Russian authors have written on the life of Ivan Kargel. Marina Sergeevna Karetnikova[7] and Irina N. Skopina[8] both divide his life into two periods, a Russian period and a Ukrainian period. Because of the inaccessibility of German documents to these writers, they have not been able to give much attention to the other aspects of Ivan Kargel's life among the Germans, Bulgarians, Finns, and Estonians.

The third writer, Dimitry Turchaninov,[9] is apparently unaware of Kargel's life prior to his arrival in Saint Petersburg in 1875. In his biography, Turchaninov claims that when Kargel first appeared there in his mid-twenties he was not yet an evangelical believer. Turchaninov describes how the young Kargel was wandering the streets of Saint Petersburg when he stumbled across some Pashkovites (named after Colonel Vasily Alexandrovich Pashkov). The young man listened to their evangelical message, repented, and began a life of ministry.[10]

---

5. See Noll, *The Rise of Evangelicalism*.

6. For Holiness streams in England in the nineteenth century, see Bebbington, *Holiness in Nineteenth-Century England*.

7. See Karetnikova, "Ivan Veniaminovich Kargel," 684–88 as well as various other reprints and editions, including her paper given on the seventieth anniversary of Kargel's death, Karetnikova, "Biografiya I. V. Kargelya" and her paper given on the 150th anniversary of Kargel's birth, Karetnikova, "Velikij Duxovnyj Uchitel.'"

8. Skopina, "Iz Biografii I. V. Kargelya," 689–701.

9. Turchaninov, "Vospominanie o Zhizni i Sluzhenii Kargelya."

10. Ibid., para. 1.

In reality, however, when Johann Kargel arrived in Saint Petersburg in 1875, he had already been a student at Johann Oncken's Baptist Mission School in Hamburg and had served as a Baptist pastor in the Volhynia region of the Russian Empire.[11] Johann Kargel committed himself to full-time Christian ministry while in the Molotschna Settlement in 1873 when attending a conference convened by the emerging Mennonite Brethren, a revivalist offshoot of the Mennonite movement.[12]

These three biographies of Kargel, because they were researched during the Soviet period, did not have access to the primary sources that are now available. A fourth work on Kargel, however, was completed recently. In 2009, Miriam Kuznetsova completed her doctoral dissertation "Early Russian Evangelicals (1874–1929): Historical Background and Hermeneutical Tendencies based on I. V. Kargel's written Heritage." Her purpose was to explore the "hermeneutical principles [which] guided the reading and understanding of Scripture by the Russian evangelicals, specifically by I. V. Kargel."[13] The work contains some very useful material as it examines the writings of Kargel to define his hermeneutical approach to Scripture and theology. Because of the focused nature of her work, Kuznetsova chose to rely on the writings of Karetnikova, Skopina, and Turchaninov for much of her background material. She does however manage to challenge or reconcile some of their findings in light of newer evidence.[14]

Some details of the early years of Johann Kargel's ministry were reported among the many stories about the German Baptists that were printed in journals such as *Missionsblatt aus der Brüdergemeine* (*Missionsblatt*), *Wahrheitszeuge*, *The Baptist Missionary Magazine*, and *Quarterly Reporter of the German Baptist Mission*.[15] *Missionsblatt*

---

11. For Johann Oncken, see Balders, *Theurer Bruder Oncken*.
12. Kargel, *Zwischen den Enden*, viii; Kargel, "Soroczin," 83–88.
13. Kuznetsova, "Early Russian Evangelicals," 14.
14. For evidence of this see Kuznetsova, "Early Russian Evangelicals," 282, 285, 296, 306, 310.
15. *Missionsblatt aus der Brüdergemeine* was renamed *Wahrheitszeuge* in 1880. *The Quarterly Reporter of the German Baptist Mission* translated and reprinted much from *Missionsblatt* and *Wahrheitszeuge*. *The Missionary Magazine* was renamed *The Baptist Missionary Magazine* in 1872 and was published by the American Baptist Missionary Union.

described some of Kargel's time in Volhynia.[16] Accounts of his early years in Saint Petersburg in the 1870s were published in *Quarterly Reporter of the German Baptist Mission*,[17] *The Baptist Missionary Magazine*,[18] and *Wahrheitszeuge*.[19] His move to Bulgaria in 1880 was extensively depicted in *Wahrheitszeuge*[20] and *Quarterly Reporter of the German Baptist Mission*.[21] By 1884, when Kargel moved back to Russia, the German Baptists were no longer reporting on his ministry. Beginning in 1895, *Zionsbote*, the German-language journal published in the United States by the Mennonite Churches of North America, began to publish numerous works by Johann Kargel and these were still being published in 1904.[22] These publications were not about his life and ministry, but were theological writings that exhibited the strong influence of the evangelical Holiness tradition. At no time has anyone been able to bring together the German and Russian sources to produce a comprehensive narrative and analysis of the life and thought of Johann G. Kargel.

As I have examined the sources and attempted to piece Kargel's history together, I have perceived two perspectives regarding the beginnings of the Russian Baptists.[23] One perspective tends to downplay the international connections: this protected the Baptists and other evangelicals from the Russian Orthodox and later Soviet accusation of being an imported sect of non-Russian origin.[24] These authors tend to highlight the influence of the Orthodox breakaway group, the Molokans,[25] seeing them as being closely associated with the development of Russian Baptist theology.[26] They often play down the German

16. Kargel, "Soroczin," 83–88.
17. Kargel, "Russia, Further News," 4–6; "Work in St. Petersburg," 8–9.
18. "Mission to the Germans," 270–73; "Recognition of the Church," 124–25.
19. "Erste Fruechte," 54.
20. "Eine Reise nach Kasanlik [part one]," 94; "Eine Reise nach Kasanlik [part two]," 104; Kargel, "Bulgarei," 59–61.
21. "Bulgaria," 11–13.
22. Kargel, "Pura," 1; Kargel,"Ein Guter Anfang [part two]," 1.
23. For a detailed analysis of the two perspectives see Nesdoly, "Evangelical Sectarianism in Russia," chapter 3.
24. Beeson, *Discretion and Valour*, 98–101. He places the Baptists under his section entitled "Sects of Soviet Origin."
25. This term was first used after the 1654 reforms of Patriarch Nikon.
26. Hebly, *Protestants in Russia*, 74–83.

influence.²⁷ In an extreme version of this perspective, the start of the Baptist movement has been explained as a "Christian reform" that occurred in Russia.²⁸

The second perspective has tended to highlight the Western roots of the Baptists. This view was used by some to argue that the Baptists were indeed an imported sect from the West with no legitimacy in Russia.²⁹ Others have used this perspective to suggest that while the Russian Baptists have roots outside Russian soil, they were not a dangerous sect but evolved through natural contacts with the international community as a "synthesis of Western Protestantism with Russian-Ukrainian piety."³⁰ This view highlights organic links with outsiders such as the Anabaptists, English Puritans, and German Baptists.³¹ Using this perspective, some have shown the benefits of the Baptists within Russian society, calling them the "backbone of Russian Protestantism."³²

Prior to the fall of Communism in Eastern Europe, writers from within the worldwide evangelical community had to be careful not to write in such a way as further to endanger vulnerable evangelicals living within Communist lands. Additionally, much of the primary historical material that could have shed light on the Baptist story was locked away within the Soviet Union. Since the fall of Communism, writers from the 1990s onwards have gained access to many primary sources that are shedding new light on the varied beginnings of the Baptist movement. The opening of Russian archives has also enabled

---

27. Nesdoly, "Evangelical Sectarianism in Russia," 135–97; Shubin, *A History of Russian Christianity*, vol. III, 160–61.

28. Savinskij, *Istoriya Russko-Ukrainskogo Baptizma*, 17.

29. Dorodnicyn, *Yuzhno-Russkij neobaptizm, izvestnyj pod" imenem" shtundy. Po ofictial'nym" dokumentam*; Dorodnicyn, *Religiozno-racionalisticheskoe dvizhenie na Yuge Rossii vo vtoroj polovine 19-go stoletiya*; Pobedonostsev to Vasilij Alexandrovich, December 1884, *Pism'a Pobedonosteva k Aleksandru III*, M. N. Pokrovskij, editor (Moskva, 1923), vol. II, 158–60, as cited in Heier, *Religious Schism*, 139–42. *Missionerskoe Obozrenie* and *Obzor" Sektantskoj Literatury* were two journals dedicated to covering the activities of non-Orthodox groups and proving that they had no legitimacy in Russian. For an explanation of the works by Dorodnicyn see Wardin, *Evangelical Sectarianism*, 81–83.

30. Kolarz, *Religion in the Soviet Union*, 283.

31. Struve, "Other Christian Denominations," 135; Kuznetsova, "Early Russian Evangelicals," 62.

32. Bolshakoff, *Russian Nonconformity*, 128.

authors to explore new territory in regard to sectarianism,[33] dissenting movements,[34] and folk religions[35] in Russia. These fresh perspectives have provided new sources of primary material. Their interpretations of the Russian sources have highlighted areas that overlap with Russian evangelical studies, such as Russian morality, little-known religious sects, and the migration of people groups within the Russian Empire and the Soviet Union. Mennonite Brethren have also become more open in their acknowledgement of the significant role that the German Baptists played in their own formation in Ukraine.[36] These factors have contributed to a new freedom to enter into an atmosphere of open dialogue and ground-breaking research among those involved in the study of the multi-faceted Free Church expression of Christianity within Russian lands.[37]

The historians who have told the story of the Free Church movement in the Russian Empire often speak of three streams that converged to form the present-day Evangelical Christians-Baptists Union. The three streams are often summarized as: Baptists in the Caucasus, Stundism in Ukraine, and the Pashkovite movement in Saint Petersburg.[38] This model is helpful in understanding the present-day situation, but it does not provide an adequate portrayal of spiritual continuity within the European context. There are significant similarities between the Russian story and broader progressions of evangelical history and theology, particularly in Europe, which have not yet been explored. In particular, the existence of a Holiness movement in Russian evangelical life, one that drew from wider sources but was shaped in a distinctive way in the Russian context, has never been analyzed. The story of the Holiness revival across Europe has been told by M. E. Dieter in *The Holiness Revival of the Nineteenth Century*,[39] but the Russian scene is not mentioned. In 1875, the year in which Kargel

33. See Zhuk, *Russia's Lost Reformation*.

34. See Boobbyer, *Conscience, Dissent and Reform*.

35. See Heretz, *Russia on the Eve of Modernity*.

36. Wardin, "Mennonite Brethren and German Baptists in Russia," 101.

37. For a fuller discussion of these ideas see Corrado, "In Search of an Eastern European Identity," 7–13.

38. Sawatsky, *Soviet Evangelicals*, 33; Steeves, "The Russian Baptist Union," chapter 1; Belousov, "Tri Kolybeli Bratstva," 9–19; Coleman, *Russian Baptists and Spiritual Revolution*, chapter 1; Kolarz, *Religion in the Soviet Union*, 283.

39. See Dieter, *The Holiness Revival of the Nineteenth Century*.

began his ministry in Saint Petersburg, the Keswick Convention began in the English Lake District. Interdenominational Holiness teaching began to spread from this increasingly influential annual convention and similar conventions elsewhere.[40] I want to explore in this work the extent to which Kargel can be seen as a shaping leader of a Holiness movement within the Russian Empire.

PIETISTIC AND EVANGELICAL MOVEMENTS

Holiness thinking had a pre-history. An important strand that can be traced from the eighteenth century onwards was Pietism. The Pietist movement, as W. R. Ward argues in *The Protestant Evangelical Awakening*, owes much to the work of the Lutheran pastor Philip Spener, although there were others within his circle in the seventeenth century who shared his concerns. In 1675 Spener published an introduction to some devotional sermons by Johann Arndt, a Lutheran theologian, and then went on to produce what was to become his best known work, with the title *Pia Desideria, or Heartfelt Desires for an Improvement of the True Evangelical Church Pleasing to God, with Some Christian Proposals to That End*. In the English-speaking world this book was to become known as *Pious Wishes*. It is from this title that the term "Pietism"—used initially by Spener's opponents—came into popular use.[41]

Pietism introduced two fresh ideas into Protestantism. First, as it developed, it allowed, and indeed encouraged, interdenominational relationships based on the idea of unity in the essentials of the faith and diversity in non-essentials. Second, Pietism gave the Protestant churches affected by it an understanding that "heart knowledge" was more important than "head knowledge."[42] The emergence of the Pietist movement was a pivotal point in the history of wider European Protestantism and later, especially through German communities, Pietism was to have a bearing on the shape of Russian evangelical life.

In a sermon in 1669 Spener called for the opportunity for Lutheran laymen to meet together—in groups that were termed

40. For Keswick see Barabas, *So Great Salvation*; Pollock, *The Keswick Story*; Price and Randall, *Transforming Keswick*.

41. Ward, *The Protestant Evangelical Awakening*, 57.

42. For an introduction to Pietism see Stoeffler, *German Pietism during the Eighteenth Century*.

collegia pietatis—and lay aside their glasses of beer, cards, and dice to think about Christ in each other.[43] Pietism developed and spread from the German and wider continental Lutheran Church, affecting other Christian movements. A major missionary thrust came from the Herrnhut community in Germany in the eighteenth century. The patron and spiritual guide of the community, Count Nicolas Von Zinzendorf, was a graduate of the University of Halle, a center in the spread of Pietism. In 1722 Zinzendorf opened his estate in southeast Saxony to a group of Protestant refugees from Bohemia and Moravia.[44] In 1727 the Herrnhut community experienced an intense spiritual awakening.[45] The Renewed Unity of the Brethren, or the Moravian movement,[46] was founded, which embraced a worldwide missionary vision.[47] A number of the emphases to be found in Pietism, notably the crucial place of spiritual experience, were to characterize the ministry of Kargel.

The experience of spiritual renewal that found expression in the eighteenth-century Evangelical Revival in Britain, and, in America, in the Great Awakening, is also central to an understanding of the currents that shaped Kargel. David Bebbington describes in *Evangelicalism in Modern Britain* how the decade beginning in 1734 "witnessed in the English-speaking world a more important development than any other, before or after, in the history of Protestant Christianity: the emergence of the movement that became Evangelicalism."[48] Studies of evangelicalism over recent years have generally followed the argument advanced by Bebbington that evangelicalism—molded in its early period by leaders such as Jonathan Edwards, John Wesley, and George Whitefield—is a movement comprising all those who stress conversion, the cross, the Bible, and activism.[49] Each of these emphases is evident in Kargel's thinking.

Writing about relationship with God, Kargel remarked that Martin Luther was not "saved" when he entered the monastery,

---

43. Spener, *Pia Desideria*, 13.
44. For Zinzendorf see Lewis, *Zinzendorf: The Ecumenical Pioneer*.
45. Podmore, *The Moravian Church in England*, 6.
46. For a standard history see Hutton, *A History of the Moravian Church*.
47. Mason, *The Moravian Church and the Missionary Awakening in England*, 6.
48. Bebbington, *Evangelicalism in Modern Britain*, 20.
49. Ibid., 2–17.

despite the fact that he knew many things.[50] Without a point of conversion, Kargel doubted whether there was true salvation. The cross of Christ was vital to Kargel's theology. In his personal letters, he referred to sharing "the Word of the cross."[51] Kargel wrote that the power of sin could be broken and remain broken if a person, with a living faith, came to the cross to receive pardon and ascended to the cross with Christ to be crucified with him.[52] Kargel's theology was biblical. He believed that the Bible was "daily spiritual food" for the Christian.[53] Every declaration in his Confession of Faith,[54] which was written in 1913 and widely accepted by Russian evangelicals, is accompanied by verses from Scripture, pointing to his belief that ultimate authority is found in the Bible. Finally, there is activism, which springs from Kargel's belief that action should be a result of the conversion experience. Evangelical spirituality has often been marked by "a round of ceaseless activity."[55] This was true of Kargel, as he travelled relentlessly, preaching and teaching across the Russian Empire.

THE HOLINESS EMPHASIS

In addition to Pietism and evangelicalism, I will argue that Kargel advocated the tenets of Holiness theology as expressed particularly in the Keswick Convention.[56] The Holiness or "Higher Life" movement (as it was called) was shaped by a number of nineteenth-century figures. Under the influence of speakers and writers such as Phoebe Palmer with her "Tuesday Meetings for the Promotion of Holiness" in New York City in the 1830s, Wesleyan ideas of perfection were

50. Kargel, "V Kakom Ty Otnoshenii k Duxu Svyatomu?" 116.

51. I. V. Kargel to "Dear brother in Christ" [V. A. Pashkov], 26 May, 1884, 2/13/025, Pashkov Papers.

52. Kargel, "Grex Kak Zlo Vsex Zol v Etom Mire," 34.

53. Kargel, "Xristos Osvyashhenie Nashe," 92.

54. This Confession of Faith was originally written by Ivan Kargel when he served as pastor for the Second Evangelical Congregation of Saint Petersburg. It was adopted by the All-Union Council of Evangelical Christians-Baptists in 1966 as their official doctrinal statement and it remained so until 1984. It will be discussed further in chapter 8; an English translation of the 1913 Confession of Faith is included as an appendix to this book.

55. Bebbington, *Holiness in Nineteenth-Century England*, 40.

56. The Keswick links to the German Holiness movement, particularly in Blankenburg, will be mentioned in the final chapter as an area for further research.

transformed into the ideas of "laying all on the altar" and a "baptism of the Holy Spirit." W. E. Boardman's book *The Higher Christian Life*, which appeared in 1858, was important. Gradually this new thrust made inroads into British Christianity. It was felt in the Evangelical Alliance, which encouraged a prayer union for all who had the "purity of the church" and the "welfare of the soul at heart."[57] The ministry of an American couple, Robert Pearsall Smith, and his wife, Hannah Whitall Smith, contributed much to the emergence of a British Holiness movement outside the Wesleyan tradition. In 1875, Hannah Whitall Smith's book, *The Christian's Secret of a Happy Life*, was published; this has been considered to be the "most influential book of all in the origins of Keswick."[58] Hannah and Robert made several trips to England. "Union Meetings for Consecration" were held, such as the "Oxford Union for the Promotion of Scriptural Holiness" in 1874, which was attended by 1,500 people from various denominations. The participants included English society figures and ministers and leaders from several countries, including Britain, Germany, France, Switzerland, and America.[59]

The British Holiness movement took an enduring form in 1875. After huge meetings in Brighton at which Hannah Whitall Smith was a much-acclaimed speaker, the Keswick Convention was launched. Bebbington sees the characteristics of Keswick as including poetic inclinations, the appeal of nature, an exaltation of faith, an internal sense of peace, repression of sin, an element of crisis, and a premillennial view of the eschaton. He refers to "Romantic affinities," such as admiration for William Wordsworth, and describes some of those who influenced Keswick, such as [Robert] Pearsall Smith and Charles Fox, as being on the verge of the "mystical" in their inclinations.[60] Another related characteristic of Keswick spirituality was that faith was viewed as the means to sanctification. Ian Randall notes: "Evangelical conceptions of holy living achieved through sustained struggle were replaced, in the spirituality purveyed at Keswick, by the idea that sanctification, like justification, was attained through faith, not works."[61] Keswick's

---

57. Dieter, *The Holiness Revival of the Nineteenth Century*, 157.
58. Bebbington, *Holiness in Nineteenth-Century England*, 76–77.
59. Dieter, *The Holiness Revival of the Nineteenth Century*, 166–67.
60. Bebbington, *Holiness in Nineteenth-Century England*, 79.
61. Randall, *Evangelical Experiences*, 14.

concept of sanctification was that of a "rest of faith."[62] Sanctification was not to be found in a human struggle against sin but by the power of God, which enabled victory over sin. Similarly, for Kargel, the faith that led to a silent and untroubled rest was the mark of true faith in a believer.[63] Keswick taught the repression or counteraction of the sinful nature rather than its eradication, thus denying widespread Wesleyan eradicationist convictions.[64] The view that the sinful nature is suppressed rather than eliminated will be seen to be the stance taken by Kargel.

Often the way into the deeper holy life was through a moment of crisis. Thus, "Keswick stressed that holiness came by personal consecration."[65] This was not simply a verbal commitment made by an individual, but was a full surrender and dedication with a resolve to submit to the demands of God. It involved human co-operation with God, but not co-operation through human effort. Rather, there was a desire to "abide in Christ." Kargel subscribed to this idea of consecration. He wrote that many believers did not know power because they "never declared a claim to the promise of it as our own property."[66] In his later writings, as will be seen, this idea of declaring a claim was replaced by the idea of an ongoing and active process of consecration. This also resonates with Keswick spirituality, which held that there were recurring times when a person needed to experience a special filling. Kargel wrote that "only one thing is necessary," which for him was "to give yourself entirely to the Holy Spirit daily."[67]

The final characteristic of Keswick theology, according to Bebbington, was a premillennial view of the Second Coming of Christ. Belief in the personal return of Jesus fitted the strong Holiness emphasis on power over sin. Jesus might personally appear at any time as the "heroic deliverer," taking his place "on the stage of the world to set everything right."[68] Bible teachers associated with Keswick were

---

62. For an explanation of the Quaker roots of this term see Bebbington, *Evangelicalism in Modern Britain*, 155–57.
63. Kargel, "Xristos Osvyashhenie Nashe," 97.
64. Bebbington, *Evangelicalism in Modern Britain*, 173–74.
65. Randall, *Evangelical Experiences*, 27.
66. Kargel, "V Kakom Ty Otnoshenii k Duxu Svyatomu?" 122.
67. Ibid., 150.
68. Bebbington, *Holiness in Nineteenth-Century England*, 83.

speakers at major prophetic gatherings.[69] The international Keswick movement, combining distinctive elements regarding the spiritual life, was to affect evangelical thinking in Russia, and Kargel was a crucial conduit.

THE RUSSIAN ORTHODOX CONTEXT

The Russian Orthodox Church was the cultural and religious backdrop for many Baptists in the Russian Empire, including Kargel. The Russian Orthodox Church has been an integral part of Russian culture and experience since 988. Although Kargel was not raised in an Orthodox home, most of his life was spent in an Orthodox country as a naturalized citizen. The Orthodox Church, in its theological and spiritual teaching, has not emphasized a rational systematic theology.[70] Orthodoxy considers its liturgy as a "source and expression" of its theology, rather than looking to an external source such as the "magisterium or the Bible."[71] It is deeply held within Orthodox spirituality that elements of the Christian faith must remain a mystery; no human mind is capable of fully comprehending God. Through the practice of *katharsis* (purification) the Orthodox believer uses "negative theology" (stating what God is not) to contemplate Truth.[72] Within Orthodoxy, salvation is viewed as a process called deification or *theosis*. This process takes place exclusively within the Orthodox Church, primarily through the sacraments by which "the Holy Spirit works to give grace and deify people."[73]

The Orthodox Church is inseparable from its national culture in lands that have adopted the Orthodox faith. Konstantin Pobedonostsev, **Ober**-Procurator (General Director) of the Most Holy Synod of the Russian Orthodox Church from 1880 until 1905, held that "Russian nationalism" was "the purpose of the ROC [Russian

---

69. Marsden, *Understanding Fundamentalism and Evangelicalism*, 37, 72, 79; Sandeen, *The Roots of Fundamentalism*, 132–44.

70. Ware, *The Orthodox Way*, 12–32.

71. Meyendorff, *Byzantine Theology*, 115. Meyendorff, in this same work, states that theology should be based on Scripture yet "able to reach beyond the letter of Scripture." See page 13.

72. Ibid., 11–13.

73. Fairbairn, *Eastern Orthodoxy through Western Eyes*, 88.

Orthodox Church] and the imperial monarchy."[74] In the period when Baptists emerged and grew in Russia, the Orthodox Church "often interpreted peasant activism as a negative consequence of secular enlightenment that ultimately would harm the Orthodox faith."[75] In some cases, the activism was connected with literacy and lay interpretation of Scripture.[76] The link with Baptist life was, therefore, close.

It is difficult to make a definitive statement about the Orthodox spirituality that affected the lives of those with whom Kargel was connected, but it does not seem that he himself was significantly influenced by the Orthodox ethos that surrounded him.[77] His works did influence some Orthodox Christians. In a review of one of his books, the Orthodox author quotes extensively from Kargel, stating that this book was the first sectarian work he had read that did not show an intolerance towards Orthodoxy but rather echoed "Orthodox humility and modesty" in regard to the process of salvation.[78] Some of those with whom Kargel worked, such as Ivan Stepanovich Prokhanov[79] and Vasily G. Pavlov,[80] were raised in Molokan families, and therefore had a good grasp of Orthodox spirituality. Vasily Pashkov, in Saint Petersburg, was part of a wealthy Russian and thus Orthodox circle, largely aristocratic. Several of those with whom Kargel was connected, however, especially in his early period of ministry, were Germans. A significant number were Baptists, and others, such as Johann Wieler, were part of the German Mennonite movement. Although the Mennonites and other Germans lived in an Orthodox country, they were not permitted to interact with the Orthodox at a religious level.[81] For Germans in the Russian Empire, there was very little opportunity (or perceived need) to delve into Orthodox theology. As time went on, Kargel had more and more to do with those from an Orthodox background, from the aristocracy to the peasants. However, in the case of

74. Shubin, *A History of Russian Christianity*, vol. III, 118.
75. Chulos, *Converging Worlds*, 6.
76. Ibid.
77. The similarities of Kargel's thoughts on sanctification and the Orthodox theology of deification will be mentioned in the final chapter of this book as an area for further research.
78. Chepurina, "Ispoved' I. V. Kargelya," 509.
79. Prokhanoff, *In the Cauldron of Russia*, 9–41.
80. Pavlof, "An Autobiography," 95.
81. Dyck, "Moulding the Brotherhood," 92–93.

many, such as Mikhail Ratushnyi and Ivan Riaboshapka, two leaders of the Baptist movement who came from peasant backgrounds, he was dealing with those who had left Orthodoxy in search of another expression of Christianity.[82]

While Orthodoxy is often portrayed as a seamless unity, there have been several significant groups that have left the Russian Orthodox fold. The Molokans evolved out of Russian Orthodoxy because they could no longer accept all the teachings of the Orthodox Church. They were indebted to another movement, the Dukhobors, who believed in the presence of an "inner light" or "inner revelation" that guided them in their worship and daily life. The Dukhobors rejected any form of hierarchy, including the need for a local priest. In the mid-eighteenth century, a Dukhobor named Simon Uklein of Tambov began to teach the supremacy of the Bible over the light of inner revelation. His emphasis on the place of Scripture was innovative. He gathered a following around him who began to search the Scriptures. They became known as Molokans, a name probably taken from the fact that they drank *moloko* (milk) on Orthodox days of fasting. They typically displayed a disdain for other forms of Orthodoxy.[83] The Molokans continued the Dukhobors' opposition to the Orthodox Church's high regard for the sacraments, rituals, and the veneration of the saints and icons, on the grounds that the Christian faith was to be an inner faith.[84] Molokans preferred to call themselves "Spiritual Christians."[85] They rejected outward demonstrations of piety such as wearing a cross or icon.[86] They held communal meals in place of Holy Communion and confessed their sins to elders. Molokan meetings were very simple: elders reading the Bible and giving a sermon based on the reading, and singing.[87]

The Molokans were significant for Russian Baptist life. On 20 August 1867, Martin Kalweit baptized Nikita Isaevich Voronin, a wealthy Molokan merchant, in a mill stream of the Kura River in the Caucasus region of southern Russia, near Tiflis (now Tbilisi, the

---

82. Zhuk, *Russia's Lost Reformation*, 164–71.
83. Karev, "The Russian Evangelical Baptist Movement," 56.
84. Zhuk, *Russia's Lost Reformation*, 175; Hebly, *Protestants in Russia*, 78.
85. Kolarz, *Religion in the Soviet Union*, 349.
86. Shubin, *A History of Russian Christianity*, vol. III, 71.
87. Ibid., 79–80.

capital of Georgia). Martin Kalweit was born into a Lutheran family in Lithuania, and after having experienced evangelical conversion through German Baptist work he was baptized as a believer in 1858.[88] The baptism in 1867 of Voronin, who had been studying the Scriptures on the question of baptism for some time, is the first known immersion baptism of an adult Russian citizen in Tsarist Russia; Voronin is celebrated by Russian Baptists as the first Russian Baptist.[89] Voronin encouraged other Molokans to be baptized, and a group of Baptists slowly grew in Tiflis. They used the name "Baptist" because that was the name given to them by Kalweit. After four years the Baptist membership still only numbered about a dozen, but three of these early Russian Baptists were to be crucial figures in Baptist advance. Johann Kargel joined the group in 1869. A crucial role was also played by Vasily G. Pavlov, who as a sixteen-year-old was baptized by Voronin in 1871. The third person was Vasily V. Ivanov, who first heard about believer's baptism in 1866.[90] In 1870 he visited Tiflis. The message he heard within the Baptist congregation there was that he must have "personal fellowship with God and assurance of the forgiveness of sins through Jesus Christ," and in October 1871 he was baptized. He went on to organize the second congregation of Baptists in the Caucasus.[91] Early Baptist life in Russia, including that part of Baptist life with which Kargel was connected, drew from the Molokan background.

The southwestern territorial expansion of the Russian empire after the Russo-Turkish wars of the 1730s created communities that were home to people seeking freedom and emancipation. The Russian southern frontier was also an experiment in Russian colonization. The Russian government recruited whole villages to resettle in the sparsely inhabited steppes of Novorossiia.[92] Between the 1760s and 1820s,

---

88. Sawatsky, *Soviet Evangelicals*, 27–33.

89. "Ot Vsesoyuznogo Soveta Evangel'skix Xristian-Baptistov," 4.

90. A descendant of Vasily Ivanov renamed himself Ivanov-Klyshnikov in memory of his Molokan ancestors who had escaped persecution by hiding under the common surname of Ivanov. Some scholars have used the surname Ivanov-Klyshnikov when referring to this person. See Coleman, *Russian Baptists and Spiritual Revolution*, 129 n. 3; Kolarz, *Religion in the Soviet Union*, 285.

91. N. V. Odintsov, "Obrazets dlia vernyx," *Baptist*, No 2 (1929) 10, as cited in Steeves, "The Russian Baptist Union," 5.

92. Many of the villages were composed of Old Believers, a sect of the Russian Orthodox Church formed in reaction to Patriarch Nikon's reforms in the seventeenth century.

many thousands of foreigners—Germans, Serbs, Poles, Jews, French, and Swedes—settled in southern Ukraine.[93] In addition to these foreigners, Russian peasants moved to the area to escape a life of indentured serfdom.[94] Soon, the foreign population began to experience economic growth. This was especially true for some of the German colonies, which held special privileges and practiced advanced agricultural techniques. Many of these Germans were Mennonites; others were Lutheran and Reformed. Soon, the foreigners held more land than the Russians.[95] To some Russian peasants, the Germans were a people to emulate because of their economic prowess. The peasants also realized that the religious life of the Germans was different from the religious life they experienced in the Russian Orthodox Church. The peasants knew many corrupt priests, interested in serving themselves and the local administration. Bishop Leonid, in 1862, in Ekaterinoslav Province, was charged with accepting bribes of 100 to 500 rubles from a priest who wanted to receive a certain parish.[96] In 1864, three priests were convicted of being involved in illegal alcohol production and extortion in the Zvenigorodka district.[97] Zhuk's *Russia's Lost Reformation* is filled with documented cases of corruption, drunkenness, and sexual misbehavior by Orthodox priests on the southern frontier.[98] Orthodox believers were legally prohibited from converting to another type of faith, but many Russians became curious about the faith of their German neighbors. It was in this context that Baptist growth was most rapid.

An example is in Rohrbach, a Reformed parish in the northeast region of Odessa Province. The Reformed Church pastor, Karl Bonekemper, had been influenced by pietistic thinking and he attracted the attention of Orthodox peasants including Mikhail Ratushnyi, one of the few literate laborers and one who had managed to read the Bible. Later, Ratushnyi influenced other Russians with the

---

93. Zhuk, *Russia's Lost Reformation*, 36.

94. These peasants were followed by others who were officially emancipated in 1861 after the agrarian reforms.

95. RIGA, f, 1263, op.1,d.478, 1.1–2, as cited in Zhuk, *Russia's Lost Reformation*, 39.

96. Zhuk, *Russia's Lost Reformation*, 65.

97. Ibid., 66.

98. Ibid., 64–74.

message that he was learning from the Bible.[99] On 11 June 1869, Abraham Unger, a Mennonite Brethren leader, baptized thirty converts in the German colony of Stari Danzig. Efim Tsymbal, a Russian peasant, managed to slip into the line of those to be baptized, becoming the first south Russian to commit himself to the baptistic faith. Tsymbal travelled to a nearby village and baptized Ivan Riaboshapka, a Ukrainian. Riaboshapka soon baptized forty-eight others in the nearby vicinity of Odessa, including Mikhail Ratushnyi in 1871.[100] The Stundo-baptist[101] movement soon spread throughout the south of Russia.[102] All of the Russian attendees can be assumed to have been members of the Russian Orthodox Church. Gradually more and more were baptized, joining the Mennonite Brethren and later the Baptist movement as it spread in southern Russia. Although Kargel received his baptism in Tiflis, later he would meet with Riaboshapka and Ratushnyi, helping them develop their ministries and keeping them within the broader movements of Baptist and evangelical faith.

SOURCES AND STYLE

Throughout this work, I will be quoting extensively from the letters of Johann Kargel and his wife Anna. The original letters are found in the Pashkov Papers, held at the University of Birmingham. An authorized microfiche copy is held at the International Baptist Theological Seminary, Prague, Czech Republic. Each letter is given a reference number, which I will use to refer to the letters. These letters have not been used previously for academic purposes. Many of them are handwritten using the old German style and therefore are difficult to read. I am deeply indebted to Maria Schellenberg (Detmold, Germany) and Vera Pätkau (Bielefeld, Germany) for their transliteration of the letters into modern German. In much of the correspondence between Kargel and Pashkov, they maintained the habit of using both the Old Style Russian dates (Julian calendar) and the New Style European dates (Gregorian calendar). I have tried to maintain a consistency through-

---

99. Wardin, "How Indigenous was the Baptist Movement in the Russian Empire?" 31.

100. V. P., "Pravda o Baptistax," *Baptist* 42 (12 October 1911) 332, as cited in Coleman, *Russian Baptists and Spiritual Revolution*, 16.

101. This term will be discussed in chapter 2.

102. See Nesdoly, "Evangelical Sectarianism in Russia."

out this work by referring only to the Gregorian calendar date, which is twelve (before 1900) or thirteen (after 1900) days ahead of the Julian calendar. If an Old Style date is given in a direct quotation, I have used [o.s.] to indicate it as Old Style.

Where there is a translation from the Russian, it is my original translation, since no English translation of the works or the letters of Kargel exists except for his 1913 Confession of Faith.[103] In the translation I have tried to remain as close to Kargel's wording as possible and have also tried to convey the tone of his writing. The works of Kargel have been published in various forms over the years, both in German and Russian. I have chosen to use the recently published Russian versions of his writings for ease of access. They are found in *Sobranie Sochinenij* [The Collected Works]. At times there is a need to transliterate the Cyrillic letters of the Russian alphabet for words that are not commonly used in English. I have chosen to use the GOST 7.79 B as the standard for my transliteration. At times I have used the names of cities and proper names as written by Kargel, who often used the German spelling. Otherwise, I have chosen to use the consistency list of the *Modern Encyclopedia of Religions in Russia and Eurasia* (MERRE), edited by Paul Steeves. The name of the city of Saint Petersburg, Russia, was Petrograd from 1914 until 1924, and Leningrad from 1924 until 1991. I have chosen to use the name Saint Petersburg throughout this work in order to maintain consistency. I have used the other names only when they are located within a direct quote. At some points, I have referred to material found in *Istoriya Evangel'skix Xristian-Baptistov v SSSR* [The History of Evangelical Christians-Baptists in the USSR], which I will abbreviate as HEC-B. This is the standard textbook for the story of the Evangelical Christians and Baptists, from the Tsarist period through to the end of the Soviet period, as the story is understood in the Russian-speaking context. *HEC-B* was written by a team of Russian-speaking scholars[104] and

---

103. See Parker, *Baptists in Europe*, 154–58 for Maria Vogel's translation; de Chalandeau, *The Christians in the USSR*, 59–62 for de Chalandeau's translation. I have amended the translation of Maria Vogel and included it as an appendix to this book.

104. The primary author for the first seven chapters was Sergei Nikitovich Savinsky. Chapter 8, on the contemporary period, was initiated and written mainly by Pavel Dmitrievich Savchenko. Chapter 9, on Moldova, was written by Karl Stanislavovich Sedletsky; chapter 10, on Estonia, was written by Robert Vosu; chapter

draws on primary sources, including archives and Russian-language journals.

THE STRUCTURE OF THE BOOK

This book will largely follow Kargel's life chronologically, as he moved from a primarily German-speaking context to a Russian-speaking context. Throughout, I will highlight details of his personal life as they influenced his understanding of the Christian faith. In chapter 2, I show how Johann Kargel developed as a Baptist leader. Although baptized in Tiflis along with Russian speakers, he was a native German speaker. I show that in his early ministry, his focus was on German speakers living within the Russian Empire. Beginning in 1874, when he came into contact with the aristocratic revivals in Saint Petersburg, he began to shift to a Russian-oriented ministry. This is explained in chapter 3. In chapter 4, I examine Kargel's move to Bulgaria to start the Bulgarian Baptist community. It was during his time in Bulgaria that he sought and found a deeper relationship with Christ. Also, increasingly, he embraced an interdenominational perspective of ministry. Chapter 5 looks at his return to Russia to assist Vasily Pashkov in a variety of pan-evangelical enterprises. Chapter 6 shows the influence Kargel had as he continued to travel and work on behalf of Pashkov, often with Friedrich Baedeker, preaching in prisons and assisting evangelical believers who were experiencing persecution. Chapter 7 will analyze Kargel's theological contribution as he helped in the formation of the Evangelical Christian Union and as he became a central teacher in their Bible College in Saint Petersburg. Kargel's mature understanding of the sanctified life is explored in chapter 8, and this shows that he taught from the perspective of Keswick spirituality. The final era in Kargel's life is examined in chapter 9. As Kargel grew older, he became a sought-after sage. He was uniquely influential in constructing what I consider to be Russian Holiness theology.

11, on Latvia, was written by Janis Tervits; chapter 12, on Lithuania, was written by Jonas Inkenas; chapter 13, on Belorussia, was written by Ivan Vasilievich Bukatyi and V. Ya. Kanatush; chapter 14, on the Pentecostals, was written by Dmitri Leontievich Vosniuk; and chapter 15, on the Mennonite Brethren was written by Johannes Dyck. This information is courtesy of Johannes Dyck.

CONCLUSION

Current work on Russian Baptist history suggests that a number of streams contributed to the emergence of Russian Baptist life. The most important of these were: first, Baptist missionary activity in the Caucasus region, associated with the German Baptist movement; second, Stundism or Stundo-baptism, which linked Russians with revivalism among the Mennonites in southern Russia; and third, the evangelical movement in Saint Petersburg. All of these joined together eventually to form the Union of Evangelical Christians-Baptists. This work will show the ways in which Kargel was connected with each of these streams and how—as he drew from them—he developed a distinct expression of spirituality within the Russian-speaking evangelical context. Using a framework proposed by Philip Sheldrake in *Spirituality and History*, spirituality is seen as concerned with the conjunction of theology, communion with God, and practical Christianity.[105] Kargel's expression of spirituality was evangelical, within the definition of evangelicalism formulated in David Bebbington's quadrilateral—conversionist, crucicentric, biblicist, and activist. Furthermore, I will seek to show that Kargel's distinct expression of evangelical spirituality reflected the emphases present within the Holiness movement, in particular those expressed by the Keswick movement. With this distinct expression of evangelical spirituality as the shaping force in his life, I will show how Ivan Kargel became a uniquely influential preacher, theologian, and writer within the Russian-speaking Baptist and evangelical environment.

---

105. Sheldrake, *Spirituality and History*, 52.

2

The Shaping of a Baptist Leader

(1849–1874)

JOHANN G. KARGEL WAS born in the Caucasus region in 1849. It is most likely that his father was German and his mother was Armenian.¹ There is no evidence available that could prove or disprove this, but it is the most common explanation of his background. The Russian *otchestvo* (patronymic) that Ivan Kargel used was Veniaminovich (son of Benjamin). When Kargel communicated with non-Russian speakers he used his German name, Johann. When he communicated with Russian speakers he used Ivan. Benjamin was most likely the name of his father.² Despite its Hebrew roots, Benjamin would have been a common name for a German man at this time. It appears that his father may have been a non-Mennonite German colonist who lived in the Russian Empire. According to Princess Sophia Lieven, a Saint Petersburg aristocrat who knew Kargel well, Kargel's daughters thought he might have had Scottish ancestry.³ This should probably be taken to mean that the Kargel family of Germany was considered to be descendants of Cargills in Scotland. The family name Cargill is common in Scotland, but given the fact that Kargel's given name was Johann and his mother tongue was German, it is fairly certain that, if the family did originally come from Scotland, over several generations they had been Germanized—as the spelling Kargel also suggests. It is possible that Johann Kargel had a Turkish passport from birth,⁴ but

---

1. Brandenburg, *The Meek and the Mighty*, 131.

2. It is conceivable that he adopted Benjamin as his patronymic so that he would be called "of the tribe of Benjamin."

3. Lieven, "Kratkij ocherk zhizni i deyatel'nosti brata I. V. Kargelya," 8.

4. Bender, "Kargel, Johann," 1099; Brandenburg, *The Meek and the Mighty*, 131.

some speculate that he became a naturalized Bulgarian citizen.⁵ *The Mennonite Encyclopedia* records that Kargel was the "son of a German father and an Armenian mother (birthplace unknown) [who] came to Russia from Bulgaria, which was then under Turkish rule, and thus had Turkish citizenship."⁶

Some have suggested that Kargel studied in Germany and received a technical engineering degree and that he lived with his parents in England for a time.⁷ However, these statements are not based on credible evidence. The root of this problem of evidence will be discussed in the following chapter as I look at information in "Folder 4/51" found in the AUCEC-B's Moscow Archives. This archive does state that, as a child, Johann Kargel and his immediate family moved from the Caucasus to Germany and then back to the Caucasus, and that Kargel studied in Germany and received a mechanical engineering degree.⁸ To date, no birth certificates or marriage licenses have been found that record the immediate family of Johann Kargel. In his brief personal testimony, which was published as an introduction to his book *Zwischen den Enden der Erde: Unter Bruedern in Ketten* [To the Ends of the Earth: Among the Brothers in Chains],⁹ no personal data is given.¹⁰ The purpose of this chapter is not to deal with Kargel's earliest years but rather to focus on what is known about his spiritual development, particularly within the German and Russian Baptist contexts of the early 1870s. In chapter 3, I will attempt to show the origins of the conflicting sources regarding Johann Kargel's early life.

---

5. Skopina, "Iz Biografii I. V. Kargelya," 690.

6. Bender, "Kargel, Johann," 1099.

7. Karetnikova, "Biografiya I. V. Kargelya," para. 1; Skopina, "Iz Biografii I. V. Kargelya," 689; Kuznetsova, "Early Russian Evangelicals," 276. Kuznetsova refers to a statement in one of Kargel's books as proof that he was in London. However, the statement does not specifically state that he was in London. It simply states that he was aware of the events in London which he gained "only from the newspaper." See Kargel, "Se, Gryadu Skoro . . . ," 398.

8. Golobashhenko, *Istoriya Evangel'sko-Baptistskogo Dvizheniya v Ukraine*, 48.

9. Kargel, *Zwischen den Enden*.

10. I have tried throughout this work to piece together snippets about his early life, but nothing conclusive can be said regarding the time before his conversion and baptism in 1869 at the age of twenty.

JOHANN KARGEL'S BAPTIST BEGINNINGS

According to a statement in one of Johann Kargel's sermons, he experienced an evangelical conversion around 1869.[11] In a letter dated 12 May 1886, Kargel wrote, "The next day I took the train to Sevastopol and at 1:00 left for Batum. During the whole trip we witnessed for our Lord on the steam boat. For me it was all the more joyful because it was the same steam boat on which, seventeen years ago, I had first heard the new gospel of Christ which also brought me to repentance."[12] It would seem that Johann Kargel first comprehended the "new gospel of Christ" as a twenty-year-old as he travelled from Sevastopol to Batum in 1869. The dates would indicate that soon after hearing the message, he was baptized in Tiflis Baptist church; a mere two years after that congregation's first baptism had taken place. After his baptism, he soon began an active ministry— an evidence of typical evangelical activism. Eventually this ministry would take Kargel into many parts of the Russian Empire.

Princess Sophia Lieven wrote in her short tribute to Kargel, which was published after his death, that she remembered him describing some details of his conversion. She states that he told her that while he was singing in a church choir, the words of the hymn he was singing brought him to an awareness of his personal sin, and so to repentance.[13] I do not consider it likely that this event happened in the small Baptist church of Tiflis. In 1869, when he started to attend this congregation, there were fewer than a dozen members.[14] It is very unlikely that a church of that size would have had a choir. It is more likely that the choir Kargel spoke of was in a German Lutheran church. Probably this event preceded his "steam boat" experience. His conversion was probably a process that culminated in 1869.

The story of the Tiflis church in which Kargel was baptized was linked (as noted in the previous chapter) with Martin Kalweit, who, with eleven others, had set out from the German Baptist church in Memel (today Klaipeda, Lithuania) in search of work.[15] The Memel

11. Kargel, *Klagen und Fragen*, 7.
12. J. G. Kargel to "Friend and brother in Christ" [V. A. Pashkov], 12 May 1886, 2/13/049/, Pashkov Papers.
13. Lieven, "Kratkij ocherk zhizni i deyatel'nosti brata I. V. Kargelya," 8.
14. Steeves, "The Russian Baptist Union," 4.
15. It is also reported that Kalweit was from the church in Ichsken, in Prussia. See "Extension of the German Baptist Mission into Asia and Africa," 381.

church was the mother church of much of the Baptist work in Lithuania and Latvia, as well as having connections further afield. In 1875, the year that Kargel arrived in Saint Petersburg, the Memel Baptist church had twenty-seven preaching stations and 2,780 members.[16] Most of the members of the group from Memel of which Kalweit was a part were drawn to the port city of Odessa. Others arrived in Tiflis and were greeted by Kalweit's relatives who lived outside the city. They decided to settle in Tiflis to find work.[17] Kalweit and three colleagues found, as he put it later in a letter to Johann Oncken on 22 July 1869 ("Extension of the German Baptist work in Asia and Africa"), that "work is plentiful and wages good; but [we are] without friends, without Christian fellowship, without even *Missionsblatt* [a magazine that reported on the happenings within the German Baptist Union]; we felt as if forsaken of God."[18] It was this rather disconsolate group that Kargel joined, although it may well be that he did not view the group in the same manner as Kalweit because he was a new convert and had not left a flourishing Baptist church.

What is particularly interesting about this letter by Kalweit to Oncken is that it shows that neither Kalweit nor the German Baptist Union realized the historical implications of what was happening in Tiflis. The fact that a Baptist congregation had been planted was in itself significant. Even more significant were discussions that Kalweit had with Voronin about baptism, which led (as noted in the previous chapter) to the latter's baptism. Kalweit, however, seemed to bemoan in his letter to Oncken the fact that he was not on the "front-line" of ministry as Baptist expansion took place. He wrote: "We rejoice thus to get intelligence of beloved brethren in Germany and especially to read of all that is going on for the spread of the Kingdom of Christ and we long to take part in it; but, hitherto we have not mustered courage to send our mite to Europe for this purpose."[19] However, the German-Russian Baptist congregation in Tiflis did send their

---

16. Lysenkaite, "Baptist Beginnings in the Baltic Countries," 2.

17. Martin Kalweit arrived in Tiflis in 1862. See Byford, *Peasants and Prophets*, 79.

18. This account is based on a letter that Kalweit wrote to J. G. Oncken on 22 July 1869, as "Extension of the German Baptist Mission into Asia and Africa," 381–83.

19. Ibid., 382.

"mite"—ten Russian rubles—with this letter to Oncken, as a contribution to German Baptist work in China and Spain.

For Kalweit the real advance, which he wanted to support, was "in Asia and Africa." Kalweit had a typical evangelical vision for expansion. It was this evangelical vision that Kargel would absorb. Kalweit and his wife remained as significant members of the Baptist movement in the Caucasus. He was sent into exile to Gerusi [Armenia] in 1891 while his wife remained in Tiflis.[20] During his trips to the Caucasus, Kargel would check on Mrs. Kalweit and send information back to Pashkov concerning the Kalweit family.

When Nikita Voronin had first begun to seek answers concerning baptism, he approached a colporteur named Yakov Deliakovich Deliakov [Jacob Dilakoff]. Deliakov was a Persian bookseller who had learned Russian and would later be employed by the British and Foreign Bible Society. It was Deliakov who introduced Voronin to Kalweit. Voronin tried to introduce more Molokans to Baptist beliefs, but his success was limited and the local Molokans eventually excluded those who joined the Baptist ranks. Soon after Voronin's baptism, he was "not allowed to sit in the place where he had formerly sat" in the Molokan congregation and was not allowed to speak.[21] Yet despite the slow growth, the congregation nurtured leaders such as Kargel, V. G. Pavlov and V. V. Ivanov.[22]

In 1869 Kalweit described the Baptist meeting as follows: "As some of us are Russian and some German we use both languages in our service and sing hymns from a Russian collection as well as from the *Glaubenstimme*. Some of the hymns are the same and suit the same tune, but the German are the favorites even with those who understand Russian best, as the words are simpler and the tunes more lively."[23] Also in 1869, Kargel was baptized. One source that mentions Kargel's 1869 experience is a short biography published as a foreword to one of his books. This simply states that he was "born again" (*bekehrt*) in 1869 in

---

20. Steeves, "The Russian Baptist Union," 34; Dilakoff, "The Autobiography of Jacob Dilakoff," 11.

21. Dilakoff, "The Autobiography of Jacob Dilakoff," 12.

22. Brandenburg, *The Meek and the Mighty*, 100.

23. "Extension of the German Baptist Mission into Asia and Africa," 382. Kalweit asked for more German hymnals to be sent to him in this article and in 1870 asked that a German hymn and some of Spurgeon's sermons be translated into Russian and sent to him. See Kalweit, "Letter from Mr. Kalweit," 21.

Tiflis.²⁴ Kargel did not specifically mention his baptism in any of his writings but there is primary evidence about this event. Karl Kalweit, brother of Martin Kalweit, wrote that he and Kargel were baptized by Martin Kalweit on October 6, 1869 [o.s.] at 11.00 p. m. in the Kura River in Tiflis.²⁵ At this time, there were only eleven members in the Tiflis congregation.²⁶

The Tiflis church brought Kargel into contact with German Baptist life. After several years among the Tiflis Baptist members, he was (as will be seen) sent to the six-month training course offered by the German Baptists at their school in Hamburg. Although there was a Russian element in the Tiflis congregation, Kargel's knowledge of the Russian evangelical scene was probably limited due to the lack of communication within this isolated corner of the Russian Empire. Kargel later commented that he was not familiar with the Russian believers and their work until 1877.²⁷ Russian was not Kargel's first language. At the age of twenty-seven, when in Saint Petersburg, he was not confident enough in the Russian language to be able to speak publicly using it. In those early meetings among the Russian evangelical Christians in Saint Petersburg, Count Alexis Pavlovich Bobrinsky, at one time Russian Minister of Transportation, served as Kargel's translator.²⁸ Even as late as 1884, when he corresponded with Pashkov concerning a conference of the Baptists in Russia and the Caucasus, Kargel wrote in German. The Tiflis Baptist church, which influenced Johann Kargel and in which he was baptized by immersion, also introduced him to the active and growing German Baptist movement in Europe.

GERMAN BAPTIST DEVELOPMENTS

The father figure of the wider German Baptist movement, Johann Oncken, was born in Oldenburg, Germany, in 1800.²⁹ He was baptized into the Lutheran Church and later confirmed.³⁰ At the young age of

---

24. Kargel, *Zwischen den Enden*, viii.

25. Val'kevich, *Zapiska o Propagande Protestantskix' Sekt' v' Rossii*, appendix #5, 29.

26. "Extension of the German Baptist Mission into Asia and Africa," 382.

27. Ibid.

28. Kargel, *Zwischen den Enden*, ix–x.

29. For more on the life of J. G. Oncken see Balders, *Theurer Bruder Oncken*.

30. Rushbrooke, *The Baptist Movement in the Continent of Europe*, 18. For a re-

thirteen, he was offered an apprenticeship by a Scottish businessman and worked for several years in Edinburgh.[31] During his nine years in Scotland he became "deeply impressed by the Scottish piety."[32] He then moved to London where he lodged with a family whose "tone of prayer" and their "public worship at the Independent chapel arrested him."[33] It was at a Methodist service that, in an echo of John Wesley's experience, he received an assurance of salvation. Upon his arrival home one night, he recorded "an inexpressible blessing."[34] He immediately began to share his faith through tracts and preaching. By the end of 1823, Oncken's vibrant witness and his German background attracted the attention of the interdenominational Continental Society for the Diffusion of Religious Knowledge over the Continent of Europe (Continental Society).[35] The organization asked him to be a colporteur in Hamburg. An English connection was found in Hamburg: the English Reformed Church, where T. W. Matthews was pastor. Oncken was given opportunity to preach in English in this church but felt his true calling was to be among Germans. At first his activities were curtailed because he was not a citizen of Hamburg, but in 1828 he was granted citizenship.

As early as 1826, Johann Oncken was beginning to have questions concerning baptism. He began to meet with a small group to study the Bible and discuss the issue. He recorded, "In a shoemaker's work shop in 1829, those whose hearts were separated from the state church, gathered themselves to study the holy writings, particularly the book of Acts which, alone, is the infallible church history. Here we soon recognized that the church of Christ can only be composed of converted persons who have made a confession of their faith in

---

cent survey of the wider Baptist movement in Europe see Randall, *Communities of Conviction*.

31. McBeth, *The Baptist Heritage*, 471.
32. Gunnar, *The Free Church through the Ages*, 284.
33. Rushbrooke, *The Baptist Movement in the Continent of Europe*, 19.
34. H. Luckey, *Gerhard Oncken*, 42, as cited in Wagner, *New Move Forward in Europe*, 5.
35. The society was founded by Henry Drummond in 1819 to mobilize resources in England to revive "the vital goodness" of evangelical Christianity, particularly within the continent of Europe. For more on the Continental Society see Stewart, *Restoring the Reformation*, 160–92; Stunt, *From Awakening to Secession*, 111.

His death by being baptized."[36] Matthews, the pastor of the Hamburg English Reformed Church, resigned and returned to England to receive believer's baptism. Oncken, however, was not willing to take time away from his itinerant preaching schedule to leave Hamburg to be baptized. When he asked for guidance from the Baptists in Scotland, some encouraged him to baptize himself, but for Oncken this would have been unbiblical.[37] He waited five years until Barnas Sears,[38] a Baptist pastor from America, was in Germany, and on 22 April 1834 Sears baptized Oncken, along with his wife Sarah and a few friends, in the Elbe River—under cover of darkness. This marks the beginning of the modern Baptist story in Europe.

Oncken's early ministry in Hamburg was interdenominational, supported by the Continental Society. Following the baptisms in the Elbe, however, Oncken's ministry became denominational in its emphasis; a Baptist church was founded with Oncken as its pastor.[39] The church's evangelistic activities soon attracted the attention of the city officials and the Lutheran Church. Two of those who were baptized with Oncken, who had been among his first converts when he was working within the Reformed Church, were Diedrich Lange (a shoemaker) and his wife Henrietta Lange. Diedrich became one of the first deacons in the Baptist Church. Diedrich Lange, Oncken, and Julius Köbner, another early member of the church, were later imprisoned together in the Winserbaum prison for their illegal religious work; Lang and Köbner were released after eight days while Oncken remained for several weeks.[40] This did not deter them. Further evangelistic work took place.

In 1836, just two years after his own baptism, Oncken baptized a group of believers in the Berlin area. Julius Köbner, the son of a Jewish rabbi, born on the Danish island of Funen, began Baptist work in Denmark. Oncken and Köbner experimented with methods

---

36. H. B. Motel, *Glieder an Einem Leib*, 100, as cited in Wagner, *New Move Forward in Europe*, 6.

37. Cooke, *Johann Gerhard Oncken*, 57.

38. At the time, Sears was professor of Biblical Theology at Hamilton Literary and Theological Institution in New York State. Previously he had served as the pastor in the First Baptist Church of Hartford, Connecticut. For more on Barnas Sears see Hovey, *Barnas Sears*.

39. Rushbrooke, *The Baptist Movement in the Continent of Europe*, 76.

40. Ibid., 24.

of training among the Baptists and also crafted the original doctrinal statement, which was foundational to Baptist theology in mainland Europe. Within fourteen years of Oncken's baptism, twenty-six German Baptist churches had been started. Oncken also realized the need to train missionaries and pastors. The Baptist church in Berlin appointed Gottfried W. Lehmann to be their pastor, and Lehmann invited representatives of the Baptist churches to meet together in July 1848. Out of this meeting emerged the German Baptist Union, which made early decisions in favor of missionary outreach, dedicating one-third of the Union's mission budget to foreign mission. German Baptist mission led Baptist growth across continental Europe.[41]

Meanwhile, in Hamburg, the Baptist congregation soon outgrew its facilities and relocated to a three-floor granary. That move proved serendipitous. During the same week—in May 1842—in which the congregation moved to the new facility, an immense fire broke out in Hamburg. The marginalized Hamburg Baptists soon volunteered to assist in the care of the city's homeless people. Their newly acquired facility was transformed into a hostel and hospital that ministered to Hamburg's many injured. This level of care could not be ignored by city officials. When a mob attacked the church shortly afterwards the police were protective.[42] Some years later Oncken's group received full government protection and in 1857 was granted legal status as a church.

Not only did the tragedy of the Hamburg fire provide an opportunity for Baptists to offer care to needy fellow-citizens; the events following the fire also proved to be significant for the wider Baptist story in Europe, particularly Eastern Europe. Laborers from a number of countries came to Hamburg to rebuild the city. Oncken and his church took the opportunity to convey the evangelical message to these men. They also offered the temporary workers hospitality, recognizing that they were separated from their families. Many of these laborers became convinced of the need for believer's baptism. A high proportion of those baptized in the Hamburg Baptist Church in this period were such "travelling men."[43] When they returned to their home countries,

---

41. Coleman, *Russian Baptists and Spiritual Revolution*, 94.
42. For more see Cooke, *Johann Gerhard Oncken*.
43. Randall, "Every Apostolic Church a Mission Society," 283.

a number of them became lay Baptist church planters. In this way, Baptist life spread into many areas of Europe.

The first Baptist church in Russia is considered by some to be the Adamov German Baptist congregation in the Volhynia region of Western Ukraine, which began in 1861.[44] The Adamov congregation came into being as a result of the work of Wilhelm Weist, who was appointed by the German Baptists to the eastern part of Europe. He travelled extensively and conducted baptisms in Western Ukraine in 1858. Among those baptized was Gottfried Alf, who became the Baptist "apostle" to the German colonists in the region of Volhynia (located today in eastern Poland and western Ukraine).[45] Alf travelled to Germany for six months of training in the Hamburg Mission School under Oncken and Köbner. By 1867, Alf had endured imprisonment "more or less ten times for God's Word."[46] In 1882 Alf stated that he had been imprisoned thirty times and "was ready to go again whenever needed."[47]

German Baptists were also active by the end of the 1860s among the emerging Mennonite Brethren congregations of southern Russia. Of the three most important early leaders of the Mennonite Brethren—Abraham Unger, Gerhard Wieler, and Johann Wieler—two were greatly influenced by Oncken. Unger was first exposed to German Baptist influences in 1859 through a booklet published in Hamburg. Through personal correspondence with Oncken, Unger was won over to the Baptist cause.[48] During a visit by Oncken in 1869

44. Wardin, "Baptists (German) in Russian and USSR," 193. Some might not consider this accurate because the congregation was ethnically German and the Adamov church could be considered to be located in Catholic Poland rather than in present-day Russia. It could be argued that the first Baptist church in Russia was founded in 1856 in the Åland Islands, in the Grand Duchy of Finland, which was part of the Russian Empire. It is also important to note that the German Baptist church in Hortschik was founded on 7 May 1864 [o.s.] and that the German Baptist church in Sorotschin, where Kargel later served, was founded on 10 May 1864. Both of these are located in present-day Ukraine which was part of the Soviet Union. In this work I have suggested that in 1879 Kargel registered the first Baptist church in Orthodox Russia, in Saint Petersburg.

45. For a fuller description of Volhynia see Schroeder, *Mennonite Historical Atlas*, 135–36.

46. *Missionsblatt* (October, 1867) 151, as cited in Wardin, *Gottfried F. Alf*, 55.

47. *Quarterly Reporter of the German Baptist Mission* (October 1882) 5, as cited in Wardin, *Gottfried F. Alf*, 55.

48. Karev, "The Russian Evangelical Baptist Movement," 15.

to the Mennonite communities of Einlage, Oncken ordained Unger.[49] Johann Wieler, who was a member of the Einlage Mennonite Church, established contacts with Oncken and the German Baptists and spent one year in Hamburg and Switzerland.[50]

As with all Baptists, and like evangelicals in other denominations, the German Baptists stressed biblical authority and the necessity of a conversion experience.[51] They also taught that believers should be immersed as a sign of their personal faith and should join a Baptist congregation as committed members. Unlike some other Baptist groups in the nineteenth century, the German Baptists were united around a strong and detailed confession of faith and a strong ecclesiastical structure. They also believed in closed communion—for baptized believers only.[52] Oncken and Köbner crafted the original doctrinal statement of faith in 1837. It underwent revisions by Lehmann and was adopted in 1847 by all the German Baptist churches.[53] It was criticized from inside the movement for its strongly Calvinistic stance but, in the end, Oncken's views prevailed.[54]

There were regional German Baptist associations that belonged to the national Union or *Bund*. This structure provided a corporate unity.[55] One major activity that held the regional associations and Union together was conferences, especially the Triennial Conference (*Bundes Conferenz*). It was during these conferences that money was discussed, ministries were assigned, connections were made, and reports were given. It was an event most German Baptist leaders would not miss. The Hamburg Mission School was also instrumental in maintaining unity. Those trained there were sent out not only to plant churches in Germany but also as missionaries to German-speaking communities elsewhere. When new Baptist causes were started, local leaders were identified and asked to come to Hamburg to receive training. After the

49. Toews, "Baptists and Mennonite Brethren in Russia," 86.

50. Klippenstein, "Johann Wieler (1839–1889) among Russian Evangelicals," 49; Dyck, "Moulding the Brotherhood," 37–38.

51. Wardin, "Mennonite Brethren and German Baptists in Russia," 97.

52. For comparison with England see Briggs, *The English Baptists of the Nineteenth Century*, 41–53.

53. For a fuller discussion of the process see Lumpkin, *Baptist Confessions of Faith*, 402.

54. Parker, *Baptists in Europe*, 56.

55. Wardin, "Mennonite Brethren and German Baptists in Russia," 98.

training, they were commissioned to be Baptist missionaries in their area.[56] For some, funding was arranged so that they could be full-time missionaries and not be tied to one congregation. We will see later how this dynamic German Baptist milieu shaped Kargel's early years of evangelical experience.

BAPTISTS AND MENNONITES

This wider mission of the German Baptists included engagement with Mennonites living in southern Russia whose roots lay in the sixteenth-century Anabaptist movement. In 1763, Catherine II had offered potential European settlers land and special rights in Ukraine,[57] within the framework of a *Privilegium*.[58] The original *Privilegium* status extended significant privileges to the Mennonite settlers,[59] which remained securely intact until Paul I inherited the throne of Catherine II upon her death in 1796. The Mennonites of Khortitsa sent a delegation to Saint Petersburg at that point to seek to receive a written guarantee that their former rights would remain under the new ruler. The delegates returned in 1800 with the written guarantee that their special status as settlers was confirmed in perpetuity.[60] The Russian administration was familiar with the success of the Quakers, Mennonites, and Moravians who were becoming settled in North America.[61] In 1836 there were forty-six Mennonite villages along the Molotschna River and by 1863 the number had grown to fifty-seven.[62] This Mennonite community would be significant in Kargel's early ministry.

As early as 1866, Oncken and his missionary preachers were working among the Mennonite Brethren in southern Russia. The Mennonite Brethren had emerged as a separate Mennonite group, owing much to the ministry of Eduard Wuest, a German Lutheran preacher deeply steeped in Pietist spirituality, and to several Baptist tracts that found their way into the Mennonite community. From 1845

---

56. See Coleman, *Russian Baptists and Spiritual Revolution*, 97.

57. For a full English translation of the original Manifesto see Stumpp, *The Emigration from Germany to Russia*, 15–18.

58. Toews, *Czars, Soviets, and Mennonites*, 3.

59. Smith, *The Coming of the Russian Mennonites*, 23.

60. Ibid., 26.

61. Zhuk, *Russia's Lost Reformation*, 40–41.

62. Kolarz, *Religion in the Soviet Union*, 275.

onwards Wuest began to gain a following through his call for spiritual renewal and authentic relationship to Jesus Christ.[63] This preaching produced a division within the Mennonite ranks, with the revivalist Mennonite Brethren, who produced their own creed in 1860, splitting off from the traditional Mennonites.

The Mennonite Brethren called their first conference in July 1872. Three Mennonites, Johann Wieler, his brother Gerhard, and Abraham Unger are the leaders credited with the emergence of the Mennonite Brethren in the Khortitsa settlement.[64] The two Wieler brothers were "the only one[s] of the original brethren who had a good command of spoken and written Russian."[65] Eventually, Johann Wieler settled in the Molotschna Settlement.[66] It was forbidden to proselytize among the Russian population, but as early as 1860 Johann Wieler was engaged in precisely this kind of activity.[67] Wieler was placed on the missions committee of the Mennonite Brethren early in their history.[68] Johann Kargel lived with the Wieler family for several months in 1872,[69] and Kargel and Wieler later worked under the direction of Vasily Pashkov.

It was during the formative Mennonite Brethren period in the 1860s and early 1870s that Oncken had particular influence on the movement. In a report to the American Baptists in 1869, Oncken stated:

> The prospects in Russia among my countrymen, both in the Baltic province and in the South, on the Molotschna [River], among the Maronites[70] and Lutherans, are glorious indeed.

63. de Chalandeau, *The Christians in the USSR*, 2–3.

64. Karev, "The Russian Evangelical Baptist Movement," 16. Toews adds Heinrich Neufeld to the list of those with the greatest influence on the Mennonite Brethren. See Toews, "Early Mennonite Brethren and Evangelism in Russia," 195. Toews also states that Gerhard Wieler eventually became a leader in an exuberant movement (the "jumpers") among the Mennonite Brethren and at one point excommunicated his brother Johann. See Toews, "Early Mennonite Brethren and Evangelism in Russia," 197 n. 26.

65. Friesen, *The Mennonite Brotherhood in Russia*, 278.

66. All further references to Wieler will be to Johann Wieler.

67. Klippenstein, "Johann Wieler (1839–1889) among Russian Evangelicals," 48.

68. Dueck, *Moving beyond Secession*, 50.

69. Martens, "Grossmutter's Brief," 4.

70. This is the actual word used in the article and should be considered a typographical or linguistic error. The reference is to the Mennonites and not to the Maronites, an ancient form of Christianity based in Lebanon holding strictly to the Council of Chalcedon of 451.

> I have at present with me a brother from the South, who is passing through a course of instruction to be initiated into the practical workings of a New Testament church. He will return in May or June (D. V.) and if I possibly can, I propose to accompany him. Numbers of converts are waiting there to be baptized and be united into the Churches of Christ, I have no doubt in my own mind that these churches are destined by the Head of the Church, ultimately to [A]ffect the first breach in the great Greek [Orthodox] Church of the Russian Empire.[71]

It would seem that not all those "waiting to be baptized," were members of the Orthodox Church but that they also included traditional Mennonites who, having been baptized by pouring, rather than immersion, were now to receive baptism by immersion and join the ranks of the Mennonite Brethren or the Baptists.

As the teachings of the Mennonite Brethren spread, their liturgy and patterns of worship developed. Their Bible studies, prayer meetings, song festivals, evangelistic meetings, publication efforts, and conference organization all became a part of the developing evangelical scene. The Mennonite Brethren adopted practices that they learned from the German Baptists. This included scheduled business meetings, standardized worship services, a mission strategy,[72] and an overarching conference structure—all elements of the German Baptist Union.[73] A particular feature of some German groups was Bible studies and prayer meetings normally lasting an hour, which produced the term *Stundist*, deriving from the German word for "hour." "Stundist" also began to be applied to Russian groups that followed the German model.[74] One term that I learned from Lawrence Klippenstein that was used by Orthodox writers in the nineteenth century is "Stundobaptist." It is the term that Abe J. Dueck uses in the English translation of the "Minutes of the Mennonite Brethren-Baptist Convention in Rückenau, May 21–23, 1882."[75]

---

71. "Mission to Germany [1869]," 278; also see "Letters from Mr. Oncken in Russia," 797–806, for a full report.

72. The strategy was to establish a mother church, which would then develop preaching stations that were later to become self-sustaining churches.

73. Toews, "Baptists and Mennonite Brethren in Russia," 95.

74. For a description of the cultural change within the Stundists see Zhuk, "A Separate Nation," 139–60.

75. Dueck, *Moving beyond Secession*, 37–54.

In 1877, F. M. Dostoevsky, the famous Russian writer, in an article entitled *Mirages: Stunda and Radstockists,* offered a commonly held view of Stundism:

> What is the meaning of this poor Stunda, anyway? A few Russian farm-hands working for German settlers understood that the Germans live better [richer] than the Russians because they have a different established order. The [German] pastors who happened to be here explained that their order is better because their faith is different . . . It's the everlasting story, old as can be, which originated a lot earlier than Martin Ivanovich Luther, but is repeated almost exactly, according to immutable historical laws, in our Stunda. It is known that they are already falling apart; they quibble over letters; they interpret the Gospel at their own risk and by their own conscience . . . —poor, miserable, ignorant people! . . . There is no reason to fear the Stunda, although we can very much pity it. The Stunda has no future, it won't go far, it will soon come to an end, and will probably blend in with one of the benighted Russian sects . . .[76]

Oncken's perspective on what was happening was quite different. His trip to southern Russia was all he had expected it to be. He wrote back to Germany, "Throughout southern Russia, both among the Germans and Russians, there is a most inviting field for missionary labor. And were my age 30 instead of 70, I would devote my life to cultivate this neglected but promising land. Pray ye the Lord of the harvest that He would send his own appointed laborers hither too."[77] New opportunities were opening up for Baptist growth in Russia, and Kargel would take advantage of them.

Regarding Kargel's shaping as a Baptist and then as a leader in the wider evangelical movement, an important factor was his relationship with Johann Wieler, who, as noted above, was keen to witness to ethnic Russians. The roots of their friendship are unclear, but the friendship was well established by 1872 and would last until Wieler's early death in 1889—the result of a construction accident connected with building a church.

Wieler was approximately ten years older than Kargel. Wieler married in May 1872 and he and his wife settled in Odessa. Kargel

---

76. Dostoevsky, *Polnoe Sobranie Sochinenij,* vol. XXV, 10–12.
77. "Letters from Mr. Oncken in Russia," 804.

appears to have lodged with them from July 1872 until Easter 1873.[78] On his arrival in Odessa in July 1872, Kargel brought greetings and correspondence to the Baptist congregation[79] in Odessa from the Tiflis church.[80] Although only recently baptized, Kargel preached the day after his arrival and throughout his time in Odessa.[81] He made an extended trip to the Molotschna Settlement, returning on 9 December 1872.[82] It is highly likely that this trip was Kargel's first exposure to the Mennonite Brethren.

Another friendship was with Karl Ondra. At about the time when Kargel was nearing the end of his stay in the Wielers' home, Karl Ondra, a German Baptist, arrived in Odessa, fresh from a visit to Hamburg.[83] Ondra was a Baptist missionary pastor from the Volhynia area. He became the pastor of Neudorf German Baptist Church, the "mother Baptist church" of the German colonists in the Volhynia region. In May 1873, Ondra and Kargel attended the Mennonite Brethren conference held in the Molotschna village of Klippenfeld. This was to prove a turning-point. It was in this ecclesiastically mixed situation that Johann Kargel began his first pastorate. His awareness of the different streams of evangelical life in Russia, even at this early stage in his evangelical experience, was to have significant implications later in his ministry.

SOROTSCHIN: KARGEL'S FIRST PASTORATE

It seems that the members of the Tiflis church had hoped that Kargel would start a course at the Hamburg Mission School in 1870, but war broke out with France and no new students began in that year. A later starting date was proposed for 1872, but again there were delays. Kargel, however, did not waste his time waiting for the Hamburg classes to begin, nor did he return to the Tiflis congregation. From Odessa he made his way, with Ondra, to the Mennonite Brethren's

---

78. Martens, "Grossmutter's Brief," 4.

79. The Baptist Church in Odessa was formed by Johann Wieler and in March 1871 the congregation had ten members. See Dyck, "Moulding the Brotherhood," 43–45.

80. Wieler, "Tagebuch vom ersten Januar 1872 bis 1883," 20.

81. Ibid., 21, 22, 54, 55, 57.

82. Ibid., 53.

83. Ondra, "Poland and Russia," 58.

1873 conference. His horizons were being broadened as he engaged with streams within the wider evangelical community. Kargel writes, "It was in the month of May [1873] that I met Brother Ondra on our way to the conference in Molotschna. He then found out about my intentions to do mission work. As I shared my desire at the conference, it was suggested that I either stay in the Molotschna region, work with the colonists in Einlage, or as Brother Ondra suggested I could join him on his trip to Volhynia. I chose the latter as I felt close to him, as Jonathan to David."[84]

It is likely that it was among the Mennonite Brethren, influenced as they were by Pietism, that Kargel's sense of having a calling to full-time ministry and mission was confirmed.[85] As Kargel spoke to Karl Ondra during the conference about his future, Ondra probably set out a vision for the twenty-three-year-old Kargel. By 1873 Ondra had been in ministry ten years and had already baptized over 600 people.[86] Kargel himself pointed to the 1873 conference in the Molotschna Settlement as the occasion of—or perhaps the confirmation of—his call to the ministry. In his short autobiography he notes that the incentive to begin his ministry in Volhynia came from the conference in Klippenfeld.[87] Although Ondra was an ordained Baptist minister, he was significantly involved in Mennonite Brethren affairs. The boundary lines between the two groups at this time were fluid. Later Kargel was to lament Baptist denominational rigidity, but this was not the reality in Ondra's case.

At this point it appears that the Tiflis church, Kargel's home congregation, had little involvement in the direction of Kargel's life. It was not a particularly organized group. V. V. Ivanov, from Tiflis, was bemused during a trip to Poland by the contrast between what he knew in Tiflis and what he saw among the German Baptists residing closer to Germany. He wrote of his own discouragement as he compared the Russian Baptists with the other, more organized, Baptist movements.[88] It may be that tensions in Tiflis grew between the Russian-speakers

---

84. Kargel, "Soroczin," 83.

85. Ibid., 83–88.

86. Miller, *In the Midst of Wolves*, 13.

87. Kargel, *Zwischen den Enden*, viii.

88. "Gosudarstvennyi muzei istorii religii," Koll. I, op.8, folder 1, l. 287, as cited in Heather J. Coleman, *Russian Baptists and Spiritual Revolution*, 97.

and the German-speakers.[89] Ivanov complained that in Tiflis "Russian Baptists wanted to hold many Molokan practices in the service, such as singing Psalms in the Molokan way, and performance of bows during singing and prayers and so on. The Germans wanted to toss out everything that was Russian and Molokan from the service and set up everything in the German manner."[90]

By contrast, Ondra had a clear vision. He was keenly aware of opportunities in the southwest region of the Russian Empire among German-speakers. Ondra convinced Kargel that he should lead the Sorotschin German Baptist Church. Sorotschin, then in the far western part of the Russian Empire, is in present-day Ukraine. The Baptist church was founded and cared for by Matthew Kelm, who in 1860 had been baptized as a believer—at fifty-three years of age—by Gottfried Alf. Two years later, Kelm took up ministry in Sorotschin. Alf made a journey from Warsaw to (for him) this remote area in 1862 to help Kelm make connections with German Baptist immigrants moving into the area. The village was over 800 kilometers by horse and wagon from Warsaw, the final stretch through a road-less forest.[91] German Baptist influence was spreading. Kelm settled in the area but wrote to Oncken in 1863 that "The moral and spiritual degradation with which we are surrounded here is beyond description! On every hand, and especially by those who call themselves Christians, we are ridiculed and annoyed. The members of the Lutheran and Greek [Orthodox] churches would destroy us, 'the sooner the better' if it were in their power."[92] However, a Baptist church was established in Sorotschin and this grew to over 240 members under Kelm's leadership. During Kelm's time as pastor, he led the church through difficult times of persecution by the Lutherans in the area, including public ridicule and beatings.[93]

There was a strong connection between Karl Ondra and the Sorotschin church, since Ondra and his step-brother August Meereis (an important figure in German Baptist life) were baptized by Kelm. The events illustrate how German Baptist networks operated. Kelm

---

89. Coleman, *Russian Baptists and Spiritual Revolution*, 92–100.

90. "Gosudarstvennyi muzei istorii religii," Koll. I, op.8, d. 516, l. 24ob, as cited in Coleman, *Russian Baptists and Spiritual Revolution*, 96.

91. Wardin, *Gottfried F. Alf*, 78.

92. Kelm, "Russia, Letter from the Polish Emigrants," 13.

93. Ibid., 61.

had officially retired from his ministry before Ondra and Kargel met, and Ondra was keen to ensure ongoing leadership in Sorotschin. He saw in Kargel, despite his inexperience, someone who could help to meet the needs of the church. After the May Mennonite Brethren conference Kargel went to the Volhynia region with Ondra. Kargel wrote: "We enjoyed wonderful days and a love feast and also some time in Annenthal near Odessa. Then the train took us onto Berdiczew and to Zhitomir and then to here. Once we arrived at the church in Neudorf,[94] they suggested that I visit all the preaching stations."[95] The idea that Ondra had conceived came to fruition. While he was in the region, Kargel was called to be the pastor at Sorotschin. He began his ministry in 1873. The Sorotschin church could have been considered to be on the untamed frontier, and it might not have been attractive to some German ministers. As a young man, Kargel was open to new challenges, and his vision was being expanded rapidly. Kargel's early ministry in Sorotschin was noted by Rushbrooke: "Baptists secured a footing in Volhynia through the incoming of preachers from Germany and Poland, S. Lehmann and Kargel being among the earliest missionaries."[96] When Kargel took over the work in Sorotschin, the church had sixteen preaching stations and 244 members.[97] In 1874, the membership was 296.[98] In addition to preaching and pastoral work, Kargel also performed marriages.[99]

Johann Kargel was pastor in Sorotschin for less than twenty-four months, five of which were spent in Hamburg at Oncken's school. He was not yet ordained. While Kargel was in Hamburg attending classes, Ondra looked after the congregation, baptizing several people in

---

94. One of the preaching stations of Neudorf was Solodyri in the Volhynia Region. When in the village of Solodyri, nearly a decade later, Kargel made the statement that his mother and brother were living "here in the Volhynia Region." This could, in the future, shed some light on the family of Johann Kargel. See J. G. Kargel to "Dear friend and brother in Christ" [V. A. Pashkov], 4 June 1885, 2/13/016, Pashkov Papers.

95. Kargel, "Soroczin," 84.

96. Rushbrooke, *The Baptist Movement in the Continent of Europe*, 131.

97. "Statistics of Continental Baptist Churches [1873]," 62.

98. "Statistics of Continental Baptist Churches [1875]," 16.

99. It is recorded that he signed the marriage certificate of John Klemm, Albert W. Wardin, Jr.'s great-grandfather. See Miller, *In the Midst of Wolves*, xiv. The foreword is written by Albert W. Wardin, Jr.

Sorotschin and in Neudorf.[100] In early 1875, Kargel took a three-month trip to Saint Petersburg to assist with the German Baptist work there, only to decide to remain there rather than returning to Volhynia, as will be seen in more detail in the next chapter. His tendency to move on to new challenges was evident. Kargel's departure from Sorotschin after a relatively short time as pastor, and without giving the congregation notice, caused "some tensions and hard feelings in the Sorotschin church toward him."[101] The Sorotschin congregation was without a pastor until Adam Reinhold Schiewe arrived in 1876. Schiewe stayed five years before moving to Saint Petersburg to replace Kargel, who by this time had moved to Bulgaria. This move will be further discussed in chapter 4. By 1881, despite the pastoral uncertainties, the Sorotschin church numbered over 700 members. At that stage it released 323 members to form nine new preaching stations.[102] Later in Kargel's life, he returned to Sorotschin, and the memory of his rapid departure seems to have faded. He reported that when he returned in October 1889 he spoke at a conference with 1,200 in attendance.[103]

The growing Europe-wide, German-speaking Baptist community was—as noted above—held together by triennial conferences and by the Hamburg Mission School. The school was important for Kargel's ministry. Although it was hoped that he would have enrolled for training at the school in 1870, that did not happen. In what appear to be minutes concerning the Hamburg school signed by Emil Windolf, there is the following explanation: "In the autumn of 1869, twenty brothers were accepted to start the Hamburg school in 1870. But war broke out with France and that year's school was postponed. In a meeting on 28 August 1871, it was decided to start the school in February 1872. This revised date did not come to fruition due to the Hamburg Baptist internal struggles. The Altona [Baptist] church had pulled all the churches into the struggle and there was not sufficient financing to pay for the school."[104]

---

100. Ondra, "Polen und Russland," 178.
101. Miller, *In the Midst of Wolves*, 62.
102. Ibid., 59.
103. Ivan Kargel to "My dear friend and brother in the Lord Jesus Christ" [V. A. Pashkov], 23 October 1889, 2/13/081, Pashkov Papers.
104. Windolf, "Verschiedenes zur Geschichte des Seminars," 9.

The internal struggles concerned the question of the authority of the pastor of a church over the deacons. Oncken took the view that the deacons in the Hamburg church were not active enough in house visiting, and therefore exercised his authority and terminated their ministry. This produced a split in the Hamburg church, and the formation of a second congregation. Julius Köbner was one of those seeking reconciliation in the early 1870s.[105] At the time, Kargel may have not been aware of these struggles, although he knew that the school was not accepting new students in the years 1870 to 1873. The "Hamburg Struggle" lasted throughout his studies in Hamburg and he was aware of the conflict at its close.

After his training in Hamburg, Kargel was firmly within the wider German Baptist orbit and would remain there until he came into contact with the Pashkovites in Saint Petersburg. The school deserves examination, because of its place in Kargel's development.

THE HAMBURG MISSION SCHOOL

The school in Hamburg was at the heart of the German Baptist plan for mission across continental Europe. It was founded in 1849 (the year of Kargel's birth) following the German Baptist Union's conference of that year where it was decided that steps should be taken to train mission workers.[106] The German Baptists referred to it simply as "*die Missionsschule*" (The Mission School)[107] until 1880, when it became the "Hamburg Baptist Seminary." The school provided a six-month training course for missionaries, preachers, and evangelists. Between 1849 and 1880, 100 students graduated.[108] The program was "not aiming at any great show of learning," but rather sought to provide instruction by "experienced ministers" so that students would be enabled to "preach throughout the length and breadth of the land" and "speak and write their own language with correctness and fluency."[109]

---

105. Balders, *Theurer Bruder Oncken*, 147–48.

106. Wagner, *New Move Forward in Europe*, 23.

107. Some have also referred to it as "The Preacher's School." I will refer to it as the "Hamburg Mission School."

108. Wagner, *New Move Forward in Europe*, 23.

109. M., "Missionary Students in Hamburg," 92.

In 1880, the six-month program, which had a particular emphasis on mission, was changed to a three-year program.[110] During the time Kargel was there, the teaching was done by several pastors: Oncken and Gülzau taught Biblical Exposition and Homiletics; Willraht taught Church History, German, and Reading; and Dengel taught Mathematics, Writing, Geography, and Singing.[111] It was noted in 1874 that up to that point the school had trained eighty-five students in these nine topics and that many of those who had been at the school were currently successful preachers and evangelists.[112] parallel Baptist training college in England was C. H. Spurgeon's Pastors' College and through the friendship that grew up between Spurgeon and Oncken there was sharing of information. The Pastors' College report in 1872 stated that "(s)everal German gentlemen have requested admission."[113] This was, no doubt, because of the problems in Hamburg during that time.

Donald Miller notes that the students who joined the school in 1872 included Joseph C. Herb, Julius Hermann, Adam Reinhold Schiewe, Johann Kargel, Julius Vogel, and Eduard Aschendorf.[114] However, this intake did not take place. *Missionsblatt* announced that sixteen students had graduated from the school in September 1874, following the re-starting of the school in that year.[115] Their names are recorded in a set of unpublished minutes: A. Kühn of Reetz, J. Marcks of Hamburg, J. A. Rumberg of Riga, O. Langer of Braunschweig, J. H. Jansen of Ihren, H. Siemens of Ihren, J. G. Kargel of Sorotschin, J. Hermann of Rossitten, F. Götke of Templin, L. Hellm of Templin, E. Aschendorf of Zezulin, J. G. Herb of Kazin, J. Vogel of Kazin, S. Lehmann of Bremen, F. Neuschaefer of Hessen, and M. Riess of Libau.[116] The minutes state that there was a seventeenth student but the name is not given.[117] *Missionsblatt* mentioned that one student

110. Barnes, *Truth is Immortal*, 24.

111. Neuschaefer, "Schlubfeier der Missionsschule," 170; Windolf, "Verschiedenes zur Geschichte des Seminars," 9. Only the family names are recorded in these sources.

112. Windolf, "Verschiedenes zur Geschichte des Seminars," 10.

113. Annual Paper descriptive of the Lord's Work connected with the Pastor's College, 1871, 6–7, as cited in Randall, "The World is our Parish," 74.

114. Miller, *In the Midst of Wolves*, 150.

115. Neuschaefer, "Schlubfeier der Missionsschule," 170.

116. See Donat, *Das Waschsende Werk*, 258.

117. Windolf, "Verschiedenes zur Geschichte des Seminars," 9–10.

(Langer) was "on his deathbed," but Langer's name is included in the minutes. It is very possible that the seventeenth student was Adam Reinhold Schiewe,[118] the pastor in Lodz from 1872 until 1876. He was ordained in December 1874, three months after the 1874 class completed their studies. Kargel was also ordained at the end of his studies. Schiewe served as pastor in Sorotschin and then in Saint Petersburg. After his ministry in Russia, Adam Schiewe returned to Hamburg and had connections with the seminary from 1908 until 1911.[119] Karl Ondra went with Kargel to Hamburg in 1874 but his name is not on the list of 1874 graduating students. It can be safely assumed that he no longer needed the courses since he had attended previously.

The classes in the Hamburg Mission School at that time followed this pattern:[120]

	7:30–8:30	8:30–9:30	10:00–12:00	2:00–4:00	4:30–6:30
Monday	Arithmetic	Reading	Scripture Exegesis	German	Writing and Composition
Tuesday	Singing	Church History	Scripture Exegesis	German	Sketches of Sermons
Wednesday	Singing	History	Scripture Exegesis	German	Writing and Composition
Thursday	Singing	Reading	Scripture Exegesis	German	Sketches of Sermons
Friday	Accounting	Church History	Scripture Exegesis	German	Arithmetic and Church History
Saturday	German	German	Scripture Exegesis	Free	Free
Sunday					

Some significant gaps in the curriculum exist, at least from the point of view of traditional German theology. There were no classes in systematic theology, for example. The emphasis was on a biblical rather than a systematic approach to the faith. This is not to suggest that Oncken lacked awareness of theological traditions. He espoused—as

---

118. Schiewe's name appears on Donald Miller's list. Miller is citing an undocumented student list of 1871.

119. Wagner, *New Move Forward in Europe*, 27.

120. M., "Missionary Students in Hamburg," 92.

did Spurgeon—an evangelical Calvinist position. This was not a position promoted by all the German Baptist leaders. Another influence was Moravian piety. German Baptists sang Moravian hymns, as well as Lutheran chorales and new songs, and the stress on singing in the school's curriculum is notable. Presumably, Kargel would have gained a basic understanding of Calvinistic theology while in Hamburg, but the stress on biblical exegesis and the lack of systematic theology are significant. Later in his life, Kargel would be known for his ability to "inspire [others] with a deep knowledge of the Lord and Scripture."[121] As one of the best known biblical expositors of the Russian-speaking world, Kargel would advocate a biblical rather than a systematic understanding of the faith. That is not to say that he shut himself off from theological issues. In 1924, in a letter to a church in America, he warned them of the "higher criticism" being generated from their seminaries.[122] But his concern was to promote unity rather than emphasize theological differences.

In any case, although the Hamburg school did seek to provide solid biblical instruction, there was strong emphasis on the practice of ministry and mission. German Baptist ecclesiastical methods, approaches to worship, mission strategies, and commitment to interchurch fellowship through a conference structure,[123] were all doubtless imbibed by Kargel during his period in Hamburg. The practical nature of the training was to prove an issue later in Kargel's ministry when he was asked about documentation to prove his education in Hamburg. By this time (in the 1880s) he was working primarily within the Russian evangelical environment, and there was talk of a new initiative for a school in Tultscha, Romania. This would (as will be seen in chapter 6) have involved finding qualified teachers. Kargel wrote regarding the production of a diploma as evidence of his education that "I cannot come up with one of those, because the seminary in Hamburg, from where I received my education, did not have one, as it was mainly a school with religious tendencies, namely Baptist, which were not accepted by the State, and therefore I could not receive a report card from the state; only at the end of the course were we ordained as preachers and dismissed in that way. Whether this is enough for the

121. Lieven, *Duxovnoe Probuzhdenie V Rossii*, 106.
122. "Svedeniya o Dele Bozhiem," 14.
123. Toews, "Baptists and Mennonite Brethren in Russia," 95.

Romanians, for our purposes, is questionable."[124] In fact, having only spent six months in training, a diploma would not have been expected or appropriate. From this statement of Kargel's, it can be assumed that he possessed no other educational qualification, disproving the claims by some that he had been trained as an engineer,[125] or had some other form of higher education.[126] His educational experience, which was to remain important to him, was within a German Baptist setting.

CONCLUSION

Johann Kargel was brought into Baptist life in Tiflis, in a church that was influenced by both German Baptist and Russian traditions. German Baptist worship was mixed with Molokan tradition, which reflected something of the ceremony and mystery of Orthodoxy.[127] Kargel also made contact with Johann Wieler and through him met Karl Ondra. These two men brought the young Kargel into the heart of the developing Mennonite Brethren circle, with its German-speaking baptistic revivalism. As a result of these encounters, Kargel was drawn into a leadership position. Despite the fact that he was serving as the pastor of the German Baptist church in Sorotschin, he maintained an interdenominational ministry through his contact with the Mennonite Brethren.[128] It was while he was in Hamburg as a student that Johann Kargel, by then in his mid-twenties, began to understand more deeply German Baptist ways. He absorbed these and returned to ministry as a more informed German Baptist, implementing the approach to church leadership that he had learned while in Hamburg. He also gained connections through his classmates and other members of the German Union. These relationships were maintained, as will be seen in the next chapter. Yet wider evangelical sympathies were develop-

---

124. J. G. Kargel to "My beloved brother" [V. A. Pashkov], 11 January, 1894, 2/13/100, Pashkov Papers.

125. Karetnikova, *Almanax po Istorii Russkogo Baptisma, vypusk 4*, 5; Skopina, "Iz Biografii I. V. Kargelya," 689.

126. Sawatsky, *Soviet Evangelicals*, 448; Kuznetsova, "Early Russian Evangelicals," 278.

127. See Coleman, *Russian Baptists and Spiritual Revolution*, 100–104.

128. During the next period of his life, when he served as pastor to the German Baptist congregation in Saint Petersburg, Kargel still travelled to the Mennonite Brethren as an itinerant preacher. See Harms, *Geschichte Der Mennoniten Bruedergemeinde*, 60.

ing. However, in his mid-twenties Johann Kargel was firmly situated within the German Baptist Union, focused on ministry among the German population abroad, and operating according to the prevailing German Baptist method of ministry.

3

First Saint Petersburg Period

Exposed to Evangelicalism

(1875–1880)

THE NEXT PHASE OF Johann Kargel's life and ministry began with a move from Sorotschin to Saint Petersburg. In early 1875 Kargel felt called to Saint Petersburg to be involved in the German Baptist church there. The move was highly significant. At this time, Saint Petersburg was one of the three leading centers for the social life of the European aristocracy. It seems that he was won over by the life of the city, the possibilities for ministry, and the denominational freedom that he felt as he travelled in and around Saint Petersburg. From the early 1860s, a small group of evangelicals in Saint Petersburg from different denominational backgrounds—mainly Germans, though some were Russian—all of whom had an interest in mission, started meeting each Monday evening for prayer, to read devotional books and to hear missionary reports from several missions including the Basle Mission and the Moravians. One of the members attended an Evangelical Alliance conference in Geneva in 1861, and when information about the Alliance was shared with the group the members decided to associate themselves with the annual international concert of prayer that was organized by the Evangelical Alliances in different countries during the first week of January.[1]

When the Evangelical Alliance was founded in England in 1846, Oncken was present, promoting the idea that British Christians needed to show greater concern for mainland Europe. Oncken stated

---

1. *Evangelical Christendom*, vol. 17 (March 1863) 128, as cited in Randall, "Eastern European Baptists and the Evangelical Alliance," 19.

that in his view such knowledge was "sadly deficient."[2] The Alliance was founded for the purpose of launching, as it was stated, "a definite organization for the expression of unity among Christian individuals belonging to different churches."[3] The Alliance's vision for unity was to be important for Eastern European Baptists.[4] Erich Geldbach, in his examination of the approach of Köbner, notes that Köbner believed that "(a)ll who believe in Christ are part of God's people which is why he eagerly participated in early ecumenical attempts as they found expression in the Evangelical Alliance."[5] G. W. Lehmann and Eduard Kuntze, a Lutheran pastor who had been a curate at the German Savoy Church in London, were also active in the Evangelical Alliance.[6]

Against the background of these international evangelical links, Johann Oncken made a trip to Saint Petersburg in 1864 to make an appeal for action to be taken in support of German evangelicals who were being persecuted in the Volhynia region. He secured an interview with a Count Sievers, representing the Russian Ministry of the Interior, and in the course of the conversation Sievers emphasized that no conversion to Baptist beliefs from among Russian Orthodox Church members was permissible.[7] Oncken stayed in the city five weeks and baptized eight people from the German-speaking evangelical community.[8]

By the late 1860s Saint Petersburg was becoming the scene of increasing evangelical activity. Kargel's experiences in the city in the later 1870s were to prove pivotal to his spiritual development.

GERMAN BAPTIST LIFE IN SAINT PETERSBURG

In 1872, the American Baptist Missionary Union, based on information provided by the German Baptist Union, listed five German Baptist

---

2. Report of the Proceedings of the Conference held at Freemasons' Hall, London, from August 19th to September 2nd Inclusive, 1846 (London, 1847), 242, as cited in Randall and Hilborn, *One Body in Christ*, 61.
3. Howard, *The Dream that would Not Die*, 7.
4. Randall, "Eastern European Baptists and the Evangelical Alliance," 14–33.
5. Geldbach, "Julius Köbner 's Contribution to Baptist Identity," 68.
6. Randall and Hilborn, *One Body in Christ*, 160.
7. Byford, "The Movement in Russia," 74.
8. Byford, *The Soul of Russia*, 341–42.

First Saint Petersburg Period   49

churches in Russia. These five churches were: Horssazik [Hortschik],[9] founded in 1864; Soroczin [Sorotschin], founded in 1864; Neudorf, founded in 1866; Alt Danzig, founded in 1869; and Odessa, founded in 1870.[10] Saint Petersburg was not listed as having a German Baptist congregation. The first known Baptist witness in Saint Petersburg began in October 1855 when C. Plonus, a tailor from the Baptist Church in Memel, moved to the Russian capital.[11] Plonus reached out to other Germans in the city and soon a small Bible study began.[12] It has also been suggested that Plonus was the person who gave a tract to a Mennonite that inspired some Mennonites to explore believer's baptism by immersion and subsequently to create the Mennonite Brethren.[13] The origins of the Mennonite Brethren are much more complex than that, as has been seen, but it is clear that Plonus was engaging in robust witness within the Saint Petersburg evangelical milieu. This early Saint Petersburg group is not to be considered as an organized Baptist church but rather a preaching station of the Memel Baptist Church.

In their reports on Baptist expansion, the German Baptist Union leaders highlighted the possibility of Baptist expansion further east from their foothold in Volhynia. Oncken himself, as stated previously, had reported in 1869 on the "glorious" prospects in Russia, although he had not mentioned Saint Petersburg specifically.[14] An important development that was to affect Kargel took place in 1873, and this is explained in a letter written by Karl Ondra.[15] A German merchant named J. Schulz was travelling to Saint Petersburg in that year and, in addition to pursuing his business interests in the city, he was carrying a letter from Ondra, who had helped to place Kargel in Sorotschin. It seems that in the early 1870s the German Baptist leadership had become anxious to renew contact with the German Baptists living in Saint Petersburg. There was no Baptist pastor in the city and they felt

9. Alternate spellings used are Horczik and Horstschick. See Wardin, *Gottfried F. Alf*, 78 and Miller, *In the Midst of Wolves*, 37.

10. "Mission to Germany [1872]," 286.

11. Wardin, "Baptists (German) in Russian and USSR," 193.

12. Wardin, *Gottfried F. Alf*, 19.

13. See Stassen, "Anabaptist Influence in the Origin of the Particular Baptists," 322–48.

14. "Mission to Germany [1869]," 278.

15. Ondra, "Russland and Polen," 192–95.

on their own. Ondra mentioned that there had been visits by German Baptists in the past but that there "had been no outsider to visit them in a long time." The last visit to the Baptist group, according to Ondra, was made by two people, Wieler and Baumgärtner.[16] German Baptist movement were clearly keen to see the Baptist group, which was still attached to Memel, become a church in its own right.

Schultz had difficulty finding the members of the small Baptist community and had to resort to asking the Lutheran pastor for help in locating them. Once the letter from Ondra to the Baptist group was delivered and read, there was discussion within the group as to whether they needed someone—perhaps Ondra himself—to come and visit them. Schultz suggested to them that a visit from Ondra would help in discussion of Baptist principles. After taking a vote, the congregation decided to invite Ondra to come.[17] It was to become clear that there were considerable tensions in the community. Perhaps they recognized that someone from outside might wish them to be more explicit in their witness, giving greater emphasis to Baptist distinctives, and to moves that would establish them as a church. When Oncken met with Sievers he had not mentioned Baptist commitment to believer's baptism, but had told the Count (who may or may not have understood all that Oncken was saying) that Baptists were seeking to "win souls to Christ" through spreading their message "among the millions throughout Europe, who have rejected all revealed truth and who form a most dangerous element to all good governments."[18] The manner in which Oncken chose to focus on Baptists as part of a wider evangelical community and on their ability to contribute to social stability was, arguably, somewhat disingenuous. Oncken and the German Baptist movement wanted, in fact, to set up Baptist churches in as many places as possible.[19] It was this that Ondra hoped would be the result in Saint Petersburg.

Even though Ondra received the invitation from Saint Petersburg, an invitation he had himself—at least in part—engineered, he was not able to visit the city in 1873 because of the pressures of his local ministry in the Volhynia region. Eventually, after consulting Oncken and

16. Ibid., 193.
17. Ibid.
18. Cooke, *Johann Gerhard Oncken*, 146–48.
19. Randall, "Every Apostolic Church a Mission Society," 281–301.

Brother Gülzau (one of the teachers at the Hamburg Mission School), Ondra felt convinced that he had to make the time to visit the group in Saint Petersburg to see what was happening and he set out on 23 June 1874. He arrived at the home of a "Brother Schwan" in Saint Petersburg on 30 June 1874. J. Schwan had already been known to the wider German Baptist world for some years. He was an Estonian who had been one of those baptized by Oncken in Saint Petersburg in 1864 and at times had ministered on the Estonian Island of Saaremaa.[20] In 1866 it had been reported that Schwan, who was a land surveyor, had been accused of being a self-constituted priest. Russian police were posted around his house every Sunday to prevent visitors from entering the house for meetings. He was also, in this period, fined fifteen silver rubles.[21] It is clear that he was the leader of an evangelical group—almost certainly a continuation of the Plonus group—and that he was a Baptist, but he does not seem to have been functioning as the pastor of a Baptist congregation.

When Ondra found Schwan, a reasonably encouraging sight greeted him. Several men were present in Schwan's home, engaged in a Bible study. Over the next several days, however, Ondra became very discouraged and even embarrassed about the spiritual state of the group. "After I became more personally involved in the serious situations of the people's personal lives," he wrote, "I was so embarrassed and wanted to pack my bags and return home. If it would not have looked like I was running from a difficult situation, I would have left."[22]

1 Corinthians 13:13.[23] It was a message about love and unity. The reaction from the congregation was heartening to Ondra. During the sermon and throughout the afternoon members of the group poured out confessions, offering and receiving forgiveness with evident sincerity. Later, Ondra was able to report, "There was hardly a dry eye and the people began to get up and confess openly to each other. Even in the afternoon, there was much openness with much reconciliation and forgiveness. It is easy when God directs the hearts. I think I was part of something lasting. May God let it be so. God also let us take part in

20. Pilli, "Baptists in Estonia 1884–1940," 27.
21. "Livonia and Esthonia," 150.
22. Ondra, "Russland and Polen," 194.
23. The text speaks of faith, hope, and love, with love being the greatest of these.

the confession of two believing souls about their need for baptism. I learned something about the Lord's Day that day."[24]

The Saint Petersburg group, now enlivened, wanted to take as much advantage as possible of the ministry of an ordained Baptist visitor. They organized a baptism for Monday (the day after Ondra's sermon) at a lake across the Finnish Bay.[25] There Ondra baptized five people. The rest of the day was spent in teaching and in enjoying the view across the water of Saint Petersburg. There were subsequent visits to some local *dachas* (summer residences) presumably owned by members of the group. After several enjoyable days, Ondra had to return home. He had gathered enough information about the situation in Saint Petersburg and could now give his wholehearted endorsement to the small Baptist group. As he said his goodbyes, two women came to him with tears in their eyes. They had wanted to be baptized but their circumstances had not allowed them to participate in the service. Ondra, as a visiting missionary, was torn: he felt the needs of this community yet he was aware of the needs of his own post. He prayed again for the group, asking God's blessing.[26]

It is evident that Ondra did not forget the group, since within a few months he asked Johann Kargel to travel from Sorotschin to Saint Petersburg. The purpose of the trip was twofold. The German Baptist Union seems to have identified Kargel as a capable leader, since in September 1874 Kargel was asked by them to travel to Saint Petersburg to petition the Russian government for a formal recognition of the German Baptists who were experiencing persecution.[27] Ondra was part of this decision and he also wanted Kargel to continue the ministry that he had started earlier that year. This excursion opened up a whole new world to Kargel. To his own surprise, he remained in the city rather than returning to Sorotschin. The change was enormous. It is difficult to say whether it was the city life, ministry possibilities, or guidance from Ondra that had most weight in convincing Kargel to stay. Certainly mission was central. Two years after his arrival, Kargel

---

24. Ondra, "Russland and Polen," 194.

25. Ondra states that the lake was near Pargalova and Kablowfa. Kargel states that Lake Schuwalowo had been used for baptisms prior to Kargel performing a baptism there in 1876.

26. Ondra, "Russland and Polen," 194–95.

27. "Donesenie o sezde nemeckih menonitov i baptistov," para. 8.

estimated that in terms of mission to Germans there were between 45,000 and 50,000 Germans living in Saint Petersburg.[28] He was a young man with new adventures beckoning. In Saint Petersburg his thoughts and experiences were to be broadened considerably.

BLESSING AND ENJOYMENT: KARGEL'S SAINT PETERSBURG PASTORATE

Kargel experienced success in his new location. The new experiences appeared to stimulate him. He was taken into a very different world during this phase of his life and he stated in 1876, after having been in the city a year, "The past year has been one of blessing and enjoyment in Saint Petersburg. Happily, the little band that formerly was much tossed to and fro by internal differences are now fused into a harmonious whole, so that we can now say, 'Behold how good and pleasant it is for brethren to dwell together in unity.'"[29] The theme of unity was one that would become very important to Kargel, but one that would also, ironically, create spiritual tensions.

By the spring of 1876, Kargel had conducted eleven baptisms, established a membership structure, and instituted a procedure for discipline and restored those under discipline. The church at that point numbered thirty-four members.[30] Kargel attended the tenth Triennial Conference of the German Baptist Union in 1876. Kargel reported that his friends who had studied with him in Hamburg were excited to learn more about his work in Saint Petersburg. Baptist outreach in the capital city of Russia, led by a recent student of the Hamburg Mission School, was arousing considerable interest in the wider German Baptist community.[31] The 1876 *Bundes Conferenz* was also concerned with internal struggles within the Germany Union. August Liebig, a participant, explained that the structure of the German Baptist Union was like children's shoes that had been outgrown and needed to be changed.[32] According to the published minutes of the conference, Kargel, with his concern for unity, wanted the German Baptist Union

---

28. Kargel, "Russia, St. Petersburg [1876]," 9.
29. Ibid., 7.
30. Ibid., 8.
31. Kargel, "Russia, Further News," 4–6.
32. *Auszug aus dem Protokoll der zehnten Bundes-Conferenz*, 57.

to "shed more light" on the problems.³³ Others called for clarification as well, but details were not given in the minutes.

While at the Triennial Conference, Kargel was asked to write an article about the work that he had undertaken which was to be published in the Union's *Missionsblatt*. This extended article, published in 1877, is instructive and worth examining at some length, since it shows Kargel's spiritual priorities at this point. The first thing that is clear in the article is that Kargel and the congregation gave priority to evangelical conversion. Kargel noted that during the eight weeks he was away from the city, three of the church leaders, "brothers Plonus, Nickels, and Jacobson," conducted the services "by turns" in the church. Kargel then related the "first joyful news brought to me on my return," which was that:

> two dear brethren, a youth and an old man, had found the Lord. This rejoiced my soul exceedingly. And I do not know how to thank the Lord enough. These, however, were not to be the only ones. A few days later I heard that another person had found peace and again such and such a person had given their heart to the Savior. Until one day Brother Jacobson came to me to say that two Estonian women were converted and wished to be baptized. The Sunday came when these dear friends should acknowledge their faith before the congregation. How sweet it is to listen to the diverse ways which our Lord chooses to bring the lambs into His fold again. How he chastises the one and wins the heart of another by His loving and gentle guidance.³⁴

Kargel clearly placed considerable stress on the individual spiritual experience of these people. There is no suggestion of a set pattern of conversion. The expectation was that each person would be able to give testimony—an important part of the evangelical tradition—and Kargel believed that the testimonies illustrated the "diverse ways" in which God deals with people.

Linked to this was ethnic diversity. Kargel spoke in his article of being "particularly moved" as he heard how the two Estonian women had been converted. "Most of us," he commented, "could not understand one word of their language, as they could not speak German and spoke with the aid of a translator."³⁵ In fact, four language-specific

---

33. Ibid., 58.
34. Kargel, "Russia, Further News," 4–5.
35. Ibid., 5.

Baptist congregations were eventually to develop in Saint Petersburg—German, Estonian, Lettish (Latvian), and Swedish.[36] Kargel spoke of "Brother Jacobson, who after the usual German service holds one in the Estonian language," but added somewhat judgmentally that, "(t)his race that inhabits the southern coast of the Gulf of Finland has peculiar characteristics and particularly that of adhering firmly to their old belief and superstition."[37]

Alongside the holding of spiritual priorities that belonged to the wider evangelical movement, it is clear that the church in Saint Petersburg was firmly Baptist. On the day set for baptizing new converts, the baptismal service was performed, Kargel reported, "according to the ancient form." No doubt by this he meant by immersion—an echo of some of the debates that had taken place in the Mennonite community regarding pouring or immersion. The Saint Petersburg Baptists used Lake Schuwalowo for their baptisms. On the occasion reported by Kargel in his article, an initial group of about twenty people took the train from the city out to the lake where they erected tents. The account is full of fascinating detail. The tents were formed, he wrote,

> by fastening some large sheets to four trees, which served us instead of posts. While these preparations were going on, a crowd of onlookers had assembled who were curious to see what would happen. When all were ready we stepped down to the water's edge where a small clear space enabled us easily to perform the holy ceremony. We formed a half circle and sang a hymn together, which although very weak had the effect of assembling more people. A large number of ladies and gentlemen came from the beautiful villas situated around the lake to see what was going on. Some only looked from a distance whilst others sailed about in boats or came close to where we were standing. After the hymn I read Matthew 3 and held a short discourse about it. And then brother Jacobson sang and gave a short address in Estonian. We all knelt down together and thanked God for the mercy he had shown us in opening our eyes by His Holy Spirit to our great sin. The prayer ended, we performed the Holy ceremony, which I trust brought a blessing not only to us but to the many onlookers.[38]

36. Latimer, *With Christ in Russia*, 40.
37. Kargel, "Russia, Further News," 5.
38. Ibid., 5–6.

The language of "Holy ceremony" perhaps reflects something of the influence of Orthodox spirituality, although it may also be derived from a Lutheran view of the sacraments. However, the emphasis on baptism as a witness to others of a changed life is typically Baptist. German Baptists followed Oncken's lead in this emphasis.[39]

The description by Kargel speaks of ladies and gentleman "from the beautiful villas" coming to see what was going on. Kargel was impressed and surprised by their respectful behavior. Evidently, he had seen some different behavior towards Baptists elsewhere. He commented that "they did not offer one scornful word or cause the least disturbance." Instead the men stood with "uncovered heads and serious faces" and they "remained quietly looking on until the ceremony was concluded."[40] In fact, in this period, evangelical meetings in Saint Petersburg, as reported in British Evangelical Alliance circles, were attracting the "elite of the Russian aristocracy."[41] Kargel's account confirms this interest. He reported:

> Then a young Russian lord came up to our tent and addressed brother Plonus. He asked what we had been doing. Brother P. told him that we had been baptizing according to God's word. But he said: "Do you mean to say that if these people had died unbaptized they would have been lost forever?" Brother P. then explained to him that it was not the ceremony itself which saved us . . . and advised him to study for himself from the Bible the way to gain eternal life. But the whole thing seemed a puzzle to this young Russian, and I then tried to explain to him that the Apostles had never baptized children, but only adults, and although the customs in God's church were different nowadays we still follow the old custom; but that after all "belief in the crucified Lord" was the only true way to Salvation.[42]

There is a balance in this reply between a strong affirmation of the Baptist distinctive of believer's baptism and an acknowledgement that more important than the question of baptism is the question of

---

39. At baptismal services Oncken asked each candidate, "What are you willing to do for Christ?" This impressed C. H. Spurgeon when he visited Hamburg. See Randall, *Communities of Conviction*, 67. For Spurgeon on baptism see Grass and Randall, "Spurgeon on the Sacraments," 55–75.

40. Kargel, "Russia, Further News," 6.

41. *Evangelical Christendom*, vol. 28 (July 1874) 201–3, as cited in Randall, "Eastern European Baptists and the Evangelical Alliance," 24.

42. Kargel, "Russia, Further News," 6.

the "true way to Salvation," which was seen as being through faith in Christ, not through any outward ceremony. Influential Baptists such as Oncken and Spurgeon opposed the idea that baptism contributed to salvation. In 1864 Spurgeon preached a controversial and widely-read sermon on this topic, "Baptismal Regeneration."[43] This was a clear attack on the Church of England, including evangelicals in the Church of England, and it led to Spurgeon's resignation from the Evangelical Alliance. He was later reconciled to the Alliance, but retained a facility to provoke controversy.[44] Spurgeon's robust stance does not seem to have been one that influenced Kargel, who was to find himself increasingly drawn to a more inclusive form of evangelical life.

THE INFLUENCE OF LORD RADSTOCK

The most prominent individual bringing evangelical ideas from England to Saint Petersburg in the years just prior to Kargel's arrival was Granville Augustus William Waldegrave, or Lord Radstock. He was the only son of the second Baron, Vice-Admiral Lord Radstock, who retired from the British Navy in 1815.[45] Upon his father's death, Granville, at the age of twenty-seven, became the third Lord Radstock. Two years before that he had married Susan Calcraft, the daughter of the fifth Duke of Manchester.[46] Waldegrave studied at Oxford University and in 1855 travelled to Crimea as an officer. While in Crimea, he became very ill with a fever and it was this experience that contributed to his evangelical conversion.[47] After his conversion, in typical evangelical fashion, Radstock took up evangelistic activities. He began to visit Middlesex Hospital, for example, praying with the sick and dying. He and his wife, who joined him in his evangelical journey, held small Bible readings in their house after Saturday-evening military drills. A group of officers sat around a table and commented on various biblical passages.[48]

---

43. Spurgeon, "Baptismal Regeneration," 313–28.
44. See Randall and Hilborn, *One Body in Christ*, 113–18.
45. Trotter, *Lord Radstock*, 3.
46. Ibid., 12.
47. Heier, *Religious Schism*, 34.
48. Trotter, *Lord Radstock*, 15–17.

In line with his interest in lay ministry, Radstock became associated with the Brethren movement.[49] The Brethren were committed to a simple form of worship in which believers met for the Lord's Supper (the "breaking of bread") without clerical leadership. Radstock was associated with the Open Brethren, to be distinguished from those who were usually termed the "Exclusive Brethren," led by J. N. Darby.[50] There were highly respected members of the Open Brethren in this period, such as George Müller, well known for his orphanage work in Bristol and his belief in the "faith principle"— praying for, rather than soliciting, funds. The idea of congregational life in which Christian workers depended on God for funds was an expression of this principle of "living by faith."[51] Because of their strong stress on basic evangelical distinctives regarding conversion, the Bible, the cross, and active evangelism, Bebbington has described the Brethren as "evangelicals of the evangelicals."[52]

In 1865 Radstock joined the Evangelical Alliance, which—after having been suspicious of the Brethren—had by this time recognized that the Open Brethren had a place in the wider evangelical world. The Alliance and its links would become a vehicle for Radstock's work in Russia.[53] He also began to preach locally in Weston-super-Mare, described in one history of the Evangelical Alliance as a "fashionable watering place where he had taken a house."[54] It was here, in 1866, through the influence of Radstock, that the German-born Friedrich (Frederick) Baedeker dedicated his life to Christ.[55] Dr. Baedeker[56] would eventually travel to Russia, Siberia and the Caucasus preaching

49. For a history of the Brethren see Grass, *Gathering to His Name*.

50. Ibid. See chapter 4 for the division within the Brethren.

51. For more on Müller and on the "faith principle" see Rowdon, "The Concept of 'Living by Faith,'" 339–56; Summerton, "George Müller and the Financing of the Scriptural Knowledge Institution," 49–79.

52. Bebbington, "The Place of the Brethren Movement in International Evangelicalism," 260.

53. Ewing, *Goodly Fellowship*, 140.

54. Ibid., 152.

55. For a full description of the life and work of Baedeker see Latimer, *Dr. Baedeker*.

56. The title of Doctor may have been granted due to his medical training in surgery, which he received in Bristol, as well as a degree in philosophy, which he earned at the University of Freiburg, and further studies at the Bonn University. See Latimer, *Dr. Baedeker*, 24.

to nobility, peasants, and prisoners, and would become an important colleague of Kargel's.

In 1868 Radstock spoke about the evangelical faith to several members of the Russian aristocracy who were in Paris.[57] Radstock was fluent in French, using it in social settings. His contacts resulted in Radstock visiting Saint Petersburg, his arrival coinciding with Holy Week, 1874. Strict state laws limited his earliest preaching and he was able to speak only in the American Chapel on Post Office Street.[58] This was used by the German Lutheran and the Congregational congregations of the city. These early meetings were attended by a few of the members of the aristocracy whom Radstock had met in Paris. Later Radstock was able to move his meetings to the salons or drawing rooms of his friends among the nobility. These luxurious residences gave stimulus to his activity. He drew upon the Sunday night ministry he had undertaken among fellow officers in England. Within a short time his meetings in Saint Petersburg were attended by an "enormous mass of listeners."[59] A number of wealthy and influential figures became devout evangelicals, including Count Alexis Pavlovich Bobrinsky, Count Modest M. Korff, Natalia Lieven, and Colonel Vasily A. Pashkov.[60]

The immediate success of Radstock's ministry can be attributed to two factors. First, he was exclusively centered on scripture and brought spiritual nourishment to Russians who belonged to the Orthodox Church.[61] Second, the Russians appreciated his sincerity and modesty. Some in Russian society found his French "imperfect," his habits of prayer "English," and his requests to come to him the next day "to find Christ" curious, yet he attracted "cultivated Russians to accept his message."[62] Because he sought no respect, respect was given to him by Russian people who held humility to be the primary Christian virtue.

---

57. Trotter, *Lord Radstock*, 187–88. According to Robert Sloan Latimer, the meetings took place in Switzerland. See Latimer, *Under Three Tsars*, 73.

58. Brandenburg, *The Meek and the Mighty*, 106.

59. Latimer, *Under Three Tsars*, 73.

60. Trotter, *Lord Radstock*, 188–200; Rushbrooke, *The Baptist Movement in the Continent of Europe*, 138–39.

61. Trotter, *Lord Radstock*, 191.

62. Stead, *Truth about Russia*, 355.

As previously mentioned, in 1876 Kargel had a conversation with a member of the Russian nobility about issues connected with baptism. Kargel would have been aware that, through Radstock, a number of aristocrats were by that time becoming well versed in evangelical beliefs. Kargel reported the conversation with the "young Russian lord":

> "I know," he [the young Russian lord] said, "that the Apostles baptized adults in the river as you are doing. But how is it that there is such a great difference in age among these present?" (He must have thought we belonged to the Mennonites who baptize their children when they are grown up, but at a fixed age. Or could he have thought that the Apostles did so?) I pointed out that God's word nowhere prescribes a certain age for baptism, but simply demands faith. When a man acquires faith, be it in his youth or in his old age, he is thereby a fit candidate for baptism. He who has not acquired faith, must, according to God's word, be kept back from this sacred ordinance. This accounts for the difference of age among those baptized. The young Russian, having learned something, then left us. Oh, that the Lord might open his eyes and those of all present.[63]

Kargel was most impressed by this conversation and by evangelicals he was meeting from these aristocratic circles. In May 1878 he wrote in *Missionsblatt*, "I visited with Sister W. but before that I met W. who invited me to the gathering at Count K.'s [Korff]. When I told Sister W. that I was going to the Russian gathering that evening; she promised to come along."[64] It is clear that by this time Kargel was prepared not only to go to these broader, interdenominational, evangelical meetings and to mix with people whose backgrounds were very different from his own, but also to invite others to do so. Dostoevsky remarked on "the coincidence of the appearance of both our sects at the same time: the Stunda—among the common people, and the Radstockists—among the most elegant society" and argued that "they undoubtedly came from one and the same ignorance, that is to say—from the absolute lack of knowledge of their [Russian] religion."[65] Kargel was acquainted with both the Stundists and the Radstockists,

---

63. Kargel, "Russia, Further News," 6.
64. "Russland. St. Petersburg. Nachrichten Von Br. Kargel," 183.
65. Dostoevsky, *Polnoe Sobranie Sochinenij*, vol. XXV, 10–12.

but unlike Dostoevsky, he saw them both as genuine movements of God.

Kargel was particularly fascinated by the deeply personal relationship with Jesus being expressed in these meetings in Saint Petersburg in the later 1870s. His report in *Missionsblatt* in 1878 described how, when he reached one meeting place—"Count R.'s place"—the people were gathering in the courtyard. "A young man offered to take me upstairs. I asked if he loved Jesus and he answered yes with a beaming smile."[66] This young man described to Kargel his thrill at hearing God's word being explained in Saint Petersburg and also in his own language [Russian]. He had, he explained to Kargel, been to Kargel's services and although not understanding the [German] language completely, the young man said that he "felt God's presence as if it was in his own life."[67]

The interdenominational meetings made a lasting impression on Kargel. As well as Radstock, George Müller was to visit Saint Petersburg, speaking at 112 meetings in eleven weeks.[68] Although Radstock and Müller did not promote Brethren ideas, they spoke to audiences as lay people. Radstock showed no interest in forming the kind of Baptist ecclesial life to which Kargel was committed at that time.

ALL THE CHURCHES:
KARGEL AND THE GERMAN BAPTIST UNION

Although Kargel was making new discoveries and connections that would later lead him in a new direction, his primary connection in this period was still with the German Baptist Union. He regularly reported on his activities in *Missionsblatt* and also updated the Union on his financial situation. These reports in turn were sent on to *Quarterly Reporter of the German Baptist Mission* and published in English in the United States. In his report of March 1876 Kargel wrote, "I myself have been at work nearly a year without any pay except the most insignificant sums, which have been given to me. While here nothing better presents itself for the coming year; elsewhere the prospect is much more inviting. My former charge in Volhynia is making every effort

66. "Russland. St. Petersburg. Nachrichten Von Br. Kargel," 183.
67. Ibid.
68. Corrado, "The Philosophy of Ministry of Colonel Vasiliy Pashkov," 107.

to get me back."⁶⁹ He acknowledges being torn between a ministry that can financially support him and the work already started among the "forty-five to fifty thousand Germans" living in Saint Petersburg.⁷⁰ It is noteworthy that within the capital city there was not enough money forthcoming from the Baptist congregation, which was admittedly still small, to supply Kargel with sufficient financial support. In response, Lehmann wrote a well-crafted appeal on Kargel's behalf to the American Baptist Missionary Union, which was published in May 1876. He said:

> Of those who from there [Russia] stretch their hands toward us, I mention now the church of Saint Petersburg. After a series of years in which individual believers acknowledged the truth of baptism and joined together in Christian fellowship, the time seems to have come now, when, with a larger number of believers, they can constitute a regular church. They have called a very dear and talented brother, Mr. Kargel, who for some time received religious instruction in Hamburg. He has accepted the call. They have applied to your German Committee to solicit some aid for the salary of their pastor from the funds derived from the Union.⁷¹

Lehmann explained that the German Committee had hoped to give help to the Saint Petersburg cause but that this had not proved possible. He concluded on an eloquent note: "Oh how painful is this blow to us! We had hoped that at length in the centre of yonder immense dominion [Russia] the glorious gospel in its full truth would be proclaimed, and would celebrate its victories."⁷² As a result of this appeal, in July 1876 the American Baptist Missionary Union, which took a keen interest in Oncken's enterprises, began to support Kargel's work in Saint Petersburg. Kargel was fully dependent on his German Baptist connections.

This correspondence was reprinted in the German Baptist Mission's 1876 annual report, along with a vivid report recently received from Saint Petersburg including descriptions by Kargel of some support from the aristocracy, of persecutions, and of baptisms

---

69. Kargel, "Russia, St. Petersburg [1876]," 8.
70. Ibid., 9.
71. "Mission to Germany, Appeal from the German Committee," 77.
72. Ibid., 78.

taking place. Kargel reported: "It is of special interest, that a Russian general's wife, with whom I had only become acquainted a few days previous, together with a lady of the imperial court, was present at our last baptism."[73] One instance of persecution was related to a wedding celebrated on 1 March 1876 in the village of Natjagailowka. This wedding was celebrated, said Kargel, "exactly in the middle of the great fasting time, to the greatest vexation of the Orthodox. The peasants, infuriated, dragged the guilty ones to the magistrate; but, not finding him at home, they resolved to punish the 'Stundisten' after their own laws. Thus the beating began: the chief criminal received about one hundred and fifty stripes."[74] It is not clear how these Stundists were connected with Kargel's congregation, but he was evidently intent on emphasizing, for German and American readers, the importance of supporting work that was subject to severe repression. He also reported that on 15 March 1876, "we were again permitted to baptize three dear friends; thus there have fourteen been added to the little flock since my arrival."[75]

A year later, Kargel expressed once more his sense of strong connection with the German Baptist Union. He quoted from St. Paul's instructions, "On the authority of these words: 'If one member be honored, all members rejoice,' I write these lines. Now I thank all the dear brethren and sisters and all the churches for their kind gifts toward the expenses of my journey to Germany. May the Lord bless you a thousand fold for your donations! Kindest greetings to you from this small community and your humble fellow servant."[76]

Two years after the commencement of Kargel's ministry, there were forty-five members in the German Baptist church in Saint Petersburg, with more people in attendance. A report by Joseph Lehmann in 1877, designed to be widely read in Baptist circles, stated: "Brother Kargel has not labored in vain during the cold winter season. A new harvest of souls has appeared with the return of spring, so that it was permitted to baptize eight persons, more than ever at one time, at Saint Petersburg, on the 5th of May."[77] The German Baptist church

73. "Mission to the Germans," 273.
74. Ibid.
75. Ibid.
76. Kargel, "Russia, Further News," 6.
77. Lehmann, "Letter from Rev. Joseph Lehmann," 376.

continued to grow and eventually took up residence in a four-storey building located at 4 Serpuchiowska Street. The early Baptist witness of Plonus and the Bible study led by Schwan had developed into a Baptist church under the leadership of Johann Kargel.

Kargel went through a long process in 1877 to become "naturalized in Russia." The reason stated was so that "he could not be banished from the country in case of persecution."[78] Ondra, Schiewe, and others had been banished to "obscure places in Poland, where they had no friends and relations, while [others] were deposited on the Austrian frontier."[79] Donald Thompson noted that "a German might take out naturalization papers in another country without losing his citizenship in Germany."[80] Once naturalized, Kargel held rights in Russia and secured a guarantee against being exiled.[81]

In 1879, Kargel took advantage of a period of greater religious freedom in Russia to register his German Baptist congregation with the government officials. As a naturalized Russian citizen and a minister of the German Baptist Church in Saint Petersburg, Kargel saw this registration as significant "not only for the Baptists at [Saint] Petersburg but also for all Baptists in the Russian Empire."[82] In the process of registering his church, he also took an oath of allegiance to the Tsar. The experience was detailed in *Wahrheitszeuge*[83] and translated into English in *The Baptist Missionary Magazine*.[84] By this action, Kargel registered the first Baptist church in Orthodox Russia.[85] At the time, the congregation was composed of sixty members.[86] He wrote: "First of all the [Baptist] churches in Russia *we* had everything

---

78. Ibid.

79. Ibid., 377.

80. Thompson, *Donald Thompson in Russia*, xiv.

81. Because it is yet to be determined which passport Johann Kargel held from birth, it is therefore difficult to explore the contractual arrangements with the governments of that period. It is also yet to be determined what his status was after the Russians changed their passport system during the Soviet period.

82. "Recognition of the Church," 124.

83. "Erste Fruechte," 54.

84. "Recognition of the Church," 124–25. Also see Latimer, *Under Three Tsars*, 99–100.

85. It may not be considered by some to be the first Baptist church in Russia because the congregation was of German extraction.

86. "Recognition of the Church," 125.

[correct], for which we are much indebted to the excellent and kind bearing of the authorities towards us."[87] Lehmann wrote that Kargel "sings a Te Deum for the new liberty."[88] The registration ceremony was described in detail. Kargel was, according to the law, to kiss the cross and the Bible. He stated, however, that he had no cross and that Baptists did not kiss the Bible, at which point he was told simply to sign a document and report any heresies in Baptist communities.[89]

As a result of the process of legal recognition of the Baptists in Saint Petersburg, there were new freedoms. Baptists were granted permission to go directly to the "censor" to print a hymnal in the Lettish (Latvian) language without having to go through Lutheran channels as had previously been the required procedure. Kargel also noted that "the soul of the Christian movement at St. Petersburg has given three hundred Russian rubles from the funds of the Society of Christian Knowledge to assist our brethren in Leifland and Courland to publish Lettish tracts. All he stipulated was that they should not contain anything denominational."[90]

The expression "the soul of the Christian movement" is fascinating. There seems little doubt that the reference is to Vasily Pashkov, who took on the leadership of the evangelical movement that owed its beginnings to Radstock. Pashkov was enormously wealthy and was committed to producing and promoting evangelical literature. Kargel had an increasing desire to use such literature. He drew together the young people in his congregation and taught them to pass out literature in the streets of the capital.[91] He also engaged in a great deal of pastoral work. He wrote in 1877: "I spend much of my time in house visitation, conversing with the unconverted and the careless in their home, with the aged poor in the workhouse, and with some of high rank who from time to time attend our services."[92] The church membership in the 1870s did not become large. In 1878 he spoke about having fifty members.[93] However, as a result of the greater freedom

---

87. Ibid., 124.
88. Ibid.
89. Ibid.
90. Ibid., 125.
91. Kargel, "Russland. St. Petersburg," 126.
92. "Annual Report," 3.
93. "Russia, St. Petersburg," 7.

he organized larger events—"love feasts"—and at these he explained to his audiences, in robust Baptist fashion, how "[B]aptist views appeared in Germany through brother Oncken and thence spread over the whole continent."[94]

THE PASHKOVITES

The influence of Colonel Pashkov in Kargel's spiritual development cannot be overstated. Vasily Alexandrovich Pashkov was born in 1813 into an aristocratic Russian family. The family, one of the wealthiest and most socially prominent in Russia, was truly *boyarin*—a Russian term which means that the family's ancestry was traceable to medieval times.[95] Vasily Pashkov received the best education possible. He then chose to enter the military and eventually become Captain of the Cavalry and aide-de-camp to the Emperor. He retired as a colonel and gave attention to the lands he owned in Saint Petersburg, Novgorod, Moscow, Tambov, Orenburg, and to large copper mines in the Urals. His wife, Alexandra Ivanovna Pashkov, welcomed Lord Radstock to one of the Pashkov residences in 1874 but Colonel Pashkov, irritated by Radstock's presence, left to visit his estates in Moscow. When he returned, the English evangelist was still in Saint Petersburg and was using the Pashkov estate for meetings.

One evening, Alexandra Ivanovna Pashkov invited Radstock to dinner. Colonel Pashkov was unable to excuse himself politely and sat listening to Radstock making various comments about Saint Paul's letter to the Romans. At the conclusion of the meal, the evangelist asked if he could pray for the family. Radstock invited the Pashkovs to kneel with him on the floor and he began an extemporaneous prayer.[96]
Prayer affected Vasily Pashkov deeply and the meeting with Radstock proved to be a turning-point in Pashkov's life. Vasily Pashkov now threw himself and his possessions fully into the propagation of the evangelical message.

Beginning in 1878, the Russian evangelical movement centered in Saint Petersburg increasingly became known as Pashkovism. The Pashkov palace on Gagarin Quay[97] became a center for evangelical

94. Kargel, "Russia, St. Petersburg [1876]," 8.

95. Korff, *Am Zarenhof*, 31.

96. Lieven, *Eine Saat*, 13–14.

97. *Gagarinskaya Naberezhnaya* is the Russian name of the street. *Naberezhnaya* can be translated as quay or embankment.

ministry. This occurred despite the Russian Imperial government giving orders to the police to prevent people from preaching the Word of God "who are not duly appointed to do so by the Church authority."[98] The Pashkov home could hold over 1,000 people and was used for larger evangelical meetings. Radstock continued to preach in other areas of the Russian Empire as well as in Scandinavia, particularly in Stockholm, Copenhagen, and Helsinki, until 1878.[99] Although Pashkov was new to the evangelical faith, he was a natural leader who commanded huge respect. At many of the drawing room meetings Alexandra Pashkov played the organ and their daughters sang.

The upper class Pashkovites attempted to maintain their relationships with the Orthodox Church but as the revival spread, the attitude of the authorities changed. Konstantin Pobedonostsev, at the time a tutor for the young Alexander Alexandrovich (the future Tsar and son of Alexander II) attended several of Pashkov's meetings in 1876. He was alarmed by the evangelical teaching but was unable to stop the meetings because Alexander II was a close friend of the Pashkov family. A. E. Timashev, the Minister of Internal Affairs, and General Trepov, the governor of Saint Petersburg, were relatives of Pashkov and supported him. Timashev was convinced that the moral and ethical teaching which Pashkov offered was beneficial to Russia. He once exclaimed: "If Pashkov succeeds, we [the Russian society] are all saved."[100]

Concern for Russian society led Pashkov to broaden the original ministry of Radstock to include the lower classes. It became commonplace for the meetings of the Pashkovites to have princes and peasants, drunkards and court gentlemen, women of the streets and women of the court. Pashkov himself had a particular concern for the *izvozchiki* [cab drivers] who would leave their families and farms in the winter to drive cabs in the city. The Colonel would pass out scriptures and tracts to all the drivers he met. This developed into a distribution system to

---

98. Stead, *Truth about Russia*, 376.

99. Heier, *Religious Schism*, 112. Heier and others have claimed that Radstock was expelled or banished from the Russian Empire, but according to my personal correspondence with Albert W. Wardin, Jr., there seem to be no primary sources that corroborate this statement.

100. Gutsche, *Westliche Quellen Des Russischen Stundism*, 64. Also see Heier, *Religious Schism*, 113, which states that it was General Trepov who made the exclamation about Pashkov.

take Bibles, tracts, and hymnals to the outlying villages when the drivers returned home for the summer. Because of his personal wealth, Pashkov was able to subsidize these ventures.

The Society for the Encouragement of Spiritual and Ethical Reading (SESER) was founded by the Pashkovites in 1876 and produced inexpensive reading material. It was a new idea. Pashkov and his acquaintances used the trade fairs held in Nizhniy Novgorod and the Moscow Exhibition to distribute their literature.[101] Heier writes that the SESER preceded similar ventures by Tolstoy by eight years. "Indeed," he observes, "the society of Pashkov served as a stimulus and model for all others."[102] At a time when many Russians were learning to read, the SESER offered affordable reading material.

It was as the Pashkovite movement spread that links were developed with the Baptists. From having been someone who attended some of the Pashkovite meetings, Kargel found himself drawn into its inner circle. He wrote: "In 1877 I began to become more familiar with the Russian believers."[103] He spoke of situations occurring that caused "all who were searching for God" to draw closer together.[104] There were several factors, such as discovery of a common evangelicalism and also, according to Kargel, "the political situation," which meant that "all those who loved the Lord, were forced to be close knit."[105] There were revolutionary sentiments in Russia, for example, among students, and the Pashkovites developed restaurants directed towards students and others. Pashkov stated, "I feed thousands of people daily with the best food our northern capital can offer."[106]

However, Kargel's reference to the political situation probably had more to do with the recent massacre of thousands of Bulgarians under Ottoman rule. Pashkov was aware of talks between Britain and Russia about a coalition in support of the Bulgarians and against the Ottoman rulers. Such talk, said Kargel, prompted Pashkov to invite people to come together to pray that God would not allow a blood

101. For more information on the publication efforts of Pashkov see Corrado, "The Philosophy of Ministry of Colonel Vasiliy Pashkov," 129–47.

102. Heier, *Religious Schism*, 121.

103. Kargel, *Zwischen den Enden*, ix.

104. Ibid.

105. Ibid.

106. T. I. Butkevich, *Obzor Russkix Sekt*, 471, as cited in Heier, *Religious Schism*, 116.

bath. It was in this context that the Pashkovite meetings became more international, including Latvians, Swedes, and Germans, as well as Russians. This gave Kargel a higher profile. He reported: "I attended the Pashkovite gatherings and spoke to them. Bobrinsky translated my first speech. Although I knew Russian somewhat, I did not dare to do a speech in Russian and therefore I asked for a translator."[107]

The coming closer together of the Baptists and the Pashkovites was also a response to growing persecution. In 1878, Orthodox authorities had curtailed Radstock's activities in Saint Petersburg and ordered Pashkov and his followers to "abandon their erroneous ways and return to the Orthodox Church."[108] Early in the 1880s, Pobedonostsev had shaped "Anti-Pashkovism," which sought to prevent the evangelical message from spreading throughout the Russian Empire.[109] The areas where there was a concentrated effort by this task force were the areas around Tambov, Rjazan, Moscow, Kiev, Saint Petersburg, Nikolayev, Tula, Tver, Novgorod, Voronezh, Jaroslav, Olents, and Warsaw.[110] In a number of these places links were established between the Pashkovites and Baptists. Alongside Pashkov, Korff was an important figure, and by the end of the 1870s, through a visit to Switzerland, he had met Baptists outside Russia and had embraced Baptist beliefs.

After the assassination of Tsar Alexander II in 1881 the government intensified its control on all groups that were seen as subversive. Alexander III, on 3 May 1883, issued an *ukase* [proclamation] which seemingly granted religious nonconformists the right to worship. The proclamation included an important prerequisite for this freedom of worship, however, which was that all religious teaching was to be free from any errors and the teaching was to be monitored by the Orthodox Church. This restraining prerequisite "gave almost unlimited opportunities for the persecution of the Stundists, Baptists and Pashkovites."[111] The prerequisite was a direct result of the influence of Konstantin Pobedonostsev, who became Ober-Procurator (General Director) of the Most Holy Synod of the Russian Orthodox Church in

---

107. Kargel, *Zwischen den Enden*, ix.

108. Terletskij, G. "Sekta pashkovtsev," *Pravoslavnoe obozrenie* (Jan.), II, 5–6, as cited in Heier, *Religious Schism*, 112.

109. For further reading on Anti-Pashkovism see Heier, *Religious Schism*, 125–37.

110. Heier, *Religious Schism*, 118.

111. *Istoriya Evangel'skix Xristian-Baptistov*, 98.

1880. By the close of 1884, the major Pashkovite leaders were either in prison in Siberia, exiled from Russia, or had been killed.

JOHANN AND ANNA KARGEL AND THEIR DAUGHTERS

It is important to be clear about the precise influence that Pashkov had on Johann Kargel. As stated earlier, Turchaninov, due to limited access to documents, has suggested that it was through Pashkov that Kargel became a missionary and that he was later baptized in Tiflis and ministered there.[112] This story was also retold by A. V. Suyarko in her biography of Kargel written in 1995.[113] These Russian historians (among others) have used a document in the All-Union Council of Evangelical Christians-Baptists' Moscow Archives as their source.[114] This section of the AUCEC-B's Moscow Archives will be referred to henceforth as "Folder 4/51." Some of the material in Folder 4/51 seems to be based on one article written by Sophia Lieven that was published after Kargel's death in the journal *Evangel'skaya Vera*.[115]

Folder 4/51 states that Kargel was converted and left his work and became a missionary through his contact with Pashkov.[116] Kargel's first meeting with the Pashkovites did make an impression on him, as we have seen, and it is quite possible that Pashkov suggested to Kargel and other German Baptists that they attend the Pashkovite meetings. However, Kargel's first encounter with the Pashkovites occurred after Kargel had been baptized, trained in Hamburg, received Baptist ordination, and served as pastor to two Baptist churches.

This is not to play down the huge impact of Pashkov on Kargel. His life was never the same after his encounter with the Pashkovites. It is difficult to overestimate the adjustment that Kargel had to make when entering the highest levels of Russian society. No other German Baptist pastor had managed to make contacts at this level. For Kargel, there was a blending of both spiritual and social fascination, as

---

112. Turchaninov, "Vospominanie o Zhizni i Sluzhenii Kargelya," para. 1.

113. Suyarko, "Vospominanie o Zhizni i Sluzhenii Kargelya," para. 4–5.

114. For the portion of this archive relating to Ivan Kargel see Golobashhenko, *Istoriya Evangel'sko-Baptistskogo Dvizheniya v Ukraine*, 48–50. It is stated that the material is taken from folder 51 of the archive. For the full folder number see Golobashhenko, "Karev, A. V. Istoriya Xristianstva Evangel'sko-Baptistskogo Dvizheniya v Ukraine," D:/files/books/book_002/0045_t.html.

115. Lieven, "Kratkij ocherk zhizni i deyatel'nosti brata I. V. Kargelya," 8–10.

116. Golobashhenko, *Istoriya Evangel'sko-Baptistskogo Dvizheniya*, 51.

indicated in this report by Kargel about a Pashkovite meeting. He wrote in 1878, "After about twenty were gathered, we were sent to another room where the Count awaited us. After we all sat down, the Count stood up and said a wonderful prayer to begin our study. It was a thrilling feeling to hear a prayer by such a person in high standing prayed in another [the Russian] language."[117] Here was a circle of powerful people who provided Kargel with support of a spiritual, and later, a material kind. They welcomed him into their midst upon the simple declaration that he loved Jesus.

Although neither Radstock nor Pashkov were interested in starting a Brethren community in Saint Petersburg, they did reflect some Brethren ideals. Kuznetsova, tracing the hermeneutical tendencies of the early Russian evangelicals believes "the Brethren movement seems to be the most influential in regard to the theology and practice of St. Petersburg Pashkovites."[118] Pashkov would have concluded that the Brethren ideals of church would correspond well to the emerging Russian intelligentsia which viewed the established church as "one of the oppressive structures which [hu]mankind needed liberation from."[119] It was frequently insisted among the Brethren that they should "receive all whom Christ had received."[120] It seems that the Pashkovites met to celebrate the Lord's Supper weekly and welcomed all believers to the Lord's Table.[121] Kargel was being exposed to a new kind of fellowship.

One of the most significant events in the life of Kargel, which came about as a result of his encounter with the Pashkovites, was meeting Anna Semenova,[122] his future wife. He later wrote somewhat obliquely: "God gave me a helper in the Russian circle and the bonds became closer but only for a short time because in 1880, the year of my marriage to that helper, I was called to Bulgaria."[123] Kargel's wife, Anna Alexandrovna Semenova, born in 1852 in Saint Petersburg, was

---

117. "Russland. St. Petersburg. Nachrichten Von Br. Kargel," 184.

118. Kuznetsova, "Early Russian Evangelicals," 91.

119. Boobbyer, *Conscience, Dissent and Reform*, 16.

120. Grass, *Gathering to His Name*, 92.

121. Anna Kargel to Alexandra Ivanovna [Pashkov], 12 January 1882, 2/13/006, Pashkov Papers.

122. An alternative spelling could be Semenoff which is what Johann Kargel used in German.

123. Kargel, *Zwischen den Enden*, x.

a friend of the Pashkovs, although there is no suggestion that she was from the aristocracy. The friendship probably developed within the evangelical community in Saint Petersburg. Kargel later wrote that Anna had "a [teaching] diploma from Ekaterinin Institute of Saint Petersburg," which qualified her to be a *Domashnyaya Uchitel'nice*,[124] and had worked as a teacher.[125] There is no doubting the significance of the marriage, which tied Johann Kargel firmly to the Pashkovs and the Russian Pashkovite movement. As the next chapter shows, Anna was very dependent on the Pashkovs in the early years of the marriage. Their early married life was in Bulgaria, which was to prove rewarding in unexpected ways, but also difficult. Kargel wrote that in 1880, the year of his marriage to his "helper," he was called to Bulgaria and was absent from Saint Petersburg for four years.[126] During those years Anna Kargel wrote a number of letters to the Pashkovs in which she spoke in a very personal way about her feelings. She told Alexandra Ivanovna Pashkov how she missed Saint Petersburg, the Christian community there, and the fellowship around the Lord's Table.[127]

The Kargels married in 1880. Folder 4/51 states that they were married in Finland.[128] This has been re-stated in several works on Kargel.[129] Primary sources indicate differently. In a Bulgarian journal in 1920 there is one of the earliest accounts of the start of the Bulgarian Baptist story. It was written by Georgi M. Chomonev, an early convert of Kargel's who remained a friend.[130] Chomonev, after speaking of appeals made by Bulgarians in Kazanluk for baptism, stated,

---

124. *Domashnyaya Uchitel'nice* [home tutor] was the type of teacher used by some families to educate their children outside of the schools used by the general population. It is very possible that Anna Alexandrovna Semenova was in close contact with the aristocracy of Saint Petersburg because she was a private tutor to some of their children.

125. Ivan Kargel to "Dear beloved brother" [V. A. Pashkov], 11 January 1894, 2/13/100, Pashkov Papers.

126. Kargel, *Zwischen den Enden*, x.

127. Anna Kargel to Alexandra Ivanovna [Pashkov], 12 January 1882, 2/13/006, Pashkov Papers.

128. Golobashhenko, *Istoriya Evangel'sko-Baptistskogo Dvizheniya*, 50.

129. Suyarko, "Vospominanie o Zhizni i Sluzhenii Kargelya," para. 7; Turchaninov, "Vospominanie o Zhizni i Sluzhenii Kargelya," para. 1; Karetnikova, *Almanax po Istorii Russkogo Baptisma*, vypusk 4, 19.

130. Georgi M. Chomonev to Vasily Alexandrovich Pashkov, 2 August 1882, 2/13/010, Pashkov Papers.

"Br. Ivan Kargel was sent with his fiancée[131] to be married to her in the Tultscha Baptist Church and then to go to Kazanluk, to look after those Bulgarians, if they were ready to be baptized, and if so, to baptize them. After they were married in Tultscha, br. and sister Kargel came to Ruse [Rustchuk]."[132] It is also clear from a letter written by Johann that he and Anna were married outside the Russian Empire: he states that "she came to me in *Ausland* to be married."[133] The most likely reason for their marriage taking place outside of Russia is that they could not be married in an Orthodox church because they were both evangelicals. When Anna was leaving the country to be married, her teaching diploma was taken by the Foreigners' Office in Odessa. She received a Foreigner's Pass in return.[134]

The exact chronology of events is difficult to establish, but probably Johann Kargel travelled to Bulgaria alone in early September 1880. He then met Anna who travelled overland from Odessa. In mid-September Anna and Johann were married in Tultscha (now in Romania).[135] After their marriage they travelled back to Saint

---

131. The Bulgarian word used here is *raninitsa* which is an archaic Bulgarian word used to designate someone as being under another's care.

132. Chomonev, "Poyavyavaneto na Baptizma v Bulgariya," 2.

133. J. G. Kargel to "My beloved brother" [V. A. Pashkov], 11 January, 1894, 2/13/100, Pashkov Papers.

134. Ibid. Later Anna wrote to Pashkov stating that she was still in possession of her Foreigner's Pass; see Anna Kargel to Vasily Alexandrovich [Pashkov], 11 February 1894, 2/13/102, Pashkov Papers.

135. In a personal letter to the author dated 30 September 2008, Dr. Albert W. Wardin, Jr. wrote: "The German Baptist Church in which they were married was actually at Catului (currently known as Cataloi, Romania), a short distance south of Tulcha (Tultscha) which is currently known as Tulcea, Romania. The Catalui Church was in Dobrudja, which in 1878 was taken from Turkey and annexed to Romania. This church had its beginnings in 1864–66 when the Russian government exiled immersed believers from the German colony of Neu-Danzig in Ukraine to Dobrudja. On his return to Germany from his trip in Russia in 1869, Oncken went to Catalui where he organized the Catalui Church with August Liebig as pastor. In 1873 August's brother, Ludwig Liebig, will become pastor of the Catalui Church and will remain as pastor until 1884. I therefore assume that Ludwig Liebig married Kargel and his wife. I know that already in the 1860s the Romanian government gave German Baptists the right of registration of births, marriages, etc., and I therefore assume the marriage was registered in the registry of the Catalui Church." The fact that Tultscha was at one time under Turkish control and the location of Kargel's marriage might explain why his daughters were considered to be Turkish. See Lieven, "Kratkij ocherk zhizni i deyatel'nosti brata I. V. Kargelya," 8.

Petersburg and then left the city on 17 November, arriving together in Rustchuk, Bulgaria, on 28 November 1880.[136]

The Kargels had four daughters. I will cover the lives of three of the daughters more fully in chapter 9, but here I want to clarify certain issues regarding the family. There has been misinformation due to a lack of resources available to previous researchers and the inaccurate document (File 4/51). The information I have gathered comes from personal letters written by Anna Kargel and Ivan Kargel. In a letter dated 11 May 1882, Anna expresses thanks to the Lord for a visit to Saint Petersburg and adds that "during the trip [to Balta] the child became sick and is still suffering." Later in the letter she writes that she is terribly tired and hopes that she and the "poor little girl" can get some rest.[137] It seems that the first of the Kargel daughters, Natasha, was born in Saint Petersburg sometime in February or March 1882. The first time that Natasha's name is mentioned in a letter is to Mrs. Pashkov on September 1882. She had been taken to a doctor because she was losing weight.[138] Of the daughters named in the letters written by Anna in the early 1880s and held in the Pashkov Archives, Natasha's is the one that occurs most often. Johann Kargel was also deeply attached to Natasha. In May 1883 he wrote to Pashkov that "since I have left my dear Anna and our little darling behind, I will be speeding home."[139]

The Kargels' second daughter was Elena. In some Russian writings, she is wrongly referred to as the first born. This comes from Folder 4/51 which states, "In the same city of Rustchuk his [Kargel's] first daughter Elena was born—on July 13, 1883."[140] Elena may well have been born on that date, but she was the second daughter. Beginning in

---

136. Anna Kargel to Vasily Alexandrovich [Pashkov], 1 December, 1880, 2/13/002, Pashkov Papers.

137. Anna Kargel to Vasily Alexandrovich [Pashkov], 11 May, 1882, 2/13/007, Pashkov Papers.

138. Anna Kargel to Alexandra Ivanovna [Pashkov], 18 September 1882, 2/013/012, Pashkov Papers.

139. Ivan Kargel to "My dear friend and brother in the Christ Jesus" [V. A. Pashkov], 4 May 1883, 2/13/018, Pashkov Papers.

140. Golobashhenko, *Istoriya Evangel'sko-Baptistskogo Dvizheniya*, 50.

September 1883, Anna began to use the plural—girls.[141] In February 1884 Anna clearly states "both girls."[142]

The Kargels' third daughter, Maria, was born in 1886. Kargel, writing from Saint Petersburg to Pashkov in March 1886, stated, "If the Lord permits, I will be taking my family to Hapsal [Estonia] on 16 May and I will have to stay there until my dear wife gives birth. I would much rather be here over the summer alone because of the cost, however I feel it is my duty toward my wife and children especially the latter who are not developing very strongly."[143] In a letter dated September 1886 Kargel wrote that the Lord had blessed him that past summer with a third daughter.[144] Folder 4/51 mistakenly states that "the second daughter, Maria, was born in 1886 in Hapsal [Gansel], Estonia."

Folder 4/51 also states: "The third daughter, Elizaveta, was born in 1887 in Petersburg."[145] Elizaveta was the fourth daughter. Kargel wrote to Pashkov in March 1888, stating quite clearly: "As I am sure you are aware of, he [God] gave us a fourth daughter. How this happened continues to be a miracle in front of our eyes. Imagine this that a half an hour before the birth, my wife entertained guests, walked around the room, and did laundry. Half an hour later, it was finished. O, how good our God is."[146] Anna also mentioned four daughters in a letter that she wrote from Krekshino in July 1890: "The children already are doing very well; it is a joy to look at them. Only poor old Grigorii is suffering from them. All four are with him from morning until evening."[147]

---

141. Anna Kargel to Vasily Alexandrovich [Pashkov], 23 September, 188, 2/13/020, Pashkov Papers.

142. Anna Kargel to Vasily Alexandrovich [Pashkov], 27 February, 1884, 2/13/024, Pashkov Papers.

143. Ivan Kargel to "Dear friend and brother in Christ Jesus" [V. A. Pashkov], 17 March, 1886, 2/13/050, Pashkov Papers.

144. Ivan Kargel to "Dear brother in Christ Jesus" [V. A. Pashkov], 23 September, 1886, 2/13/053, Pashkov Papers.

145. Golobashhenko, *Istoriya Evangel'sko-Baptistskogo Dvizheniya*, 50.

146. Ivan Kargel to "Dear friend and brother in Christ Jesus" [V. A. Pashkov], 14 March 1888, 2/13/058, Pashkov Papers.

147. Anna Kargel to Vasily Alexandrovich [Pashkov], 14 July, 1890, 2/13/084, Pashkov Papers.

Another complication that biographers of Kargel have had to deal with is a reference in Folder 4/51 to "a fourth daughter Anna, born in Saint Petersburg."[148] Folder 4/51 seems to have drawn from the memories of Princess Sophia Lieven who incorrectly identified the oldest daughter of Ivan and Anna Kargel as "Anna Ivanovna."[149] The personal letters of the Kargel family, however, clearly show four daughters named Natasha, Elena, Maria, and Elizaveta, with no direct reference to an additional daughter named Anna.[150] Folder 4/51 suggests that "Anna Ivanovna," whom Lieven named as the oldest,[151] was the youngest and died when she was nineteen years of age.[152] This has been taken up by researchers, most recently by Marina Sergeevna Karetnikova.[153] Karetnikova points to a sentence in Kargel's book *Behold, I am Coming Soon*[154] and uses it to attempt to prove that the data found in "Folder 4/51 in reference to 'Anna Ivanovna' is correct. In this book, Kargel states 'about nine years ago . . . I buried my dear daughter.'"[155] The most likely scenario is that the book was written in

148. Golobashhenko, *Istoriya Evangel'sko-Baptistskogo Dvizheniya*, 50.

149. Lieven, "Kratkij ocherk zhizni i deyatel'nosti brata I. V. Kargelya," 9.

150. There is the possibility that Ivan Kargel referred to Natasha as "Anna" or "Annchen" in German. See J. G. Kargel to "Dear beloved brother in Christ" [V. A. Pashkov], 16 September 1895, 2/2/1202, Pashkov Papers; J. G. Kargel to "Dear and beloved brother in the Lord Jesus Christ" [V. A. Pashkov], 17 April 1889, 2/13/071, Pashkov Papers; J. G. Kargel to "Dear brother in Christ Jesus" [V. A. Pashkov], 23 September 1886, 2/13/053, Pashkov Papers.

151. Lieven states: "Moving from one community to another, [Ivan Kargel] appeared in the Sumy region where his oldest daughter, Anna Ivanovna, died during the great suffering." See Lieven, "Kratkij ocherk zhizni i deyatel'nosti brata I. V. Kargelya," 9. I believe that Lieven's statement is referring to Kargel's oldest daughter who is actually Natasha (misidentified as Anna Ivanovna) who would have been about thirty-six during the great sufferings of the Russian Revolution and famine.

152. Golobashhenko, *Istoriya Evangel'sko-Baptistskogo Dvizheniya*, 50. If Folder 4/51 is correct in stating that a daughter died at the age of nineteen, it may have been Natasha, who would then have been nineteen years of age and died circa 1901, which is close to her mother's death. If Folder 4/51 is correct in stating that the Kargels' youngest daughter died at the age of nineteen, it would suggest that the Kargels had a fifth daughter named Anna, who died when she was nineteen years old. But there is no reliable evidence for this.

153. Karetnikova, *Almanax po Istorii Russkogo Baptisma*, vypusk 4, 22–25.

154. "Se, gryadu skoro..." This book will be discussed in chapter 7 in the section about Kargel's publishing efforts.

155. In this book, Kargel states, "about nine years ago . . . I buried my dear daughter." See Kargel, "Se, Gryadu Skoro . . . ," 423. Elsewhere in the book he states that

1928 and that Natasha, the oldest Kargel daughter, died around 1919, when she was thirty-six years old, and this is the daughter to whom he referred in his book.

Three of the Kargel daughters survived to adulthood and their names are well known to the Russian-speakers who have taken an interest in Ivan Kargel: Elena, Maria, and Elizaveta. These three daughters often accompanied Kargel throughout his life. The last letter that I have found that was written by Anna Alexandrovna Kargel is dated 11 February 1894. It is written from the Finnish city of Vyborg[156] and addressed to Vasily Pashkov. In this letter she wrote in hopeful tones about the future, partly because of a possible opening for her to teach in a school that the evangelicals might open in Romania.[157] In May 1896 Johann Kargel speaks of picking up a letter from his wife that was waiting for him at the post office.[158] After this date, I have found no primary documents that refer to Anna being alive.

The Kargel family moved from Vyborg to Saint Petersburg in 1898.[159] Sophia Lieven wrote that "Ivan Veniaminovich Kargel returned [to Saint Petersburg] from Finland with his wife and four daughters, and resided with us in our home."[160] Folder 4/51 of the AUCEC-B's Moscow Archives states: "Unfortunately, during a time when Kargel was abroad with his two oldest[161] daughters, his

---

for "nine years" Palestine has been under British rule. See Kargel, "Se, Gryadu Skoro ...," 388. This implies a publishing date of 1928. Therefore, Kargel buried a daughter sometime around 1919. However, Karetnikova dates the book as 1909 and this suggests that the death of the daughter was in 1900. See Karetnikova, *Almanax po Istorii Russkogo Baptisma, vypusk 4*, 41–42, 58.

156. Vyborg is a Finnish city on the Karelian Isthmus near the head of the Bay of Vyborg, which is currently within Russia. It is the city to which the Kargels moved circa 1891.

157. Anna Kargel to Vasily Alexandrovich [Pashkov], 11 February, 1894, 2/13/102, Pashkov Papers.

158. Ivan Kargel to "Dear and deeply loved friend" [V. A. Pashkov], 9 May, 1896, 2/13/110, Pashkov Papers.

159. Lieven states: "at the end of the 1880s, [Ivan Kargel] moved with his family to Finland where he lived and worked for about ten years after which he returned to [Saint] Petersburg." See Lieven, "Kratkij ocherk zhizni i deyatel'nosti brata I. V. Kargelya," 8. Karetnikova clarifies the date and states that Kargel returned to Saint Petersburg in 1898. See Karetnikova, *Almanax po Istorii Russkogo Baptisma, vypusk 4*, 34, 58.

160. Lieven, *Duxovnoe Probuzhdenie V Rossii*, 81.

161. There is a typographical error that printed *strashim* (frightened) rather

loving wife Anna Alexandrovna became ill with diphtheria and died ..."[162] After 1898, while residing in Saint Petersburg, Ivan Kargel often travelled abroad, allowing for the possibility that Anna died after the family's return. It can be reasonably concluded that Ivan Kargel's wife, Anna, died sometime between 1898 and 1901[163] after he returned to Saint Petersburg with his wife and daughters.

CONCLUSION

In 1875, Johann Kargel moved from his pastoral work in a church in the western reaches of the Russian Empire to its capital city. This move had huge implications. It placed him in an influential position within the life of the German Baptist Union, which was looking for opportunities to expand into Russia. He was the first to register successfully a Baptist congregation under the Russian government's religious procedures, which Lehmann highlighted as something the German Baptists had "waited for so long and have worked for so much."[164] The Baptist congregation in the capital was small, and Kargel was constantly looking for new avenues of outreach.[165] Alongside Kargel's German Baptist ministry and links, however, he came into contact with a new movement. The ministry of Lord Radstock brought to Saint Petersburg an evangelicalism that grew within the upper class of Russian society. Colonel Pashkov, who became the first Russian leader of the evangelicals in Saint Petersburg, was to become a strategic figure in Kargel's spiritual journey. Through the Pashkovite meetings, Kargel encountered a form of Christianity that was not tied to one denomination and in particular he came to believe "that the Lord's Supper belongs to all the children of God."[166] He also began to move into and be accepted within the highest level of Russian society. During this period, too, he became a naturalized Russian citizen. A crucial role in Ivan Kargel's life, and specifically in the development of his evangelical spirituality,

---

than *starshimi* (oldest). See Lieven, "Kratkij ocherk zhizni i deyatel'nosti brata I. V. Kargelya," 9; Golobashhenko, *Istoriya Evangel'sko-Baptistskogo Dvizheniya*, 50.

162. Golobashhenko, *Istoriya Evangel'sko-Baptistskogo Dvizheniya*, 50.

163. For an explanation of the 1901 date, see page [?].

164. "Recognition of the Church," 124.

165. Kargel, "Russia, St. Petersburg [1878]," 8.

166. J. G. Kargel to "Dear brother in Christ Jesus" [V. A. Pashkov], 24 September 1886, 2/13/052, Pashkov Papers.

was played by his wife Anna Alexandrovna. She was a major link with the Pashkovites. Their daughters were also to become closely connected with Ivan's ministry. In the following chapter it will be seen how significant Anna's influence was in the development of Ivan Kargel's distinct expression of evangelical spirituality.

4

Bulgarian Period

Released from Spiritual Narrowness

(1880–1884)

THIS CHAPTER WILL EXAMINE the way in which Johann Kargel carried out his work in Bulgaria. His inner journey will also be explored. This period of his life was one in which his wife, Anna, had a powerful impact on his spiritual experience. A considerable amount of the information about Kargel's developing spirituality is gleaned from letters that he, and especially his wife, wrote to Vasily Pashkov and his wife Alexandra Ivanovna Pashkov.

When the Kargels left Saint Petersburg in 1880, Johann had been the pastor of the German Baptist congregation there for five years. During his time in Bulgaria—the first half of the 1880s—he worked extensively among the Bulgarian and German populations of the area. In Kazanluk, in 1880, he baptized a group of people who then formed the first Baptist church in Bulgaria. Kazanluk is to the south of the Balkans. Kargel also served as pastor of the German Baptist congregation in Rustchuk.[1] Over this period, however, his relationship with Pashkov deepened. Financial as well as spiritual support from Pashkov and the Pashkovite circle became more central. Towards the end of the Kargels' time in Bulgaria, Pashkov and Korff were exiled from Russia. Meanwhile, in Bulgaria, Kargel reached a point of crisis in his spiritual

---

1. "Kazanluk" is the spelling I will be using for the town, which is also spelled Kasanlik, Kasanik, Kasanlyk, Kasanluk, and Kazanlyk. I am also using the name Rustchuk which is the Turkish name for the Bulgarian town of Ruse. Kazanluk is located south of the Balkan Mountains, which divide Bulgaria laterally, and north of the Sredia Mountains, in a valley known for growing roses.

journey as he grew weary of the internal conflicts among some of the Baptists in both Russia and Bulgaria as they struggled to find their denominational identity. For him, especially as he listened to Anna, the problem was that there was too great an emphasis on being Baptist. Kargel's answer to this problem was to be found in a focus on Christ and on an evangelical spirituality that transcended denominations.

BAPTISTS IN BULGARIA: THE EVANGELICAL DOCTRINE

Early Protestant missionaries in Bulgaria in the 1850s became keenly aware of the strong Orthodox roots that helped to mould the national identity of the Bulgarians.[2] Non-Orthodox Christian missionaries were not readily accepted, because associating with Protestantism meant the loss of one's Bulgarian identity. Methodist, Congregational, and Baptist mission efforts faced this sort of resistance as they started to work in Bulgaria. The Free Church movement in Bulgaria, which owed a great deal in its first phase to American missionaries, started in 1857. The Methodists and the Congregationalists, in a display of Christian unity—at least on a pragmatic level—divided the country between themselves.[3] The Balkan Mountains were generally used as the boundary, with Methodists working to the west and north of the mountains and Congregationalists active in the south and east. By 1862, the Congregationalists had established three preaching stations in Bulgaria.[4] The first recorded Protestant church was established by the Congregationalists in 1870.[5] The administrative relationship between the Methodists and Congregationalists seemed to work until 1866 when Baptist colporteurs began to enter the country.[6] It is perhaps significant that Kargel's developing vision during his years in Bulgaria included a desire to embrace more fully evangelicals outside the Baptist community.

---

2. For the history, including the religious history see Crampton, *A Concise History of Bulgaria*.

3. The American Board of Commissioners for Foreign Missions was predominantly Congregational.

4. Wardin, "The Baptists in Bulgaria," 148.

5. Mojzes, "A History of the Congregational and Methodist Churches in Bulgaria and Yugoslavia," 93.

6. Angelov, "The Baptist Movement in Bulgaria," 8.

In 1876 a Bulgarian rebellion against Ottoman rule was harshly suppressed and over 100 villages and five monasteries were destroyed. In one village alone, 5,000 Bulgarians were massacred.[7] The scenes of slaughter shocked the world. During the subsequent Russo-Turkish War (1877–1878) Russian troops enlisted the support of Bulgarian patriots and together they liberated Bulgaria, forging a bond between the two peoples. This period was to be crucial for Baptist life in Bulgaria in general and for Kargel in particular.

In the late 1860s German families had begun to arrive in Bulgaria. Some Baptists settled in Dobruja [Dobrudja], between the Black Sea and the Danube, an area which in 1878 became part of Romania. The Turkish government allowed Germans, some of whom were Baptists, to live in Tultscha near the Danube River. Kristin Polk, August Fisher, Jacob Klundt, and Martin Heringer, were among the early settlers. There was significant Bible Society activity among this group. Heringer, for example, served with the British and Foreign Bible Society (BFBS) in Bulgaria for thirty years, from 1871 until his death.[8] In 1875 the Bulgarian Evangelical Society was formed. The Bulgarian Baptist movement, with leadership from Kargel in its early phase, found a place in this wider evangelical context.

The first Baptist church in Bulgaria came out of Congregational mission work in Kazanluk. Several members of the Congregational cause came to the conviction that baptism was for adult believers only. This was a challenge to the Congregational practice of the baptism of infants. Some of the members of this group decided in 1874 to find someone who would baptize them. Lewis Bond, the Congregational missionary working in Kazanluk, tried to explain that such baptism was not necessary. Several from the Kazanluk congregation had heard that German Baptists lived in the northern part of Bulgaria and they decided to cross the mountains in search of someone who could baptize them. They did not find the Baptists, but they found out more about the theology of the Baptists and were given an address. Soon the Kazanluk group was writing letters, appealing to German Baptists in various countries for help. The appeals went unanswered for several years. In 1879 one of the Kazanluk members, Grigor B.

---

7. Crampton, *A Concise History of Bulgaria*, 81.

8. For more see Oprenov, "The Origins and Early Development of Baptists in Bulgaria," 10; Rushbrooke, *The Baptist Movement in the Continent of Europe*, 168.

Drumnikov (Duminkoff) wrote a letter to the German Baptist Union. Stephen Kurdov, another Bulgarian, who heard the evangelical message preached by Armenian refugees in Istanbul in 1867[9] and became a colporteur for the American Bible Society, was an important influence on Drumnikov.[10]

Grigor Drumnikov's letter to the German Baptist Union was published in October 1880 in *Wahrheitszeuge* as well as in *Quarterly Reporter of the German Baptist Mission* in an article entitled, "The Macedonian Cry Re-Echoed from Macedonia Itself."[11] In Drumnikov's appeal, which was signed by twenty-two people, he wrote: "the Bulgarian church at Kazanluk has accepted the Evangelical doctrine for four years past inasmuch as they have acknowledged and accepted the baptism of believers according to the teaching of the Word of God. They have therefore rejected infant baptism because it can nowhere be proved from the New Testament."[12] It is noteworthy that Drumnikov referred to Baptist beliefs as "the Evangelical doctrine." Drumnikov explained that his group had previously sent letters to German Baptists in Rustchuk, Tultscha, and Catalui.[13]

In the meantime, at the 1879 German Baptist Triennial Conference in Hamburg, August Liebig shared the news and the request from Bulgaria with the entire conference. Liebig had first received the appeal from the Kazanluk group while he was in Odessa.[14] Johann Kargel was at the Triennial Conference and heard the appeal. He was already considering his future, as the weather in Saint Petersburg was causing his health to suffer.[15] One report noted that "Brother Kargel's health is very delicate, and he appears unable to bear the severity of

---

9. Kirkilanov, "Kratka Istoriya na Evangelskata Baptistska Tsurkva v Grad Kazanluck," *Evangelist* 4, no. 9–10 (1924) 5, as cited in Oprenov, "The Origins and Early Development of Baptists in Bulgaria," 10. Oprenov uses "Tsarigrad" for the city of Istanbul (Constantinople).

10. Angelov, "The Baptist Movement in Bulgaria," 9.

11. "The Macedonian Cry Re-Echoed from Macedonia Itself," 1–2 and "Ein macedonischer Ruf," 142–43.

12. "The Macedonian Cry Re-Echoed from Macedonia," 2.

13. Catalui is in Turkey. These letters must have been addressed to literature depots or Baptist groups because there were no Baptist churches in these towns at that time.

14. Wardin, "The Baptists in Bulgaria," 149.

15. "St. Petersburg," 9.

the Russian winters."[16] Also, Kargel was already interested in Bulgaria through being part of Pashkov's special prayer meetings for the violent events taking place in that country. Later Kargel wrote that in 1880 "I was called to Bulgaria . . . There God saw fit to start the groundwork for a mission work which is still in existence right now."[17]

There seem, therefore, to have been three factors that motivated Kargel to move to Bulgaria: he heard of the need at the German Baptist Union's Triennial Conference; he was finding the climate in Saint Petersburg difficult; and he had prayed about the needs in Bulgaria with Pashkov and his circle. However the different reasons are interpreted, Kargel decided to travel to Bulgaria just before his wedding. This decision was unknown to the Kazanluk group. Indeed, Kargel had arrived in Kazanluk in September 1880, before the appeal from Drumnikov was printed in *Quarterly Reporter of the German Baptist Mission*. Kargel went to Bulgaria as a Baptist pioneer, but he was not sent by the German Baptist Union. His work appears to have been largely funded from this point on by Pashkov and his circle in Saint Petersburg.[18]

This is suggested in a report to American Baptists by P. Z. Easton, a Presbyterian missionary to Persia, who wrote, "In Saint Petersburg I made the acquaintance of Mr. Kargel, pastor of the German Baptist congregation, who had also been a member of the Tiflis congregation and like Pavlov, had gone to Hamburg to study for the ministry . . . Some two years ago, on account of health, he was obliged to leave Saint Petersburg, and went to Bulgaria. His zeal and faithfulness in his former work had won for him such a good reputation that Pashkov contributed to his support in his new field."[19] Although Kargel was still committed to Baptist life, he was beginning to find a new home within the wider evangelical community in Russia.

NO ONE SHOULD RESIST THE WATER

As Johann Kargel made his way to Kazanluk, he travelled for part of the journey by boat and stopped in Rustchuk, which is located on the current Romanian border and lies on the Danube River. It was one of

16. "Work in St. Petersburg," 9 and "Erste Fruechte," 54.
17. Kargel, *Zwischen den Enden*, x.
18. Ibid.
19. Easton, "Baptist Work in Russia and the Caucasus," 35.

Bulgaria's wealthiest and most sophisticated cities in the nineteenth century.[20] Because of its location on the main trade route between the Black Sea and Germany, Rustchuk was Bulgaria's gateway to Europe as well as the location of a sizable German community. It was also the location of a Bible depot established by the British and Foreign Bible Society in 1878.[21] Kargel arrived in Rustchuk on 4 September 1880. His detailed account of the trip was printed in serial form in German in *Der Wahrheitszeuge*[22] and an abbreviated version was published in English in *Quarterly Reporter of the German Baptist Mission*.[23] These articles state that Kargel was not sure how he would travel through Bulgaria to Kazanluk and that he did not speak Bulgarian.[24] There is reason to pause here and consider statements made by some which claim that Kargel came to Russia from Bulgaria.[25] It would seem highly unlikely that Kargel had previously spent time in Bulgaria; as *Wahrheitszeuge* put it in May 1881, "Kargel entered the country [Bulgaria] without knowing the language and did not know what he would do."[26]

As he stepped off the boat in Rustchuk, Kargel was met by Martin Heringer of the British and Foreign Bible Society. Heringer volunteered to be Kargel's guide and translator. He had been travelling in Bulgaria for several years and was accustomed to the difficulties. The road over the mountains to Kazanluk was dangerous with many check points and the constant threat of robbery.[27] Displaced Turks, as well as Bulgarian soldiers trained in mountain warfare who were out of work at this time, were a particular threat to travelers. Kargel described his first impressions of the Bulgarian people, writing that the villagers reminded him of people in the Caucasus, with their Asian appearance, while the town's folk looked more European. He noted that the women did not cover their faces according to Islamic tradition. They

20. Otfinoski, *Bulgaria*, 95.
21. Wardin, "The Baptists in Bulgaria," 148.
22. "Eine Reise nach Kasanlik [part one]," 94 and "Eine Reise nach Kasanlik [part two]," 104.
23. "Bulgaria," 11–13.
24. Ibid., 11.
25. Brandenburg, *The Meek and the Mighty*, 131; Bender, "Kargel, Johann," 1099.
26. "Eine Reise nach Kasanlik [part one]," 94.
27. Their first night was in Bjela, where Kargel mentions that they ate a sparse meal and slept on straw infested with fleas.

wore "men's leggings under their dresses" and "carried babies on their back as they do in Africa." The village women were very industrious and were often seen spinning wool. Kargel's attention to detail shows that he was studying the culture and people. He felt deeply the poverty gripping the area. Coming from the wealth of Saint Petersburg, Kargel was troubled not only by the poverty but also by the poor planning of the villages. In many cases the streets were too narrow for two wagons to pass and the roofs of the houses were overhanging, creating a "dismal atmosphere." During the trip to Kazanluk, horses were difficult to find and at times they travelled on foot.[28] Although Kargel had been somewhat discontented in Saint Petersburg, he did not fully comprehend what he would face in Bulgaria. New challenges brought him to a profound sense of spiritual need.

Kargel and Heringer arrived in Kazanluk on Friday 5 September 1880 and were greeted by Grigor Drumnikov. The next day Kargel began to interview the Bulgarians who wanted to be baptized with the assistance of Heringer who translated for him from German to Bulgarian. Kargel began with words adapted from Acts 10:29, "So when I was sent for, I came without objection. I ask then why you sent for me."[29] Over the course of Saturday and Sunday, eight people sought baptism and six were approved. Of these six, one decided not be baptized after discussion with the Congregational missionary, Lewis Bond, who saw the baptisms as "re-baptism" of those baptized as infants.[30] Bond had been in Bulgaria since 1871.[31] He held heated discussions with Heringer and Kargel over the issue of baptism. Not surprisingly, he did not invite Kargel to preach in his church. Kargel records a difficult conversation. "I put myself in his [Bond's] position and felt that if I had won souls for the Lord and others had come to avert them [steer them away] from me, there would be a great unending pain. On the other hand, I also saw clearly that the law of the Lord that tells me that no one should resist the water, that those who have received the Holy Ghost, just the same as we, should be baptized."[32]

28. "Eine Reise nach Kasanlik [part one]," 94.
29. "Bulgaria," 11.
30. Ibid., 12.
31. Mojzes, "A History of the Congregational and Methodist Churches in Bulgaria and Yugoslavia," 94.
32. Kargel, "Bulgarei," 60.

Kargel understood Bond's position as a fellow-evangelical, but ultimately Kargel's own spiritual convictions as an evangelical and also a Baptist meant that he had to follow what he saw as biblical teaching.

Sunday 7 September 1880 saw the beginning of the Baptist congregation in Kazanluk, Bulgaria, which is considered to be the first Bulgarian Baptist Church. At night, under a full moon, Kargel baptized five Bulgarians in the river.[33] Their names are Toshka Pateva, Marijka Belcheva, Nikola Patev, Grigor Drumnikov, and Petko Kurkelanov.[34] The baptisms seem to have confirmed strongly to Kargel that he should not return to Saint Petersburg but should bring his bride to Bulgaria.[35]

There was also, however, realism about what could be done in a foreign country. The German community on the north side of the Balkans provided a lifestyle better fitted to Kargel and his wife than did Kazanluk and they decided to settle in Rustchuk. The existence of the Bible Depot in Rustchuk also played a role in this decision. Johann travelled to Saint Petersburg with Anna after their wedding and they arrived in Rustchuk on 28 November 1880, after a nine-day trip from Saint Petersburg. Anna was not prepared for the difficult trip and arrived feeling lonely, dispirited, and unwell.[36] Life in Rustchuk for Anna, a woman who may have been somewhat pampered by her life in Saint Petersburg, was trying. Within the first few days, however, Anna was anxious to learn Bulgarian, stating in a letter to Pashkov: "I can understand everything. Bulgarians also understand Russian and like Russians very much."[37] In these early days she was excited about working with the varied local population. In the same letter she wrote: "The Turkish people are different from what I knew about them before; they are an honest and work-loving people."[38]

---

33. Ibid.

34. Angelov, "The Baptist Movement in Bulgaria," 10.

35. Kargel stated that "my wife and I" have determined to move to Bulgaria to learn the language in his report describing the original baptisms in Kazanluk on 7 September 1880. This report was not written immediately after the baptism in Kazanluk because he was not married until after he performed the baptisms. See "Bulgaria," 12.

36. Chomonev, "Poyavyavaneto na Baptizma v Bulgariya," 2.

37. Anna Kargel to Vasily Alexandrovich [Pashkov], 1 December 1880, 2/13/002, Pashkov Papers.

38. Ibid.

Over the course of the first year, Rustchuk became the main church for the Bulgarian Baptist movement and Kazanluk became the associated preaching station. Rustchuk offered a multi-national population that was less tied to the Orthodox Church and therefore more open to Baptist ideas. Johann Kargel preached in German and also in "Bulgarian mixed with Russian."[39] It seems that he was progressing in his proficiency in Russian and it is likely that this was the commonly spoken language in the home. Anna's level of German is unknown. Anna wrote all her letters in Russian while Johann often chose to write to Pashkov in German. For Anna, the loss of the Russian environment was serious. She told Pashkov that "my heart is in Petersburg."[40] However, the Kargels pressed on with the work. Turkish and Bulgarian neighbors began to visit their home.[41] Anna tells of visiting various homes as she made new friends in town.[42] In 1882 Johann Kargel baptized nine people in Rustchuk.[43]

But there was a severe reaction. In November of that same year, several of the church members were beaten and taken to court where they spent twelve days in jail. Anna reported in a letter to Pashkov that stones were thrown through the windows of the Kargels' house.[44] Baptisms provoked particular opposition, although they also attracted those who were interested in the message that Kargel was preaching. In 1882 a public baptismal service was broken up by hooligans. The event was finally moved to a private piece of land, but even then the police tried to disrupt the service. The police eventually arrested the owner of the property. In the end, Kargel, after searching for the chief of police and finding him in a card game, managed to get the property owner released. Throughout the process he explained to those who would listen the meaning of the gospel and of baptism.[45]

---

39. Chomonev, "Poyavyavaneto na Baptizma v Bulgariya," 2.

40. Anna Kargel to Vasily Alexandrovich [Pashkov], 1 December 1880, 2/13/002, Pashkov Papers.

41. Ibid.

42. Anna Kargel to Vasily Alexandrovich [Pashkov], 25 December 1880, 2/13/004, Pashkov Papers.

43. "Statistik 1883 der vereinigten Gemeinden Getaufen Christen."

44. Anna Kargel to Vasily Alexandrovich [Pashkov], 18 November 1882, 2/13/013, Pashkov Papers.

45. Ibid.

In July 1882, the Kargels reported to Pashkov that five Bulgarians and one German had been baptized.[46] In September, a letter to Pashkov spoke of ten Bulgarians, a German, and a Hungarian who had professed repentance and faith. Anna Kargel also spoke about a Jewish man and his wife having been baptized.[47] In 1883, two baptismal services were held: on 26 August and on 7 September, which was celebrated as the third anniversary of the first baptisms in Kazanluk.[48] Altogether, the Kargels reported that fourteen people had been baptized in 1883: ten were Bulgarian, two were Jewish, and two were German.[49] A multi-cultural Baptist community was gradually being established.

MINISTRY IN WORD AND DEED

Johann Kargel aspired to develop the Baptist community in Bulgaria, yet he also had a wider vision for the evangelical world—a vision formed in Saint Petersburg among the Pashkovites. After Johann and Anna settled in Rustchuk, they kept Pashkov in touch with the situation. They mentioned attending a Methodist meeting, which appealed to Pashkov's interdenominational interests.[50] Kargel reported to Pashkov on the situation concerning tracts at the Bible Depot, telling Pashkov that the selection was not what he had hoped for and that there might be a possibility of printing new tracts in Rustchuk.[51] Within a month of arriving in Rustchuk, Anna Kargel spoke of witnessing to a Turkish man and giving him a Bible. The literature distribution was not limited to any one section of the population. On market days, when Bulgarian villagers would travel into Rustchuk, Anna made a special effort to pass out tracts containing the evangelical message. She also took books to the soldiers in the barracks. She

---

46. Anna Kargel to Vasily Alexandrovich [Pashkov], 20 July, 1882, 2/13/009, Pashkov Papers.

47. Anna Kargel to Vasily Alexandrovich [Pashkov], 18 September 1882, 2/13/011, Pashkov Papers.

48. Oprenov, "The Origins and Early Development of Baptists in Bulgaria," 18.

49. Kargel, "Conflicts in Bulgaria (Continued)," 7.

50. Anna Kargel to Vasily Alexandrovich [Pashkov], 1 December 1880, 2/13/002, Pashkov Papers. The last two pages (7 and 8) of this letter appear to be misfiled and actually belong to another letter. This quotation is from page 7 of this letter.

51. J. G. Kargel to "Dear friend and brother in Christ" [V. A. Pashkov], 2 December 1880, 2/13/003, Pashkov Papers.

asked Pashkov to send more Russian New Testaments to distribute among the Russians in town.[52] The denominational tensions that had been so problematic in Kazanluk, when the Congregational pastor in Kazanluk reacted strongly against Kargel and believer's baptism, were largely absent in Rustchuk. By the end of 1881, Kargel was preaching at the Methodist meeting in the morning and the German Baptist group in the afternoon.[53] His commitment to active evangelical co-operation was growing.

At the same time, Kargel was aware of many needs. In 1881 he wrote in *Quarterly Reporter of the German Baptist Mission* about his sense of spiritual need: "May the Lord clothe me with His Spirit's might that I may proclaim His word." He then added: "My support is indeed guaranteed, but a colporteur is much wanted who would visit the outlying villages and small towns with tracts in Bulgarian and for this means are needed."[54] Kargel believed that more resources were needed for the Bulgarian work: "I would lay it on the hearts of those who may read this letter and . . . have a heart for the kingdom of God, not to forget Bulgaria with their gifts. You will indeed be casting your bread on the water, but you will find it again after many days, and if not here, at all events in a joyous and glorious eternity."[55] This request was addressed to Baptists, but it is clear that much of the Kargels' support by now was coming from Pashkov.

Kargel travelled on behalf of Pashkov in this period. However, the need during such travels was for good contacts, and often these were provided by Baptists. Thus in April 1882, the Kargels, along with Liebig and others from the German Baptist church in Odessa, travelled to distribute aid to the Jews in Balta, then on the Polish-Turkish border.[56]

This 1882 trip highlights another aspect of the Kargels' work: humanitarian aid. On 10 April 1882 a pogrom took place in Balta in which over 1,200 Jewish homes and shops were completely destroyed. All the Jewish homes except for sixteen were attacked. During the

52. Anna Kargel to Vasily Alexandrovich [Pashkov], 25 December 1880, 2/13/004, Pashkov Papers.

53. Anna Kargel to Vasily Alexandrovich [Pashkov], 22 November 1881, 2/13/005, Pashkov Papers.

54. "Bulgaria," 12.

55. Ibid., 12–13.

56. Balta is in southwest Ukraine, in the north of Odessa Province.

attacks, nine Jews were killed and 211 were injured, with thirty-nine sustaining serious injury. Many women were raped and terrorized.[57] The Jewish population had outnumbered the Christian population three to one, but many of the 15,000 Jews began to leave.[58]

Anna Kargel relates the story of the Baptist team's trip to Balta. Within hours of the arrival of the Baptist group, a rabbi came to visit them and learn the reason for their trip. The rabbi listened to Kargel talking about the food supplies and money that he wanted to distribute to the needy. The rabbi also read the scriptures and prayed with the team. News of the supplies they carried soon spread throughout the town and by midnight there was a frenzied scene in front of the hotel where the team was staying. The police had to disperse the crowd. It was decided that no food would be given on the street but rather people would be visited at home so that their needs could be assessed. For five days the team distributed aid to the town. These days were quite chaotic as the need was overwhelming. On the sixth day, after the supplies and money were gone, the team slipped out of town quietly for fear of a riot.[59] Pashkov was interested in the distribution of the aid and possibly the finances came from him. The evangelical witness was seen as being expressed in deed as well as word.

The vision that the Kargels had of reaching out to the various groups around them in Bulgaria was hard to translate into reality. It seems that a focus on the Turkish members of the community may have been driven by Anna.[60] In her opinion, the Bulgarians mistreated the Turks and that elicited her compassion. The early desire on the part of Anna to reach the Turks may have also been due to the fact that, like the Turks, the Kargels were foreigners in Bulgaria. Anna was keen to learn Turkish and Bulgarian. She felt that her native Russian tongue gave her the ability to learn Bulgarian and she wanted to speak to the Bulgarians in their heart language.[61] But disappointment soon

57. *Le Temps*, 21 April and 13 May 1882, as cited in David Vital, *The Origins of Zionism*, 52–53.

58. Dubnow, *History of the Jews in Russia and Poland*, 352.

59. Anna Kargel to Vasily Alexandrovich [Pashkov], 11 May 1882, 2/13/007, Pashkov Papers.

60. Anna Kargel to Vasily Alexandrovich [Pashkov], 1 December 1880, 2/13/002, Pashkov Papers.

61. Anna Kargel to Vasily Alexandrovich [Pashkov], 25 December 1880, 2/13/004, Pashkov Papers.

replaced her early hopes. In 1881 Anna wrote that "when they [the local Bulgarians] knew that my husband came for God's work, they began to look at us differently. Bulgarians considered us no better than dogs; to preach in a home was not possible . . . Protestants, as we're called here, are not allowed in their homes . . . and we are considered almost as pagans."[62] It is likely that in the Pashkov circle Anna had not heard much about Protestantism. In November 1882 the Kargels' housekeeper left them, afraid that she would be beaten for working for Protestants. The only helper that the Kargels could find was a converted bandit who was, it seems, very reluctant to take a bath.[63] Anna reported in 1882 that it was rumored that the Kargels kept a special book and that when a person's name was written in it, that person could never escape. Some locals were even afraid to pass by their gate.[64] Much appeared unpromising.

THE WORK OF THE HOLY SPIRIT

Although there were many disappointments, Anna also believed she saw the Holy Spirit at work. In 1882, the Rustchuk congregation registered forty-nine members with four preaching stations.[65] Anna reported after the Balta trip in July of 1882 that: "From the time of our return, my husband baptized five Bulgarians and one German. Three Bulgarians and one Romanian woman were also converted. In this revival, my husband sees his answer and will stay in Bulgaria."[66] Two months later she reported: "My husband is preaching in many cities around Bulgaria and everywhere seeing a response to the Word of the Lord. The local Orthodox bishop complained that we were baptizing Orthodox believers and the bishop instructed his people to throw stones at us but we are still alive and healthy and two were converted in the event."[67]

---

62. Anna Kargel to Vasily Alexandrovich [Pashkov], 22 November 1881, 2/13/005, Pashkov Papers.

63 Anna Kargel to Alexandra Ivanovna [Pashkov], 18 September 1882, 2/13/012, Pashkov Papers.

64. Ibid.

65. "Statistik 1883 der vereinigten Gemeinden Getaufen Christen."

66. Anna Kargel to Vasily Alexandrovich [Pashkov], 20 September 1882, 2/13/009, Pashkov Papers.

67. Anna Kargel to Vasily Alexandrovich [Pashkov], 18 September 1882, 2/13/011, Pashkov Papers.

Anna was also seeking a definite role for herself. There was talk of a mission school being opened in Bulgaria and she wrote to Pashkov: "We turn to you with the request to give us advice and also to ask our Father clearly to show His will. Here there could be a job for me, but I say again: let His will be."[68] In another letter, penned after visiting Odessa, she said that while she was there she had some work to do, but in Rustchuk there was nothing for her to do.[69] Her human desire was for Pashkov to give her some direction, while her faith in "our Father" led her to trust that the will of God would ultimately be clear.

Some of Anna Kargel's concerns for those around her were redirected after she became a mother. In a letter in 1882 she told the Pashkovs: "Yesterday we arrived in Rustchuk, I thank the Lord that we're finally in one place, especially for the poor girl, and here she'll get a rest."[70] This was immediately after the trip to Balta. But in the summer of 1883 she was again questioning why there seemed to be no work or ministry for her. She wrote: "I gave all to the Lord but it is difficult for me here without work. One thought comes to me, when the Lord gave me an opportunity to work for him, maybe I wasn't faithful to Him and He could not leave me in a dear and honoring position for my service."[71]

Anna was questioning what she had done previously. Had she been faithful? Was God unwilling to give her any further ministry? The spiritual anguish was intense, but cannot be separated from the massive changes occurring in her life as children arrived. There were also some tensions between Johann and Anna. She seems to have had little sympathy with the Baptist life with which she was now involved. In 1882 she wrote to Alexandra Pashkov: "Every splitting and tearing of Christ's true church disturbs and deeply grieves me and it is more painful that my husband supports some of them."[72] Anna described how she and Johann had talked often about the "unity of all God's

---

68. Anna Kargel to Vasily Alexandrovich [Pashkov], 22 November 1881, 2/13/005, Pashkov Papers.

69. Anna Kargel to Vasily Alexandrovich [Pashkov], 11 May 1882, 2/13/007, Pashkov Papers.

70. Ibid.

71. Anna Kargel to Vasily Alexandrovich [Pashkov], 23 September 1883, 2/13/020, Pashkov Papers.

72. Anna Kargel to Alexandra Ivanovna [Pashkov], 12 January 1882, 2/13/006, Pashkov Papers.

children" and she now accepted that she had probably not talked "in love," since Johann had asked Anna not to speak about this.[73]

It is clear that Anna was trying to draw Johann away from his traditional Baptist views and towards a more open evangelical perspective. One issue was probably the "open Table" that was practiced by the Pashkovites. The practice of the German Baptists was to restrict the Lord's Table to those who had been baptized by immersion on profession of faith.[74] Although she agreed not to talk about this, Anna continued to pray for Johann's attitude to change. "During this time," she wrote to Alexandra Pashkov, "I asked the Lord to reveal to him [Johann] His will and remove his hard stubbornness. I know the Lord has heard my prayer."[75] It seems that, somewhat against his will, Johann had been challenged in late 1881 or early 1882 by letters from the Pashkovs: they had "stirred him deeply" and he hoped to reply. "The dear Lord taught me," wrote Anna, "to be cautious and when I was reading your [Pashkov] letters, he [Johann] said to me that he wished greatly to break bread with all of you, and when I asked him, who and what are the obstacles for him, he began to bring some proofs in his defense, but they were weak, human ones."[76] Anna prayed for a "deeper work of God" within her husband.[77] What is indicated here is a complex relationship between Johann and Anna. The issue was whether or not he would take the path that she wanted him to take, moving from what she saw as restrictive Baptist practice to an open, interdenominational evangelical spirituality.

Nearly one year later, both Johann and Anna experienced a profound inner change. On the Orthodox Christmas of 1883, Anna wrote about this in vivid terms. The trials and pressures of the first years of marriage and of ministry in Bulgaria had forced them both to a point of searching and surrender. While expressing hopes for her husband to abandon his "weak, human" way of looking at the church, she knew that she was also in need. She wrote to Pashkov: "For some time, the Lord has given my husband and me a thirst for the Holy Spirit. We

73. Ibid.

74. One could further speculate as to Anna's baptism. I have found no reference to this.

75. Anna Kargel to Alexandra Ivanovna [Pashkov], 12 January 1882, 2/13/006, Pashkov Papers.

76. Ibid.

77. Ibid.

both asked the Lord to give us this completely and to fully dwell in Him; and to sink in us His Spirit, asking that He completely and fully accomplish in us the work that was started by Him. We ask and wait for it to come soon. We also pray this for all God's children and therefore we turn to you and ask that you, dear friend, join with us in this request."[78]

This prayer request shows the couple's deep desire for spiritual renewal. The language, "a thirst for the Holy Spirit," was common in the Holiness movements of the time in Europe. It would appear that Anna had become aware that although she felt she had an understanding of spirituality her husband lacked, nevertheless she also needed God to "complete fully" what he had begun in her as well as in her husband.

This request from Anna to Vasily Pashkov to join in prayer about the spiritual experience of the Kargels was no doubt taken seriously by Pashkov and his circle. Two months after she made the request, a further letter from Anna had quite a different tone. "Let us all together, more persistently, more and more solicit from God with faith and thanksgiving, from now to clothe us with all His power that hides us in him, hidden in the unshakable rock and also to allow us to glorify Him in all fullness and keep His word." Once more the language suggests an acquaintance with Holiness spirituality, particularly in the phrase "clothe us with all His power." The letter continued with even more striking language. "Let us look to everything that is going on around us as already perfect as victors."[79] While most evangelicals did not want to use the language of "perfection," such language was used in Wesleyan Holiness thinking. The idea of being "victors over sin" was spreading within the branches of evangelicalism that were open to the Holiness movement. Anna admitted that "we are all weak," but saw that "even here there is joy for us, we can even boast in our weakness because Christ's power then dwells in us."[80]

What appears to have happened is that the Kargels had experienced a full surrender to God. This was not an experience that was

---

78. Anna Kargel to Vasily Alexandrovich [Pashkov], 7 January 1883, 2/13/015, Pashkov Papers.

79. Anna Kargel to Vasily Alexandrovich [Pashkov], 10 March 1883, 2/13/017, Pashkov Papers.

80. Ibid.

advocated within German Baptist circles and it therefore constituted a challenge to the tradition in which Kargel had been shaped. Writing much later, in *Christ—our Sanctification*,[81] Johann Kargel spoke of how, during this time [in 1883], he found the sanctification he had been seeking.[82] A change of focus in Kargel's work, from a specifically Baptist allegiance to a wider interdenominational vision, was described by Anna in a letter to Pashkov written two years after the initial request for prayer. She wrote on 1 February 1884:

> Our dear miraculous faithful Father released my husband from any spiritual narrowness; he does not want to work with any particular church but just to be God's worker where and with whom, it does not matter; only to get the souls of sinners for the Lord. He seeks now a connection with God's children. O how I thank the Lord; and he says that already for two months he has felt some kind of need to go to Russia to work in the south or on the Volga, wherever God wills, but not in the Baptist community where there is no peace.[83]

This letter is explicit—and blunt—concerning the issues that had been troubling Anna. Johann Kargel's view of the church was shaped primarily by his Baptist experience, while Anna's views were shaped by her experiences with the Pashkovites. For her the Baptist view represented "spiritual narrowness." She had no interest in the structures of the church and saw the key elements in Christian community as the community members' relationship to Christ and to each other around an open communion table. The relief in her statement is palpable. Johann does not want to be in the Baptist community, "where there is no peace." Johann Kargel apparently now accepted that God's guidance would not lead them in a "narrowly" Baptist direction. In the same letter Anna asked Pashkov if true workers for the Lord should "arrange systematic rules" or rather "proclaim from one side of the earth to the other His eternal gospel."[84] The question provided its own answer.

---

81. *Xristos Osvyashhenie Nashe*. This book will be discussed in chapter 7 in the section concerning Kargel's publishing efforts. Karetnikova states that it was first published in 1912. See Karetnikova, *Almanax po Istorii Russkogo Baptisma, vypusk 4*, 43. It was also published in serial form in 1926 in the journal *Xristianin*.

82. Kargel, "Xristos Osvyashhenie Nashe," 80–82.

83. Anna Kargel to Vasily Alexandrovich [Pashkov], 1 February 1884, 2/13/022, Pashkov Papers.

84. Ibid.

CONTINUING BAPTIST LINKS

For Kargel, however, the Baptist community continued to offer wide connections. He valued his links with German Baptists in Odessa, a cosmopolitan city which was considered to be the Saint Petersburg of the south. It had a significant German population with a thriving Baptist fellowship. At one point the German Baptists of Odessa asked Johann and Anna Kargel to stay in Odessa permanently.[85] Although they refused this offer, the opportunities within the Odessa German Baptist congregation were felt by Kargel throughout his time in Bulgaria. It is clear from Anna's letters that Johann spent a considerable amount of time in Odessa. One of his longest trips there, in 1883, lasted three months, from September to December. Although such trips, which took Johann away from the family, must have been difficult for Anna, she recognized that Odessa provided a stimulus for Johann and spoke positively about his work there.[86] Johann Kargel was a typical evangelical activist who was unhappy without activity. Anna spoke about Johann being "in a huge confusion" because there was more work to do in Odessa than in Bulgaria.[87] Presumably the confusion was about priorities.

Although Anna found Baptists difficult, her mentors, the Pashkovs, did not have the same reservations as she expressed. Kargel reported back to Pashkov about his meetings with Baptist leaders in Odessa and there is no sign of Pashkov wishing to steer Kargel away from Baptist life. In May 1883 Kargel reported to Pashkov that he had met with Ivan Riaboshapka and Mikhail Ratushnyi, two Baptist leaders, and discussed the persecution of Russian Baptist leaders, among others, in the south of Russia.[88] Johann Kargel also received encouragement through Baptist conferences. He preached at a Baptist conference in Zhitomir and reported, "We received great blessings during our conference. The Lord sent his Holy Spirit down and there was great movement. There were tears of repentance as well as of great

---

85. Anna Kargel to Vasily Alexandrovich [Pashkov], 11 May 1882, 2/13/007, Pashkov Papers.

86. Anna Kargel to Vasily Alexandrovich [Pashkov], 23 September 1883, 2/13/020, Pashkov Papers.

87. Anna Kargel to Vasily Alexandrovich [Pashkov], 18 September 1882, 2/13/011, Pashkov Papers.

88. J. G. Kargel to "Dear friend and brother in Christ" [V. A. Pashkov], 19 May 1883, 2/13/019, Pashkov Papers.

joy, shed by many sinners, and in the end about thirty souls found peace and forgiveness in the blood of Christ, while even more than that stayed behind who had not found Christ yet."[89] Most of Johann Kargel's travel destinations outside Bulgaria were areas (often villages) associated with German settlements in Russia, such as Volhynia Province, Taurida Province, the Molotschna Settlement, Rückenau, Friedensfeld, Zhitomir, Astrakhanka, and often to Tiege which was Johann Wieler's place of residence. He also made frequent trips across the Danube to Romania. Together with D. Schwegler, he officiated in the opening of a Baptist Church in Bucharest in 1882 and baptized Johann Hammerschmidt who eventually became the pastor of that congregation.[90] In many ways Kargel's work in these German communities was fruitful, as reported in his letters to Pashkov. But the combination of his own inner turmoil and his wife's unhappiness with being outside Russia meant that he began to consider returning to Saint Petersburg.

It is apparent that in later 1883 and early 1884 Pashkov had in mind Kargel taking the co-pastorate of the German Baptist Congregation in Saint Petersburg. During an earlier trip to Saint Petersburg, Kargel, prompted by Pashkov, approached Adam Schiewe, who had replaced Kargel as pastor of the German Baptist congregation there, with a proposal that Kargel assist him in building up the congregation.[91] This suggestion was not well received by Schiewe, who sent a letter of protest to the German Baptist Union.

As Anna Kargel explained to Pashkov (in February 1884), deep problems had developed in the Saint Petersburg church. She wrote, "Those members of the church [Saint Petersburg German Baptist Church] who contact him [Johann] do so only to complain about Shive [Schiewe], but such work is not for God's children. As I said, I only knew this from him and only when I read your letters, where you write pointing to the Baptist community."[92] Anna reported that Johann believed it was impossible for him to work with Schiewe. When Schiewe complained to the German Baptist Union about

---

89. Ibid.

90. Donat, *Das Waschsende Werk*, 384.

91. Anna Kargel to Vasily Alexandrovich [Pashkov], 1 February 1884, 2/13/022, Pashkov Papers.

92. Ibid.

Kargel, Liebig was able to defend him. Anna wrote: "Thank the Lord that brother Libich [sic] was in Germany for a time for a conference and could justify my husband a bit and disentangle him from the gossip that was due to Shive [Schiewe]."[93]

The theme of "seeking peace" emerges again in Anna's letter: "I write you of this that you could know that it is not stubbornness[94] or any other force that causes my husband to separate himself from this community, but only a desire for peace."[95] Pashkov repeated his suggestion that Kargel might work in the German Baptist congregation.[96] It may be that Pashkov had felt confident that Kargel, if he had become involved again, could have solved the problems—as he had done previously. Kargel was not convinced. A vision that reached beyond the Baptist community was now re-shaping Kargel's spirituality.

LEAVING BULGARIA

During their earliest period in Bulgaria, the country was seen by the Kargels as a location for "work without end."[97] But this was not to be the case. Johann Kargel's health problems returned, with Anna complaining in January 1882 that he had been ill for three weeks and was unable to function.[98] In July of the same year, he was again ill. He had to cut short a planned six-week stay in Kazanluk in order to return home to Rustchuk. Later he left for Bucharest but was "barely well."[99] Two months later, Anna was nursing him again, this time due to bronchitis.[100] It is clear that the climate in Bulgaria, which was supposed to help Johann's health, had not achieved what had been hoped. It was,

---

93. Ibid.

94. *Kaprizny* [capricious]

95. Anna Kargel to Vasily Alexandrovich [Pashkov], 1 February 1884, 2/13/022, Pashkov Papers.

96. J. G. Kargel to "Dear friend and brother in Christ" [V. A. Pashkov], 29 November 1884, 2/13/032, Pashkov Papers.

97. Anna Kargel to Vasily Alexandrovich [Pashkov], 25 December 1880, 2/13/004, Pashkov Papers.

98. Anna Kargel to Alexandra Ivanovna [Pashkov], 12 January 1882, 2/13/006, Pashkov Papers.

99. Anna Kargel to Alexandra Ivanovna [Pashkov], 1 July 1882, 2/13/008, Pashkov Papers.

100. Anna Kargel to Alexandra Ivanovna [Pashkov], 18 September 1882, 2/13/012, Pashkov Papers.

too, almost inevitable that Kargel's travel schedule and the pressure of the wider ministry would take their toll on his body. In addition to his international travel, Kargel was travelling within Bulgaria, most often to Kazanluk but also to Lompalanka, Bazarjik [Pazardjik], and Varna.

By 1882 there were discussions within the family about leaving Rustchuk. A combination of factors converged to motivate them seriously to consider moving back to Russia: Johann's poor health, Anna's desire to work, her longing to return to friends (and presumably family)[101] in Saint Petersburg, and the tensions concerning spirituality. The possibility of moving away from Bulgaria was increasingly mooted. The idea must have been mentioned publicly, because members of the Bulgarian congregations expressed their dissatisfaction with the notion and asked Pashkov not to remove the Kargels from Bulgaria.[102] Clearly in their minds the fact that Pashkov was providing funds meant that he was the deciding figure.

The Bulgarians' problem was that Anna was the conduit for all communication to the Pashkovs and all their letters had to pass through her hands and be translated into Russian. She wrote to the Pashkovs about her dilemma: "All of Rustchuk will write to you and I will translate it but I will do it opposite [with the opposite meaning]. I'll ask that somehow we be able to be freed from here."[103] One example of the attempts made by the Rustchuk congregation to retain the Kargels was a letter sent to Pashkov from Rustchuk signed by Georgi Chomonev, dated August 1882. It was written and translated by Anna. Chomonev stated that he had been converted to the Christian faith through Kargel and he went on to list towns all over Bulgaria where the evangelical message was required, seeking to prove that the need was not to remove Kargel but rather that more people like him should be sent to Bulgaria. Chomonev wrote, through Anna: "I am a Bulgarian and it is an insult that you call Kargel back to Russia."[104] One can imagine the tension that Anna felt as she penned these words to Pashkov.

---

101. It is interesting to note that in all her personal letters to the Pashkovs, her own extended family is never mentioned.

102. Georgi M. Chomonev to Vasily Alexandrovich Pashkov, 2 August 1882, 2/13/010, Pashkov Papers.

103. Anna Kargel to Alexandra Ivanovna [Pashkov], 18 September 1882, 2/13/012, Pashkov Papers.

104. Georgi M. Chomonev to Vasily Alexandrovich Pashkov, 2 August 1882, 2/13/010, Pashkov Papers.

Both the Kargels were well aware that the needs of the country were immense. It was not easy for Johann, in particular, to consider leaving Bulgaria, an area that showed so much potential.

In 1883 Kargel sent Vasil Khristov Marchev, a Bulgarian and potential leader of the Baptist work in Bulgaria, to Germany to attend the Hamburg Mission School. In May 1883, writing from Zhitomir, Kargel said to Pashkov:

> Concerning our return to Russia, I can tell you that I am convinced that it will happen and it is only a matter time. We would come immediately if we were not needed in Bulgaria. The work of the Lord is as follows here: As we returned last year, we found that the Lord was plucking one soul after another, and we could count fifteen new dear redeemed ones in our fellowship. Up to now in this year there are eight. These are very inexperienced in the ways of God, and we fear that without any leadership they may stray as did Stundism, where a few stray ideas have come in, and I fear we would bear some of the responsibility in that.[105]

Anna was soon aware of the turmoil and wrote in July 1883 from Rustchuk: "My husband sees clearly that he should leave but doesn't dare, not knowing God's will."[106] Her approach was less pastorally sensitive than was her husband's.

Anna's view prevailed. By January 1884 the Kargels had spoken openly about their intention to leave Bulgaria. This was not well received by the Bulgarian congregations. Anna wrote: "When we told the local congregation [that we were returning to Russia] and announced that we were selling our house, a whole storm rose up. They want to keep us here, literally by force, at least for three more years, until the preacher [Marchev] that was sent to Hamburg to the mission school returns."[107]

The Bulgarian Baptists again appealed directly to Pashkov to leave the Kargels in Bulgaria, but Anna Kargel wrote her own letter to Pashkov asking that he "respond to them decisively that every laborer should be eager to work where there is more work and where

---

105. J. G. Kargel to "Dear friend and brother in Christ" [V. A. Pashkov], 19 May 1883, 2/13/019, Pashkov Papers.

106. Anna Kargel to Vasily Alexandrovich [Pashkov], 23 September 1883, 2/13/020, Pashkov Papers.

107. Anna Kargel to Vasily Alexandrovich [Pashkov], 16 January 1884, 2/13/021, Pashkov Papers.

the Master calls, but not to sit without any work, comforting others."[108] Later in 1884, Kargel read in the newspaper of Pashkov's exile from Russia.[109] Pashkov and Korff had been told to sign a document that promised that they would not preach, organize meetings, engage in free prayer, or continue relationships with Stundists and other religious communities.[110] When they refused to sign it, they were both exiled. This may have confirmed to Kargel the sense of being needed back in Russia.

In this period Kargel was travelling and preaching among Lutherans and Baptists but found the latter to be "unclean and split from each other."[111] He and Anna were looking for a fresh start. Anna had indirectly to ask the Pashkovs for financial help as the family prepared to leave Rustchuk. She spoke in January 1884 of having no money for the trip, indeed "no money at all," since the house was not sold and "there is no other source."[112] She must have received a guarantee of money from Pashkov because she wrote in February 1884: "I don't have the words to thank you and never could, nor can I express my heart on paper . . . I will always consider that I owe a debt."[113] Johann had harbored some thoughts of returning to Germany, but by May 1884 he had dismissed them.[114]

Anna was desperate to leave Rustchuk and return to Saint Petersburg. She wrote: "I can't believe that soon I will be leaving this place and I count the minutes. We ask the Lord to bless our departure on 19 March and it seems that we will not make it earlier."[115] Johann, by

---

108. Anna Kargel to Vasily Alexandrovich [Pashkov], 16 January 1884, 2/13/001, Pashkov Papers. The final pages of the letter are not in chronological order and contain no greeting. It is clear from the content that it is the continuation of the 16 January 1884 letter, which is found at 2/13/21 in the Pashkov Papers.

109. J. G. Kargel to "Dear friend and brother in Christ" [unknown], 31 June 1884, 2/13/026, Pashkov Papers.

110. Ibid., 113; Korff, *Am Zarenhof*, 62–64.

111. J. G. Kargel to "Dear friend and brother in Christ" [unknown], 31 June 1884, 2/13/026, Pashkov Papers.

112. Anna Kargel to Vasily Alexandrovich [Pashkov], 16 January 1884, 2/13/001, Pashkov Papers.

113. Anna Kargel to Vasily Alexandrovich [Pashkov], 27 February 1884, 2/13/024, Pashkov Papers.

114. J. G. Kargel to "Dear friend and brother in Christ" [Pashkov], 3 May 1884, 2/13/040, Pashkov Papers.

115. Anna Kargel to Vasily Alexandrovich [Pashkov], 27 February 1884, 2/13/024, Pashkov Papers.

contrast, was aware that his departure left the three-year-old churches in Kazanluk and Rustchuk in a vulnerable position. By 1885 the Rustchuk congregation had three preaching stations and thirty-five members.[116] Even in the midst of the preparations to leave Bulgaria, Kargel planned a late winter trip over the mountains to Kazanluk to check on the congregation there, which had about twenty members.[117]

After the family's departure from Rustchuk in March 1884, Kargel still maintained contact with the Bulgarian churches. He intended to travel back to Rustchuk and Kazanluk in February 1885 but poor weather made this impossible.[118] Once the weather improved, Kargel again thought of visiting the congregations in the summer of 1885, but now there were new issues to consider. Writing to Pashkov he stated:

> Now I am sure you would like to know why I did not go to Bulgaria, where I so wanted to go. I am not able to tell you the main reason, though I will allude to it. The situation has become so difficult in the past five to six weeks here in Petersburg that I had reason to believe that if I would cross the border it would not be easy for me to return, and in the end, possibly not at all. Added to this I had a certain Word from God that I feel I understood well. Also an American Missionary in Constantinople visited my work in Bulgaria and wrote about it. This visit . . . helped with the greatest needs. Added to this, a Bulgarian brother [Marchev] who is at the Mission school in Hamburg will be going to the field for two months so that the most important things will be seen to.[119]

This letter contains important points about Kargel's spiritual outlook. First, he was practical in his thinking. He was aware the

---

116. "Statistik 1886 der vereinigten Gemeinden Getaufen Christen." For further statistics see "Statistik 1882 der vereinigten Gemeinden Getaufen Christen"; "Statistik 1883 der vereinigten Gemeinden Getaufen Christen"; Wardin, "The Baptists in Bulgaria," 149. The numbers quoted by Wardin probably represent Rustchuk and its preaching stations without the inclusion of Kazanluk. There is no discussion of a decline in church membership in any of Anna or Johann Kargel's letters during this period.

117. Anna Kargel to Vasily Alexandrovich [Pashkov], 16 January 1884, 2/13/001 Pashkov Papers.

118. J. G. Kargel to "Dear friend and brother in Christ" [V. A. Pashkov], 22 February 1885, 2/13/037, Pashkov Papers.

119. J. G. Kargel to "Dear friend and brother in Christ" [V. A. Pashkov], 4 June 1885, 2/13/016, Pashkov Papers. This letter is mislabeled as 1883 but the handwriting states 1885.

government might not have allowed him back into Russia if he had left. Second, he was open to direct guidance—the "certain Word from God." Third, he continued to feel a responsibility to the Bulgarian Baptist congregations. He was delighted that pastoral care was continuing. Vasil Marchev, the Bulgarian studying in Hamburg, was soon to return to Bulgaria. Kargel, having had dramatic experiences in terms of his inner spiritual experience, remained a pastor.

CONCLUSION

Johann Kargel, with his wife Anna, moved to Bulgaria hoping that it would prove to be congenial to his health and that he would be able to establish Baptist work there. His years in Bulgaria did not turn out as he had expected. He did not regain his health and while his wife threw herself into their work initially, she soon became frustrated and critical of the Baptists. She saw a spiritual narrowness in Baptists, including her husband. Anna's increasing desire was to return to Saint Petersburg. The establishment of Baptist work in Bulgaria was significant, but equally significant for Johann Kargel was that he experienced a turning point in his own spiritual life. The actual details of the crisis are recorded by Kargel in his book *Christ—our Sanctification* which was published in 1926 in the journal *Xristianin*.[120] Kargel's interest in Bulgaria continued. In October 1888 he returned to Rustchuk on the way home to Saint Petersburg and was joyfully welcomed. Kargel wrote to Pashkov: "Oh dear brother, I am thanking the Lord that he brought me home this route as I see how that He was able to use me here. I give Him praise, thanks and honor for this."[121] Kargel was now fully open to the broader perspectives of the Pashkovites. From the mid-1880s onwards he became the most influential figure working to bring unity among the various expressions of the evangelical faith in Russia.

---

120. Karetnikova states that the book was first published in 1912. See Karetnikova, *Almanax po Istorii Russkogo Baptisma*, vypusk 4, 43.

121. J. G. Kargel to "Dear friend and brother in Christ" [V. A. Pashkov], 25 October 1888, 2/13/060, Pashkov Papers.

5

Second Saint Petersburg Period

Part of the Pashkovite Circle

(1884–1887)

WHEN THE KARGELS ARRIVED back in Saint Petersburg in 1884, Ivan Kargel (as I will now refer to him) did not reconnect with the German Baptist church of which he had previously been pastor. This can be seen as evidence of a break with his previous Baptist commitment and as being in line with his developing perspective on evangelical spirituality. It was also the case that the tensions within the German Baptist congregation had increased since his departure four years previously. However, Kargel was not being drawn away from Baptist life at the instigation of Vasily Pashkov. Indeed Pashkov may have considered the possibility that the German Baptists and the Pashkovites could share a building. It seems that a Pashkovite group was meeting in various homes around the city, but the police were locating and disturbing evangelicals wherever they met.[1] From this point on, Kargel's ministry was to be among Russian-speaking evangelicals. This chapter will examine Kargel's local ministry in Saint Petersburg, as he took on the leadership of the Pashkovites in 1884 within what I will now refer to as the "Saint Petersburg Evangelicals."[2]

---

1. J. G. Kargel to "Dear friend and brother in Christ" [V. A. Pashkov], 29 November 1884, 2/13/032, Pashkov Papers.

2. Up until this point, I have referred to this group as "Pashkovites." It does not seem appropriate to continue to refer to them as such following the departure of Pashkov from Russia. From this point on I will refer to the group as the "Saint Petersburg Evangelicals." On most occasions, when I refer to them in this chapter, I will be referring to the actual group in the capital. But increasingly the movement had adherents throughout the Russian Empire. The use of the city is not so much a

It will also look at the way he was making international links that led to a broadening of his work across Europe. Kargel's continuing Bulgarian contacts will also be investigated. The chapter will analyze the attempts made to form a wider Baptist-evangelical unity in Russia, and the role of Kargel—alongside Pashkov and Johann Wieler—in that process. Kargel's own spiritual development continued, and as this is traced it will be seen to be central to all that took place.

MINISTRY IN SAINT PETERSBURG

Ivan and Anna Kargel were actively involved with the Saint Petersburg Evangelicals in Saint Petersburg during a three-year period beginning in 1884. Despite the pressure from the government, Ivan Kargel managed to oversee their home Bible studies and their celebrations of the Lord's Supper. By this stage the Brethren term "breaking of bread" was being commonly used. Kargel compared the Saint Petersburg Evangelicals, after the departure of Pashkov, to sheep scattered without a shepherd.[3] In August 1884 he described the closing of some of their meeting places by the government, as the authorities become more active in suppressing the activities of the group. Kargel still managed at that stage to preach on Sundays in various locations despite the persecutions.[4] By November 1884, however, the Saint Petersburg Evangelicals were finding it very difficult to hold their meetings.[5] The courts were under Pobedonostsev's control and it was clear that they would punish those who "had forsaken the faith of their fathers for the absurd teachings of the ephemeral sectarians," whether of the nobility or peasantry.[6] Kargel wrote to Pashkov: "We broke bread here and there in homes just as in the book of Acts, but everywhere we met the police soon started questioning and we had to change locations." Later in that same letter, Kargel stated: "I will continue to have ministry here

---

marker of their location as a marker of their origin. I will clarify when I use the term in reference to Pashkovites residing outside Saint Petersburg.

3. J. G. Kargel to "Dear friend and brother in Christ" [unknown], 31 June 1884, 2/13/026, Pashkov Papers.

4. J. G. Kargel to "Dear friend and brother in Christ" [V. A. Pashkov], 8 August 1884, 2/13/027, Pashkov Papers.

5. For a comparison of the Pashkovite meetings before and after the exile of Pashkov see Ignat'ev, "Pashkovcy-Baptisty v' Petersburg," 184–92.

6. Heier, *Religious Schism*, 146.

[Saint Petersburg] and want to stay here longer, until the Lord shows me otherwise. He will guide us with His eyes, so that we can't miss His ways. We continue to pray for you [Pashkov] and your family, as well as for your return."[7]

Ivan Kargel did remain involved in leadership and preaching among the Saint Petersburg Evangelicals and was recognized as their "shepherd."[8] The Kargel family lived for periods of time at the Lieven Palace on Bol'shaya Morskaya 43. Sophia Lieven was the daughter of Natalia Lieven; Natalia's sister was Vera Gagarina. With the most prominent male leaders in exile, Natalia Lieven, Vera Gagarina, and Elizaveta Chertkova took leadership within the evangelical movement. Chertkova's husband was not exiled but died in 1884. Lieven and Chertkova were reportedly sentenced to go into exile but "the tsar remained adamant that 'his widows' be left alone."[9] In November 1884, Anna thanked the Pashkovs for the use of their apartment on Vyborgskaya Street where Anna had settled in with her two girls (Natasha, aged two and Elena, aged one) while Johann was in Odessa.[10]

In early 1885, the Saint Petersburg Evangelicals experienced a split, as part of the group felt they could not continue without congregational rules and argued in favor of forming a church with elected elders. Kargel visited the breakaway group several times and tried to bring them back to the Pashkovite ideals of an evangelical fellowship without a denominational structure. Kargel reported to Pashkov on the situation, using words that showed something of the influence of Brethren thinking on his own views: "Now, you know my opinion concerning the church, that it is God's will that the church should follow the example of the New Testament and be founded upon this. I am not able to discern the will of the Lord in this situation; whether I am to do something about it or not. I have also told the brothers and the

---

7. J. G. Kargel to "Dear friend and brother in Christ" [V. A. Pashkov], 29 November 1884, 2/13/032, Pashkov Papers.

8. Latimer, *With Christ in Russia*, 39. Latimer also mentions that Kargel and other Christian leaders of Saint Petersburg preached in the city's main hall before large crowds. See Latimer, *With Christ in Russia*, 17.

9. Corrado, "The Philosophy of Ministry of Colonel Vasiliy Pashkov," 169.

10. Anna Kargel to Vasily Alexandrovich [Pashkov], 14 November 1884, 2/13/031, Pashkov Papers.

sisters here [Saint Petersburg] about the situation. They are making me accountable to God to at least give them advice."[11]

Kargel did not mention the details of the conflict, but Pashkov did in his correspondence with I. Rozov, who would be elected by the breakaway group as their presbyter. Pashkov wrote to Rozov in March 1885: "We do not see in the Word that presbyters were elected by the Church. They were appointed by the Apostles or their delegates. Therefore *an election* of anybody to this position would be a deviation from the Word."[12] Baptists, who elected leaders, took a contrary position.

Pashkov and Kargel do not seem opposed to the general idea of elders within a congregation but Pashkov particularly opposed the election of leaders by the congregation. In April 1885 Pashkov advised the breakaway group against elections, because it would be a "deviation from the Lord's instruction."[13] The vacuum caused by Pashkov's exile produced problems. Puzynin suggests that Pashkov may have planned to appoint Kargel to succeed him in leadership, but Kargel did not want to be restricted to Saint Petersburg.[14] On one side of the conflict about leadership were Pashkov and Kargel who—in line with Brethren thinking and, as they saw it, with the New Testament—did not agree that the congregation should elect its own pastor. On the other side was a group that felt they needed a leader.

In May 1886 Kargel was still struggling with issues among the Saint Petersburg Evangelicals, including a case of immorality.[15] The group, however, had no formal membership and no obvious disciplinary procedure. Kargel was not recognized as an ordained minister and was not able to exercise authority in the way that might have been possible in a Baptist congregation. The authorities, however, still regarded Kargel as a Baptist minister, and in 1885 officials questioned Adam

---

11. J. G. Kargel to "Dear friend and brother in Christ" [V. A. Pashkov], 24 January 1885, 2/13/035, Pashkov Papers.

12. "Your Loving Brother V. P." [V. A. Pashkov] to "Dear Friend Rozov," 1/13 March 1885, 2/1/b/045, Pashkov Paper.

13. [V. A. Pashkov] to "Dear Petersburg Brothers and Sisters," 2/14 April 1885, 2/1/b/66, Pashkov Papers.

14. See Puzynin, "The Tradition of the Gospel Christians," 119.

15. J. G. Kargel to "Dear friend and brother in Christ" [V. A. Pashkov], 12 May 1885, 2/13/049, Pashkov Papers.

Reinhold Schiewe several times about Kargel's income.[16] The relationship between the two men was strained, but evidently was healed by September 1886, when Kargel and Schiewe travelled together to the island of Dagö[17] and villages near Hapsal in Estonia.[18] Schiewe was influential in molding Estonian Baptist theological views. On 23 February 1884, at the request of some evangelical believers in the country, he baptized seventeen people in the Ungru River, not far from Hapsal.[19] This event marks the beginnings of the Baptist community in Estonia. Kargel still had important Baptist links.

Although Kargel enjoyed wider opportunities for ministry, his enthusiasm for travel was not shared by the Saint Petersburg Evangelicals who looked to him for leadership. In early 1885 the group appealed to Kargel to stay in Saint Petersburg and serve them. A letter from Anna Kargel to Pashkov outlined the struggles that they felt as Ivan Kargel tried to come to terms with the requests from outside the city to engage in wider ministry and the needs being expressed by the local congregations.[20] Perhaps this could have been dealt with if there had been a structure of accountability in the Saint Petersburg evangelical community, but it seems that Kargel was unwilling to initiate such a structure. It appears that to a large extent Kargel left the Saint Petersburg congregations to sort their affairs out on their own. At the end of May 1885, when the local needs in Saint Petersburg were very apparent, he was in Taurida Province at Astrakhanka.[21] During the summer of 1885, he spent ten weeks on a preaching trip to the Molotschna Colony, Riga, and Volhynia. These trips were followed by five weeks in Poland. When he finally returned to Saint Petersburg, he wrote: "After I returned from Poland to Marino, I had intended to go to Saint Petersburg with my family. He [God] urged me out again. I

---

16. J. G. Kargel to "Dear brother in the Lord" [V. A. Pashkov], 5 August 1885, 2/13/043, Pashkov Papers.

17. Hiiumaa is the Estonian island referred to in German and Swedish as Dagö.

18. J. G. Kargel to "Dear brother in the Lord" [V. A. Pashkov], 23 September 1886, 2/13/ 53, Pashkov Papers.

19. Pilli, "Baptists in Estonia 1884–1940," 28.

20. Anna Kargel to Vasily Alexandrovich [Pashkov], 12 April 1885, 2/13/039, Pashkov Papers.

21. J. G. Kargel to "Dear friend and brother in Christ" [V. A. Pashkov], 4 June 1885, 2/13/016, Pashkov Papers. This letter is mislabeled as 1883 but the handwriting states 1885.

had no peace and I had to go. I went first to Volhynia."[22] This lack of willingness or perhaps ability to organize the Saint Petersburg circle would cost the Saint Petersburg evangelical movement dearly.

WIDER MINISTRY

Ivan Kargel's connection with the Saint Petersburg Evangelicals provided him with additional contacts with evangelicals from Western Europe, especially from Britain. Over the course of his years in Saint Petersburg he learned first-hand of evangelical practices and perspectives from a number of foreign guests who stayed in or spoke at the Lieven Palace. These guests included members of the Evangelical Alliance in Britain such as Friedrich Baedeker; teachers and preachers within the Holiness movements in Europe such as Jessie Penn-Lewis, Otto Stockmayer,[23] and H. Grattan Guinness; evangelist and Keswick missionary spokesman, Reginald Radcliffe;[24] interdenominational student leaders such as Baron Paul Nicolay and John Mott; and those involved in ministries that involved social concern, such as George Müller in Bristol and Mildred Duff of the Salvation Army.[25] These relationships expanded Kargel's view of the universal church and he also began to sense a strength and unity in organic relationships that he had not experienced in denominational structures.[26]

Kargel became closely associated with Friedrich Baedeker, a German by birth but later English by adoption. Baedeker was the cousin of Karl Baedeker, the pioneer in guide books,[27] and was a close friend of Radstock and George Müller. His own evangelical faith had been shaped by Radstock, and like Müller and Radstock he was associated with the Open Brethren. Baedeker was also involved in Holiness

---

22. J. G. Kargel to "Dear brother in Lord" [possibly Baedeker], 28 October 1885, 2/13/047, Pashkov Papers.

23. Kuznetsova suggests that Stockmayer taught the practice of healing in the Pashkovite circle in 1880 and that Pashkov, Korff, and Kargel practiced the gift of healing. See Kuznetsova, "Early Russian Evangelicals," 127.

24. Latimer, *With Christ in Russia*, 38.

25. Lieven, *Eine Saat*, 59–60; Corrado, "The Philosophy of Ministry of Colonel Vasiliy Pashkov," 107–14.

26. For a fuller description of the background of some of these individuals and their connection to the Saint Petersburg Evangelicals see Kuznetsova, "Early Russian Evangelicals," 125–36.

27. Latimer, *Dr. Baedeker*, 18.

gatherings, especially from the 1870s, and served as a translator for Robert Pearsall Smith when he presented the Holiness message to thousands in Germany.[28] He was involved in the Evangelical Alliance's outreach to Russia[29] and worked with Pashkov in attempting to form a Russian Evangelical Alliance. He also possessed a unique authorization by the Russian government to visit the prisons throughout Russia and supply the convicts with copies of the Bible.[30] When Baedeker spoke in the Lieven home, he used Kargel as his translator into Russian.[31] As a translator, Kargel would have had to grasp the details of the messages being delivered. The relationship between Ivan Kargel and Baedeker became strong as together they undertook extensive travels. Baedeker was highly significant in Kargel's continued exploration of the relationship between authentic spirituality and effective ministry.

In July 1885 Baedeker was in Saint Petersburg assisting Kargel in the task of preaching to the evangelical Christians—of various churches—scattered throughout the city. The travelling partnership between Kargel and Baedeker may have begun a month later. Kargel reported to Pashkov in August that he was in Warsaw with Baedeker for a conference.[32] In a letter to Baedeker soon after this Polish trip, Kargel clearly showed the influence that Baedeker had exerted on him: "Would it not be wonderful if you could come to Russia and Poland and speak to them about holiness in the gatherings? I am convinced that if the people are brought into the correct position, the Lord would do miracles among the non-converted."[33] This expresses a classic aspiration found in Holiness circles. Believers needed to be brought to a "correct position" in terms of the understanding and practice of holy living, and as a result there would be a powerful ministry to those outside the church. Several months later, in a letter probably written to Baedeker, Kargel expressed thanks for subscriptions to *The Christian*, which was the most widely read interdenominational evangelical weekly newspaper in Britain, and *The Golden Lamp*, a Brethren

---

28. *Earnest Christianity*, I (July, 1875), 444, quoting "a Berlin paper," as cited in Dieter, *The Holiness Revival of the Nineteenth Century*, 171.

29. Randall and Hilborn, *One Body in Christ*, 171.

30. Latimer, *With Christ in Russia*, 44.

31. Lieven, *Duxovnoe Probuzhdenie V Rossii*, 81.

32. J. G. Kargel to "Dear friend and brother in Christ" [V. A. Pashkov], 5 August 1885, 2/13/043, Pashkov Papers.

33. J. G. Kargel to Dr. Baedeker, 24 August 1885, 2/13/044, Pashkov Papers.

publication (with a typically Brethren sub-title of "truth in love for the children of God"). The letter to Baedeker is in German, but it is clear that Kargel could read English. His ability in English is also referred to by Sophia Lieven as she recounts how Kargel translated Baedeker's English into Russian.[34] *The Christian* would have introduced Kargel to the writings of many of those within the Keswick network, although *The Golden Lamp* was especially noted by Kargel as containing "sweet truths."[35]

In March 1886, Kargel and Baedeker travelled from Saint Petersburg to the Caucasus with the intention of preaching wherever possible and gathering information about evangelical Christians sent into exile. They travelled together by way of Moscow, Kharkov, and Sevastopol. On the way to Sevastopol, they took a trip to Novo-Grigorivka to meet with a man named Sacharoff [Sakharov]. The government surveillance was so pervasive that their telegram was intercepted and a *pristav* (police officer) met them upon arrival. To ensure that their freedom was restricted, he stayed the entire night with them at the Sakharov home. As they entered the Crimean Peninsula, Baedeker continued on to Sevastopol to hold meetings there and Kargel went to the Molotschna village of Rückenau where he "shared the good news with hundreds."[36] The two joined up in Sevastopol and from there took the steamship across the Black Sea to Batum.[37] From Batum they travelled to Tiflis, where they arrived on Easter Sunday, 12 April 1886.

Kargel, attempting to find the Baptists in Tiflis, his own home community, only managed to find the Kalweits' apartment. When he arrived at their apartment, he found that the Kalweits had already left for the morning's worship and Kargel was unable to locate the Baptist meeting place.[38] We know from Russian sources that Kargel assisted in officiating over the founding of the Tiflis Baptist Church

---

34. Lieven, *Duxovnoe Probuzhdenie V Rossii*, 81.

35. J. G. Kargel to "Dear brother in the Lord" [possibly Baedeker], 28 October 1885, 2/13/047, Pashkov Papers.

36. J. G. Kargel to "Dear friend and brother in Christ" [V. A. Pashkov], 12 May 1886, 2/13/049, Pashkov Papers.

37. Kargel also mentions that this was the same ship in which he had first heard and responded to the gospel.

38. J. G. Kargel to "Dear friend and brother in Christ" [V. A. Pashkov], 12 May 1886, 2/13/049, Pashkov Papers.

and the ordinations of V. G. Pavlov, S. G. Rodionov, A. M. Mazaev, and M. K. Kalweit in August 1880.[39] The problem in finding the meeting place in 1886 may be an indication of the measures that the Baptists in Tiflis took to maintain a low profile during the difficult days of Pobedonostsev. Baedeker and Kargel eventually managed to speak at Baptist meetings, and were greatly appreciated.[40]

In Tiflis Baedeker visited the "Colony Church" [the Lutheran Church] and was asked to deliver a series of lectures for the church, which Kargel translated from German into Russian. The pair spent two and a half weeks preaching and teaching in the Tiflis area and making journeys to outlying villages. Writing to Pashkov, Kargel gives some insights into the topics they covered and the nature of the meetings:

> Especially blessed were the meetings that were exclusively for believers. Here the theme was, "Why we are not growing," and "How can we be mature in Christ?" There were free dialogues, spurred on by me, and then continued by all who had something to say about the themes . . . The dear brothers were deeply touched, which became evident over the succeeding days as they eagerly asked questions such as, "How can we live a life in constant fellowship with Christ?" Others confessed, "We thought we were very good Christians and now we see that we are not." We have ample reason to thank the Lord for our two and a half weeks in Tiflis.[41]

Baedeker would often "engage a hall and issue his bills [hang posters] for public services."[42] If he was challenged as to the legality of a foreigner preaching without permission, he asked if he could give a lecture instead. If that was acceptable, the old bills were replaced with new ones announcing that "Dr. Baedeker from England" would be lecturing on "Sin and Salvation."[43] Meanwhile, Kargel would often meet Russian believers in exile. Because of his broad range of contacts with Pashkovites, Baptists, Mennonite Brethren, and Molokans, he was well suited for the task. Kargel mentions many lectures taking

---

39. *Istoriya Evangel'skix Xristian—Baptistov*, 78; Popov, "Iz Istorii Nashego Bratstva," 65.

40. "Germany Reports," 430.

41. J. G. Kargel to "Dear friend and brother in Christ" [V. A. Pashkov], 12 May 1886, 2/13/049, Pashkov Papers.

42. Latimer, *Dr. Baedeker*, 69.

43. Ibid., 70.

place.[44] It seems that these were rather like extensions of the Keswick Conference, mini-Keswick Conferences taken to Russian and German speakers who were in exile.

From Tiflis, Kargel and Baedeker travelled to Vladikavkaz, where they held many meetings with both Germans and Russians. On 5 May 1886, they arrived in Rostov, with the possibility of going on to Berdjansk. Kargel, however, decided to return to Saint Petersburg to complete his family's move to Hapsal, Estonia, in that month, prior to the birth of their third child, Maria.[45] On his longer journeys, many of them by train, Kargel passed out Bibles to fellow passengers and engaged in discussions about religious matters. On 28 October 1885, for example, he wrote that, "In the train wagon, the Lord gave me opportunity to witness to a young man on his way to Jerusalem, but he did not know about the heavenly Jerusalem."[46]

During these years, Kargel's travel schedule seems to have increased and I have calculated that he was away from his family approximately 35 percent of the time between 1885 and 1888. His travels often took him to Saratov and the German villages along the Volga. He also spent considerable time near the Molotschna Colony and in the Volhynia region. He began to press into new areas to the northeast. He also took numerous trips to Poland. Even though he was now reasonably comfortable speaking in Russian, the destinations indicate that he was still drawn to German speakers within the Russian Empire.

During these years of travel, the family spent periods of time, especially in the summer, in Hapsal. Anna Kargel mentions that a doctor recommended removing the family from the city for their health.[47] Even during the quiet summer months, however, Kargel was active. In 1887 he took trips to Liban (Poland), Kovno (Latvia), and Dagö Island (Estonia).[48] Here was evangelical activism operating at full strength.

---

44. J. G. Kargel to "Dear friend and brother in Christ" [V. A. Pashkov], 12 May 1886, 2/13/049, Pashkov Papers.

45. J. G. Kargel to "Dear brother in Christ Jesus" [V. A. Pashkov], 23 September 1886, 2/13/053, Pashkov Papers.

46. J. G. Kargel to "Dear brother in Lord" [possibly Baedeker], 28 October 1885, 2/13/047, Pashkov Papers.

47. Anna Kargel to Vasily Alexandrovich [Pashkov], 18 January 1890, 2/13/082, Pashkov Papers.

48. J. G. Kargel to "Dear friend and brother in Christ" [V. A. Pashkov], 13 August 1887, 2/13/057, Pashkov Papers.

He was also continually writing reports of the trips to Pashkov and Baedeker. In addition, he carried money as gifts, no doubt from Pashkov, to support needy believers. In March 1886 Kargel reported the joy and thanks that Riaboshapka had expressed as Kargel handed him gifts of 1,220 rubles and another 500 rubles—the latter for the completion of a barn, which possibly would have been used as a meeting place.[49] Kargel kept in touch with his mother and his brother when he returned to the Volhynia region, where they both lived. In a letter dated June 1885,[50] he reported: "God gave me great joy in the past year. My mother, for whom I have prayed for years, lives here in Volynshen [Volhynia], has found the Lord and is happy and joyful in Christ." In the same letter he talks about his brother, who attended meetings conducted by Kargel and gave his life to Christ, but who, says Kargel, does not yet "feel the great joy inside."[51] In 1886 Kargel returned to the Saint Petersburg German Baptist Church for several months. Adam Schiewe was travelling in America to raise money, and asked Kargel to care for the church in his absence.[52] In April 1887, however, Anna wrote to Pashkov that she was hoping to find "a corner somewhere near the Finland. Zh. D."[53] It would appear that Anna and the family were seeking a new residence, perhaps to escape the pressure of persecution.[54]

---

49. J. G. Kargel to "Dear friend and brother in Christ" [V. A. Pashkov], 17 March 1886, 2/13/050, Pashkov Papers.

50. This letter is incorrectly filed as 1883 due to the archive's misjudgment of the handwriting.

51. J. G. Kargel to "Dear friend and brother in Christ" [V. A. Pashkov], 4 June 1885, 2/13/016, Pashkov Papers. This letter is mislabeled as 1883 but the handwriting states 1885.

52. J. G. Kargel to "Dear brother in Christ Jesus" [V. A. Pashkov], 23 September 1886, 2/13/053, Pashkov Papers.

53. Anna Kargel to Vasily Alexandrovich [Pashkov], 22 May 1887, 2/13/056, Pashkov Papers.

54. There is a train station in Saint Petersburg named "Finlandia." In her letter, she used "Zh. D." which is a common Russian abbreviation for a train station but perhaps she was signaling to the Pashkovs her desire to leave Russia. Four months after this letter was written the Kargel family were residing outside Saint Petersburg in Hapsal, a quiet seaside town in present-day Estonia.

A BEAUTIFUL GARDEN: CONTACT WITH BULGARIA

Ivan Kargel continued to take a keen interest in Bulgaria. The Rustchuk church, of which he had been a pastor, struggled for three years after he left, but in 1887, when Vasil Marchev returned from training in Hamburg, the work was revived. New Baptist churches were formed in Bulgaria. Three decades later, the Baptist Union of Bulgaria was established in the town of Rustchuk. Kargel had been influential in three of the five founding churches of the Baptist Union of Bulgaria—Rustchuk, Kazanluk, and Lompalanka.[55] Kargel returned to Rustchuk in 1888, and commended Marchev, the new pastor. He wrote to Pashkov that "the brother who was sent to the school in Hamburg has returned and is a faithful worker."[56] While on this trip, Kargel and Marchev travelled to Lompalanka, passing out tracts and New Testaments and speaking at every possible opportunity. Kargel did not report to Pashkov on the founding of the Lompalanka church, but the Baptist congregation there was founded around the time of Kargel's visit (October 1888) and it was begun as a daughter of the Rustchuk Baptist church.[57]

Kargel's excitement at being back in Bulgaria and seeing evangelistic opportunities present themselves is clear in his report to Pashkov on his trip:

> I became aware of the fact that there are not very many good tracts available. Brother Martscheff [Marchev], to whom I gave the tracts from the Salvation Army, started translating "Buried alive" while he was waiting for our ship. He is hopeful that he will be able to finish it very soon. We will be hard pressed to finance the printing of a few thousand. As he started to translate it (in the public house) the people around wanted to know what it was he was doing and he translated it orally, and it made a big impression on them so that he was able to speak to a full room for more than two hours . . . O, I rejoice as I know that God will do great things here.[58]

---

55. See Wardin, "The Baptists in Bulgaria," 149–50; Angelov, "The Baptist Movement in Bulgaria," 11.

56. J. G. Kargel to "Dear brother in the Lord" [V. A. Pashkov], 25 October 1888, 2/13/60, Pashkov Papers.

57. Oprenov, "The Origins and Early Development of Baptists in Bulgaria," 20.

58. J. G. Kargel to "Dear friend and brother in Christ" [V. A. Pashkov], 29 October 1888, 2/13/061, Pashkov Papers.

Vasil Marchev had been critical of some aspects of the Baptist community in Bulgaria following the Kargels' departure. After the 1888 trip, Ivan Kargel assured Pashkov that Marchev was competent to carry on the work that he had started. Kargel was glad that he had had the opportunity to return because he was aware of particular theological errors that he had to address. It is not clear what they were, although in the context of Kargel's own development an interpretation can be offered. Here are Kargel's words: "I did find a deficiency concerning the recognition of full salvation in Jesus, as well as in the care for the souls, those who are already His; I was also able to do away with some of the narrow minded ideas of one of the brothers, which could have done some harm to them. The brothers have learned much, according to their own words. Especially they learned to carry one another with love and to see each other through Jesus."[59] These words might imply legalism in the church, and that is quite possible, but it is more likely that Kargel wanted to emphasize "full salvation in Jesus" in the sense of the deeper Christian life, or as Anna had put it when they were in Bulgaria, the knowledge that God could "complete fully" his work in believers. It is clear that Kargel was delighted at the outcome of his teaching.

Kargel had kept Pashkov informed during the early- and mid-1880s about what was happening in Bulgaria, and the fact that Pashkov was interested in the country was probably another reason for Kargel's continued interest. There was, in all probability, some on-going financial support for Bulgarian Baptists coming from Pashkov. In his report to Pashkov in November 1888, Kargel painted a picture of potential evangelical advance. He wrote, "In spite of what it may look like to a human eye, in its dry state, I hope that this field will become a beautiful garden to the Lord. The young, but excited worker Vasilii Martscheff (who became a Christian through my witnessing in 1881) was especially happy to see me again. It is his decision to leave all for Jesus and to serve Him. One thing I fear is that there will not be other workers for this field that have not died to themselves."[60] The theme of deeper spirituality is again noteworthy in Kargel's vision for the future. It would not be enough, in his view, to have more "workers

---

59. J. G. Kargel to "Dear friend and brother in Christ" [V. A. Pashkov], 15 November 1888, 2/13/062, Pashkov Papers.

60. Ibid.

in this field." They should be workers who have "died to themselves," a clear reference to a crisis of surrender that was seen within Holiness spirituality as separate from, and subsequent to, conversion.

During the 1888 trip to Bulgaria, Kargel was not able to go to Kazanluk, but in May 1889, on returning from an extended trip to Israel, he managed to visit the Kazanluk and Rustchuk congregations on his way to Saint Petersburg. As Kargel visited the Kazanluk area, he mentioned that travel was difficult and food was scarce.[61] He was pleased that he had finally been able to return to the congregation where he had baptized the first Baptist believers in Bulgaria, and yet he was not entirely content with their spiritual condition. He wrote to Pashkov, "Yesterday we had two blessed gatherings, and today, if the Lord so permits, we will have another, and in the end we will be breaking bread together. I am sorry that the brothers here are rather closed minded,[62] but I am hoping that the Lord will give them the light yet; I am also hoping that my passing through here, even if very short, will not be fruitless."[63]

There are three points here that are significant. The first is the use of the common Brethren term "breaking bread," rather than the normal Baptist reference to the Lord's Supper. The second is the somewhat opaque reference to the brothers as "rather closed minded." This might have to do with their unwillingness to share with each other, but it might well refer to their adherence to a policy in which only those baptized as believers could come to the Lord's Table. Third, Kargel hoped that they would receive more "light." The "light" could be a larger view of the church, one free from denominationalism.

AN ATTEMPT AT UNITY

Although Kargel's vision for interdenominational unity seems, at this point, to have had Brethren overtones, others who were seeking unity among Russian evangelicals were operating from a different perspective. In 1881 there was an evangelical conference in Saint Petersburg

---

61. J. G. Kargel to "Dear friend and brother in Christ" [V. A. Pashkov], 8 May 1889, 2/13/077, Pashkov Papers.

62. Kargel used the word *engherzig* which could also be translated petty, narrow-minded, or mean-spirited.

63. J. G. Kargel to "Dear friend and brother in Christ" [V. A. Pashkov], 8 May 1889, 2/13/077, Pashkov Papers.

at which one of the issues discussed was an "open" rather than "closed" Lord's Table.⁶⁴ In 1882, Pashkov met with evangelicals in southern Russia, including Johann Wieler.⁶⁵ Wieler eventually embraced the ideas of an open Table,⁶⁶ and in June 1883 Wieler left his teaching position at the secondary school in the Molotschna Colony and became a full-time worker funded by Pashkov.⁶⁷ In 1882 Wieler invited representatives from various evangelical communities with whom he was in contact to attend the Mennonite Brethren meetings to be held in Rückenau from 20 to 22 May. The minutes of this meeting are published in Abe Dueck's *Moving beyond Secession*.⁶⁸ According to the minutes, many of the attendees were Germans from the various communities within the Molotschna Settlement. The German settlements in Herzenberg, Puchtin, Einlage, Wiesenfeld, Friedensfeld, Sagradovka, Sergievka, and the regions of Don and Kuban were also represented, bringing the total number of Germans to sixty-two.⁶⁹ Russians were also invited to the meetings, from Russian fellowships in Novo-Vasilievka, Astrakhanka, Vladikavkaz, Tiflis, Osnova, Ignatievka, Poltavka, Mairovka, Karlovka, Lyubomirovka, Einlage, Lidiyafeldt, and Chichma in Bessarabia Province.⁷⁰ The total number of Russian representatives was eighteen. Among the Russian Baptists were Ivan Riaboshapka, Mikhail Ratushnyi, Grigorii Kushnerenko, and Alexander Kapustin. Also present were Minai Chanin, a baptized Molokan, and Andrej Markovich Mazaev, a leader in the Tiflis Baptist Church.⁷¹

---

64. Dyck, "Moulding the Brotherhood," 76.

65. Anna Kargel to Vasily Alexandrovich [Pashkov], 20 July 1882, 2/13/009, Pashkov Papers.

66. Friesen, *The Mennonite Brotherhood in Russia*, 499.

67. Martens, "Grossmutter's Brief," 9.

68. Dueck, *Moving beyond Secession*, 37–54.

69. The number is sometimes given as sixty-four, if the two guest missionaries, Christian Fisher and Yakov Deliakov, are included.

70. Dueck, *Moving beyond Secession*, 41–43.

71. There is a slight discrepancy about the exact number of attendees. Reshetnikov and Sannikov state fifty delegates, of whom nineteen were Russian or Ukrainian. See Reshetnikov and Sannikov, *Obzor Istorii Evangel'sko-Baptistskogo*, 112. Popov states that seventeen Russians and fifty-five Germans attended. See Popov, *Tserkovnii Vestnik*, 31, 1892, as cited in Dueck, *Moving beyond Secession*, 43.

This was a meeting of significant evangelicals from Baptist, Mennonite, and Molokan backgrounds. Johann Wieler was elected as chair and this event in 1882 points to an attempt on his part to merge the mission efforts of the various evangelical groups, to achieve some co-operation. The group heard reports from fifteen missionaries. These reports seem to have been evenly balanced between those working among Germans and those working among Russians. The committee also discussed a varying scale of pay for workers, based on the number of months spent as a missionary.[72] Missionaries were then appointed to geographic locations, to both Russian and German communities. Following the business portion of the meeting, an open discussion took place on various points of theological conflict. Anointing with oil was discussed. Wieler suggested that churches should practice healing prayer with anointing by oil.[73] This was a practice advocated by Radstock and possibly practiced by the Saint Petersburg Evangelicals.[74] After some discussion, it was determined to leave this to local congregations and to honor the wishes of the sick person whether to use oil or not. The issues of baptism and communion were then discussed, and according to the minutes Wieler passed on Pashkov's views about an open Table.[75] The question was raised, from a Baptist standpoint, "Why did Pashkov separate from the Orthodox Church if he believes their baptism is true?"[76] The conference failed to reach agreement over the question of whether those not baptized as believers could be admitted to the Lord's Supper, and a decision was postponed. The meetings did end with the Lord's Supper but the Germans and the Russians held separate celebrations.[77]

As Pashkov sought to influence the evangelicals of the southern Russian Empire towards an open Table, they were also having an influence on him. Early in 1883, George Müller spent an extended period of time in Saint Petersburg and Pashkov was baptized by Müller.[78]

72. Dueck, *Moving beyond Secession*, 43–46.
73. Ibid., 50–51.
74. Trotter, *Lord Radstock*, 23.
75. Dueck, *Moving beyond Secession*, 51.
76. Ibid., 52.
77. Ibid., 51–53.
78. Gutsche, *Westliche Quellen Des Russischen Stundism*, 58–60. Puzynin challenges the accuracy of Gutsche's statement that Müller baptized Pashkov by noting that there was no reference to a primary source. See Puzynin, "The Tradition of the

Pashkov's baptism was his decision, but it must be understood within the context of the pressure felt by the evangelicals of Saint Petersburg to forge a clearer identity. It should be noted that although Pashkov was in contact with many of the Baptists in the Russian Empire, he chose to be baptized by George Müller, an Open Brethren leader. This was a clear statement by Pashkov that he desired that the evangelical movement in Saint Petersburg would remain free of denominationalism. In 1883, the year of Pashkov's baptism, Wieler tried to invite Russian Baptists to Mennonite Brethren meetings, but he was blocked by the leadership of the Mennonite Brethren. The Mennonites may have feared the persecution that would result from transgressing the law regarding proselytism among the Russian Orthodox population and so refused to allow the Russian missionaries to their meeting.[79] However, P. M. Friesen states that many Mennonite Brethren "gave Br. Wieler their sympathy and supported him with their financial gifts."[80] In this period Wieler and Kargel often came into contact with each other. Both had a vision for evangelical unity, although Wieler was not particularly influenced by the Brethren. They preached together several times in the German communities along the Volga. Wieler fled from Russia in 1886. After a short time in Berlin, where his family joined him, he moved to Tultscha, Romania, in September 1887, to be the pastor of a Baptist congregation.

PASHKOV AND THE EVANGELICAL ALLIANCE

As early as 1883, Pashkov and Korff began to plan for a conference that would build relationships among the evangelically-minded groups in Russia. Their vision was similar to that of Wieler, but at this point they were operating in parallel with Wieler's efforts rather than in conjunction with him. They had communicated with the various evangelical centers they were aware of across Russia, including in Ukraine and the

---

Gospel Christians," 110–11. However, in a personal letter to Vasily Pashkov dated 18 April, 1883, Baedeker writes: "we were delighted to receive your letter and to learn from it that you have followed the Lord in the spirit of obedience by Baptism." See Baedeker to "My much loved brother" [V. A. Pashkov], 18 April 1883, 2/3/026, Pashkov Papers.

79. Friesen, *The Mennonite Brotherhood in Russia*, 514.

80. Dueck, *Moving beyond Secession*, 150. The full article is "Confession or Sect" written by P. M. Friesen in 1914 which was translated and published in this work, pages 142–57.

Caucasus. The range of evangelicals was broad and included Baptists, Mennonites, Molokans, Dukhobors, and Stundists. Some of this intelligence had been gathered or corroborated by Ivan Kargel as he travelled from his home in Bulgaria. The date for the conference was set for 1 April 1884. Pashkov and Korff provided travel expenses for those who could not afford the journey. Pashkov also provided room and board for all the attendees at what was to be a ten-day conference. Most of the delegates—seventy in all—stayed in a Saint Petersburg hotel. In addition to the Russian delegates, there were several non-Russian participants. Baedeker and his wife were in the inner circle of the conference and were lodged with the Pashkovs rather than at the hotel.[81]

Pashkov and Korff had three goals for this conference. They desired to strengthen their brothers through forging stronger bonds of unity; they wanted to see a deepened understanding of the Bible; and they wanted to provide an event that would emphasize evangelical fellowship.[82] These objectives proved to be difficult to attain. It was clear from the first meeting on 1 April 1884 that Pashkov had been too idealistic in thinking that seventy delegates could agree on previously disputed points of doctrine. It became evident that Pashkov's open-minded evangelical outlook was not shared by all.[83] One major point of division, as it had been at Wieler's conference, was who could be admitted to Holy Communion.[84] Problems became more evident as the Mennonites, Dukhobors, Molokans, Baptists, and Stundists all raised issues that emphasized their distinctives. It was hard to find common ground.[85] After several days of discussion and argument the delegation agreed to concentrate on ethical issues and steer away from theological details.[86]

Halfway through the conference the participants were starting to draw closer together. They did not realize, however, that the authori-

---

81. Dr. Baedeker's biographer notes that he and his wife were given tickets numbered one and two. See Latimer, *Dr. Baedeker*, 36.

82. Brandenburg, *The Meek and the Mighty*, 112.

83. Steeves, "The Russian Baptist Union," 24.

84. Brandenburg, *The Meek and the Mighty*, 112.

85. Pashkov's wide range of contacts among the Stundists and Dukhobors was well known to Bonch-Bruyevich, a researcher for Lenin. See Jones and Muckle, "Marginalia," 80–84.

86. Korff, *Am Zarenhof*, 57.

ties were about to strike. On 6 April, the fifth day of the conference, Pashkov, Korff, and Baedeker were waiting at the Pashkov palace for the delegation to arrive from the hotel. No delegates arrived. Preparations were being made at the Lieven estate for a large lunch for the entire delegation. The leaders waited several hours, with no news forthcoming, before Pashkov went to the hotel where the delegation was staying to discover that the group had vanished.[87]

Later that afternoon, one of the delegates was able to find Pashkov and to solve the mystery. He told the hosts that on their way home from the previous night's activities the members of the group were arrested and taken to the city's fortress of Saint Peter and Saint Paul. The police searched them for revolutionary documents, but found only Bibles and notes from the conference. The police then informed the delegates that they had no legitimate business in Saint Petersburg and had to return home. They were escorted to their hotel and then to the train station early the next morning.[88] They were forced onto the train and told they could not re-enter the city. The messenger had managed to get off at the first stop and had walked back to tell Pashkov and Princess Lieven the story.[89]

It seems that the April conference may have caused Pobedonostsev to move with all possible force against the evangelical Christians. Such a conference was viewed as a revolutionary act to subvert the Orthodox Church. The next step was that Korff and Pashkov were exiled. The Pashkov family moved to Paris, where they established a relationship with missions in France and England, including the McCall Mission, based in Paris, and the East London Missionary Training Institute (also called the Harley College) at Harley House in Bromley-by-Bow, run by Grattan and Fanny Guinness. Natalie Nikolaevna Kruzeinas was Pashkov's administrator in Saint Petersburg.[90] Pashkov continued

---

87. Latimer, *Dr. Baedeker*, 37.

88. Stead relates a slightly different story with two separate arrests occurring during the conference. The first arrest occurred on Saturday night when the entire delegation was arrested. They were freed after Pashkov and Korff intervened only to be re-arrested on Sunday night and then escorted to the train station on Monday morning. See Stead, *Truth about Russia*, 365–66.

89. Lieven, *Eine Saat*, 50.

90. Natalie Nikolaevna is referred to in Kargel's letters. Sophia Lieven gives Natalie Nikolaevna's family name as Kruzeinas in her memoirs, stating that Kruzeinas was the only non-family member to travel to Italy to attend Pashkov's funeral. See Lieven, *Duxovnoe Probuzhdenie V Rossii*, 63–64. In the German version of this book, Lieven, *Eine Saat*, Natalie Nikolaevna is not mentioned.

to advise, fund, and at times direct Ivan Kargel and Johann Wieler in the work of developing a network of evangelical Christians within the Russian-speaking world.

NOVO-VASILIEVKA, 1884

Following the abortive April 1884 conference in Saint Petersburg, Wieler and Kargel gathered together some of the attendees again in the village of Novo-Vasilievka, a Russian village south of the Molotschna Settlement where Wieler lived.[91] The destination was far enough away from the German Mennonites to permit the Russians safe travel and close enough to Wieler's home to arrange a large meeting. It was also the home of a Russian Baptist congregation whose leadership had attended previous meetings. The purpose of this conference was, again, to organize the mission work of evangelicals within the Russian Empire. This time, however, of the thirty-three delegates, only six were Mennonite Brethren, with the majority being from a Russian background.[92]

This meeting is considered by the Russian Baptist Union to be the origin of their denomination.[93] The Baptists had previously held a conference in October 1879 in Tiflis but the results fell short of their hopes and are not considered the start of the denomination.[94] The starting of a new denomination was not Wieler's intention and the meetings carried no legal standing.[95] Remarkably, Wieler and Kargel, both Germans and neither of them at the center of Baptist life, were elected as chairman and vice-chairman of the conference. Their leadership gifts were clearly affirmed. It is significant that the name chosen for the conference was "The Russian Conference of the Union of Believers, Baptized Christians, or as they are called, Baptists, of South Russia and the Caucasus." The meeting was, in fact, a blend of Russian

---

91. Kolarz states that it is near the city of Berdyansk in Zaporozh'e Province. See Kolarz, *Religion in the Soviet Union*, 285.

92. For a full list of the delegates compare Karev, "Russkoe Evangel'sko-Baptistskoe Dvizhenie," 7; Diedrich, *Urspruenge Und Anfaenge Russischen Freikirchentums*, 454–55; and Nikolaevskij, "K" Istorii Russkogo Sektanstva," 42–59.

93. Koval'kov and Chernopyatov, "Ivan Veniaminovich Kargel," 47.

94. Balousov, "Pervyj Nazidatel'nyj S"ezd Baptistov v Omske Sibir,'" 38; Savinskij, *Istoriya Russko-Ukrainskogo Baptizma*, 340.

95. Steeves, "The Russian Baptist Union," 28.

Stundo-baptists, Russian Baptists, German Mennonite Brethren, and German Baptist communities.[96]

An extended report on the conference was written by Kargel and sent to Pashkov.[97] Kargel wrote the report from Tiege, presumably from Wieler's home, on 3 May 1884.[98] He described how he and Wieler had arrived on 28 April in Astrakhanka[99] to finish the preparations for the conference. When they arrived, they found Ivan Riaboshapka and another Ukrainian waiting for them. Wieler and Kargel were informed that the *upravnik* (local government manager) of Novo-Vasilievka had been drinking excessively and was making threats against the planned conference. This, along with an unusual gathering of five *pristavniki* (police officers) in Melitopol, caused the locals to be fearful of government action. Their fear is understandable, considering that only three weeks previously some of them had attended the Saint Petersburg conference and had been deported. Kargel and Wieler were escorted out of the Russian village that day to a nearby German community (presumably the Molotschna Colony) where they spent the next two days preaching in several villages. Meanwhile, in Novo-Vasilievka, a very large crowd of over 2,500 believers gathered on Sunday 29 April. Molokans, Orthodox, Lutherans, Mennonites, and Baptists were among them. Various preachers took turns speaking. An offering was collected for mission work that amounted to seventy-six rubles.[100]

---

96. J. G. Kargel to "Dear brother in the Lord" [V. A. Pashkov], 3 May 1884, 2/13/040, Pashkov Papers. It can be seen in this letter that there are representatives of each of the categories listed.

97. The following account is based on the letter, "J. G. Kargel to Dear brother in the Lord [V. A. Pashkov], 3 May 1884, 2/13/040, Pashkov Papers," which is also translated and printed in Klippenstein, "Russian Evangelicalism Revisited," 42–48. This letter is twenty pages in length.

98. *Istoriya Evangel'skix Xristian-Baptistov*, 99 states that Kargel came from Bulgaria to attend these meetings. This is incorrect. It is clear from his letters that his family was in Saint Petersburg and from previously discussed material we know that the Kargel family left Bulgaria in the middle of March. Kargel was in Saint Petersburg for Pashkov's April Conference. Koval'kov and Chernopyatov correctly state that Kargel was travelling from Saint Petersburg. See Koval'kov and Chernopyatov, "Ivan Veniaminovich Kargel," 47.

99. Astrakhanka is a Russian village on the southern edge of the Molotschna Settlement.

100. J. G. Kargel to "Dear brother in the Lord" [V. A. Pashkov], 3 May 1884, 2/13/040, Pashkov Papers.

On Monday, despite anxieties, the conference began, with thirty-three delegates in attendance and six guests, three of whom were Molokans with the family name of Sakharov [Sacharoff],[101] from Astrakhanka.[102] The conference members elected Wieler and Kargel as chairman and vice-chairman respectively. The parallels with the Mennonite Brethren meetings of 1882 can easily be seen. The first part of the meetings opened with a report of finances followed by missionary reports. Kargel reported that "the whole area from Kiev on to Rostoff and from there up to the Caspian Sea would be covered."[103] The second half of the meetings was dedicated to an open discussion of the various issues the groups were facing. As was common in both Mennonite and Baptist circles, attention was given to discipline. They discussed the issue of the remarriage of someone deserted by their spouse and decided that abandonment must be accompanied by evidence of the death of the deserter before the abandoned partner could remarry. It was also decided that those who were under discipline could still be married in the church, provided they were not living contrary to the church's teaching.[104]

Other issues related only to the Mennonites present. Some conference members raised the issue of "jumpers" [German: *Fröhliche*, Russian: *Prigunstvo*]. They were an enthusiastic group of believers who exhibited physical signs of joy, such as jumping, laughing, or dancing.[105] The conference decided that the group was a heretical sect.[106] As the Russians listened to Mennonite perspectives, they were indirectly learning some of the Anabaptist/Mennonite distinctives. The Mennonite practices of foot washing and of banning (shunning) were discussed. Kargel noted that the churches in Ukraine and in the

---

101. The Sakharov [Zakharov] family name is associated with the development of the Novo-Molokan (New Molokan) movement which was a mixture of Molokan, Baptist, and Mennonite elements. See Shubin, *A History of Russian Christianity*, vol. III, 138–39.

102. Karev, "Russkoe Evangel'sko-Baptistskoe Dvizhenie," 7.

103. J. G. Kargel to "Dear brother in the Lord" [V. A. Pashkov], 3 May 1884, 2/13/040, Pashkov Papers.

104. Klippenstein, "Russian Evangelicalism Revisited," 45–46.

105. It is difficult to determine if this ecstatic expression was related only to the Mennonites because it also was present among the Molokans. See Bolshakoff, *Russian Nonconformity*, 109–10. For a fuller description of the movement among the Mennonite Brethren see Loewen, "Echoes of Drumbeats," 118–27.

106. Klippenstein, "Russian Evangelicalism Revisited," 45.

Caucasus, which were Baptist in outlook, did not observe foot washing, while those from the Molokan background did. Even though the Ukrainians had been heavily influenced by the Mennonites, they did not adopt this custom. The issue of foot washing was possibly brought up by Johann Wieler but more probably by some of the Molokans who attended the meetings. Some felt that the practice was essential to church life, whereas Kargel seems to have disagreed. He wrote to Pashkov, "The Ukrainians and those from the Caucasus do not observe it [foot washing], while the Molokans do."[107] After discussing the meaning of John 13, the group decided that churches were permitted to practice the washing of feet if they wished.[108] It was decided that foot washing and the use of shunning in church discipline should not be reasons for division and that different perspectives would be tolerated on these issues.[109]

Two other major issues that were discussed were ordination and communion. The influence of the German Baptist ethos was evident in the discussion on the ordination of ministers. Ordination was described simply as "according to the Holy Scriptures."[110] At this stage neither Pashkov nor Kargel would have been enthusiastic about this point. The Brethren position was one of opposition to ordained clergy, but Kargel was not prepared to make this an issue of division. On the question of open or closed communion, as at all the gatherings of Russian evangelicals in this period there were those who held different views. Indeed this was part of a larger debate about baptism—about the mode, whether immersion or pouring, and about the subjects, whether only believing adults could be baptized or whether infants could receive baptism. Kargel was pleased to report to Pashkov that a feeling of openness prevailed. The conference, to Kargel's delight, decided to encourage everyone to have patience with those who held differing views. It is interesting to note how Kargel seemed to have steered the discussion. He focused on the question "Can one partake in the Lord's Supper with those who have a different perspective

---

107. J. G. Kargel to "Dear brother in the Lord" [V. A. Pashkov], 3 May 1884, 2/13/040, Pashkov Papers.

108. Ibid.

109. Toews, "Baptists and Mennonite Brethren in Russia," 88.

110. J. G. Kargel to "Dear brother in the Lord" [V. A. Pashkov], 3 May 1884, 2/13/040, Pashkov Papers.

on baptism?"¹¹¹ Had the question been "Can one admit to the table someone who has not been baptized?" there would have been far more problems to deal with. In encouraging willingness to "exercise patience toward a few brethren who were decidedly of another point of view,"¹¹² Kargel and Wieler managed to steer a path towards greater openness.

After the issues were discussed, the participants explored the authority of the assembly. They asked if decisions made at meetings such as Novo-Vasilievka were to be binding on the congregations represented in the meetings. Wieler and Kargel suggested thinking in terms of three categories of final decisions that might be made. The first category would cover issues connected to mission.¹¹³ It was agreed that decisions made about mission, such as where outreach and church planting would take place, were binding because the conference group was a *Vereinigung* (fellowship) and could come to a common mind on such matters. The second category would cover issues of a dogmatic nature.¹¹⁴ On theological issues, the conference group hoped to find a consensus on some of the issues discussed, but even if that did happen, the statements concerning theological issues were not to be seen as binding. Here a Baptist view was evident: each congregation was seen as free and able to make its own decisions as the members saw fit after having sought God's will. The third category would cover issues of an external nature. Again, decisions were not binding.¹¹⁵ Presumably this category included relationships with the state, matters regarding buildings, and funding. The conference had functioned—and could function in the future—as a forum to exchange information and share wisdom, but its authority was limited.

AN AMBIGUOUS OUTCOME

The outcome of the Novo-Vasilievka conference was ambiguous. Wieler and Kargel achieved some of what they wished to see among Russian evangelicals. They had been able to steer the conference

---

111. Klippenstein, "Russian Evangelicalism Revisited," 45.

112. Ibid.

113. Ibid. 46.

114. J. G. Kargel to "Dear brother in the Lord" [V. A. Pashkov], 3 May 1884, 2/13/040, Pashkov Papers.

115. Klippenstein, "Russian Evangelicalism Revisited," 46.

towards commitment to common action while at the same time there was an acceptance of diversity. Wieler and Kargel wanted to build into this conference an attitude of inclusion. For example, they saw—as did Pashkov—the potential of the New Molokans[116] as a key ingredient in a future Russian Evangelical Alliance. With the growth of the Baptists, the Molokans themselves had been somewhat marginalized among Russian evangelicals. But Kargel and Wieler were keen for the Molokan Sakharov brothers to attend the conference.[117] The Sakharov brothers stayed at the Novo-Vasilievka meetings for the first day and departed on Tuesday "when the main items dealing with mission had been dealt with," but as they left they expressed their view that the Baptists should hold—as the Molokans did—to a "closed" Table. In Kargel's letter there was no hint of disappointment over their unwillingness to consider an open Table. On the contrary, he seemed happy that the "brethren [Sakharov brothers] left us with the impression that they had been richly blessed, and that their hearts were brought together as never before." Indeed, the Molokan brothers requested that Pashkov himself hold a conference among them. Kargel pressed Pashkov to take them up the offer because it would help further the cause of union.[118]

Although Pashkov was not physically present in Novo-Vasilievka and was not able to be present at subsequent meetings, he was nevertheless active from a distance, taking a keen interest in this conference and its outcome. His two close associates, Wieler and Kargel, ran the meeting, and he had given a large sum of money to enable the conference to take place.[119] Kargel was careful to report to Pashkov: "The whole assembly was overjoyed to see the large sum of money available to undertake this work."[120] Kargel saw himself as continuing the dream of Pashkov in trying to create an Evangelical Alliance in Russia. After the meetings, Kargel reported that the work was advancing and that the "believers are united as never before."[121] He assured Pashkov that

116. For a brief explanation of the New Molokan, see page [? – ?].
117. J. G. Kargel to "Dear brother in the Lord" [V. A. Pashkov], 3 May 1884, 2/13/040, Pashkov Papers.
118. Klippenstein, "Russian Evangelicalism Revisited," 46.
119. Ibid., 44.
120. Ibid., 45.
121. J. G. Kargel to "Dear brother in the Lord" [V. A. Pashkov], 3 May 1884, 2/13/040, Pashkov Papers.

a union would be possible in the not-so-distant future. It is not clear whether Kargel was fully convinced about this or whether he was, at least in part, saying what Pashkov wanted to hear.

After the Novo-Vasilievka conference, Kargel stayed with the Molotschna Colony developing relationships for another week. We know that in November 1884, Kargel and Wieler organized a three-day consultation in Galka (Saratov Province) to unite the baptistic mission efforts. Twenty-eight missionaries were assigned to five regions spreading from Saratov to Tsaritsyn[122] and agreed to preach one to two months without pay with the goal to plant new churches.[123] It is not clear if "The Russian Conference of the Union of Believers, Baptized Christians, or as they are called, Baptists, of South Russia and the Caucasus" met again in the following year, but the Baptists were becoming more organized and Kargel, despite the fact that he had been on a journey away from Baptist life, exercised significant leadership among Russian Baptists in the late 1880s. Wieler was unable to take a leadership role due to police action against him. The bond between Kargel and Wieler remained strong. Wieler's daughter states that Johann Kargel invited Wieler to travel with him to Jerusalem in early 1889,[124] but Wieler failed to regain the strength necessary for the trip after his accident. Wieler died in July 1889 in Romania and soon after his family returned to the Molotschna Settlement.[125]

In May 1885 Kargel attended a conference in Astrakhanka, which is very near Novo-Vasilievka. In his report to Pashkov he mentioned the mission situation in various locations as well as the whereabouts of certain individuals. However, the sense of enthusiasm and unity that characterized the 1884 meeting is lacking. He wrote:

> One could feel that the works of the Lord continue to go forth with blessings. However, to me it seems that while it is spreading, there is a lack of depth. I am afraid there are many weeds among the wheat, and there is too quick an acceptance of new members from the Lutheran churches as well as from the others . . . I am not writing to you so that I can criticize, but that you, dear brother in the Lord, can bring this before the Lord;

122. Tsaritsyn is currently known as Volgograd, Russia.

123. J. W. [Johann Wieler] to "Deeply respected and dear brother in Christ" [V. A. Pashkov], 18 October 1884, 2/25/7, Pashkov Papers.

124. Klippenstein, "Salvation on the Steppe," 31.

125. Klippenstein, "Johann Wieler (1839–1889) among Russian Evangelicals," 57.

so that He will get rid of all hindrances among the Russian brothers, to His glory.¹²⁶

At the close of the letter he mentioned that the government had increased its pressure on the Germans, forbidding them to gather in homes, limiting travel and making mission virtually impossible. The cleansing of Russia of all non-Orthodox sects, as directed by Pobedonostsev, had reached into even the smaller villages of Russian Empire. It is quite possible that this was the reason for Wieler's absence from the 1885 Astrakhanka meetings. He should have been there as chair of the conference.

German-Russian tensions, which were not so apparent when Kargel and Wieler were giving leadership to the Russian evangelicals, came to a head among the Russian Baptists in 1885 and 1886. The Russians, without the consent of the German Baptists, elected a Russian, Dei Ivanovich Mazaev, as their president. Mazaev was from a Molokan family and was a successful businessman. He was to remain a dominant Russian Baptist leader for the next thirty years. The German-speakers were unable to accept this move and eventually disengaged from the Russian-speaking churches and established a separate German Baptist Union;¹²⁷ this focused exclusively on the German-speaking population of the Russian Empire.¹²⁸ Kargel, somewhat surprisingly, was not opposed to this division among the Baptists. He knew that the tensions between the Germans and Russians reflected a deeper problem of control and not simply a problem in understanding each other's language. Writing from Warsaw, Poland, in September 1885, to a "dear friend in the Lord" (in Berlin), he spoke of the "constitution of the union" and referred to the position with "the brothers here."¹²⁹ We can infer that he was with several leaders of the German Baptist work who had gathered in Warsaw to

---

126. J. G. Kargel to "Dear brother in Christ" [V. A. Pashkov], 4 June 1885, 2/13/016, Pashkov Papers.

127. Sawatsky, *Soviet Evangelicals*, 97.

128. The German-speaking Baptist Union of Russia remained active until the anti-German sentiment of the mid 1940s forced them to curtail their activities. In the 1950s, what remained of the German-speaking Baptist Union of Russia was gradually absorbed fully into the All-Union Council of Evangelical Christians-Baptists, ending this chapter in Baptist history.

129. J. G. Kargel to "Dear friend in Berlin," 7 September 1885, 2/13/046, Pashkov Papers.

discuss the possible formation of a new German Union in the territory of the Russian Empire.

In his letter of September 1885, Kargel foresaw that there would be "many difficulties with the uniting of the brothers [Russians and Germans] as a whole since we [Germans] are lacking men who have enough energy to embrace the work wholeheartedly."[130] It appears that Kargel was still working for a wider unity, as he normally did. However, he was not optimistic. Although the Russian Baptists were understandably seeking their own organization, there is evidence that part of the problem—perhaps a large part—lay in the unwillingness of the Germans to recognize the aspirations of the Russians. This was a problem across the regions of Europe where German Baptist influence was strong: for example, there was little or no vision for holding worship in the majority languages.[131] Kargel suggested that by the next German Baptist Union conference, to be held in Koeningburg, there might be voices that would be heard on behalf of the Russians and that "there may be some who will regret that the matter was pushed this far." It would make sense, he argued, to have a conference for the Russian Union. He hoped for "a unified work and that they [different parts of the Baptist community] would be bonded together."[132] In this case, Kargel chose the option for peace rather than any use of "political" force to save the control which the strong German Baptist Union had—often in an unacknowledged way—asserted over their Russian members.

Although this letter was sent to Berlin by Kargel and it has been thought that it might have been a letter to Lehmann, later in the letter he wishes the recipient a "blessed trip to England." Baedeker is the most likely recipient. It would appear from this letter that Kargel and Baedeker were in contact with the German Baptist Union and perhaps were making an attempt to unite the Polish Baptists with the Russian Baptists and then to cement wider unity within the German Baptist Union. This would again point to the ideals of the Evangelical Alliance, as absorbed by Kargel, to unite movements and form bonds of unity whenever possible. Despite Kargel's journey away from

130. Ibid.

131. Coleman, *Russian Baptists and Spiritual Revolution*, 93–95.

132. J. G. Kargel to "Dear friend in Berlin," 7 September 1885, 2/13/046, Pashkov Papers.

German Baptist life, he continued working on their behalf to develop unity among the Baptists. Kargel was still speaking in Russian and in German Baptist churches. He included them in his reports to Pashkov and maintained a desire to see them in full fellowship with the other evangelicals in the Russian Empire. In July 1885, Kargel and Baedeker were preaching in the Baptist church in Riga, Latvia, and were involved in a youth conference.[133] J. A. Rumberg in Riga had been a classmate of Kargel's in Hamburg. In August 1886, Kargel reported that the tracts and New Testaments that Pashkov had given to the Baptist church in Kovno, Lithuania, had been distributed, that he (Kargel) had been welcomed in the pulpit and there was much potential for the work of the Lord.[134] In August 1887, as will be seen in more detail in the next chapter, Kargel and Baedeker were preaching for and working with the Baptist congregations in Hapsal, Estonia, with both the Russians and the Estonians welcoming Kargel and Baedeker to participate in their meetings.[135] In the aftermath of the 1884 conference Kargel's vision for unity across boundaries continued to be one that he sought to realize in practice.

COMPLETE HEALING OF SPIRIT, SOUL AND BODY

As far as Baptist spirituality was concerned, however, Kargel found much of it discouraging. All too often, in his letters to Pashkov, he found himself relating stories of splits or potential splits. In May 1884, soon after the Novo-Vasilievka meetings, Kargel learned of a situation in Saratov where a Baptist elder was apparently intent on splitting the congregation and Kargel had been called in to attempt to bring peace and prevent division.[136] He arrived in the Saratov area in June 1884 and was horrified by what he found. He reported to Baedeker that "The Baptists have become unclean and have split from each other so that there are two groups."[137]

133. J. G. Kargel to "Dear brother in Christ" [V. A. Pashkov], 8 July 1885, 2/13/042, Pashkov Papers.

134. J. G. Kargel to "Dear friend and brother in Christ Jesus" [V. A. Pashkov], 26 August 1884, 2/13/028, Pashkov Papers.

135. J. G. Kargel to "Dear brother in Christ Jesus" [V. A. Pashkov], 13 August 1887, 2/13/057, Pashkov Papers.

136. J. G. Kargel to "Dear brother in Christ" [V. A. Pashkov], 26 May 1884, 2/13/025, Pashkov Papers.

137. J. G. Kargel to "Dear brother in the Lord" [Baedeker], 31 June 1884, 2/13/026, Pashkov Papers.

The use of the word "unclean" is consistent with his commitment to Holiness spirituality. He later explained the elements at the root of the problem, as he saw it. Partly, the complications were due to the fact that the spiritual life of the Baptists was "a mixed up one." They had not "stood on the Hamburg Creed," but were made aware of baptism through Mennonite believers—and presumably allowed baptism by pouring. However, this was not the deepest problem. It seems that after the church was formed it took a wrong direction. Kargel wrote, "They then were led astray and eventually members fell into public sin. Though many were sobered after this event, they still portray a sad existence. They do not have organized fellowship. Everyone does what is right in his own eyes, there is hardly a mission mindset, and though they were led in a special way to pray for others, they mostly pray for themselves."[138] Kargel was concerned for unity, holiness, and mission. Each of these seemed to be lacking in at least some of the Baptist congregations with which he was involved.

The spiritual renewal which Kargel had experienced in Bulgaria seemed to drive him on in a search for an even deeper relationship with God. In July 1885, reporting on a trip with Baedeker, he spoke of how he was inspired when he met with those who wanted "the higher life" and "a more intimate relationship with Christ." The vocabulary he used is significant. "Many times we were asked about the higher life and a more intimate relationship with Christ, and my soul rejoices about these first signs of the dawning of a new day. O that all the people of God would find this, the place in which Jesus' blood has placed them, so that they can reflect him to the world again. O how much is lacking, even in the recognition of salvation."[139] In a letter dated August 1885, Kargel told Baedeker that he was convinced that the key to reaching the unconverted was to preach to gatherings of believers concerning "holiness."[140] The evidence suggests that the Holiness message was taking a deeper hold of Kargel personally, and it appears that this perspective on the Christian life was reinforced through his increasingly close relationship with Baedeker in the later 1880s. In contrast to Baedeker's spirituality, which Kargel found so attractive,

138. Ibid.

139. J. G. Kargel to "Dear brother in Christ" [V. A. Pashkov], 8 July 1885, 2/13/042, Pashkov Papers.

140. J. G. Kargel to Dr. Baedeker, 24 August 1885, 2/13/044, Pashkov Papers.

the spirituality that Kargel perceived in many Baptist situations was actually a hindrance to God's work. In Warsaw, in 1885, Kargel complained that the Polish Baptists were difficult to understand: some of them wanted an open Table, others were not willing to make such a change, and still others did not want to discuss it for fear of division.[141] Perhaps Kargel was a little unfair in stating that he could not understand them. In his own life, under the guidance of a powerful Russian aristocrat and his own wife, it took him several years to become receptive to the idea of an open Table. What is clear is that in 1885 he was firmly committed to a broader view of spirituality than that espoused by German and Russian Baptists.

In September 1886, having clearly given further thought to the issue of closed communion as practiced among Baptists, Kargel explained in a letter to Pashkov why, in his opinion, Baptists were so reluctant to open their communion table to Christians who held to different views of baptism. He wrote:

> By the way, I have come to my own conclusion, after two and a half years of personal experience, that what the Baptists need to hear is not so much about the Lord's Supper, but the full commitment and submission of our entire heart to Christ, for the complete healing of spirit, soul and body. If the dear souls would come to this point, their hearts would be opened more, and they would be filled with the Holy Spirit's love. May God be forever thanked for He has healed me from every kind of division, but he did not do it by convincing me through anyone that the Lord's Supper belongs to all the children of God, but through my willing submission to Him; and there was then room for Him to live in me.[142]

In this statement, we find evidence of the change that took place in the philosophy of ministry of Kargel. He moved to a new baptistic perspective.[143] Kargel's view of an open communion Table put him at

---

141. J. G. Kargel to "Dear brother in Christ" [V. A. Pashkov], 7 September 1885, 2/13/045, Pashkov Papers.

142. J. G. Kargel to "Dear brother in Christ Jesus" [V. A. Pashkov], 24 September 1886, 2/13/052, Pashkov Papers.

143. One way of describing this is move would be to say that Kargel moved from a "credal baptistic position" to a "non-credal baptistic position." This transition implies that an evangelical conversion experience, not a mental assent to a statement of faith (such as the Hamburg Statement of Faith) is the critical mark of membership for a baptistic community.

odds with many of his fellow Baptists, but as he saw the issue now, it was not primarily about church order, but about a lack among Baptists of "full commitment and submission of our entire heart to Christ, for the complete healing of spirit, soul and body." In this period, while teaching with Baedeker at their mini-Keswick meetings, Kargel wrote:

> I want to tell you that in the past seventeen years since I have known Jesus as my Lord, I have not experienced his great power as I have in the last four weeks. O, this total dying to sin, the power in and through Him to withstand temptation, and to come out triumphant against the powers of Satan, and to have full joy and full peace in a childlike faith in his personal presence and the total fulfillment of all of his promises—that for me is a reality. "Yes and Amen." This is more than I could have ever imagined. To Him be all praise and glory for eternity, Amen.[144]

This is a powerful statement, full of Keswick ideas. In Keswick teaching sanctification and justification were both centered in the work of Christ, who redeemed humanity from sin through his death. "Man cannot become holy without the cross" and to continue with the Keswick thought, "[i]f the cross is the ground, the Holy Spirit is the Agent of our sanctification."[145] Kargel particularly focused on victory over sin through faith in Christ. This message of holiness was now central to Kargel's thinking.

During this period, in the later 1880s, Kargel gave much more attention than he had done before to the place of spiritual experience in the life of evangelical communities. It is not that he gave up his evangelistic drive. He was active in travelling and preaching across the Russian Empire. From the time of his departure from Bulgaria until Pashkov's death in 1902, Kargel spent approximately 18 percent of his time on itinerant preaching trips.[146] He spent long hours with individuals and families, speaking about the need for conversion, and

---

144. J. G. Kargel to "Dear friend and brother in Christ Jesus" [V. A. Pashkov], 12 May 1886, 2/13/049, Pashkov Papers.

145. Barabas, *So Great Salvation*, 94.

146. Using only his correspondence with Pashkov found in the Pashkov Papers, Kargel spent 138 weeks out of 736 on preaching trips. This figure excludes Kargel's itinerant preaching in Estonia and Finland when he and his family lived in Hapsal and Vyborg. It also excludes ten weeks that he spent receiving medical care (*Kur*) in Bavaria.

was overjoyed when they responded. What was evident, however, was that in his ministry he was drawing on a distinct strand of Holiness spirituality—the spirituality of the sanctified life. Where he had opportunity, he delivered this Holiness message.

While staying in a guest house on a trip to the Volga region in 1884, for example, he wrote: "The brother who was with me sang a beautiful soprano[147] and I sang bass, and so we sang the Gospel out of the Sankey songbooks. Soon the whole room was filled with Germans and Russians, and they all wanted to listen to the singing. After we had sung for a time, I began to speak to them about the joy of belonging to Christ.[148] The Sankey songbooks were used at the meetings led by the American evangelist D. L. Moody and his co-evangelist and singer, Ira Sankey. Moody had undergone a deep spiritual experience, like a "second conversion," in 1871, but he feared division over the issue of holiness.[149] Kargel wrote to Pashkov in 1887 explaining his need of a tract on the life of Moody written by Baedeker entitled *Moody, the Blood and Heaven* as well as Sankey songbooks.[150] Moody, like Baedeker, exemplified for Kargel a life of submission to Christ which led to evangelistic endeavor.

CONCLUSION

Ivan Kargel returned to Saint Petersburg from Bulgaria without a clear idea of what he was to do. In the early years after Pashkov's exile he provided some guidance to the Saint Petersburg Evangelicals—the Pashkovite circle—but gave more energy to wider ministry across the Russian Empire. Against a background of persecution, Kargel's prayer was that "the Lord would open the eyes of the emperor, so that he will see the light of the Gospel for his salvation and for the wellbeing of the land." He hoped that "the Lord will let his salvation flow over the whole country of Russia, so that no power or might will be able to stand against him, and that all will bow at the feet of our wonderful Savior

---

147. It is possible that "sang a beautiful soprano" was intended to mean that the man sang the melody line.

148. J. G. Kargel to "Dear friend and brother in Christ Jesus" [V. A. Pashkov], 29 November 1884, 2/13/032, Pashkov Papers.

149. Findlay, *Dwight L Moody*, 132. For more on Moody's relationship with the Holiness movement see Bebbington, *Evangelicalism in Modern Britain*, 162–64.

150. J. G. Kargel to "Dear brother in Christ Jesus" [V. A. Pashkov], 13 August 1887, 2/13/057, Pashkov Papers.

and Lord."¹⁵¹ Kargel was dependent for his ministry on Pashkov's support. In November 1888 Kargel told Pashkov of his thankfulness "for every opportunity to serve the Lord and all the material needs and the whole wellbeing of my life and my house comes from the Lord's grace through your dear giving hands."¹⁵² Pashkov's desire to bring Christians together in fellowship around the Lord's Table, regardless of denominational differences, became Kargel's dream. In the wake of Pashkov's 1884 attempt to form a wider evangelical alliance in Russia, Kargel assisted in leading the conference, which was seminal in the formation of the Russian Baptist Union. At a time when there were tensions between the Russian and German expressions of the Baptist faith in Russia, Kargel maintained—in a unique way—relationships with both groups. At the same time, he was developing the wider evangelical network in Russia. He was aware of the changes which had taken place in his understanding of spirituality and wrote: "Gone is legalism. The stick of the slave master is broken and in its place reigns the quiet soft murmur of His Holy Spirit."¹⁵³ Kargel became increasingly connected to the Keswick expression of spirituality, especially through spending significant amounts of time in ministry with Baedeker. Kargel was intent on developing cooperation between evangelicals in Russia who could unite around an open Table, who would embrace Holiness spirituality, and who would be effective in mission across the Russian Empire.

---

151. J. G. Kargel to "Dear friend and brother in Christ" [V. A. Pashkov], 29 November 1884, 2/13/032, Pashkov Papers.

152. J. G. Kargel to "Dear and beloved friend and brother in the Lord" [V. A. Pashkov], 15 November 1888, 2/13/062, Pashkov Papers.

153. J. G. Kargel to "Dear brother in Christ" [V. A. Pashkov], 8 July 1885, 2/13/042, Pashkov Papers.

6

Reaching the Russian Empire

(1887–1898)

During this period (1887–98) in Ivan Kargel's life, six years were spent, with the family, based in the Finnish and Estonian areas of the Russian Empire.¹ The Kargel family moved for a time to Hapsal, Estonia² in the summer of 1887 because of struggles with health issues. In 1888, with the pressures on the Saint Petersburg Evangelicals mounting, the Kargels explored the possibility of leaving Russia yet continuing with Ivan's current ministry. The ministry in Saint Petersburg was still fruitful. In 1889 Kargel reported that twelve people had come to know Christ in one week.³ By the close of 1890, however, the persecution of evangelicals by Pobedonostsev had further intensified and it became almost impossible for the Saint Petersburg Evangelicals to meet in any fashion. In the summer of 1891, Kargel reported to Pashkov that the evangelicals were not faring well. He himself was under constant surveillance.⁴ The option the

---

1. The Finnish city of Vyborg was ceded to the Russians in 1721. It became part of the Grand Duchy of Finland, an autonomous region within the Russian Empire. Later, it was a part of Leningrad Province within the Soviet Union. It is currently within Russia. Estonia was ceded to the Russians in 1721 and was part of the Russian Empire. Following the fall of the Russian Empire it gained its independence, which lasted until 1944 when the Soviet Union occupied it. Estonia regained its independence in 1991. The Finnish city of Vyborg and the Estonian city of Hapsal were both cities in which the Kargel family resided.

2. Kargel's letters use "Haus Elbing" as his address. See J. G. Kargel to "Dear brother in the Lord Jesus Christ" [V. A. Pashkov], 13 August 1887, 2/13/057, Pashkov Papers.

3. J. G. Kargel to "Dear brother in the Lord Jesus Christ" [V. A. Pashkov], 23 February 1889, 2/13/065, Pashkov Papers.

4. J. G. Kargel to "Dear brother in the Lord Jesus Christ" [V. A. Pashkov], 24 July 1891, 2/13/095, Pashkov Papers.

Kargels chose was to move to the Finnish city of Vyborg near the end of 1891. He remained free to travel throughout the Russian Empire while based in Vyborg and conducted major preaching trips—in Russia (as far as Siberia, with a return trip through Japan and Egypt), Germany, Poland, Romania, Bulgaria, and Israel. He also spent time in Saint Petersburg. He had an impact, too, on the Russian evangelicals in Finland. By now Kargel was in his forties. Aspects of his ministry in this period included an emigration assistance plan and prison ministry, usually with Friedrich Baedeker, and it was during these years that he started his writing, which I will further explore in chapter 7. The evangelical links Kargel had developed from the later 1870s onwards sustained him in all that he did during this period as he attempted to reach the Russian Empire.

MINISTRY IN ESTONIA

At the end of summer 1887, Ivan Kargel wrote: "This summer I have been held, totally against my will, here in Hapsal [Estonia], however, thank the Lord, not against His will."[5] The first task that he felt called to accomplish, at that point, in Estonia was to bring together four separate groups of evangelical believers,[6] including Baptists and Moravian Brethren, with the possible goal of some sort of alliance. He began his work by starting a mid-week meeting and inviting all the evangelical Christians in Hapsal "so that the gifts that the Lord has given to the believers could be used jointly."[7] This was typical of Kargel's concern for unity and for the movement of the Holy Spirit—as suggested by his reference to the "gifts that the Lord has given to the believers."

Members of each of the four groups attended as a result of Ivan Kargel's encouragement, though many of them found it difficult to say anything in the meetings. Over time, however, they began to speak more openly with each other. Once genuine fellowship was established between the groups, Kargel added a Saturday night prayer time where

---

5. J. G. Kargel to "Dear brother in the Lord Jesus Christ" [V. A. Pashkov], 13 August 1887, 2/13/057, Pashkov Papers.

6. In this letter, he mentions Baptists and Brethren members by name, as well as Estonians, Russians, and Germans.

7. J. G. Kargel to "Dear brother in the Lord Jesus Christ" [V. A. Pashkov], 13 August 1887, 2/13/057, Pashkov Papers. He additionally points to 1 Corinthians 12 and 14, which deal with the gifts of the Holy Spirit.

the participants were to pray for personal requests. Over the summer, Kargel transformed the relationships between the groups. Part of the motivation for fostering this joint activity was the impending arrival of Baedeker in Hapsal. Kargel wrote: "And since we were awaiting the arrival of Dr. Baedeker, we asked that the Lord would prepare the soil so that he could share the Gospel with many here. The Lord answered with much grace. There are many signs that the people here are beginning to open up. I found some who were willing to give their lives totally over to Him and have begun to work for Him already."[8]

The meetings in Hapsal were carried out in Estonian and thus were attractive to Estonian speakers. There was translation from Estonian into Russian. There were also Germans who began to attend, and when Kargel noticed that the Germans were looking bored as they listened to translations, he started to preach in German on Sundays. The group grew from thirty people to over eighty during the course of the summer.[9] Kargel's intent was not to form a new evangelical congregation; he simply wanted to draw people together, regardless of their denominational affiliation.

In addition to the work in Hapsal, Kargel felt that it was God's will for him during the summer of 1887 to travel to the islands in the area. He had plans to travel to the island of Dagö,[10] to work among the Estonians, and to Nukki[11] and Worms,[12] to preach among the Swedes. Kargel was supposed to be spending time with the family, but his preaching work had priority.[13]

When Baedeker arrived in Hapsal, he was able to speak several times to crowds of over 200, composed of Estonians, Russians, and Germans. From Hapsal, Kargel and Baedeker travelled to the island

---

8. J. G. Kargel to "Dear brother in the Lord Jesus Christ" [V. A. Pashkov], 13 August 1887, 2/13/057, Pashkov Papers.

9. Ibid.

10. Dagö Island is both the German and Swedish name for the second largest island in Estonia named Hiiumaa, which saw revivals among Baptists and other Free Churches at the turn of the nineteenth century.

11. Nukki is probably the extension of the peninsula of Nuckö (Swedish) / Noarootsi (Estonian), which is a mainland peninsula extending to an island.

12. Worms Island is Vormsi (Estonian) /Ormsö (Swedish), a small island between Hiimaa and mainland Estonia.

13. It seems that some women did not know that Anna Kargel was Johann's wife and they invited Anna to attend the meetings.

of Dagö, where they preached to factory workers. In a report Kargel mentioned that there was a Baptist congregation on the island but that the factory workers were hesitant to attend the Baptist church.[14] In describing the meetings, Kargel stated: "The Lord gave the grace to speak of God's love to them, which seeks the lost and brings holiness. There was a great movement among the group, and there were not a few tears, and as we bowed again there was much sobbing to be heard during the quiet time before the Lord."[15] The crowds swelled in the three days of preaching to over 500 and attracted the attention of the factory owner, Baron Sternberg, who summoned Kargel to his office. The Baron was familiar with religious developments in Russia and asked Kargel about the circumstances of an event involving Baedeker and the police. Baron Sternberg showed his intimate awareness of the political and religious situation when he asked if Pashkov was planning to remain in Russia.[16] The Baron knew that Colonel Pashkov was in Russia at that very moment, with the permission of Alexander III, the Russian Emperor, but without the permission of Pobedonostsev.[17] Kargel had little interest in Sternberg's political intrigue and in his report to Pashkov Kargel stressed, "I was able to be genuinely happy about the warm interest that this man had for the kingdom for God and wanted to bless him."[18] Pashkov remained in Russia for three months before Pobedonostsev convinced Alexander III that he should remove him. He did this, insisting that Pashkov was "never to set foot upon Russian soil again."[19]

The Holiness spirit is clearly portrayed in Kargel's description of the meetings with the factory workers in Dagö. He seems to have been pleased to hear "the quiet sound of tears" and to know that he and Baedeker had taught the people that the Lord not only seeks the lost, to bring salvation, but also brings holiness. Additionally, in this letter the influence of the Bible in Estonia was mentioned. Kargel and Baedeker had arranged for 400 Estonian New Testaments to be

14. J. G. Kargel to "Dear brother in the Lord Jesus Christ" [V. A. Pashkov], 13 August 1887, 2/13/057, Pashkov Papers. This is a twelve-page letter.
15. Ibid.
16. Ibid.
17. Heier, *Religious Schism*, 141.
18. J. G. Kargel to "Dear brother in the Lord Jesus Christ" [V. A. Pashkov], 13 August 1887, 2/13/057, Pashkov Papers.
19. Latimer, *Dr. Baedeker*, 36.

shipped into Estonia for distribution among the crowds. The New Testaments were also to be used at the new Sunday school that had been started in Hapsal during the summer. About eighty children were coming to hear Bible stories and were delighted to hear that they would be receiving the New Testaments in their own language.[20]

Over the course of this summer, Kargel exhibited several traits that would characterize his ministry during this period that identified him as part of the wider Holiness movement within evangelicalism. He sought to unite the various groups of Christians into a cohesive spiritual group. He preached a message that emphasized the process of sanctification and the demands of holiness. Finally, he showed his commitment to the proclamation of the gospel as he travelled to outlying islands.

THE MOVE TO THE GRAND DUCHY OF FINLAND

Portions of the area known today as Finland were controlled by the Swedes until the Russian Empire expanded its influence northwards. In 1809, Finland became the Grand Duchy of Finland and was considered to be an autonomous nation under the Tsar's rule. The Lutheran Church in Finland claimed the overwhelming majority of the population. The Pietist stream within Lutheranism also found strong expression there. During the "Finnish Early Awakening" of the 1830s to the 1850s, various Finnish Lutheran congregations began to hold pietistic meetings that encouraged personal Bible study. Most of these small groups stayed within the Finnish Lutheran Church. An exception was Dean Abraham Achrenius, who, in 1840, left the Lutheran Church to found the first Free Church in Finland. Eventually, however, he returned to the Lutheran Church. The Finnish Early Awakening, Aaltio notes, exhibited classic marks of the Pietist movement, with an emphasis on small-group Bible study, prayer, an earnest Christian life, and lay preaching. The movement also diminished social class distinctions.[21]

In spite of this revival movement, the people of Finland were resistant to any non-Lutheran expressions of Christianity, including Baptist. The Baptist expression of Free Church life first came to

---

20. J. G. Kargel to "Dear brother in the Lord Jesus Christ" [V. A. Pashkov], 13 August 1887, 2/13/057, Pashkov Papers.
21. Aaltio, "A History of the National Baptists in Finland," 4.

Finland through the work of Swedish missionaries on the archipelago of Åland, where in 1856 the first Baptist church was founded within the Grand Duchy of Finland. Karl Möllersvärd, from Sweden, had preached on the Åland Islands in 1854. As a result of his preaching, a revival began. After five weeks, however, the opposition became too strong and the mission came to an end. Groups affected by this revival continued to meet and in 1855 one individual visited Stockholm and returned with booklets written by a powerful Swedish Baptist leader, Anders Wiberg, on believer's baptism and church membership. Fourteen years later, the Swedes formed a Baptist church on the mainland in Jakobstad (Pietarsaari). In July 1869, *Quarterly Reporter of the German Baptist Mission* reported the baptism of a Mr. Heikel as the first Baptist in Finland.[22] The Baptists appeared in Finland during a politically difficult time. The issues of independence, as Swedish rule was replaced by Russian rule, compounded by the Russian and English conflict during the Crimean War, created an unpromising climate for foreign missionaries.

Erik Jansson also played a significant part in the Baptist story in Finland. He was a Finnish sailor, born in Pohjanmaa in 1848, who moved to the USA and settled in the Chicago area in 1871. He came to an evangelical experience under the preaching of D. L. Moody.[23] After six years in the USA, he returned home to Finland, intent on preaching the gospel in his homeland. Although his conversion under Moody and his attendance at Moody's interdenominational meetings in America might have been likely to lead him towards Finnish Free Church life and away from the more formal Lutheran approach, Jansson attended the Lutheran Church after returning to his homeland. His revivalist bent, however, eventually isolated him. Also, he became convinced that he needed to be baptized as a believer, and he travelled to Sweden to receive baptism. His travels took him on to Saint Petersburg, to Adam Schiewe and the German Baptist congregation that Johann Kargel had helped to establish. In 1889, Jansson reported on the support he had received from Schiewe and on baptisms taking place.[24] He returned to the United States to raise money

---

22. "Sweden. The First Baptist in Finland," 374.

23. Aaltio, "A History of the National Baptists in Finland," 16. Aaltio is quoting from letters written by Jansson.

24. Jannson, "Finland," 348.

for mission in Finland and in 1889 he was officially sponsored by the American Baptist Missionary Union.[25] It was in 1889 that it became possible to register officially a non-Lutheran congregation in Finland. The leaders of the new communities were required to be Finnish and approved by the district governor; members of the congregations were still expected to pay tithes to the Lutheran Church.[26]

In late 1891 the Kargel family moved to Vyborg,[27] a Finnish city on the Karelian Isthmus near the head of the Bay of Vyborg, which is currently within Russia. In the late nineteenth century, Vyborg was the center for trade and administration for the areas of current-day eastern Finland and had a sizable population of minority groups—Swedes, Russians, and Germans. Vyborg was to be one of the centers of early Pentecostalism in Finland. Frank Bartleman, an evangelist and writer from America, reported how Vyborg had received a "baptism of the Holy Spirit" before he visited it in 1913, and he noted the importance of Finnish cooperation with the evangelicals of Saint Petersburg.[28]

The Kargel family lived in Vyborg at least until October 1895 and probably until they returned to Saint Petersburg in 1898. During this time, Ivan Kargel continued his ministry as an itinerant teacher and preacher, travelling enormous distances within and beyond the borders of the Russian Empire. As the Kargel family settled into Vyborg in 1892, Ivan began to assess the local evangelical climate. He reported that he found many of "God's children" there, but that he was saddened by the linguistic and other divisions between the Swedes and the Finns. He also noted, more specifically, that there were evening fellowship circles throughout the city, as well as German-language services on Sunday, which were translated into Swedish and Finnish.[29]

Ivan Kargel is credited with the formation of the "Russian Fellowship of Evangelical Christians in Finland," which was officially

25. Aaltio, "A History of the National Baptists in Finland," 20.

26. November 1889 saw the issue of a law that gave religious communities the right to exist outside the Lutheran Church. The Baptists and the Methodists took advantage of this new law. Jansson's church was registered in October 1891 in Amossa.

27. The family first resided at Papula Haus Wolff and in 1894 they moved to Papula Haus Tulander.

28. Wardin, "Pentecostal Beginnings among the Russians in Finland and Northern Russia," 54–55.

29. J. G. Kargel to "Dear brother in the Lord Jesus Christ" [V. A. Pashkov], 22 June, 1892, 2/13/099, Pashkov Papers.

founded in 1907. But, by that year, he had already left Vyborg and returned to Saint Petersburg. His time in Vyborg, however, had given him an awareness of and connections with the various groups of evangelicals in the Finnish lands. When Maria Maksimovna Smirnova, a Finnish evangelical leader, made an appeal to the Saint Petersburg Evangelicals for assistance in starting a new church, they sent Ivan Kargel in 1907.[30] Kargel arrived and preached to the group in Helsingfors (Helsinki).

It seems that as a result of this ministry, some new converts to the evangelical faith were formed into a church. They seem to have been drawn from the Andreevska Church which met at 22 Vysokogorn Street in Helsinki.[31] This "Russian Fellowship of Evangelical Christians in Finland," as the new church was called, held their services from 1907 in the Finnish Methodist Church in Krasnogorskaya Street. During the unrest prior to the Communist Revolution, the congregation met in secret in various homes.[32] Following the 1917 Revolution, they met in a public school located at 8 Aninskaya Street. Many of the members left the Finnish region and returned to Russia during the civil unrest in 1918, when Finland attempted to remove itself from Russian influence.[33] The members who remained continued to serve among the Russians in Finnish region. The movement was officially registered in 1921 as the "Russian Evangelical Church in Finland."[34]

30. "Clenskij Kalendar' Russkoj Evangel'skoj Svobodnoj Cerkvi v Finlandii," 9. This is a typed manuscript given to the International Baptist Theological Seminary Library by Toivo Pilli who received it from Vaino Hyvonen. It is a Russian language handout from a program celebrating sixty years of the Russian Evangelical Free Church in Finland; 1907–67.

31. Ibid. It is unclear whether the conversions led to the formation of the congregation or happened within an already formed congregation. Literally, the report states that Kargel's visit "led to the conversion of the first members in the Andreevska Church." Most likely, the Andreevska Church (Church of Saint Andrew) was an existing church and Kargel preached to some of its congregation (Russians), which resulted in the formation of a new Evangelical Christian congregation.

32. Ibid.

33. Ibid., 10.

34. The document lists some leaders: Fedor Berg, K. L. Koh, Zahar Ivanovich Ivanov, Bogdanov, and sister Smirnova. On 24 June 1921 Alexander Vladimirovich Dobrynin, a missionary sent from an American mission, was chosen to be a presbyter of the church. Also in the same year, under the instigation of Koh, the community formed an unregistered circle called the "Russian Christian Circle" [Fellowship] which met on Vysokogornaya Street where Kargel first began the movement. See "Clenskij Kalendar' Russkoj Evangel'skoj Svobodnoj Cerkvi v Finlandii," 10.

This group celebrated sixty years of history in 1967 and credited Ivan Kargel with their early formation. Kargel's influence in Finland among some parts of the country's evangelical life is undeniable. Vyborg and Helsinki, cities where Kargel taught, produced some of the early leaders of Pentecostalism who came from Evangelical Christian congregations.[35] His book *Light from the Shadows of Future Blessing* is still in print in Finnish under the title *Esikuvat Puhuvat (eli Messias Vanhassa Testamentissa)*. The publishers claim that Kargel's name is well known in Finland as one who explained the scriptures and shared the Word of Life. They further state that he was respected in all the evangelical circles in Finland.[36]

THE EVANGELICAL CHRISTIANS

Despite their move to the Finnish city of Vyborg, the Kargels maintained contact with the Saint Petersburg Evangelicals, who, along with other evangelicals in Russia, were experiencing severe persecution.[37] This pressure was now being extended to all those on Russian soil, including Germans. Just before the Kargels moved to Vyborg, Ivan stated in a letter to Pashkov that three Germans[38] had been removed from Russia.[39] The Saint Petersburg Evangelicals were meeting in secret gatherings in the forests of Kolpino.[40] For Kargel, the main advantage of moving to the Finnish region was that he was not under such close scrutiny. This enabled him to travel to various regions of the Russian Empire and the bordering countries. Most of these trips were funded by Pashkov and undertaken for the purpose of teaching those who were already evangelical believers about "the deeper truths of the Christian life," of preaching the gospel to those outside evangelical churches, and of gathering information. As he travelled, Kargel

---

35. Wardin, "Pentecostal Beginnings among the Russians in Finland," 54–55.

36. "Ivan Benjaminovitsh Kargell," para. 1–4.

37. The Minister of the Interior issued a circular letter in September of 1894 calling the Stundists the "most dangerous sect." Due to this circular, all non-Orthodox groups were brought under intense scrutiny.

38. Munster, Liebig, and Peter Freissen were all sent back to Germany because of their close association with the Russian evangelicals.

39. J. G. Kargel to "Dear brother in the Lord Jesus Christ" [V. A. Pashkov], 3 December 1890, 2/13/090, Pashkov Papers.

40. J. G. Kargel to "Dear brother in the Lord Jesus Christ" [V. A. Pashkov], 24 July 1891, 2/13/095, Pashkov Papers.

reported his findings back to Pashkov. There seems to have been no over-arching systematic plan in the arrangement of these trips. However, it was clear that Pashkov was keen to keep in touch with people that he knew. Kargel kept Pashkov apprised of the situation of various leaders of the evangelical movement such as Ivan Riaboshapka, Martin Kalweit, and the family members of Dei Mazaev.[41]

As an example of his evangelistic concern, in 1889 Kargel reported to Pashkov that twenty people had been converted in Kovno, Lithuania, and he also reported on meetings that he had recently held in Moscow.[42] Reports spoke about the effectiveness of certain tracts and why they seemed to work among the Russians.[43] Kargel often travelled along the Volga River, evangelizing in the various cities along the way, most notably those that contained German populations, such as Saratov, Galka, and Kamyshin. In 1892, he made a three-month trip through the Volga region and on into Orenburg Province.[44] In a letter to Pashkov, Kargel noted that he had managed to visit thirty or forty homes a day. Perhaps because he had often travelled in the area, the police repeatedly warned him during this trip not to preach the gospel in any public place. The religious leaders of the areas he had visited also warned the populace that they were not to associate with Kargel. Nevertheless, he held meetings, visited homes, and wrote that he had been strengthened and blessed as he "wiped the tears of some who were suffering".[45] He seemed to enjoy the opportunity to display Christ's love to those who did not or could not attend public worship. Kargel did not try to suggest that all his attempts met with success and where there was resistance or no obvious result, he recorded it in his notes.[46] In 1895, Kargel informed Pashkov that the Bible Depot in

41. J. G. Kargel to "Dear brother in the Lord Jesus Christ" [V. A. Pashkov], 7 May, 1891, 2/13/094, Pashkov Papers.

42. J. G. Kargel to "Dear brother in the Lord Jesus Christ" [V. A. Pashkov], 23 February 1889, 2/13/065, Pashkov Papers.

43. J. G. Kargel to "Dear brother in the Lord Jesus Christ" [V. A. Pashkov], 14 January 1891, 2/13/091, Pashkov Papers.

44. The handwriting is not clear but this trip may have extended as far as Ispravnik in Tobolsk Province.

45. J. G. Kargel to "Dear brother in the Lord Jesus Christ" [V. A. Pashkov], 22 June 1892, 2/13/099, Pashkov Papers.

46. Ibid. In this letter, Kargel mentioned to Pashkov that since the beginning of 1892, he was brought into the work of Countess Shuvalova which may explain way he was repeatedly warned and not arrested.

Kiev had been closed and that the government was closing in on the colporteurs and their warehouse.[47]

Visiting individual believers and evangelical groups that he and Pashkov knew was an important part of Kargel's ministry in this period. Kargel repeatedly travelled to the Molotschna Colony and regularly reported to Pashkov about the situation in the small villages of Novo-Vasilievka and Astrakhanka,[48] villages that Pashkov knew and where the seminal conferences of the mid-1880s had been held.[49] Astrakhanka was home to a number of Molokan families and part of the interest that Kargel had in this community was due to Pashkov's desire to include the Molokans in the evangelical orbit. In May 1891, Kargel specifically mentioned Ivanovka as a Molokan village that he had visited in the Caucasus region.[50] On a trip to the Caucasus in 1894, Kargel located a well-known former fellow-member from Tiflis Baptist Church, Mrs. Kalweit, now in Gerusi (Goris, Armenia), who told him that her husband Martin had been exiled to Erivan (Yerevan), Armenia.[51] While among evangelicals in Taurida Province in the same year, Kargel spoke of one leader, known by Pashkov, who was under constant surveillance.[52] Persecution was causing problems for all evangelicals everywhere in the Russian Empire. Five families in the Kharkov area had been tried in court and several had been sentenced.[53] The conditions in the Caucasus had become so difficult that it was being recommended among the evangelicals that they should request to be sent to Siberia rather than the Caucasus.[54]

---

47. J. G. Kargel to Vasily Alexandrovich [Pashkov], 1895, 2/2/1191, Pashkov Papers.

48. J. G. Kargel to "Dear friend and brother in Christ Jesus" [V. A. Pashkov], 14 March 1888, 2/13/058, Pashkov Papers.

49. These have been referred to in greater detail in chapter 5.

50. J. G. Kargel to "Dear brother in the Lord Jesus Christ" [V. A. Pashkov], 7 May 1891, 2/13/094, Pashkov Papers.

51. J. G. Kargel to Vasily Alexandrovich [Pashkov], 3 November 1894, 2/2/1189, Pashkov Papers.

52. J. G. Kargel to Vasily Alexandrovich [Pashkov], 29 July 1895, 2/2/1200, Pashkov Papers.

53. J. G. Kargel to "Dear brother in the Lord Jesus Christ" [V. A. Pashkov], 11 September 1889, 2/13/080, Pashkov Papers.

54. J. G. Kargel to Vasily Alexandrovich [Pashkov], 9 February 1894, 2/13/101, Pashkov Papers.

In addition to evangelism, teaching, visiting, and gathering information, Kargel was involved in attempts at reconciliation between various evangelical groups and also in delivering money for the needy.[55] In March 1889 he spent several hours with the evangelical believers in Odessa working through a conflict that involved a local count, but in the end there were no positive results. Kargel was not surprised by this because, as he put it, "the brothers were not looking for peace from the beginning. On the contrary most of them spoke with bitterness."[56] Kargel believed that in any reconciliation process, the believers must be guided by a mutual recognition of sin and desire for repentance. Above all, he was convinced, there needed to be a movement that emphasized the Spirit-filled life. In 1894, while visiting a Molokan village in Taurida Province, Kargel attempted to mediate in a situation involving a land dispute between the Molokan families of Astrakhanka and local Orthodox families.[57] Often it was difficult for an outsider to be the mediator, since local tensions were complex, but Kargel had a measure of success—as well as a number of failures.

There were also problems with the distribution of aid. The general pattern adopted by Pashkov and Kargel involved finding a local contact who would hold the money that was given and pass it on to others according to instructions received. This procedure was not always straightforward. In Elizabethpol, in the Caucasus Region, it was discovered that after a trip in 1895 the local contact had been drawn away from the evangelical community by the influence of the teachings of Leo Tolstoy, and it had been necessary to replace him.[58] Although Kargel advocated a broadly-based Christian community, evangelical beliefs had to be central and the teachings of Tolstoy were considered to be outside those beliefs.

It is notable that there is relatively little in Kargel's letters to Pashkov during this period about the Saint Petersburg Evangelicals. In 1889 he noted that there was "a great searching" in the city, with twelve souls having come to Christ. He also noted that many wanted to

---

55. Ibid.

56. J. G. Kargel to "Dear brother in the Lord Jesus Christ" [V. A. Pashkov], 31 March 1889, 2/13/066, Pashkov Papers.

57. J. G. Kargel to Vasily Alexandrovich [Pashkov], 9 February 1894, 2/13/101, Pashkov Papers.

58. J. G. Kargel to "Dear and loved brother in the Lord" [V. A. Pashkov], 18 October 1895, 2/2/1203, Pashkov Papers.

know how they could become holy.⁵⁹ In a letter written from Vyborg, after Kargel had arrived home after teaching twenty missionaries in the Mennonite Brethren training program in Andreasfeld, Kargel told Pashkov that he was hoping soon to see "the dear ones in Saint Petersburg," referring to the Christian community.⁶⁰ Part of the reason for Kargel's reticence may have been the complex situation among the Saint Petersburg Evangelicals. Increasingly two distinct groups could be identified—those influenced by the Baptists and those who had been influenced by Pashkov. Dei Mazaev, the leader of the Russian Baptists, was seen by some to be in favor of a church hierarchy. P. S. Bezzubov, a member of the Saint Petersburg Evangelicals, wrote at the end of 1890 that he was opposed to Mazaev's approach and stated that "we have had a division within the Saint Petersburg church." He wrote of Kargel supporting the "Mazaev Reform," which called for the election of presbyters "by all those rules that Mazaev has." Bezzubov saw the majority of the Saint Petersburg Evangelicals as now being in favor of the election of presbyters, and alleged that Kargel had encouraged this and had "dismissed Christ, the chief pastor."⁶¹ It seems unlikely that Kargel would have turned his back on the position he held five years previously, when he was against electing leaders, yet some clearly placed him on the side of the Mazaev Reform. Perhaps Kargel's perspective was misunderstood in the political rhetoric, or perhaps Bezzubov misunderstood Mazaev's views.

There was also a new force in Saint Petersburg, Ivan Prokhanov, a Molokan who had been converted to the evangelical faith in the Caucasus in 1886. That same year he came to Saint Petersburg to study at the Technological Institute. Prokhanov soon started preaching among the Saint Petersburg Evangelicals.⁶² He was an outstanding teacher, and became increasingly known as a powerful evangelical leader. In 1889 Prokhanov started *Beseda*, a Christian journal designed to maintain "correspondence with Christian believers scattered

---

59. J. G. Kargel to "Dear brother in the Lord Jesus Christ" [V. A. Pashkov], 23 February 1889, 2/13/065, Pashkov Papers.

60. J. G. Kargel to Vasily Alexandrovich [Pashkov], 9 February 1894, 2/13/101, Pashkov Papers.

61. Val'kevich, *Zapiska o Propagande Protestantskix' Sekt' v' Rossii*, appendix #5, 38. Also see Steeves, "The Russian Baptist Union," 45.

62. Prokhanoff, *In the Cauldron of Russia*, 63.

in places of exile and throughout the whole country."⁶³ Prokhanov endeavored to connect believers during times of persecution. The articles and letters printed in his journal gave a sense of identity to the Saint Petersburg Evangelicals scattered throughout the Russian Empire. A common identity for these scattered evangelicals was particularly necessary at a time when the government was intent on breaking them apart. Prokhanov developed and participated in the life of *Vertograd* [The Vineyard], a Christian agricultural community in Crimea near Simferopol. *Vertograd* was created as a "special settlement [based] on Gospel principles."⁶⁴ He also sought to bond the Russian-speaking evangelicals by introducing Russian melodies that were "capable of expressing the highest joy" into their developing hymnody.⁶⁵ Pressure from Pobedonostsev eventually disrupted these efforts by Prokhanov to develop an evangelical identity forcing Prokhanov to leave Russia in January 1895.⁶⁶ Following Prokhanov's departure *Vertograd* was dissolved, the property sold, and the inhabitants emigrated or returned to their homes elsewhere in Russia.⁶⁷ Prokhanov relocated *Beseda* to Sweden. It appears that this period of persecution was not widespread. Six months after Prokhanov's departure from Russia, Kargel reported to Pashkov that there were fewer restrictions in Saint Petersburg in July [1895] than in the previous nine to twelve months. Joyously he announces that "the Lord has blessed His word and in the past winter more souls have believed on Him."⁶⁸

Kargel's main focus during these years was on work within the Russian Empire and he felt a great concern for those in this vast realm who did not have a vibrant relationship with Jesus Christ.⁶⁹ Yet he was also interested in other parts of the world, particularly through the influence of Baedeker and his increasing awareness of the wider work of the Evangelical Alliance. In February 1889 Kargel asked Pashkov for

63. Ibid., 67. Prokhanov used the spelling "Besseda" which incorrectly transliterates the Russian word *beseda* [conversation].

64. Ibid., 87.

65. Ibid., 145.

66. Ibid., 93.

67. Ibid., 90–91.

68. J. G. Kargel to Vasily Alexandrovich [Pashkov], 29 July 1895, 2/2/1200, Pashkov Papers.

69. J. G. Kargel to "Dear brother in the Lord Jesus Christ" [V. A. Pashkov], 13 September 1891, 2/13/098, Pashkov Papers.

prayer because he was to travel to Siberia with Baedeker that April.[70] The joint trip did not, however, take place. It seems that Baedeker was not able to fit this into his other plans. Kargel then asked Wieler to travel with him to Israel on a trip to evangelize the Russians who were to visit Jerusalem during the Easter pilgrimage, but because of Wieler's injury, and after checking with doctors, it was decided that he was not healthy enough to make the trip.[71] In the end, Kargel travelled alone to Israel to preach and to pass out literature during the Easter season. Speaking of the support he received, he wrote to Pashkov that the "dear sisters in Petersburg collected 107 rubles for Mr Schriften." Kargel also mentioned that he had 357 rubles worth of New Testaments. In total, he carried with him 2,386 pieces of Russian literature: 1,500 New Testaments, 501 Gospels, and 385 tracts.[72] Kargel's printed material was delayed in customs for four days. After dealing with "deception on all levels" and paying a large amount of money, it was finally delivered to him in Jerusalem on camels.[73] During his two weeks in Israel, Kargel passed out 1,020 pieces of literature.[74]

Kargel arrived in Israel later than he had hoped, due to poor connections from Odessa, but managed to be in Jaffa when an estimated 1,400 pilgrims were in the area. While on the ship from Odessa to Constantinople, before arriving in Jaffa, he spoke about the Christian faith to some of the Jewish pilgrims who travelled with him. Relating his experience on the ship, he wrote that his "heart was touched to see such a ripe large field for godly sowing."[75] Kargel also distributed this literature not only to Orthodox pilgrims who were travelling to Israel for the Easter season but also to Jewish pilgrims—presumably Russians—going for Passover. During his time in Israel, Kargel specifically sought to give Jewish people literature and communicate the story of Jesus to them. In one incident, in which an elderly Jewish man

---

70. J. G. Kargel to "Dear brother in the Lord Jesus Christ" [V. A. Pashkov], 23 February 1889, 2/13/065, Pashkov Papers.

71. Klippenstein, "Salvation on the Steppe," 31.

72. J. G. Kargel to "Dear brother in the Lord Jesus Christ" [V. A. Pashkov], 31 March 1889, 2/13/066, Pashkov Papers.

73. J. G. Kargel to "My Dear brother in the Lord" [V. A. Pashkov], 12 April 1889, 2/13/067, Pashkov Papers.

74. J. G. Kargel to "My Dear brother in the Lord" [V. A. Pashkov], 21 April 1889, 2/13/072, Pashkov Papers.

75. Ibid.

was apparently being harassed by Arab teenagers, Kargel came to the assistance of the Jewish man and as a result was invited into his place of business. It was a bookstore and Kargel reported later how he was invited to "read from the word of God and explain the Messiah."[76]

The reaction from the Russian Orthodox pilgrims to Kargel's work was mixed. Many accepted the New Testaments and asked for two. Others accused him of subversion because the Bibles were not the approved Orthodox translation with the correct stamps. This would imply that some of the pilgrims he reached out to were Orthodox Russians. Interestingly, Kargel states that "they hardly doubted that I was Russian and that helped to earn their trust."[77] The reaction of local people, including Christians, was also mixed. He was rebuked by local nuns and priests for giving out New Testaments. Some of those he met argued with him and spat on him while others ripped up his literature. Yet, others sought him, as did a Greek Orthodox priest who asked for a Greek New Testament.[78] He toured the city and gave Pashkov a description of the sites, including his surprise at finding a Christian family running a house in an Arab orphanage.[79] During his time in Israel, Kargel mentioned ministry among the Jews, the Christians, and the Arabs. Speaking about the Jewish people, he stated that he believed they were a unique part of God's plan. He wrote, "O how I am convinced that out of this people group (Jewish nation) we will see many in the Kingdom of God one day."[80] The unused literature was left in the depot of the British and Foreign Bible Society in Jerusalem. Kargel asked: "Please pray for the seeds sown."[81]

---

76. J. G. Kargel to "My Dear brother in the Lord" [V. A. Pashkov], 21 April 1889, 2/13/072, Pashkov Papers.

77. J. G. Kargel to "My Dear brother in the Lord" [V. A. Pashkov], 13 April 1889, 2/13/070, Pashkov Papers.

78. J. G. Kargel to "Dear and beloved brother in the Lord Jesus Christ" [V. A. Pashkov], 17 April 1889, 2/13/071, Pashkov Papers.

79. J. G. Kargel to "My Dear brother in the Lord" [V. A. Pashkov], 22 April 1889, 2/13/073, Pashkov Papers.

80. J. G. Kargel to "Dear brother in the Lord Jesus Christ" [V. A. Pashkov], 31 March 1889, 2/13/066, Pashkov Papers.

81. J. G. Kargel to "My Dear brother in the Lord" [V. A. Pashkov], 13 April 1889, 2/13/070, Pashkov Papers.

MINISTRY TO THE MENNONITE BRETHREN

Ivan Kargel remained in contact with, and active among, the Mennonite Brethren throughout the time he lived in Vyborg. A particular focus was on the training of leaders. The Mennonite Brethren began to train their workers through seminars utilizing itinerant teachers. By the 1890s, these seminars had developed into mission schools or Bible courses.[82] Beginning in 1888, Kargel travelled annually, in January, to Taurida Province to preach and to hold month-long training and teaching seminars within the training system developed by the Mennonite Brethren. His trips to the area are documented for 1888,[83] 1889,[84] 1890,[85] 1894,[86] and 1895.[87] In May 1893, Ivan Kargel and Samuel Lehman participated in one of the earliest Mennonite *Sängerfest* [song festival] in Russia. It was held in the village of Rückenau in the Molotschna Settlement at the Mennonite Brethren church. This event began on the Sunday morning and continued into the afternoon, with seven visiting choirs. Kargel and Lehman lead the *Gebetsstunde* [prayer meeting] in the morning, which included twenty-two choral selections and considerable congregational singing.[88] Kargel was clearly welcomed in the Mennonite Brethren circles of this area in the 1880s as a respected leader and teacher.

It was at the close of 1887 that Kargel travelled to the Molotschna Colony to answer a plea by the Mennonite Brethren for training. In his report, Kargel stated that he was invited by the local congregation to start what he called a *Missionsschule* [mission school].[89] His view of the situation was that the developing leaders among the Mennonite

---

82. For a description of the programme see Toews, "The Mennonite Brethren in Russia during the 1890s," 144.

83. J. G. Kargel to "Dear friend and brother in Christ Jesus" [V. A. Pashkov], 14 March 1888, 2/13/058, Pashkov Papers.

84. J. G. Kargel to "Dear brother in the Lord Jesus Christ" [V. A. Pashkov], 22 February 1889, 2/13/064, Pashkov Papers.

85. Toews, "The Mennonite Brethren in Russia during the 1890s," 144.

86. J. G. Kargel to Vasily Alexandrovich [Pashkov], 9 February 1894, 2/13/101, Pashkov Papers; Toews, "The Mennonite Brethren in Russia during the 1890s," 144.

87. J. G. Kargel to Vasily Alexandrovich [Pashkov], 29 July 1895, 2/2/1200, Pashkov Papers.

88. Letkemann, "The First Mennonite Sängerfest in Russia," 4.

89. J. G. Kargel to "Dear friend and brother in Christ Jesus" [V. A. Pashkov], 14 March 1888, 2/13/058, Pashkov Papers. (this is an eleven-page letter).

Brethren had a limited knowledge of what spiritual resources God had given them. He saw this lack of understanding as the reason that so many pastors and missionaries were discouraged in their work.[90] His teaching at the MB Training Seminar[91] included several Keswick themes. The topics he covered were the depravity of humankind; justification through Christ; total submission to God; holiness; the relationship of the believer to the law, sin, and the world; baptism; the condition of a mature child of God; spiritual life as written in Romans 7; and the return of the Lord.[92] The seminar was to prepare MB missionaries for ministry and much of what Kargel covered dealt with the deeper spiritual life. The reaction by some of the seventeen leaders who attended was confirmation to Kargel that he was speaking to a real need. He reported:

> With visible joy, often with tears in their eyes, the brothers opened the texts and read aloud. One dear brother who had been converted by Dr. Baedeker, who had worked for several years, read aloud one of the wonderful truths and then said, "Dr. Kargel, is it really in the Bible, it is all too wonderful. Of course it is in the Bible, I just read it aloud." Another said, "Our whole system up to this point has been overturned." Another brother from the Ekaterinoslav area said, "I was until now an adversary of these truths, but today I am convinced otherwise."[93]

This was exactly what Kargel wanted to hear. He had originally described the group as "limited in their knowledge of what [Christ] has given us" but ended with joy at their understanding of holiness and sanctification. His seminars caused quite a stir and finished with "huge crowds" who "consumed the words."[94] Not only was Kargel

---

90. Ibid.

91. I will use "MB Training Seminar" to designate the training program used by the Mennonite Brethren during this period. They were four- to eight-week classes taught in various locations by itinerant teachers who instructed Mennonite Brethren pastors and leaders on various topics. Kargel and others have called them a "Mission School" using the same name as the Hamburg school, while others have called them "Bible Courses."

92. J. G. Kargel to "Dear friend and brother in Christ Jesus" [V. A. Pashkov], 14 March 1888, 2/13/058, Pashkov Papers. (this is an eleven-page letter).

93. Ibid.

94. Ibid.

captured by the Holiness message, he was able to instill this into a future generation of leaders within the Mennonite Brethren.

At the end of the 1888 seminar, the Mennonite Brethren community gave Kargel money for his travels so that he would be "without excuse to return again."[95] The following year Kargel taught in the MB Training Seminar in Friedensfeld[96] to sixteen students. In 1890 he was back in the Molotschna Colony with thirteen students in seminars, teaching with Jakob Reimer.[97] In January 1891 it is unlikely that he taught in MB Training Seminars because he had just returned home from an extended trip to Siberia.[98] He continued to teach the Mennonite Brethren in the area, because in 1894 he reported teaching twenty students in Andreasfeld.[99]

Kargel was also teaching in the west of Russia, in Volhynia, where he began his ministry. He reported in 1889, that while in Volhynia he organized a four-and-one-half week preachers' course which was attended by ten men who were training for ministry.[100] In early 1894 and 1895 Kargel mentioned travels to the south, within the Molotschna Settlement. In 1894 he gave a report to Pashkov of a visit to Andreasfeld, where he taught two classes daily for two weeks to twenty workers, presumably an MB Training Seminar. When he arrived there was "a revival among the young people of the colony so that during the following week they would come to our quarters and ask what they should do to be saved."[101] The lessons that Kargel taught were, he told Pashkov, "looking deeper into the indescribable riches of Christ."[102]

95. Ibid.

96. Friedensfeld is currently known as Mirapol, Ukraine.

97. Toews, "The Mennonite Brethren in Russia during the 1890s," 144.

98. There is only one letter from Kargel in the Pashkov Papers dated between September 1891 and January 1894 and it does not mention the Mennonite Brethren Mission School. It is possible that their Mission School continued and that Kargel taught in it, but there is no documentation from this time.

99. J. G. Kargel to Vasily Alexandrovich [Pashkov], 9 February 1894, 2/13/101, Pashkov Papers.

100. Ivan Kargel to "My Dear Friend and brother in the Lord Jesus Christ" [V. A. Pashkov], 23 October 1889, 2/13/081, Pashkov Papers.

101. J. G. Kargel to Vasily Alexandrovich [Pashkov], 9 February 1894, 2/13/101, Pashkov Papers. (This is a twelve-page letter.) He states that fifteen came to know the Lord during that time.

102. Ibid.

In 1895 Kargel attended the Annual Meetings of the Mennonite Brethren in Taurida Province. The Mennonite Brethren experienced increased persecution in this period and Kargel believed that this was because of their more pronounced evangelistic vision.[103] This vision may well have been due to Kargel's influence on them when he started a *Missionsschule* (mission school) in the Molotschna Colony in January 1888.

EMIGRATION ASSISTANCE PLAN

In the later 1880s Kargel became increasingly interested in a scheme to assist religious internal exiles within Russia to leave the country. A movement out of Russia could have evangelistic benefits, as it would move concentrated groups of exiled believers into unreached areas of Europe. When visiting Bucharest, Romania, in 1888, Kargel reported that there was a great lack of "workers for the Kingdom of God" in Romania.[104] Kargel discussed the possibility of foreigners forming a school in Romania, perhaps in Tultscha, which had a sizable German and Russian population. Wieler had worked among Germans and Russians in the Baptist church in Tultscha after he left the Molotschna Colony when under threat. His family had lived with him in Tultscha for two years before his early death. Anna and Johann Kargel hoped that Anna might teach at the proposed school. More widely, Kargel began to discuss with Baptist and Molokan communities "the door [that] was being opened for the persecuted brothers, where they could find a refuge."[105] He gathered information from Baptists, Molokans, and Mennonite Brethren.[106] There were considerable numbers among the exiled—often known as "the banned" or "the exiled"—who were interested in leaving Russia. The problem was that they could not receive the proper documentation, a foreign pass which would permit

---

103. J. G. Kargel to Vasily Alexandrovich [Pashkov], 29 July 1895, 2/2/1200, Pashkov Papers.

104. J. G. Kargel to "Dear brother in the Lord Jesus Christ" [V. A. Pashkov], 22 October 1888, 2/13/059, Pashkov Papers.

105. J. G. Kargel to Vasily Alexandrovich [Pashkov], 9 February 1894, 2/13/101, Pashkov Papers.

106. J. G. Kargel to Vasily Alexandrovich [Pashkov], 3 April 1894, 2/13/103, Pashkov Papers; J. G. Kargel to Vasily Alexandrovich [Pashkov], 9 February 1894, 2/13/101, Pashkov Papers.

them to leave.[107] Kargel began to pursue this issue in Saint Petersburg among the aristocracy who still had influence with the government. He found some sympathetic to the idea, but to release the banned Christians from Russia was a daunting political undertaking.[108]

Kargel arrived in Saint Petersburg in March 1894 and found that Sacharoff [Sakharov], one of the key Molokan figures involved in discussing the idea of a school, had been in Saint Petersburg but had left without leaving notes concerning any decision. H. I. Fast,[109] a Mennonite, who was also working in connection with the project, had discussed the school with Sakharov and he had implied that the Molokan group was no longer interested in financially supporting the school. Kargel concluded that the Molokans were not committed to educating their children beyond the level of basic reading, and were indifferent to the needs of the children who were among the exiled.[110] A few weeks later, Kargel commented that he was convinced that the Molokans would not send their children to the school in Tultscha because it would be a luxury,[111] and that they considered they already had an adequate educational system. In addition to the Baptists, Molokans, and Mennonite Brethren, Kargel mentioned the needs of Orthodox families whose children had few opportunities for education.[112] These families were concentrated in Kherson, Kiev, and Ekaterinoslav (today Dnepropetrovsk) Provinces.[113] In Kargel's mind the school was to be an ambitious joint effort not only between Baptists, Molokans, and Mennonite Brethren, but also involving the Orthodox.

---

107. J. G. Kargel to Vasily Alexandrovich [Pashkov], 9 February 1894, 2/13/101, Pashkov Papers.

108. J. G. Kargel to "Dear and beloved brother in the Lord" [V. A. Pashkov], 7 March 1894, 2/13/106, Pashkov Papers.

109. Prokhanov states that he was the tutor to Count Orloff-Denisoff. See Prokhanoff, *In the Cauldron of Russia*, 69.

110. J. G. Kargel to "Dear and beloved brother in the Lord" [V. A. Pashkov], 7 March, 1894, 2/13/106, Pashkov Papers.

111. J. G. Kargel to Vasily Alexandrovich [Pashkov], 3 April 1894, 2/13/103, Pashkov Papers.

112. It is quite possible that Kargel is referring to those who were Orthodox Russians by birth but had been sent into exile due to their evangelical beliefs, possibly the Stundist families.

113. J. G. Kargel to Vasily Alexandrovich [Pashkov], 3 April 1894, 2/13/103, Pashkov Papers. (This is an eight-page letter.)

By April 1894, a trip was being planned by Kargel and Pashkov to send H. I. Fast to the Caucasus to prepare the exiled for emigration, but legal matters had still not been arranged. It was decided to postpone the trip until the foreign passes for the exiled who wanted to emigrate were to hand.[114] The plan seemed to be having some success. The group in Saint Petersburg had the names and the passports of banned families interested in exiting the Russian Empire.[115] The foreign passes would require further governmental permission, but they had an insider, who apparently was willing to assist them. Things went wrong, however, when Fast was interrogated by the police. They searched his house and found many letters from those in exile, along with their passports. These items were confiscated and the entire project was disrupted. To complicate this tragic twist further, Kargel was about to leave for Bavaria to receive medical treatment.[116] Following the disruption of the plans to assist the exiled in emigration from the Russian Empire, Kargel spent the next two months in Bavaria receiving treatment for his nerves.[117] Before his trip for medical treatment, he held a brief meeting with a countess who was now helping them on the political front with the foreign passes. She had no new information and they agreed to postpone the issue until Kargel's course of treatment was finished.[118] He travelled to Bavaria for the summer while his family remained in the Finnish city of Vyborg.[119]

After this break, Kargel and Baedeker travelled to visit the exiled families in the Caucasus in September 1894. It appears that Fast's letters, which were confiscated in April, had far-reaching ramifications. Kargel and Baedeker found that the banned families now had no desire to leave. Martin Kalweit seemed satisfied with his lot in Erivan,

---

114. Ibid.

115. In this letter, Kargel wrote that if a request came for one hundred or more foreign passes, it would raise suspicions. The fact that he was thinking of over one hundred requests points to a significant interest in emigration.

116. J. G. Kargel to Vasily Alexandrovich [Pashkov], 3 April 1894, 2/13/103, Pashkov Papers.

117. J. G. Kargel to "Dear and beloved brother in the Lord" [V. A. Pashkov], 9 May 1894, 2/13/105, Pashkov Papers.

118. J. G. Kargel to "Beloved brother in the Lord" [V. A. Pashkov], 30 March 1894, 2/13/107, Pashkov Papers.

119. J. G. Kargel to Vasily Alexandrovich [Pashkov], 3 April 1894, 2/13/103, Pashkov Papers.

Armenia, as did the others there with him.[120] It was noted that Ivanov,[121] who had tried for nine years to receive a foreign pass, was now apparently content to travel within the reaches of his internal passport in order to preach. Kargel and Baedeker continued to discuss the issue of emigration within the various circles of the exiled. Based on Kargel's report to Pashkov in 1894, it seems that discussions took place in Batumi, Tiflis, Baku, Elizabethpol (today Ganja, Azerbaijan), and Gerusi with Germans as well as Russians. Finally, Kargel and Baedeker concluded that even if they were permitted to leave, few of the exiled would now take advantage of the opportunity. Kargel wrote to Pashkov, "The only exception could be those who have already been in foreign countries, or those who had a desire to live there comfortably. We received the impression that only one or two would go on their own account, unless they were sent there physically."[122]

This intelligence must have come as quite a blow, but the project was not totally abandoned until Kargel and Baedeker returned from visiting the exiled evangelicals, via Odessa, at the end of October 1894. While in Odessa, they received news that the recent persecution of evangelicals had not stopped even when the evangelicals relocated to Tultscha and some had moved back to Russia. Kargel concluded: "Under these circumstances it looks as if there is no question of emigration. But perhaps the Lord, who leads all things in this great kingdom as everywhere else, and has all things in His secure hand, has chosen better plans. We are begging Him and He will do it in His time. Silently we hope that He will open the doors in their home country again."[123]

The idea of a school in Tultscha seems to have been abandoned at the end of 1894, but the issue of assisting exiles to emigrate was discussed between Kargel and Pashkov for at least another year.[124]

---

120. J. G. Kargel to Vasily Alexandrovich [Pashkov], 3 November 1894, 2/2/1189, Pashkov Papers. (This is a twenty-four-page letter.)

121. Kargel does not mention a first name or patronymic of Ivanov but he does say that Ivanov "was with [Kalweit] as a fearless worker for the Lord." It is probably Vasily V. Ivanov, early Baptist missionary and pastor in the Tiflis region.

122. J. G. Kargel to Vasily Alexandrovich [Pashkov], 3 November 1894, 2/2/1189, Pashkov Papers.

123. Ibid.

124. J. G. Kargel to Vasily Alexandrovich [Pashkov], 29 July 1895, 2/2/1200, Pashkov Papers.

In 1895, Kargel reported that in Erivan Province (Armenia) it was known that the banned could emigrate out of Russia.[125] Some of the banned in the Tiflis region were still being denied foreign passes. One well known leader, Vasily Pavlov, did move to Tultscha, Romania. He and his family had been exiled to Orenburg, where his wife and four of his five children died of cholera in 1892. Pavlov moved to Tultscha in 1895 and remained there for five years.[126] Later, he served as a pastor in Odessa and in 1909 he was to be elected President of the Russian Baptist Union. The emigration plan, which excited both Ivan and Anna Kargel, may have produced some results in assisting a few to leave Russia but it never came to fulfillment in the way it was originally intended.[127] Given his spiritual outlook, Kargel was able to comfort himself that God "still has it all in His hands."[128]

INTO ALL THE PRISONS: KARGEL'S PRISON MINISTRY

Another aspect of Kargel's ministry during this period was his work in prisons. On 29 April 1890,[129] Kargel and Baedeker set out on a trip across the Russian Empire, to Siberia.[130] The round trip lasted four months. The pair had as their goal to preach the gospel to those who were in prison for various reasons. Baedeker had been granted a special authorization by the Director of the Prisons Department of the Russian Empire which was a "special command to visit the prisons of Russia and to supply the convicts with copies of the Holy Scriptures." This authorization made "[his] name . . . in Russian and Siberia a kind of latch for the prison gates" and allowed him "free access to every prison within the dominions of the Czar, from Warsaw to the transportation settlements on the island of Saghalien [Sakhalin], and from

---

125. J. G. Kargel to "Dear beloved brother in Christ" [V. A. Pashkov], 16 September 1895, 2/2/1202, Pashkov Papers.

126. Pavlof, "An Autobiography," 99–101; Coleman, *Russian Baptists and Spiritual Revolution*, 97.

127. Kargel, in a letter to "Dear beloved brother in Christ" [V. A. Pashkov], 16 September 1895, 2/2/1202, Pashkov Papers, states that he was on a trip to Gerusi in 1895 and could find no one interested in leaving Russia.

128. Ibid.

129. The Trans-Siberian railroad was not completed until 1905.

130. For details of this trip see Latimer, *Dr. Baedeker*, 109–63.

the fortress-prisons of Caucasia in the south to the northerly desolations of icy Siberia."[131]

On 29 August 1890 they reached Nikolaevka in the far east of Russia. They had hoped to travel on to Sakhalin, but that would have taken another month of waiting due to an outbreak of cholera in Vladivostok. The cities they visited were Nishni Novgorod, Perm, Ekatherinburg, Tjirmen, Tabolsk, Tomsk, Marinsk, Atschinsk, Krasnojarsk, Kansk, Nishni Udinsk, Irkutsk, Alexandrowoski-Sarood, Werchni Udinsk, Tschita, Nertschinsk (with the silver mines) and Kara, Blagowejtschenks, Chabarrowka, and Nikolaevka.[132] In the prisons they visited it was estimated that there were approximately 25,000 prisoners.[133] On the return journey, they travelled to Tokyo, where they stayed with a friend of Baedeker.[134] They travelled back from there separately. Kargel returned via Singapore. While on the ship from Singapore to Aden, Kargel became so ill that he could not stand.[135] He spent five days feeling very poorly.[136] From Egypt, he sailed to Odessa,[137] where he was expecting time in quarantine because he had been in Singapore.[138] One month after he left Egypt, however, he was in Russia with his family. He met his family at the Pashkov Estate in the village of Krekshino, south of Moscow. He wrote: "My train didn't arrive in Moscow until late. My wife and children were staying at one

---

131. Latimer, *Dr. Baedeker*, 44. It is important to note that Ivan Kargel received this authorization upon the retirement of Baedeker in 1896.

132. J. G. Kargel to "Dear friend and brother in the Lord Jesus Christ" [V. A. Pashkov], 29 August 1890, 2/13/085, Pashkov Papers. The names reflect the actual German spellings used by Kargel.

133. Ibid. Also see Latimer, *Dr. Baedeker* and Kargel, *Zwischen den Enden*, for a full description of the trip.

134. J. G. Kargel to "Dear friend and brother in the Lord Jesus Christ" [V. A. Pashkov], 11 September 1890, 2/13/086, Pashkov Papers.

135. J. G. Kargel to "Dear friend and brother in the Lord Jesus Christ" [V. A. Pashkov], 27 October 1890, 2/13/088, Pashkov Papers.

136. J. G. Kargel to Dr. Baedeker, 3 November, 1890, 2/13/087, Pashkov Papers.

137. In the letter, J. G. Kargel to Dr. Baedeker, 3 November 1890, 2/13/087, Pashkov Papers., there is a clue to Kargel's passport situation. He mentions that he will need to see a General Consulate in Constantinople (he does not say which one), because of a change in his passport and visa. He was worried that if his documents could not be straightened out, the steamship would not wait or honor his ticket. If things turned out poorly, he would have had to go to the Russian consulate in order to be allowed to enter Russia.

138. J. G. Kargel to Dr. Baedeker, 3 November 1890, 2/13/087, Pashkov Papers.

of the Pashkov homes for the summer. I went there the day I arrived [in Moscow]. My unexpected arrival was indescribable. To telegraph them would have been impossible. For those in the Lord's ministry in those days, it was better for the family not to know where we were."[139]

Kargel's letters written between 1890 and 1900 are full of stories about his prison ministry among Russians, Poles, Jews, and Germans, men and women alike. Sometimes he found believers imprisoned for their beliefs. In 1894, he reported that while in Tiflis, he preached in the prisons and found eleven men there who had been sentenced for their evangelical faith.[140] They were accompanied by fifteen family members who were themselves free but who chose to accompany their relatives. Despite their difficult life, the Tiflis believers had nothing to say against the police and were even hopeful that they had found a lawyer who could overturn their sentences.[141]

In many cases, however, the prison ministry was evangelistic. Kargel sought to influence prisoners and guards by giving them Bibles in their own language. In a letter to Pashkov after visiting one prison, in which he spoke to 266 people, Kargel wrote that it was truly the "power of God, which makes those holy, who believe."[142] During this period, as they travelled, Baedeker arranged for "breaking of bread" meetings, Brethren style, sometimes in the hotel rooms.[143] Kargel was convinced that the drawing together of believers committed to the way of holiness was the ultimate purpose of God for human life, and that this was a message for those in prison as much as for anyone else.

On one occasion Kargel arrived at a prison in the Kursk region on a Sunday, when the Orthodox service was underway. The Orthodox priest questioned who he was, and Kargel answered, "I am travelling into all the prisons with the papers from the main prison government, in order to distribute Testaments."[144] After the Orthodox service, Kargel was allowed to preach and then give Bibles to the prisoners as they filed out of his meeting. During the trip, he tells of be-

---

139. Kargel, *Zwischen den Enden*, 178.

140. Seven were from Orenburg Province and four were from Kiev Province.

141. J. G. Kargel to Vasily Alexandrovich [Pashkov], 3 November 1894, 2/2/1189, Pashkov Papers.

142. J. G. Kargel to "Dear and deeply loved friend and brother in the Lord" [V. A. Pashkov], 9 May 1896, 2/13/110, Pashkov Papers.

143. Skopina, "Iz Biografii I. V. Kargelya," 692.

144. Ibid.

ing befriended by various prison officials, some of whom invited him into their homes where he spoke and distributed Bibles and tracts. His ministry drained the Bible depots of supplies. He was frustrated at the intermittent supply of literature and began to order ahead, asking, for example, that 7,000 New Testaments be delivered to Kharkov so that he could distribute them in the Kharkov and Poltava regions. When he arrived, however, he found that only seventy had been delivered.[145]

Many of the stories that Kargel relates to Pashkov are about newly found commitment to a changed life. He wrote: "I thank the Lord that He is sending me into this ministry with full blessings from His gospel which gives the power to save all those who believe in it."[146] He was convinced that he was experiencing "full blessings" to carry out the work and that these blessings could and should be taken by all.

In 1895 Baedeker wrote to Pashkov that he was getting too old to continue the prison ministry. He emphasized that it had been a very successful work. He had made a contact within the government, he continued, who was willing to transfer the unique authorization that had allowed Baedeker freedom to travel to the prisons to another person whom Baedeker would recommend. Baedeker suggested to Pashkov that Kargel, with whom he had worked so closely, was the right person for the post.[147] In late 1895, with Pashkov's agreement, Baedeker passed the baton to Kargel. Clearly Kargel's perspective on this ministry was shaped by the many trips he took with Baedeker. On 17 January 1896, Kargel received the appropriate documentation that would allow him freedom to "visit and distribute the Gospel in the whole of Russia" to those in prison.[148] Kargel, with typical activism, immediately approached Princess Gagarin, one of the wealthy leaders among the Saint Petersburg Evangelicals, for funding for the project.[149] He next secured a contract for discounted literature from the Bible Society.[150]

145. Ibid.
146. J. G. Kargel to "My honored, beloved friend and brother in Christ" [V. A. Pashkov], 7 June 1901, 2/13/111, Pashkov Papers.
147. F. W. Baedeker to "My honored and beloved brother" [V. A. Pashkov], 16/28 September 1895, 2/3/196, Pashkov Papers.
148. J. G. Kargel to "Dear and beloved brother in the Lord" [V. A. Pashkov], 26 January 1896, 2/13/109, Pashkov Papers.
149. Ibid.
150. Kargel received a 50 percent discount and not the 75 percent discount that was given to Baedeker, who worked through the London office.

In February 1896, Kargel was preaching among the Baptists in Lodz, Poland (at that time under the rule of the Russian Tsar), before heading on to Petrkov and Tschenstachov, with plans to visit the four "government cities" of Radom, Kielce, Lublin, and Siedlce.[151] These government cities had prisons and his newly acquired authorization would grant him access to preach among the prisoners. In April he reported on a two-week trip to the prisons in the Smolensk region near Moscow. 1896 was the year of the crowning of the new Tsar, Nicholas II, and Kargel reminded Pashkov that it was customary for a new Tsar to issue a manifesto that could release up to one-third of the prisoners in Russian prisons. Kargel was hoping to get literature to them before they were released.[152] He also mentioned that as soon as the ice on the rivers thawed many of the religious prisoners currently held in prisons in the European section of Russia would be shipped to Siberia. These factors meant that Kargel worked as quickly as possible among the prisons nearest to his home in Vyborg. In April and May 1896, he travelled extensively, reaching into the prison systems of the Russian provinces of Witevsk [Vitebsk], Smolensk, Wilma [Vilno], Minsk,[153] Kaluga, Orel, Kursk, Kharkov, Poltava, and Jekatherinoslaff [Ekaterinoslav].[154] From early 1896, Ivan Kargel's primary target locations for his itinerant preaching trips shifted to encompass those cities that had a significant prisoner population. This aspect of his ministry remained significant until Kargel left the Finnish region.

EXILED BELIEVERS

Although Kargel had involved himself in the—ultimately unsuccessful—scheme to enable internally exiled evangelical believers to leave the Russian Empire, this was never intended to be the solution for the majority of exiled evangelicals. Many more needed encouragement in their exile, and this was part of his vision. Twice during the time that the Kargels lived in Vyborg, Ivan travelled on his own to

---

151. J. G. Kargel to "Dear and beloved brother in the Lord" [V. A. Pashkov], 26 January 1896, 2/13/109, Pashkov Papers.

152. J. G. Kargel to Vasily Alexandrovich [Pashkov], 27 April 1896, 2/2/1216, Pashkov Papers.

153. Ibid.

154. J. G. Kargel to "Dear and deeply loved friend and brother in the Lord" [V. A. Pashkov], 9 May 1896, 2/13/110, Pashkov Papers.

the Caucasus region. He delivered money to the needy who had been exiled there. His commitment to supporting and assisting those in need was clearly demonstrated as he travelled. While on these trips he spent time preaching, encouraging, and gathering information. In 1891 he visited the German colonies in the Kuban region and found that the evangelical Christians were having meetings together.[155] He then travelled to Tiflis where he found seven families who had recently been imprisoned. During this trip, he visited Slavjanka, Kidarbek, Ivanovka (a Molokan village), and Saratovka.[156] He distributed money and reported back to Pashkov on the needs he found. On his return trip through Tiflis, Kargel realized that his journey had attracted the attention of the police, which in turn caused problems for those he knew in Tiflis. Soon after his departure, the police carried out an intense interrogation of the evangelical leaders in Tiflis, asking where Kargel's money came from, what his political views were, and who his contacts were.[157]

In September 1894 Kargel and Baedeker officially travelled to the prisons in the Caucasus region, but the primary reason for the trip was to visit the banned families. They left Odessa for Batum (Batumi, Georgia) on 27 September. Once in Batum, they tried to gather information concerning those in exile, but the level of persecution had risen and even their usual contacts were reluctant to give information or had no information to give because of the restrictions on travel and communication. One thing that was noted was that some who had been sent into exile had refused to obey the order to stop preaching the gospel. Their punishment was to be sent to less desirable villages, such as Artvinja, a village outside Batum which was known as a place where fever was rampant.[158] Kargel and Baedeker were told of the increasingly severe interrogations, and in particular that the police were asking about contacts with foreigners and about the political views of

---

155. J. G. Kargel to "Dear friend and brother in the Lord Jesus Christ" [V. A. Pashkov], 7 May 1891, 2/13/094, Pashkov Papers. (This is a 24 page letter.)

156. Ibid. There are two villages in Azerbaijan which have had the name Saratovka. Given the geographic proximity to the other villages, Kargel was most likely referring to present-day of Novosaratovka and not present-day Sahiloba.

157. Ibid.

158. J. G. Kargel to Vasily Alexandrovich [Pashkov], 3 November 1894, 2/2/1189, Pashkov Papers. (This is a twenty-four page letter.)

these foreigners.¹⁵⁹ Kargel and Baedeker were advised by their contacts in Batum and Tiflis not to go deeper into the territories where the banned were living. They were told that it would further endanger those in exile and would produce no results.¹⁶⁰

Ignoring the advice of those in Tiflis and Batum, Kargel and Baedeker decided to continue with their journey, although not to hold any meetings. They travelled to Elizabethpol (today Ganja, Azerbaijan), Baku, Schemacha, Shusha, and Ivanovka.¹⁶¹ They arrived in Elizabethpol on 2 October 1894, but attracted too much attention, partly because they were European and so many of the population were Asian. Kargel and Baedeker were discouraged by those in exile from holding meetings in the hotel where they were staying because it was being watched.¹⁶² They managed to meet their contacts in Helenendorf, a German colony not far from the city.¹⁶³ During conversations in Helenendorf, Kargel and Baedeker were again advised against continuing their journey, but they pressed on regardless and entered Baku. Here Baedeker contracted a high fever and they felt it was not God's will to continue. Kargel preached in the prisons of the Baku area for three days and then the pair returned to Tiflis.¹⁶⁴ Throughout the entire trip, Baedeker and Kargel felt led by the "finger of the Lord" pointing out their way. They prayed that God would "not let us go on crooked roads."¹⁶⁵ This desire for an internal sense of peace as God guided through circumstances is classic Keswick spirituality.

Kargel and Baedeker again visited the exiled in the Caucasus Region in the summer of 1895. During this trip they were able to travel deep into the region, visiting Baku, Schemacha, Shusha, and Gerusi, which they had intended to do in 1894 but had been dissuaded by Baedeker's fever and the warnings from the banned. The practice of banning had decreased somewhat, and those in exile seemed to have more freedom than the previous year.¹⁶⁶ While visiting Schemacha,

159. Ibid.
160. Ibid.
161. Ibid.
162. Ibid.
163. Helenendorf is currently known as Khanlar, Azerbaijan.
164. Ibid.
165. Ibid.
166. J. G. Kargel to "Dear and beloved brother in Christ" [V. A. Pashkov], 16 September 1895, 2/2/1202, Pashkov Papers.

Kargel found only one banned family in need. The attitude of the local government officials had also changed. During this trip, the travels of Baedeker were published in the local newspapers, where his humanitarian efforts and visits to the prisons were praised as an effective way to help the region. Because of this positive press coverage, when the pair arrived in Shusha they were given an armed and mounted escort to Gerusi. The stir created by the press over the travels of Baedeker forced the pair of evangelists to have a higher profile than they wished. They tried to refuse the escort but the local leaders insisted, claiming that when guests had travelled so far to visit them, they were responsible to see that they were well kept and returned safely.[167]

One reason for the change of approach over the course of a year may have been the death of Alexander III in 1894. With the change to the new Tsar, Nicholas II, some local policies changed. Exiled believers were now freer to meet together and some were even given money to support both themselves and family members at home who had not been exiled. Some of the brothers offered this explanation: "Our first *nachal'nik* [governor] was a Russian who used to harass us mercilessly, the second was an Armenian who was a bit easier on us . . . and this one is a Tatar, who even treats us kindly."[168]

Despite the new openness, the local officials were still vigilant. Kargel and Baedeker were greeted in Gerusi soon after their arrival by the chief city official. Baedeker did not hide the fact that he was in the town to see the exiled. The local official did not seem concerned about the purpose of their trip and even opened his home to the pair for the meetings. The offer did not suit Baedeker and Kargel but they could not refuse. They tried to meet the believers in the marketplaces and in homes, to distribute money and gather information, but the meetings were interrupted by a messenger inviting them back to the city official's home. Finally they were physically forced to spend their final ninety minutes in his home, waiting for their train to leave.

After leaving Gerusi, they had better success in Shusha, where they had previously communicated to the banned to meet them, one at a time, beginning at 7.00 am. This new tactic proved successful and

---

167. J. G. Kargel to "Dear and beloved brother in the Lord" [V. A. Pashkov], 18 October 1895, 2/2/1203, Pashkov Papers.

168. Ibid.

they were able to gather information and distribute money which was to be passed on throughout the Caucasus region.[169]

It is not entirely clear why Ivan Kargel's travels were never restricted or why he was not banned with the other evangelical activists. There are several possible reasons. First, he was often with Baedeker, who was a well known international traveler and humanitarian figure. Local newspapers often covered Baedeker's arrival and activities and possibly the police were afraid to arrest Kargel for fear of his international connections. The pair travelled with the advertised intent to visit those in the prisons and they possessed the proper authorization. When they visited those in exile, they often did it between trips to the prisons. Another possible reason why Kargel's work was never restricted was that he never baptized Orthodox Russians. Indeed, after he left Bulgaria in 1884, there are no documented events that involved Kargel baptizing anyone. A third possibility would be that he had no employer who could be censured for allowing funds to be transmitted to a "non-Orthodox sect" leader. The Kargel family was supported, but not employed, by Pashkov. A final explanation could be his passport and citizenship. He was a naturalized Russian citizen with permission to travel abroad. He acquired this status before he was married and could not easily be banished from Russia as a foreigner. Whatever the exact reasons, Kargel was able to travel in a way that was unique for anyone in the Russian evangelical community and he took full advantage of that freedom.

The journeys that were undertaken by Kargel and Baedeker were amazing feats of strength. At times they journeyed to the Caucasus only, while at other times they continued on into Siberia. Baedeker's stamina was extraordinary, as he was not a healthy man, having only one lung, curvature of the spine, and a weak heart.[170] The longer Siberian excursions required that Kargel and Baedeker had full sets of winter and summer clothing that were hauled along with them. Immense amounts of literature were picked up along the way and distributed around the prisons. Travel conditions were primitive. Overall, Kargel made at least three extended trips to visit those in exile and prison through the Caucasus and on into Siberia. Two of the trips (1890 and 1895) were with Baedeker and the last one was without

---

169. Ibid.
170. Corrado, "The Philosophy of Ministry of Colonel Vasiliy Pashkov," 109.

him (1901). The accounts of their 1890 Siberian trip were published in two separate books, one in English[171] and one in German.[172] The way in which Kargel's accounts of his journeys have continued to be published shows their enduring ability to inspire evangelical readers.[173] The trips ceased after Pashkov's death in 1902.[174] It is likely that the reason for this was lack of finances rather than lack of desire.

THE KARGEL FAMILY

The extensive travel undertaken by Ivan Kargel during this period, much of it during the time he and Anna and their daughters were based in the Finnish city of Vyborg, was difficult for the Kargel family. However, after the Pashkovs were exiled the links Anna had with Saint Petersburg were not as strong as they had been. In 1889 Anna Kargel admitted to harboring bitterness over the exile of the Pashkovs, especially over the loss of the presence of Alexandra Ivanovna.[175] The Pashkovs' forced departure and the persecution that followed must have been a severe blow to Anna. She had often written from Bulgaria about how very much she missed the Pashkovs and the fellowship of the believers in Saint Petersburg.[176] The loss was also deeply felt by Ivan, but he had his travelling ministry to bring him fulfillment. It is clear from Anna's letters that her husband was happy with his family and his work. For her part, as she commented, she had to communicate with him often by letter, instead of having him near her. She described how he would arrive home after a trip feeling exhausted and would immediately receive another invitation to travel. Kargel wanted so much, according to Anna, to have some rest at home, but there was much work everywhere that he was being asked to undertake.[177]

171. Latimer, *Dr. Baedeker*.

172. Kargel, *Zwischen den Enden*.

173. See Brandenburg, *The Meek and the Mighty*; Kahle, *Evangelische Christen in Russland und der Sowjetunion*; Lieven, *Eine Saat*; Skopina, "Iz Biografii I. V. Kargelya"; Karetnikova, *Almanax po Istorii Russkogo Baptisma, vypusk 4*.

174. Pashkov died in Rome in 1902 at the age of seventy-one. He is buried in a non-Catholic cemetery near the Cestius Pyramid.

175. Anna Kargel to Alexandra Ivanovna [Pashkov], 15 February 1889, 2/13/063, Pashkov Papers.

176. Anna Kargel to Alexandra Ivanovna [Pashkov], 12 January 1882, 2/13/006, Pashkov Papers.

177. Anna Kargel to Alexandra Ivanovna [Pashkov], 15 February 1889, 2/13/063, Pashkov Papers.

In January 1890, Anna told Pashkov that the doctors were insisting that she take the girls to a village setting for their health.[178] She had made plans to move to Ryazanskaya Province (southeast of Moscow) but the Pashkovs offered Anna accommodation on their estate near the small village of Krekshino. She accepted this offer eagerly, acknowledging: "All my family has lived by you for a long time and I will never be able to repay you."[179] At approximately the same time that Anna and the girls moved to Krekshino, her husband and Baedeker left for the far eastern edge of the Russian Empire. Ivan would not return for seven months. While she and the girls stayed at Krekshino, Anna reported that she felt "ten or eleven years younger."[180] The fresh air and quiet setting were clearly proving beneficial to Anna and also to the girls. In addition, Anna enjoyed meeting some of the members of Muscovite high society. It was with deep regret that Anna left Krekshino when her husband returned from his journey. She said she was reminded that "indeed the children of God are sheep between the wolves in this world" as she returned to Saint Petersburg.[181]

The family stayed in Saint Petersburg until July 1891 when Ivan went to Germany for three months of respite and Anna took the girls to Wartemjagi,[182] which Ivan stated was "warmer and drier" than Saint Petersburg.[183] The entire family was suffering from various illnesses during this period. In 1891, Ivan returned to Saint Petersburg after a trip to the Caucasus to find Anna very weak. She was suffering a total loss of energy and was not sleeping well. The diagnosis was that she was suffering from *Blutarmut* (a type of anemia). The local doctor suggested that Anna drink blood, which she refused to do. Instead she drank *kefir*, took ferrous salt baths, and tried to get more fresh

---

178. Anna Kargel to Vasily Alexandrovich [Pashkov], 18 January 1890, 2/13/082, Pashkov Papers.

179. Anna Kargel to Alexandra Ivanovna and Vasily Alexandrovich [Pashkov], 18 March 1890, 2/13/083, Pashkov Papers.

180. Anna Kargel to Vasily Alexandrovich [Pashkov], 14 July 1890, 2/13/084, Pashkov Papers.

181. Anna Kargel to Vasily Alexandrovich [Pashkov], 3 December 1890, 2/13/089, Pashkov Papers.

182. This is the spelling that Kargel used and it is difficult to determine exactly where this village is located. It is most likely Vartemäki (Vartemjagi), a Finnish village, which is located north of Saint Petersburg, in the Grand Duchy of Finland.

183. J. G. Kargel to "Dear and loved brother in the Lord" [V. A. Pashkov], 24 July 1891, 2/13/095, Pashkov Papers.

air.[184] The doctors also suggested that the girls needed fresh air and gymnastics and should not return to the city.

During his journey back from Siberia (his 1890 trip with Baedeker), Ivan Kargel sought the advice of doctors in Singapore about his own health. They suggested that his liver was not functioning properly.[185] Kargel sought a second opinion in Kissingen, Germany, and the diagnosis was that his gall bladder was not functioning correctly. Despite Ivan's suggestion that Anna come with him to Kissingen for treatment for her anemia,[186] she moved with the girls to Wartemjagi, while Ivan sought further medical treatment in Germany. After two months in Kissingen, Ivan believed that the baths were having a positive effect on his health.[187] His skin was less yellow.[188] Ivan's hopes were that the family would not have to return to Saint Petersburg for the winter of 1891, since the weather there seemed to be damaging their health.[189]

Before returning home from Kissingen, Ivan Kargel was able to meet Vasily Pashkov in Ischl, Austria. After this meeting, Kargel felt that his vision had been renewed. He spoke about going to those who "do not have a love for Him, our Lord" and added, "may He not only send me but may He come along with me to show me the work He has for me."[190] The inspirational influence of Pashkov on Ivan Kargel cannot be underestimated. The sadness expressed in letters by both Anna and Ivan Kargel to the Pashkovs about their not being able to see each other and work together is deep. In one moving statement,

---

184. J. G. Kargel to "Dear friend and brother in the Lord Jesus Christ" [V. A. Pashkov], 7 May 1891, 2/13/094, Pashkov Papers. *Kefir* is a cultured milk drink similar to yogurt. Ferrous salt baths (*Salz und Eisenbäder*) were used to treat iron deficiencies by taking baths in specially treated water that contained high amounts of Ferrous Sulfate.

185. Ibid.

186. J. G. Kargel to "Dear and loved brother in the Lord" [V. A. Pashkov], 24 July 1891, 2/13/095, Pashkov Papers.

187. J. G. Kargel to "Dear brother in the Lord" [V. A. Pashkov], 14 August 1891, 2/13/096, Pashkov Papers.

188. J. G. Kargel to "Dear brother in the Lord" [V. A. Pashkov], 28 August 1891, 2/13/097, Pashkov Papers.

189. J. G. Kargel to "Dear and loved brother in the Lord" [V. A. Pashkov], 24 July 1891, 2/13/095, Pashkov Papers.

190. J. G. Kargel to "Dear friend and brother in the Lord Jesus Christ" [V. A. Pashkov], 13 September 1891, 2/13/098, Pashkov Papers.

Ivan wrote about the friendship in a way that also gives an insight into Ivan's spirituality. He spoke to Pashkov about "how it hurts, that I cannot be with you any longer; only He can measure the pain that tests hearts and kidneys. But also He alone is able to soothe the longing with His nearness. In my spirit then I will accompany you constantly and will leave you in the hands of Him whose goodness is around you and whose eyes are constantly watching your steps with love."[191] This letter indicates the depths of emotion of which Kargel was capable and at the same time shows how he brought God into that emotion: "only He can measure the pain." The letter also shows Kargel's confidence in God, however difficult the circumstances of life.

Despite the move to Vyborg, Ivan Kargel's health deteriorated, and in 1894 he wrote that he had never been in such agony due to illness.[192] It was not his liver, nor his gall bladder, but his nerves. He was, as has been seen, keeping a very full travel schedule. He complained that he could not go out into the sun or hear noises without getting upset and having headaches.[193] Eventually, he decided to go to Woerishofen, Bavaria, for *Kneippkur*.[194] Midway through his time there, the doctors extended the treatment, apparently with good results.[195] Kargel's descriptions talk about the doctors, about what the waters were doing, and about the hand of the Lord. "Only God knows how far he [Dr. Kneippe] will put me back together, in any case the water will be good for me, as my whole nature longs for it and every application of it is a relief to me."[196] He wrote again: "Even if in the two months all the chronic pain is not taken care of, the removal of some of it will be guided, through the Lord's help. I am already looking

---

191. J. G. Kargel to "Dear and beloved brother in Jesus Christ" [V. A. Pashkov], 22 October 1888, 2/13/059, Pashkov Papers.

192. J. G. Kargel to "Dearly loved brother in the Lord" [V. A. Pashkov], 30 March 1894, 2/13/107, Pashkov Papers.

193. J. G. Kargel to Vasily Alexandrovich [Pashkov], 3 April 1894, 2/13/103, Pashkov Papers.

194. J. G. Kargel to "Dear brother in the Lord Jesus Christ" [V. A. Pashkov], 14 April 1894, 2/13/104, Pashkov Papers. The letter mentions that the doctor's name was Kneippe and "Kneippekur" was probably a special cure designed by Dr. Kneippe.

195. J. G. Kargel to "Dear brother in the Lord Jesus Christ" [V. A. Pashkov], 9 May 1894, 2/13/105, Pashkov Papers.

196. J. G. Kargel to "Dear brother in the Lord Jesus Christ" [V. A. Pashkov], 14 April 1894, 2/13/104, Pashkov Papers.

forward to serving the Lord unhindered."[197] However, things were difficult for his family. Kargel took up travelling again, and was in Tiflis when he received a letter which told of an injury to his wife. There was a house helper with them in Vyborg to assist Anna, especially when Ivan was away, but in September 1895 Anna suffered a severe burn to her face and right arm and hand when the house helper was absent.[198] In that letter, Ivan reported that Anna's sister came from "S. burg" to care for her.[199] She eventually seems to have recovered from the accident, because she is mentioned in letters by Kargel dated January[200] and May 1896[201] with no statements concerning her health.

As mentioned in chapter 3, during the discussion about the Kargel daughters, the last letter written by Anna Kargel to the Pashkovs is dated 11 February 1894, and the last direct reference to her in Ivan's letters is dated 9 May 1896. I have suggested that Anna died sometime after 1898 when Ivan returned from Vyborg to Saint Petersburg with his family. On 7 June 1901, Ivan Kargel wrote to Pashkov stating that he had sent his "dear ones" from Saint Petersburg to Hapsal, while he went to Siberia.[202] Anna is not mentioned by name in this letter. In this letter written in June 1901, from Kyrgan in Tobolsk Province, Ivan Kargel wrote: "The sickness sent from Him is to be seen as a way of discipline for His children, through His hands. Since I have seen you last time, He also has begun to speak to me and mine through this way." This certainly suggests that there had been serious illness in the family. He continued to write about his "dear ones," stating that they

---

197. J. G. Kargel to "Dear brother in the Lord Jesus Christ" [V. A. Pashkov], 9 May 1894, 2/13/105, Pashkov Papers.

198. J. G. Kargel to "Dear beloved brother in Christ" [V. A. Pashkov], 16 September 1895, 2/2/1202, Pashkov Papers.

199. Ibid. The handwriting is not clear but it was probably "S. burg," meaning Saint Petersburg. It is possible to read it as "L. burg," meaning Lemburg which is currently known as Lvov, Ukraine.

200. J. G. Kargel to "Dear and beloved brother in the Lord" [V. A. Pashkov], 26 January 1896, 2/13/109, Pashkov Papers.

201. J. G. Kargel to "Dear and deeply loved Friend and brother in the Lord" [V. A. Pashkov], 9 May 1896, 2/13/110, Pashkov Papers. This is the last letter from Ivan Kargel that mentions his wife specifically.

202. J. G. Kargel to "My honored, beloved friend and brother in Christ" [V. A. Pashkov], 7 June 1901, 2/13/111, Pashkov Papers. At this time, Natasha would have been nineteen, Elena would have been eighteen, Maria would have been sixteen, and Elizaveta would have been fourteen years of age.

are "now much better after their sickness has passed."[203] It is very possible that Anna Kargel and Natasha Kargel both died separately before this letter was written. However, the focus, as always with Kargel, was on what was happening spiritually. The desire Ivan Kargel expressed in this letter was that through the suffering being experienced his "old self" would be replaced by a heart filled by God in every part. True to his evangelical activism, he himself was "getting ready for my own upcoming trip" to Siberia.[204] The family was important, but in Kargel's eyes the family came second to his calling to serve God across the Russian Empire.

CONCLUSION

During the years from 1887 to 1898, Ivan Kargel continued his itinerant preaching throughout the Russian Empire. It was during this time that he relocated to the Grand Duchy of Finland with his family to avoid the constant pressure of the police enforcing the religious agenda of Pobedonostsev. During this decade, he expanded his work to include ministry to prisoners and care for those sent into exile on the fringes of the Russian Empire. He was able to travel freely through his connections with Baedeker into remote regions to talk about the message of the gospel and about personal consecration. His ministry expanded to include the areas of Estonia, Finland, and Israel. In Estonia, he formed an interdenominational, multi-lingual fellowship. He is credited with the start of the Russian evangelical movement in Finland. In Israel, he distributed massive amounts of literature. He remained in contact with the Saint Petersburg Evangelicals but due to the persecutions there his work was limited. During his trips to the German colonies and Russian cities, Kargel continued to connect with the various groups of evangelical believers in these regions. Information was sent back to Pashkov, with the hope that one day there could be a broader evangelical coalition in Russia. Kargel renewed some contact with the Baptists, both German and Russian, as well as maintaining a teaching ministry among the Mennonite Brethren in southern Russia. The plan to bring evangelical Christians out of their place of exile and relocate them into a place of relative freedom failed. The demands of

203. J. G. Kargel to "My honored, beloved friend and brother in Christ" [V. A. Pashkov], 7 June 1901, 2/13/111, Pashkov Papers.
204. Ibid.

this project, coupled with his very heavy travel schedule, had a negative effect on Ivan Kargel's health. He spent time in Germany seeing doctors and receiving treatment to regain his strength. The physical health of his wife and young daughters was also not strong. His wife Anna, who had led him into deeper evangelical spirituality, and his first born daughter Natasha, both died near the end of this period. Despite his struggles, however, Kargel's vision to promote evangelical spirituality across the Russian Empire did not waver.

7

Third Saint Petersburg Period

Evangelical Christian Endeavors

(1898–1909)

IN 1898, IVAN KARGEL moved back to Saint Petersburg along with his wife and four daughters: Natasha, aged sixteen, Elena, aged fifteen, Maria, aged twelve, and Elizaveta, aged eleven. On his return, Kargel began to take up leadership responsibilities again among the Saint Petersburg Evangelicals within the city. He spoke regularly at gatherings that took place in homes. He also continued his ministry in Russian prisons for a time. This chapter looks mainly at aspects of his work in the early twentieth century, with the date of 1909 being chosen as an end-point since the Evangelical Christian Union was established in that year. However, much that Kargel did in the first decade of the century had longer-term implications. The chapter examines his formulation of evangelical theology, which was increasingly influential. It includes an analysis of his Baptist and wider evangelical relationships, and the attempts in which Kargel was involved to organize a wider evangelical witness in Russia in a more formal way through the establishment of the Evangelical Christian Union and an Evangelical Alliance. This chapter also gives an account of the launch of a Bible College in Saint Petersburg and of initiatives that were taken in the field of publishing. Kargel continued to be a significant leader within the Russian evangelical community, as he had been in previous years, but from 1898, at which point he was about to enter his fifties, he again made Saint Petersburg his base. Compared to his previous period of extensive travel, his role now was a very different one. He did not move from the capital until the late 1920s, when he and his three daughters moved to the Ukraine. In the period examined in this chapter, as well as being active in evangelical Christian endeavors, he gave much more attention to teaching about the sanctified life, and this will be mentioned here but will be analyzed in detail in chapter 8.

KARGEL'S EVANGELICAL THEOLOGY

In the early years of the twentieth century, Kargel increasingly became seen as the leading theologian of the Russian evangelicals. He exhibited the four marks of evangelicalism outlined by David Bebbington: conversionism, the belief that lives need to be changed; crucicentrism, a stress on the sacrifice of Christ on the cross; biblicism, a particular regard for the authority of the Bible; and activism, the expression of the gospel in effort.[1] This was referred to in general terms in chapter 1, but by this stage in Kargel's life his convictions had matured and were particularly influential. It will be evident that for him, evangelical convictions were strongly connected with evangelical spirituality. Hence, they deserve to be given more detailed consideration as Kargel's role in shaping Russian evangelical spirituality is examined.

On the question of conversion, Ivan Kargel wrote an important book entitled *What is Your Relationship to the Holy Spirit?*, in which he argued that church membership, even membership of an evangelical church, was not necessarily a sign of true faith: "You can belong to one of the existing churches, be baptized, and with purpose of heart take part in the Lord's Supper; you can be present at every church service and at religious assemblies; you can correctly gather in a household prayer circle; you can have great knowledge and praiseworthy experience, but if you do not have the Spirit of Christ, you are not His."[2] This is an uncompromising statement about the necessity of conversion. In another work on the life of Moses, Kargel argued that Moses reached a clear point of decision when he moved from his Egyptian life to embrace his Jewish roots. Kargel applied this to evangelical conversion, and wrote: "If you say, as a certain woman did recently, 'I always believed,' this is the best proof that you have not come to God, and that your Christianity has never begun."[3] Repentance was the first step in conversion for Kargel, as he emphasized when he wrote, "Concerning

1. Bebbington, *Evangelicalism in Modern Britain*, 3.
2. Kargel, "V Kakom Ty Otnoshenii k Duxu Svyatomu?" 116.
3. Kargel, "Vetxozavetnye Proobrazy," 281.

the question—'Brothers, what shall we do?'—the answer to this was given on the day of Pentecost, 'Repent and receive the gift of the Holy Ghost'; this is the command of the Lord and there is no other given anywhere."[4]

As his theology developed, Kargel gave more attention to the work of the Holy Spirit in an individual's conversion. "Without the Spirit of Christ, you are not His,"[5] he wrote in 1912. In line with his emphasis on holiness, he suggested that if all the focus was on justification by faith, without sanctification, then it was possible "that some people will come to conversion, but they will never leave the carnal views of their mind." He then added, in what seems to make the matter rather more complicated, that "the Holy Spirit, from the very beginning, has removed those [carnal views] from the convert but the convert may again run back to them."[6] The ability to lead another into a conversion experience, for Kargel, was also related to the Spirit. Such ability depended on the evangelist's relationship to the Holy Spirit, and here Kargel used the first disciples of Christ as an example. After being filled with the Holy Spirit, he said, "One man [Peter] spoke more words of life than all of them had in three and a half years."[7] He used the story of the woman at the well in John 4 to show that Jesus was dependent on "other food," or the Holy Spirit, to lead another person to saving faith.[8] Clearly, Ivan Kargel placed great stress on being converted by the power of the Holy Spirit. This conversion, he believed, brought a dramatic change to the life of a person, resulting in an ability to live in a new way.

A second emphasis was on the cross of Christ. In Kargel's work on the Old Testament Tabernacle, *Light from the Shadows of Future Blessing*, which was his first published book (1896),[9] he wrote that every "true believer" has understood the just punishment from God that they deserve for their sin. But, he continued, the person who

---

4. Kargel, "V Kakom Ty Otnoshenii k Duxu Svyatomu?" 158.
5. Ibid., 116.
6. Kargel, "Xristos Osvyashhenie Nashe," 51.
7. Kargel, "V Kakom Ty Otnoshenii k Duxu Svyatomu?" 124.
8. Ibid., 125.
9. *Svet iz Teni budushhix Blag*. This book was published in German as *Licht aus dem Shatten* in 1896. This book will be discussed in chapter 7 in the section about Kargel's publishing efforts. The Russian version was republished in 1998.

understands that should then see more, that Jesus has "taken up the wages of their sin and tasted death for them." At that moment, they have "grasped a living faith."[10] Kargel attempted to show the typology of nearly every detail of the Tabernacle to be representative of the reality of sin and God's plan for salvation in Jesus Christ. The death of Jesus on the cross was the only way, as Kargel saw it, for humankind to have sin removed and separation from God brought to an end. The cross allowed an open and free relationship between the Creator and the created. However, it is not only that a believing person moves from a consciousness of sin to a realization of what Christ has done: the reverse process can also take place. Ignorance of the full meaning of the cross means that sin can remain even in believers. Kargel wrote: "The only true knowledge of the vastness of sin comes as a result of understanding and counting dear the depths and heights of the atoning sacrifice [of Christ]."[11]

This introduces an important aspect of the cross in Kargel's thinking. For Kargel, the cross was what brought about the end of separation from God, but the believer's identification with the cross of Christ should also mean a full death to sin, including a death to the power of sin. He wrote in *Law of the Spirit of Life*,[12] "If Christ lives in us—the one who once and for all condemned to death sin and the law of sin on the cross (Rom 8:3)—then the body will consider those evils to be disgraceful and will cease to pay attention to their temptations. It is paralyzed, inactive in its relation to sin and must not and cannot serve sin as it did earlier; it is dead to sin."[13] The way of the cross was a mark for Kargel of the true Christian faith. Writing about the Old Testament prototypes that he found so helpful, he stated: "So many would like to be saved, to become Christians, but faith and the offering up of sacrifice do not agree with their dogma; their faith does not cost them anything."[14] The cross was a sign of suffering as well as the death of the "old man." Kargel saw the cross as the normal Christian life. "Suffering and grief," he wrote in *Christ—Our Sanctification*, "were in the path of

10. Kargel, *Svet iz Teni budushhix Blag*, 85–86.
11. Kargel, "Grex kak Zlo vsex Zol v ehtom Mire," 6.
12. *Zakon Duxa Zhizni*. The literal meaning of this title is "The law that was given by the Spirit of Life." For ease of reference, I will simply translate the title *Law of the Spirit of Life*. This book will be discussed in chapter 7.
13. Kargel, *Zakon Duxa Zhizni*, 159.
14. Kargel, "Vetxozavetnye Proobrazy," 283.

our Lord—that is what we just saw; and our path will be the same, for there will be no other; there must not be any other, because we again hear from the lips of the Lord the instruction; hate your own life, take the cross and follow Him."[15]

Kargel went on in this book to list four reasons why the cross was necessary in a person's life. It was necessary to "terminate sin," "strengthen our faith," and "allow patience to mature."[16] But the main point, he argued, was that "only through suffering can we achieve perfection."[17] It was through obedience that Jesus fulfilled the will of the Father, obedience that included suffering and death. Kargel continued: "The deeper the suffering in the test of the glorious One, the more evident was His steady obedience and constant fidelity to the will of the Father. And when He reached the supreme degree of obedience which demanded death, God truly put His life on the altar. His obedience led to purity, as gold refined in the fire, and it was perfect. Only in this way and in no other can we be perfect. Know this, dear children of God."[18] But Kargel did not suggest that the believer achieved this obedience, this way of the cross, through human strength. In Kargel's view, the cross was related to the ministry of the Holy Spirit. When a sinner begins to "pine after the Lamb of God," this is due to the activity of the Spirit. He writes in typical Holiness language: "Soon a breaking and brokenness will take place at the cross and will echo the words of the song 'my weary soul has found peace at the cross.'"[19] It is, he says, the true knowledge of the vastness of sin that allows someone to understand the work of the cross.[20] Kargel's evangelicalism involved conversionism and crucicentrism and both, for him, were infused with a powerful experience of the Spirit.

Ivan Kargel was also profoundly biblicist. He used the Bible as the basis for several of his works. His books *Light from the Shadows of Future Blessing, Ruth the Moabitess*,[21] *Commentary on the Revelation*

15. Kargel, "Xristos Osvyashhenie Nashe," 107.
16. Ibid., 105–7.
17. Ibid., 107.
18. Ibid.
19. Kargel, "V Kakom Ty Otnoshenii k Duxu Svyatomu?" 118.
20. Kargel, "Grex kak Zlo vsex Zol v ehtom Mire," 6.

21. *Ruf' Moavityanka, ili Mezhi moi proshli po prekrasnym Mestam*. The extended title includes the words "the lines have fallen for me in pleasant places" which are taken from Psalm 16:6. This book will be discussed in chapter 7 in the section concerning Kargel's publishing efforts.

of *Saint John*,[22] and *Law of the Spirit of Life* are verse-by-verse explanations of the biblical text. He did, in areas such as his treatment of the Tabernacle, have a tendency to allegorize sections of the Old Testament, which points to a belief that hidden within the literal words are deeper meanings for the Church. The influence of the Brethren is important to note. In the introduction to *Light from the Shadows of Future Blessing*, Kargel speaks of his use of two Brethren writers, C. H. Mackintosh and Henry W. Soltau.[23] Mackintosh (often CHM) was one of the most widely-read authors of the Brethren movement and, according to Grass, "mediated Darbyite theology to the wider church."[24] Of Kargel's four commentaries, *Ruth the Moabitess* and *Light from the Shadows of Future Blessing* are verse-by-verse, highly allegorical explanations, while his commentaries on the New Testament books of Revelation and Romans are also verse-by-verse, but they do not contain allegory. When Kargel speaks of the Word of God, the Bible, he warns that no one should ever come to it as an expert on a biblical passage and think, "Ah, I already know this." He believed that the Holy Spirit could "add new revelation"—in the sense, it seems, of new insight—to the reader of the passage of Scripture.[25] Here again, experience was crucial.

It was not only in his use of the Bible but also in the statements he made about it that Kargel's approach was classically evangelical. Kuznetsova writes: "His approach to dealing with Scripture combined the classical Reformation high view of the Scripture, clear, self-explanatory, and whole (continuity between the Testaments); the Pietistic call for personal Bible study and the immediate practical outcome; the Anabaptist stress on obedience; and the Brethren typology and interpretation of future events."[26] The Bible was the source of spiritual truth for Kargel. This can be seen in his Confession of Faith of 1913. This confession will be discussed in chapter 8. The section regarding the Bible is important in understanding his views and is also a typical

---

22. *Tolkovatel' Otkrovenieya Svyatogo Ioanna Bogoslova.*

23. Puzynin has footnoted an extensive list of books published by these authors. See Puzynin, "The Tradition of the Gospel Christians," 190 n. 136.

24. Grass, *Gathering to His Name*, 151.

25. Kargel, "Xristos Osvyashhenie Nashe," 94.

26. Kuznetsova, "Early Russian Evangelicals," 408.

example of the rest of the document in that nearly every phrase is supported with a verse from the Bible.

> II. Concerning the Word of God
>
> We believe that all canonical books of the Old and New Testament as represented in the entire Bible, or the Holy Scripture (excluding the Apocrypha), are inspired by the Holy Spirit (2 Peter 1:21) and given by the Lord (Psalms 148:8–9), as indispensable, [unique] (Proverbs 30:6; Mark 7:13), [and a] completely sufficient source of knowledge [of the God of our salvation] (Hebrews 1:1–2; John 5:39; 20:31), and His will concerning our faith (Philippians 1:27) and life (Acts 20:32; 2 Timothy 3:15–17).[27]

To Kargel, the Bible was not a source of information about the faith of the Church, but a book that brought a person to know God and his will. He described the Word of God as necessary to abide in Christ and be sanctified. When explaining how to use the Word of God, he spoke of "pure milk" which allows believers to "grow spiritually."[28] Later, he added that, "It is necessary for us to find time daily to investigate the Word, allowing it to influence us, and let us rejoice in the power it contains."[29] The Word of God is the guide that keeps believers from "wandering in doctrine."[30] But the guide was not the literal words contained in the text for Kargel. He explained that for many years he used the Bible "as only a book of texts" and found that he was searching the text in order to teach others. After a time of "many tears and begging," he realized that he must first "apply the texts" to himself, and only then he could teach others their meaning.[31]

Finally, activism was clearly a mark of the spiritual life of Ivan Kargel. He was concerned that the gospel should be clearly proclaimed to all. In his entire travelling ministry, evangelism was a primary focus. When Kargel travelled by train, he would pass through the wagons, handing out New Testaments. Once a *starets* (a spiritual guide in the Russian Orthodox Church) was curious and traced the Bibles that people were reading on the train back to Kargel. He asked Kargel the

---

27. Kargel, "Confession of Faith of the Evangelical Christians-Baptists," 154.
28. Kargel, "Xristos Osvyashhenie Nashe," 91.
29. Ibid., 98.
30. Ibid., 92.
31. Ibid., 93.

reason why he had been indiscriminately handing them out. Kargel told the man: "My dear sir, I wish that others would find in this book what I have found. Only in Jesus is holiness, in Him alone is eternal life which does not begin with the grave [death] but immediately when we believe in Him."[32] Kargel believed that eternal life was not found in the Word of God as a book, but that Jesus was found there.

Kargel was also concerned for the physical wellbeing of prisoners in the prison systems of Siberia and the Caucasus. Although he followed the Brethren in a number of his biblical interests, and although he placed great emphasis on holiness, he never allowed his more inwardly-directed interests to overshadow his practical concerns.

The four evangelical distinctives were prominent in Kargel's theology, but he also took up other themes. One theme that was prominent in his thinking was the Second Advent of Christ. N. J. Poysti, a Russian/American publisher and pastor of the mid-twentieth century, recalled his early personal experience with Kargel, when Kargel returned from the Grand Duchy of Finland and preached at the Lieven Palace. Kargel's book, *What is Your Relationship to the Holy Spirit?*[33] was republished by N. J. Poysti and in the introduction to the book he suggests that Kargel's favorite subject was the "second coming of Christ" and that his second favorite subject was "the infilling of the Holy Spirit." Poysti goes on to state: "While still an unconverted youth I was much impressed by [Kargel's] preaching when I heard him expound . . . I always imagined him as being an apostle or some Old Testament prophet as he stood before us, serious of mien and profoundly earnest."[34] Kargel's teaching on the coming of Christ was similarly effective. Poysti continues:

> When he spoke about the coming of the Lord, he spoke sensitively and seriously. He frequently repeated the phrase, "I expect any day my glorified Lord." Only after my conversion did I begin to feast on his words. His preaching caused me to

32. J. G. Kargel to Dear Friend and Brother in Christ [V. A. Pashkov], 12 May 1886, 2/13/049, Pashkov Papers.

33. "V Kakom Otnoshenii Ty k Duxu Svyatomu?" This book will be discussed later in this chapter in the section concerning Kargel's publishing efforts.

34. Poysti, "We Publish a Very Important Book," 24; Kargel, *V Kakom Ty Otnoshenii k Duxu Svyatomu?* 6. Wheaton College's Special Collections possesses a rare Russian copy of this book with a four-page introduction in Russian written by N. I. Pejsti (N. J. Poysti).

determine to follow Christ and obey his words and to have room for nothing else in my heart or mouth. The return of Christ was Kargel's favorite theme. His second favorite theme was the Holy Spirit. He deeply desired the children of God to be controlled by and baptized in the Holy Spirit.[35]

N. J. Poysti also speaks about Kargel's stress on the filling of the Holy Spirit. This theme became controversial among evangelicals in the early twentieth century through the rise of Pentecostalism. Despite Pentecostalism's evangelical roots, it was not fully accepted into Keswick circles. In 1907, Alexander Boddy, Vicar of All Saints', Monkwearmouth, Sunderland, an attendee at Keswick and later a Pentecostal leader, wrote *Pentecost for England*, in an unsuccessful attempt to persuade Keswick leaders to embrace Pentecostal teachings.[36] Often evangelicals objected to the Pentecostal advocacy of speaking in tongues. In all Kargel's writings, there is no direct mention of speaking in tongues. There is a reference to prayer "without words" in the *Law of the Spirit of Life*.[37] He does not, however, seem to be concerned with *glossolalia* in any of his published works. There is, however, another work which Karetnikova and Kuznetsova have credited to Kargel titled *The Outpouring of the Holy Spirit and the Pentecostal Movement*.[38] This work is a tirade against the Pentecostal Movement and thought to possibly be a removed chapter from Kargels book *What is Your*

---

35. Kargel, *V Kakom Ty Otnoshenii k Duxu Svyatomu?* 6–7.
36. Randall, *Evangelical Experiences*, 206.
37. Kargel, *Zakon Duxa Zhizni*, 190.
38. "Izliyanie Duxa Svyatogo i Pyatidesyatnicheskoe Dvizhenie." A photocopy of this chapter was given to me by Marina S. Karetnikova. At the time, she was unsure of the origins of the chapter but thought that it may have originally been the third chapter of Kargel's book, *What is Your Relationship to the Holy Spirit?* The chapter is fifty-six typeset pages, which contains the words "Chapter 3" in the title, begins with a preface, but has no scripture verse included after the title. On the final page is the beginning of the next chapter which contains the words "Chapter 4," the title of "Filled with the Spirit," a verse of scripture, and five paragraphs of its next chapter. The average chapter size of *What is Your Relationship to the Holy Spirit?* is approximately one-third the length of this chapter. None of the book's chapters contain a preface and each of its chapters begins with a reference verse. However, the first five paragraphs of the third chapter of *What is Your Relationship to the Holy Spirit?* exactly matches the wording at the end of the typeset copy except that the typeset copy lists them as chapter 4. Karetnikova published the chapter in 2004 claiming that it was the missing or possibly removed chapter from Kargel's *What is Your Relationship to the Holy Spirit?* See Karetnikova, *Almanax po Istorii Russkogo Baptisma, vypusk 3*, 5, 11–61; "Izliyanie Duxa Svyatogo i Pyatidesyatnicheskoe Dvizhenie," [IBTS].

Relationship to the Holy Spirit? There are several references in the document to dates and people that match the life of Kargel. There are many references to "Brother K" in the third person, which was a method of Kargel's, though rarely employed. Also, it does convey some of the broad themes found in the other writings of Kargel.[39]

However, there are reasons to doubt Kargel's authorship. The text tends towards gossip, which is most unlike Kargel. Second, it pits Pentecostals against the Baptist denomination, and such denominationalism was foreign to Kargel. Third, although it contains scriptural references, Scripture is not used to the extent that is the case in most of Kargel's other works. Fourth, the writing lacks the personal and spiritual warmth that characterizes Kargel's theology. Finally, the text mentions an article from *Evangelist* which was published in 1928.[40] Kargel's *What is Your Relationship to the Holy Spirit?* was advertised for sale as early as 1912[41] making it highly unlikely that this text was one of the original chapters.

Throughout Kargel's work, the sources from which he draws are clearly within the evangelical tradition. Kargel used both German and English commentaries. The German authors that he used most often were Martin Luther, Otto Stockmayer, Frédéric Louis Godet, and Ernest G. Wolterdorff. The English-speaking authors included Brethren writers such as Mackintosh[42] and Soltau as well as renowned preachers such as Spurgeon and Moody. It is evident that the Brethren approach appealed to him. As Grass indicates, the way in which the Brethren studied Scripture was "by means of Bible readings which worked through a passage or book of Scripture," and that they "objected to theological systems which excluded true believers from fellowship."[43] Kargel also drew from David Brown of the Jamieson-Fausset-Brown commentaries.[44] Among the Keswick writers he appreciated were Andrew Murray from South Africa and Evan Hopkins, Keswick's foremost theological thinker in its early period. Kargel liked

39. Kuznetsova, "Early Russian Evangelicals," 323–25.

40. Ibid., 323.

41. *Gost'*, November 1912, 24.

42. For more on Kargel's use of Mackintosh see Kuznetsova, "Early Russian Evangelicals," 368–77.

43. Grass, *Gathering to His Name*, 171.

44. This commentary on the entire Bible was originally written in 1871 and reflects a conservative, evangelical and Reformed theological perspective.

to work with a variety of evangelical authors, which was consistent with his inclusive evangelicalism. In his work on the Old Testament person of Enoch, he compared the German, Russian, and English translations of Genesis 5:24.[45] He does not appear to have used the original biblical languages, but relied on secondary sources for insights. At times it must have been hard for him to find the books he needed, but in writing *Light from the Shadows of Future Blessing*, for example, he used the libraries of Lieven, Pashkov, and Sister Kruze.[46] Kargel's evangelical connections aided him in his work of advocating evangelical theology.

BAPTIST AND EVANGELICAL CHRISTIAN CONNECTIONS

To what extent, in the period being examined in this chapter, did Kargel maintain his Baptist connections? Several writers have claimed that Kargel travelled to the European Baptist Conference in Berlin in 1903 as a representative of the Russian Baptist Union and that he also travelled to the Baptist World Congress in London in 1905, out of which came the Baptist World Alliance (BWA). These suggestions are found in an article in 1957 by Yakov Ivanovich Zhidkov.[47] It was at meetings in the Lieven home that Zhidkov heard Kargel.[48] Later Zhidkov wrote about how, in the winter of 1902, he heard Kargel preach on the third chapter of the Gospel of John, about Nicodemus's conversion, a sermon which was the "turning point" in Zhidkov's life.[49] He came to faith in Christ and was baptized in Saint Petersburg in 1903.[50] Zhidkov has, therefore, been regarded as a primary source for information about Kargel. Other sources also speak about Kargel's international Baptist involvement. The appendix to *The History of Evangelical Christians-Baptists in the USSR* (HEC-B) lists various data about Kargel and states that he attended the 1903 Berlin meetings as a delegate. It does not mention that he attended the 1905 London

---

45. Kargel, "Vetxozavetnye Proobrazy," 268–69.
46. Karetnikova, "Ivan Veniaminovich Kargel," 684.
47. Zhidkov, "Na Putyax Edinstva," 61.
48. He also served as a Vice-President of the BWA and served on the central committee of the World Council of Churches.
49. Zhidkov, "Nemnogo o Sebe," 29.
50. Ibid. Zhidkov does not specifically state that it was Kargel who baptized him.

Congress.⁵¹ The appendix footnotes a 1979 *Bratsky Vestnik*⁵² article, which is a short biography of Kargel written by V. M. Koval'kov and M. P. Chernopyatov. In this biography, they state that Kargel was a delegate at the 1903 Berlin meetings and at the 1905 London Congress.⁵³

There are some problems, however, with this data. It seems that in 1903 F. P. Balihin was sent as a representative of Baptists in Russia to participate in three Christian conferences: the Evangelical Alliance conference in Bad Blankenburg, Germany; a Baptist conference in Berlin; and a Baptist conference in Derby, England.⁵⁴ It was assumed by the Russian writers that the 1903 Berlin conference was an all-Europe Baptist conference, when, in fact, the first all-Europe Baptist conference did not take place until 1908 in Berlin. Of the approximately 1,200 delegates at the 1908 conference, about half were from Britain. The Russian Baptist Union sent nearly one-hundred people, who "spoke glowingly of growing Baptist influence" internationally.⁵⁵ It is possible that Kargel was in this larger group of one-hundred in 1908. The *Bratsky Vestnik* article by V. M. Koval'kov and M. P. Chernopyatov states that Kargel was with Balihin in Berlin (in 1903) and then was in London in 1905 and goes on to state that Balihin and Kargel returned from London to tell the Russian believers of the "great blessings of God. The Russian Union of Baptists has been accepted into the World Union of Baptists."⁵⁶ Kargel's attendance at the 1905 Congress is reported in a biography of Kargel written in Finnish by Osmo Pöysti,⁵⁷ and by Marina Karetnikova in her work.⁵⁸ However, the proceedings of the Congress, which contain reports on Baptist work in Russia from Baron Woldemar Üxküll and D. I. Mazaev, do not mention Kargel,⁵⁹ nor is Kargel in the list of Congress attendees.⁶⁰

51. *Istoriya Evangel'skix Xristian-Baptistov*, 530.
52. *Bratsky Vestnik* [The Fraternal Herald or The Brotherly Bulletin].
53. Koval'kov and Chernopyatov, "Ivan Veniaminovich Kargel," 48.
54. *Istoriya Evangel'skix Xristian-Baptistov*, 132–33.
55. Briggs, "From 1905 to the End of the First World War," 33. See also Green, *Crossing the Boundaries*, 2–3.
56. Koval'kov and Chernopyatov, "Ivan Veniaminovich Kargel," 48.
57. Osmo Pöysti, "Ivan Veniaminovitsh Kargel," para. 18.
58. Karetnikova, *Almanax po Istorii Russkogo Baptisma*, vypusk 4, 58.
59. *Baptist World Congress, London, July 11–19, 1905: Record of Proceedings*, 7–8, 182–85.
60. Ibid., xiv–xxviii.

HEC-B apparently found the evidence for Kargel's presence at the 1905 Congress lacking; it did not list Kargel as attending. Those listed are Dei Mazaev, V. V. Ivanov, and V. G. Pavlov.[61] Those mentioned during the 1905 London Congress by Üxküll and Mazaev as being influential in Russia were Count Bobrinsky, Pashkov, Korff, Ivanov, Pavlov, and Johann Wieler.[62] It is possible that Kargel could have attended this Congress without the Baptist Union's sponsorship, but this is unlikely. Yet, on the other hand, Ya. I. Zhidkov, who had been deeply influenced by Kargel, wrote in 1957 that, "it was hard for me to hear and feel the strong words of my confessor, I. V. Kargel, who kept to his extreme Anabaptist views, and after he returned from the First World Congress of Baptists in London in 1905, gave us a report in which he told us that he regretted that he had gone there because during the congress there was little that was spiritual, and it operated more and more by decisions in the flesh."[63] Zhidkov's words have become a well-known statement that attributes Anabaptist views to Kargel. Zhidkov added that he and other young people challenged the conclusions made by Kargel by turning to "what was printed in *Bratsky Vestnik* by V. G. Pavlov in 1906." The group determined that Pavlov's positive report "more or less objectively presented all that happened at the Congress."[64]

Zhidkov's mention of Kargel's Anabaptist views may be seen as a reference to his Mennonite Brethren connections. It may also be seen as an attempt by Zhidkov to explain why Kargel would be critical of the Baptist Congress. The report by Zhidkov has a ring of authenticity. Kargel's criticisms of things that were done "in the flesh"—as opposed to done spiritually—were well known. But it is possible that Kargel was commenting on some other Baptist events or was speaking from second-hand information about the 1905 Congress. Zhidkov was young in 1905, and presumably did not know the complexities of the Baptist world. In the early 1900s Kargel was teaching in a Bible program that was established in the Lieven home and he may have made statements that compared Baptists unfavorably with the Saint Petersburg Evangelicals. It is also significant that throughout this

61. *Istoriya Evangel'skix Xristian-Baptistov*, 142.
62. *Baptist World Congress, London, July 11–19, 1905*, 182–85.
63. Zhidkov, "Na Putyax Edinstva," 61.
64. Ibid.

article Zhidkov praised Ivan Prokhanov for his unshakeable energy and his vision to unite the Baptist Union with the Evangelical Christian Union in Russia. Zhidkov also spoke in this article of Prokhanov's publishing and writing efforts and his oversight of the Saint Petersburg Evangelicals' congregation where he (Zhidkov) was a student and a co-worker.[65] Although Zhidkov was indebted to Kargel, the older leader, he was more inspired by the younger Prokhanov, and this may have colored his recollections. Zhidkov would eventually take over the leadership of the Evangelical Christian Union and would later lead the All-Union Council of Evangelical Christians-Baptists.

In seeking to assess Kargel's Baptist connections in this early twentieth-century period, it is important to examine some of the tensions among the Saint Petersburg Evangelicals after Kargel's return from the Grand Duchy of Finland. Initially, when Kargel returned, many in the Saint Petersburg Evangelical community looked once more to him for leadership.[66] Kargel was cautious, since by this time that evangelical community had experienced a number of internal conflicts. In 1890 P. S. Bezzubov had openly criticized Kargel for what Bezzubov felt was a rejection of the original Pashkovite ideals. But for Kargel, providing leadership for the group which he had been in a close relationship for over two decades was natural. In 1903, however, six or seven young people decided to leave the Saint Petersburg Evangelical congregation that Kargel was leading. The divisive issues, as they had been on many occasions, were baptism and an open Table. The group that broke away wished to emphasize Baptist distinctives.[67] There were echoes of what had happened in 1890. In late 1904, Ivan Prokhanov returned to Russia from a two-year trip to America. He quickly reconnected with his friends among the Saint Petersburg Evangelicals, whom he had known since the 1880s. One of these, V. P. Stepanov, was contemplating associating himself with the small group of people who had broken with Kargel. With some encouragement from Prokhanov, Stepanov began to lead this group.[68]

Ivan Prokhanov, like Ivan Kargel, had important connections within Baptist life, as well as within the Saint Petersburg Evangelical

65. Zhidkov, "Na Putyax Edinstva," 52–69.
66. *Istoriya Evangel'skix Xristian-Baptistov*, 149.
67. Ibid., 149–50.
68. *Istoriya Evangel'skix Xristian-Baptistov*, 149.

community. Years of travel had offered him many opportunities to make international links. In 1895 Prokhanov had moved from Saint Petersburg to England, to study at the well-known Bristol Baptist College. It was Baedeker who, although not a Baptist, recommended that he study there.[69] It was during his years in England that Prokhanov learned about different streams of Baptist life and how the Particular Baptists and the General Baptists, despite their differences, had recently been able to come together.[70] He learned that there were significant numbers of Baptists in England who believed in open communion.[71] After one year at Bristol Baptist College, he took up study in New College, a Congregational College in London. He wrote: "The reason for such a change was my desire to come into contact with other denominations. I desired to gain as comprehensive a view of all the Protestant Christian denominations of Western Europe as might be possible."[72] Prokhanov went on to do just that studying in Paris, Berlin, and Hamburg.

Prokhanov also made connections with Evangelical Alliance leaders. Despite having contacts within British and German Baptist life, Prokhanov, in a way that was reminiscent of Kargel's development, displayed a desire to practice interdenominational tolerance rather than to align himself with one Union. At an Evangelical Alliance Conference in London in 1896 celebrating fifty years of Alliance life, Baedeker and Prokhanov spoke about the situation in Russia and urged the value of representations to the Tsar about the persecution of evangelicals.[73] In 1906, Prokhanov began to print *Xristianin* [*The Christian*],[74] which was named and patterned after *The Christian*, a weekly non-denominational evangelical paper published in London. Prokhanov's journal translated articles by leading English-speaking evangelicals, such as Andrew Murray and R. A. Torrey, from the

---

69. Prokhanoff, *In the Cauldron of Russia*, 97. The Bristol Baptist College was founded in 1679 and is the oldest continuing Baptist college in the world. For a history of Bristol Baptist College see Moon, *Education for Ministry*.

70. See Payne, *The Baptist Union*, 127–55 for a discussion of the process.

71. Briggs, "Evangelical Ecumenism," 166.

72. Prokhanoff, *In the Cauldron of Russia*, 97.

73. *Jubilee of the Evangelical Alliance: Proceedings of the Tenth International Conference Held in London, June-July, 1896* (London: J. F. Shaw, 1897), 307–13, as cited in Randall, "Eastern European Baptists and the Evangelical Alliance," 32.

74. *Xristianin* [*The Christian*].

London-based journal. It also provided a channel for writers such as Prokhanov himself and Kargel to spread their views of evangelical Christianity throughout Russia.[75] Despite the shared vision of the two men, however, there were tensions. Prokhanov assumed leadership of the group in Saint Petersburg that had broken with Kargel and moved them in a new direction. In line with common Baptist thinking, Prokhanov encouraged this group to engage in "active participation in public life,"[76] which was not Kargel's approach. The lines between the Saint Petersburg Evangelicals and Baptists were not clearly drawn in this period, but for a time, as a result of this approach, Prokhanov became more acceptable to Baptists than was Kargel.

NEW EVANGELICAL INITIATIVES

Although Kargel concentrated in the early twentieth century on developments in Saint Petersburg, some wider ministry continued. In 1901 he made a trip to Siberia with Baron Paul Nikolayevich Nicolay, who was a leader of the student movement in Russia. In 1899 John Mott, chairman of the executive committee of the Student Volunteer Movement for Foreign Missions, who later presided at the World Missionary Conference in Edinburgh in 1910, visited Russia and met Nicolay and Kargel. Nicolay was described by Mott's biographer as "a Finnish nobleman and pietistic Lutheran who had been deeply touched by the Keswick spirit."[77] The young Baron had been affected by Kargel and other Pashkovites, and meetings about the student movement in Russia took place at the Lieven home. Mott saw Russia as "the most needy and difficult student field of all the world."[78] Nicolay was fluent in English, French, German, Finnish, and Swedish, and it is possible that he may have accompanied Kargel on their trip to Siberia in 1901 as a translator. The main intention of the trip seems to have been to visit prisons, in line with the commission that Kargel had taken on from Baedeker. This was the last such trip that Kargel undertook. For a

---

75. Puzynin, "The Tradition of the Gospel Christians," 153–62.

76. Skopina, "Iz Biografii I. V. Kargelya." Skopina's use of the term "public life" implies political activity.

77. Hopkins, *John R. Mott*, 250.

78. Ruth Rouse, *The World's Student Christian Federation*, 78, 161–63, as cited in Hopkins, *John R. Mott*, 251.

time Kargel turned his main attention to leading the Saint Petersburg Evangelical congregation that met in the Lieven home.[79]

Kargel, however, was unwilling to organize the wider evangelical movement in Saint Petersburg into a formally structured body. His central concern remained the encouragement of a deeper spirituality. Prokhanov, by contrast, was a natural organizer. The plans he conceived included the formation of a large Russian Christian Youth Movement and initiatives in Bible distribution.[80] In January 1905, as part of his larger vision, Prokhanov announced that a "Union of Evangelical Churches" would be formed.[81] A key element in this initiative was the group of young people who had separated from Kargel. Youth meetings were held in Saint Petersburg and then in Moscow.[82] As he sought to further his dream of widespread Bible distribution, Prokhanov approached the Russian Baptist Union's annual conference about co-operating in a biennial Bible program to be shared—he hoped—by the Russian, Ukrainian, German, and Latvian Baptists, and by the Mennonites.[83] Prokhanov held the first Congress of the "Evangelical Union of Christian Youth" in Moscow in May 1908.[84] The numbers were small, but influential younger leaders were present. One year later they gathered for the second congress, with representatives present from twenty-eight fellowships, some Baptist and some Evangelical Christian.[85]

The political and religious climate in Russia dramatically changed in 1905. The "Act of Tolerance" was issued during Easter time 1905 by Tsar Nicholas II. The act granted religious freedom for all citizens of Russia and in the light of this Pobedonostsev resigned from all his posts. The "Imperial Manifesto" that followed on 17 October 1905 essentially turned the Russian monarchy into a constitutional mon-

---

79. J. G. Kargel to "My honored, beloved friend and brother in Christ" [V. A. Pashkov], 7 June 1901, 2/13/111, Pashkov Papers; Lieven, *Eine Saat*, 63–64.

80. Prokhanoff, *In the Cauldron of Russia*, 106. Also see *Istoriya Evangel'skix Xristian-Baptistov*, 148.

81. *Istoriya Evangel'skix Xristian-Baptistov*, 150; also see Prokhanoff, *In the Cauldron of Russia*, 131.

82. Prokhanoff, *In the Cauldron of Russia*, 132.

83. *Istoriya Evangel'skix Xristian-Baptistov*, 156.

84. Ibid., 140.

85. Ibid., 150.

archy[86] by granting the State Duma final authority over the creation of any new laws.[87] The Imperial Manifesto "conceded liberty of conscience, freedom of speech, freedom to hold meetings, [and] freedom of association" to "those classes who are now completely deprived of electoral rights."[88] Among other freedoms, it permitted the registration of non-Orthodox expressions of Christianity among Russian people. Taking advantage of the October Manifesto, Prokhanov registered a congregation of evangelicals in Saint Petersburg on 26 November 1908, taking the name "Saint Petersburg Community of Evangelical Christians." On 6 January 1909, the congregation was formally organized, with an elected eldership structure, forty members and ten candidates for membership.[89] Yakov Zhidkov served as assistant to Prokhanov.[90] Following this initiative, Kargel's congregation was registered. Prokhanov then registered the "All-Russian Evangelical Christian Union" (ECU).[91] Irina Skopina states that Kargel signed the registration documents with Prokhanov.[92] Her statement could well be true since Kargel had for over thirty years been a recognized minister in Saint Petersburg, although with the German Baptists.

There were at this point varied evangelical fellowships of Russian believers—not including registered denominations such as the Lutherans, Baptists, Mennonites, Molokans, and Methodists—across Russia, for example in Sevastopol, Yalta, Ekaterinoslav, Konotop, Melitopol, and Kiev.[93] Until 1905 none of the independent evangelical

---

86. Crankshaw, *The Shadow of the Winter Palace*, 353.

87. For details concerning the events leading up to and resulting from the October Manifesto see Crankshaw, *The Shadow of the Winter Palace*, 342–59.

88. Ibid., 354.

89. *Istoriya Evangel'skix Xristian-Baptistov*, 151.

90. Durasoff, *The Russian Protestants*, 56.

91. The English translations of Prokhanov's organizations vary. The name of the original group is often translated as the "Union of the Evangelical Churches." Later, when the group was fully registered, it was given the name "All-Russian Evangelical Christian Union." See Prokhanoff, *In the Cauldron of Russia*, 132, 151. Others have preferred the English translation "Union of Evangelical Christians" (Coleman and Brandenburg), or "Union of Gospel Christians" (Puzynin), which are both valid translations. For ease of reference and historical continuity, I will use the name "Evangelical Christian Union" or ECU, as used by Steeves, Sawatsky, and Prokhanov.

92. Skopina, "Iz Biografii I. V. Kargelya," 696.

93. *Istoriya Evangel'skix Xristian-Baptistov*, 153.

congregations had been able to register.⁹⁴ With Prokhanov and Kargel's registration of the All-Russian Evangelical Christian Union in 1909, an umbrella organization was provided for these congregations. Soon other evangelical fellowships began to take advantage of the new laws and the initiatives taken by Prokhanov, taking the name "Evangelical Christian" as their identity and joining with the new Union. The Moscow Evangelical Christian fellowship, for example, was registered in 1909. The First All-Russian Congress of Evangelical Christians met in Saint Petersburg in September 1909, with twenty-four delegates from eighteen churches and over thirty visitors.⁹⁵ Prokhanov was elected as the chairman, and remained in this post until his death in 1935. At the first congress, it was explained that the new ECU would be only consultative in character and would rely on brotherly counsel instead of executive power to resolve issues. The geographical scope of the first congress was huge and there were also attempts to reach out interdenominationally within Russia.⁹⁶

At the first (1909) and second (1911) All-Russian Conferences of the Evangelical Christian Union, Kargel was not listed among the elected officials.⁹⁷ He was overshadowed for a time by the dynamic Prokhanov. Under Prokhanov's visionary leadership, his newly registered congregation grew and was known as the First Evangelical Christian congregation in Saint Petersburg, with Kargel's congregation known as the Second Evangelical Christian congregation. Princess Lieven recalled: "I don't know exactly when it happened, but one day we heard that Prokhanov's church now called itself the first, and that of brother Kargel was to be the second. So they went on living and working side by side."⁹⁸ The two congregations held many things in common, but Kargel was committed to an open Table while Prokhanov, though willing to accept an open Table, emphasized the baptism of believers.⁹⁹ By the third Congress of Evangelical Christians, however,

---

94. These were mainly fellowships connected with the Saint Petersburg Evangelicals, Stundists, or Stundo-baptists.

95. *Istoriya Evangel'skix Xristian-Baptistov*, 155.

96. This suggestion would have been warmly welcomed by Kargel and others interested in the formation of a broad Evangelical Alliance, but there were problems because it came from Prokhanov who was a powerful and dominating force.

97. *Istoriya Evangel'skix Xristian-Baptistov*, 155–57.

98. Lieven, *Eine Saat*, 93.

99. Lieven, "Kolybel' Evangel'skogo Dvizheniya v Peterburge," 73.

held in Saint Petersburg in December 1911, the separation of Kargel and Prokhanov had been dealt with and Kargel was elected vice-chair of the ECU.[100] In 1913, fresh persecution against the evangelicals began, and Prokhanov and Kargel wrote a letter to the State *Duma* regarding the legal status of the Evangelical Christians.[101] Kargel served at various times as vice-chair of the ECU. He and Prokhanov often led the closing communion services together.[102]

The ECU gained increasing support, despite the fear of some that its structures would cause local fellowships to lose some of their freedom.[103] As Russia developed ways to register religious groups, it became important to be part of a larger organization. Thus, the Brethren model of minimal structures and of house churches, which had sustained the Pashkovites, was becoming untenable. In the early years of the ECU, Prokhanov did struggle to attract some of those who had been committed Pashkovites. The ECU can be seen as seeking to forge an identity that was somewhere between the Pashkovite/ Brethren spirit on the one hand, and the Russian Baptist Union on the other.[104]

The religious freedoms of 1905 were restricted in subsequent years in various areas of the Russian Empire. Some of the local Russian evangelical congregations did not register as ECU churches or as Baptist churches and those that chose to remain outside of a registered group, for whatever reason, were to experience difficult times in the coming years. Many independent fellowships were to be destroyed by the Soviet pressure, although several remained as isolated house churches.[105]

The ECU Congresses continued to take place throughout the Russian Revolutionary period, meeting under Prokhanov's leadership, until 1921,[106] when they were interrupted by the police and Prokhanov

---

100. *Istoriya Evangel'skix Xristian-Baptistov*, 157.
101. Skopina, "Iz Biografii I. V. Kargelya," 696.
102. *Istoriya Evangel'skix Xristian-Baptistov*, 188.
103. See Steeves, "The Russian Baptist Union," 68–73.
104. For a fuller discussion of these issues see Steeves, "The Russian Baptist Union," 87–90, 87 n. 1, 88 n. 4, 89 n. 1.
105. Sawatsky, *Soviet Evangelicals*, 36.
106. In 1919, the Congress of the "Evangelical Union of Christian Youth" met simultaneously with the Sixth All Russian Congress of Evangelical Christians, which was held in Saint Petersburg.

was sent to prison for several months.[107] The last time Kargel served the ECU as an elected official was at the ninth Congress of Evangelical Christians, held in November 1923, when he was seventy-four years old.[108] But even after 1923 he was asked to address the ECU during their Congresses.[109]

Despite its claims of being an interdenominational organization, the ECU was always led by Ivan Prokhanov and Russian Baptist leaders such as Mazaev were not invited on to its Council, although Kargel himself never severed his Baptist links. The Evangelical Christian Union and the Russian Baptist Union maintained separate links with the wider Baptist world. It has been stated that both unions became members of the Baptist World Alliance at its foundation in 1905 in London.[110] However, the All-Russian Evangelical Christian Union was not founded until 1909. Prokhanov is not mentioned in the *Record of Proceedings* of the 1905 London meetings.[111] It is clear that large Russian delegations participated in the BWA's 1908 meetings in Berlin,[112] and by the BWA's Second Congress, held in Philadelphia in 1911, both Russian Unions were members. Dei Mazaev was given an opportunity to address the general session in London in 1905,[113] and V. G. Pavlov represented Russia at the Inaugural Meeting of the BWA,[114] but it was Ivan Prokhanov who was elected as a vice-president of the BWA in 1911,[115] a post that he retained until 1928. The link between the BWA and the baptistic work in Russia was largely through the ECU. The Russian Baptist Union did not have a BWA vice-president until after their merger with the Evangelical Christian Union. Yakov Zhidkov,[116] originally a leader in the Evangelical Christian Union, who

---

107. Prokhanoff, *In the Cauldron of Russia*, 192.

108. Ibid., 204.

109. Ibid., 205.

110. Kahle, *Evangelische Christen in Russland und der Sowjetunion*, 10–12, as cited in Sawatsky, *Soviet Evangelicals*, 359.

111. *Baptist World Congress, London, July 11–19, 1905*.

112. Briggs, "From 1905 to the End of the First World War," 23, 33, 35–36.

113. *Baptist World Congress, London, July 11–19, 1905*, 184–85.

114. Ibid., 321. Baron Woldemar Üxküll of Estonia, which was then part of the Russian Empire, served as a BWA vice-president, from 1905 until 1911.

115. *Baptist World Congress, Philadelphia, June 19–25, 1911*, xv.

116. Under his presidency, the AUCEC-B broke off contact with the BWA in 1947. See Sawatsky, *Soviet Evangelicals*, 360–62. For a discussion of Russian rep-

served as the first President of the All-Union Council of Evangelical Christians-Baptists (AUCEC-B), was elected as a vice-president of the BWA in 1955.[117]

Within the ECU, ordination remained informal, and Prokhanov served within the BWA without being an ordained minister. The ECU approach, however, changed in 1924, when Prokhanov travelled to Czechoslovakia and was ordained on 1 April 1924 in Prague by the ministers of the Czechoslovak Baptist Union.[118] It had been a long-time desire of his to receive ordination from representatives of the pre-Lutheran Czech Reformation, which was, in his mind, the purest reformation.[119] Beginning in 1924, Prokhanov began to ordain other ECU leaders.[120] Kargel took part in some of these ordinations, which represented a change in his practice.[121] One example of Prokhanov and Kargel ordaining together was the ordination of Mixail Akimovich Orlov, who became a leader in the ECU churches in Moscow and Saint Petersburg. He encountered the Evangelical Christians in 1908 at the Lieven home. He was a delegate to the 1923 Baptist World Alliance meetings in Stockholm and in 1924 was ordained by Prokhanov and Kargel. He went on to be vice-president of the AUCEC-B in 1944.[122] Another example was Yakov Nikitich Xodyush, who came from Dnepropetrovsk. In 1909 he attended a Bible seminary in Berlin for three years and in October 1914 was ordained by Kargel, Prokhanov, K. P. Petrov, and Johannes Reimer and was then commissioned to work in the Far East of Russia.[123] Xodyush returned to Dnepropetrovsk in 1931 and later became chairman of a regional department of the AUCEC-B. ECU practices gradually became closer to those of Baptists. Kargel's involvement in the process signals that

---

resentation in the European Baptist Federation see Jones, *The European Baptist Federation*, 236–37.

117. Pierard, *Baptists Together in Christ*, 321–23.

118. *Istoriya Evangel'skix Xristian-Baptistov*, 209.

119. Prokhanov, "Na rodine Yana Gusa i Petra Hel'chickogo," 23–24.

120. *Istoriya Evangel'skix Xristian-Baptistov*, 209.

121. Although he had participated in the founding of the Tiflis church in August 1880, there are no other recorded instances of Kargel ordaining ministers in the intervening years.

122. *Istoriya Evangel'skix Xristian-Baptistov*, 540.

123. Ibid., 551–52.

he was coming to terms with the fact that denominational structures were unavoidable.

THE VISION OF EVANGELICAL UNITY

In line with the early vision of Pashkov, Baedeker, and Kargel, Prokhanov attempted to create a Russian Evangelical Alliance. In August 1906 Prokhanov sent a letter to key evangelical figures in the city stating his intention to start a Russian Evangelical Alliance (*Russkij Evangel'skij Soyuz*).[124] In the letter, he explained that the purpose of the move was to assist in the spiritual awakening of the Russian church and to share information regarding evangelical work.[125] In the letter he laid out the general structure he envisaged, which was similar to that governing the Evangelical Alliances in other countries. It was to be for individuals to join; the Alliance would not have groups or churches in its membership.[126] The organization would provide latitude across a range of issues that were debated among Russian evangelicals and its primary focus would be on the basic tenets of the gospel. In the same year, Prokhanov also commenced a periodical which had as its stated goal "(t)he unification of all the branches of living Christianity on the principles of freedom and brotherly love."[127]

By 4 December 1906, a core group had signed a charter in readiness for the launch of the Russian Evangelical Alliance. The first signatories were Ivan Kargel, Ivan Prokhanov, Paul Nicolay, A. M. Maksimovskij, V. X. Offenberg, and N. A. Gojer.[128] By June 1907 over twenty other evangelical leaders from different groups within Russia had signed the charter. The Russian Minister of Internal Affairs authorized the charter on 16 May 1908, and on 13 January 1909 the Alliance held its inaugural meeting. A. P. Lieven, a member of one of the most highly respected evangelical families in the city, was elected chair, with Baron Paul Nicolay serving as vice-chair.

---

124. The Russian word used is *soyuz*, which is typically translated as "union." Because this organization was to be an alliance of individuals rather than a union of churches, I have used "alliance" when referring to this organization.

125. *Istoriya Evangel'skix Xristian-Baptistov*, 152.

126. Ibid.

127. Prokhanoff, *In the Cauldron of Russia*, 138–39.

128. All except Gojer were teachers in the Gospel Courses organized by Prokhanov in Saint Petersburg: see *Istoriya Evangel'skix Xristian-Baptistov*, 167, 152.

Many Russian evangelical leaders applauded the effort—such as Count Korff, the Mennonite Brethren leader P. M. Friesen, and V. A. Fetler (William Fetler, also known as Basil Malof), a Latvian who had studied at C. H. Spurgeon's Pastors' College in London—and many encouraged prayer for the Alliance and the causes it espoused.[129] Others, particularly among the Baptists, were critical. Dei Mazaev, the leader of the Russian Baptists, looked at the Alliance as a human structure that could not fulfill the purposes of the kingdom of God. In a similar vein, Andrej Markovich Mazaev, long-time deacon and missionary of the Tiflis Baptist Church, saw the structure of the Alliance as unclear and the idea vague. To these Baptists, the Alliance's individual basis of membership meant that a Baptist and a member of the Orthodox Church could be part of the same organization, and this was not acceptable.[130]

Alongside this initiative by Prokhanov, with support from Kargel and others, discussions were taking place about the possibility of another expression of evangelical unity. In late 1906, a group of evangelical leaders met in Kiev to discuss holding an "Integrated Congress" that would include the various evangelical groups across Russia.[131] The stimulus was the religious freedom that was changing the situation for evangelicals across the country at the time and the legal issues that each group was facing. The Integrated Congress took place in Saint Petersburg in Princess Lieven's house[132] from 15 January until 1 February 1907.[133] It was attended by seventy delegates from across the Empire, representing the Baptists, the varied evangelical fellowships, and the New Molokans, a progressive sub-group of the Molokans resulting from the mixture of Molokan, Baptist, and

---

129. *Istoriya Evangel'skix Xristian-Baptistov*, 152.
130. Ibid., 153.
131. Ibid., 142.
132. Sawatsky, *Soviet Evangelicals*, 78.
133. Zhidkov, "Na Putyax Edinstva," 56–57.

Mennonite elements.[134] There were delegates from Latvia and Estonia.[135] Ivan Kargel was selected as the chair of the congress, with Dei Mazaev as vice-chair.[136] The agenda (as reported in *HEC-B*) suggests that the meetings dealt mainly with issues regarding the legal requirements for buildings, record-keeping, and the qualifications of ministers.[137]

It did not turn out to be a unifying event. There was a debate about whether children held the same kind of church membership as their parents. Mazaev called for a vote, and the Baptists voted against this idea, some of them raising both hands. Ivan Kargel was not able to maintain control over the meetings. The Molokans walked out.[138] Johannes Svensson, an observer, wrote: "You felt you were in Russia, where despotism had placed its stamp on everyone and everything. He who has the power rules and pays no heed to what the others feel and think."[139]

Undoubtedly this was a blow to the dreams of enduring evangelical cooperation that Kargel and others had been working towards for so long. But the Congress did have a deeper spiritual dimension, largely due to Kargel's influence.[140] According to a report in *Bratsky Vestnik*, each day started and ended with the reading of Scripture and there was opportunity for preaching, for reflection, and for discussion about a united effort to reach Russians with the gospel.[141] The *Bratsky Vestnik* report recalled Pashkov's 1884 conference, also held in Saint

---

134. The Baptist representatives were D. I. Mazaev, V. G. Pavlov, V. V. Ivanov, F. P. Balihin, S. P. Stepanov, and V. P. Stepanov. The Evangelical Christian representatives were I. V. Kargel, I. S. Prokhanov, V. I. Dolgopolov, and E. M. Bogdanov. The New Molokan representatives were P. Zaharov, G. Zaharov, and A. Yachmenov. For the New Molokans (Novo-Molokane) see Shubin, *A History of Russian Christianity*, vol. III, 138–39.

135. For a full list of attendees see Zhidkov, "Na Putyax Edinstva," 56–57.

136. It is interesting to note that Prokhanov is recorded in the *Bratsky Vestnik* article as a voting visitor and is not listed as a representative of the Saint Petersburg Community with Kargel and others.

137. *Istoriya Evangel'skix Xristian-Baptistov*, 142–43.

138. Sawatsky, *Soviet Evangelicals*, 79; Kahle, *Evangelische Christen in Russland und der Sowjetunion*, 121.

139. Johannes Svensson, "De ewangeliska kristnas konferens i St. Petersburg den 28. Jan. – 5. Febr. 1907," Ekenäs 1907, 10, as cited in Kahle, *Evangelische Christen in Russland und der Sowjetunion*, 121.

140. Zhidkov, "Na Putyax Edinstva," 56–60.

141. Ibid., 58.

Petersburg, suggesting that the 1907 conference was only the second time that such a broad range of Russian evangelicals had united in this way.[142] However, the tensions between the Baptists and other evangelicals could not be overcome. The Russian Evangelical Alliance, despite receiving an official charter, does not seem to have held any significant meetings apart from the inaugural meeting, and does not seem to have produced any literature. Without a strong endorsement from the Russian Baptists, it was an impossible task to unite all the evangelicals of Russia. Prokhanov's vision did not gain Baptist support, perhaps in part because Prokhanov had moved ahead without sufficient consultation.

Despite the disappointments in the period 1907–9, in 1912, ECU leaders, with Kargel as ECU vice-chairman, met with Baptist leaders in Vladikavkaz to discuss the possibility of an "incorporated committee" of the two Unions.[143] The turbulence of the times prevented progress and when the Baptists held their next annual congress in 1917, tensions between the two groups had grown because members under discipline by the Baptist Union were being accepted into the ECU's ranks.[144] From 1917 until 1919 Prokhanov and Kargel made further attempts to promote unity and in 1920 the two Unions formed the Temporary All-Russian General Council of Evangelical Christians-Baptists.[145] As a result of this, in May–June 1920, the two unions held ten-day congresses in Moscow and shared most of the sessions.[146] A decision in favor of a merger took place, with the Baptists indicating that they were willing to embrace the open Lord's Table—long advocated by the Evangelical Christians—and it was decided to take the name "All-Russian Union of Evangelical Christians-Baptists."

Problems arose, however, over sharing power, and the discussion of unity was left until representatives from both Unions attended the BWA Congress in 1923 in Stockholm.[147] The BWA held a special session for the two groups at the close of the Congress.[148] After hearing

142. Ibid., 57.
143. *Istoriya Evangel'skix Xristian-Baptistov*, 192.
144. Ibid., 192–93.
145. Ibid., 193.
146. Ibid., 194.
147. Ibid., 195–96.
148. Representatives from the Evangelical Christian Union were I. S. Prokhanov, V. T. Pelevin, A. L. Andreev, V. I. Bykov, and I. N. Koloskov. Representatives from

from both sides, the BWA leadership advised them to coordinate their efforts and to improve communication, but not to force merger.[149] This advice was taken. When considering Kargel's role in the events of this period, it is clear that he did not play a major role in the organizational aspects. His aspirations, as had always been the case, were for spiritual renewal and spiritual unity.

THE SAINT PETERSBURG BIBLE COLLEGE

The commitment Kargel felt to evangelical theology and his concern for the health of the Russian evangelical community in this period is seen in his teaching at a Bible College in Saint Petersburg, which was established by Ivan Prokhanov. The preparation for ministry among the various evangelical churches in Russia was carried on by means of local Bible or missionary courses, usually taught locally during seasons of the year which, in a largely agricultural context, were not so busy. Kargel, Wieler, and others travelled to various areas to teach month-long courses. Beginning in 1905, that model began to change. One of the first things that Prokhanov did upon his return to Russia after his extended studies abroad was to form a "Council of Educational Affairs," in October 1905. The Council sent a letter to a number of evangelical ministers inviting potential students—male only—to Saint Petersburg for six weeks of classes on preaching and "general educational knowledge and useful information from the experience of Christians from various nationalities."[150] Prokhanov then arranged a six-week course of residential study in Saint Petersburg which he named "Two-month Gospel Courses."[151] He offered the training specifically in order to develop leaders within the evangelical circles with which he was connected. The classes were designed to be practical in nature, preparing men for the sowing of God's word in the fields of Russia.[152]

---

the Russian Baptist Union were P. V. Pavlov, M. D. Timoshenko, I. N. Shilov, S. V. Belousov, A. P. Kostyukov, and P. K. Mordovia. See *Istoriya Evangel'skix Xristian-Baptistov*, 196.

149. *Istoriya Evangel'skix Xristian-Baptistov*, 196.
150. Ibid.
151. Ibid., 167. Also see Prokhanoff, *In the Cauldron of Russia*, 139.
152. *Istoriya Evangel'skix Xristian-Baptistov*, 168.

His teaching in the "Two-month Gospel Courses" helped to develop Kargel's reputation as the ablest Russian evangelical theologian of his generation. He expounded a theological approach that was clearly evangelical and within that framework called believers to a deeper understanding of their union with Jesus Christ. Kargel was often accompanied in the classroom by his daughter Maria, who also worked as a translator.[153] His daughters helped Ivan in classroom discussions, perhaps when he had to move between Russian and German.[154] Additionally, in his later years, his health may have been an issue and Maria may have stepped in to lead classes when her father was feeling tired. In the early years the classes were attended by students from various evangelical communities, including the Baptists.[155] Saint Petersburg was an ideal city due to the various venues available for the classes, such as the Lieven home. There were also unique opportunities in the city for students to attend evangelical services where Kargel and others preached every Sunday.

The program of the courses included Sin and Sanctification, and Homiletics, both taught by Kargel; The Doctrine of God, The Gospel of John, and The History of the Worldwide Evangelical Movement taught by Prokhanov; The Holy Spirit taught by T. F. Stanberg; The Analysis of the Parables taught by Paul Nicolay; and The Spiritual Life taught by Straightman.[156] General education was also included with lectures on literature, geography, world history, and Russian history.[157] The cost of the classes was to be covered by the congregations sending the students. The first classes were held from December 1905 to January 1906. During the second set of classes Kargel taught on the book of Revelation, as well as "Sin and Sanctification."[158] Arithmetic and grammar were also taught in the program.[159]

There were some discussions about de-centralized training. Baron Woldemar Üxküll, the Baptist leader in Estonia, was keen to

---

153. Skopina, "Iz Biografii I. V. Kargelya," 690.

154. Personal interviews conducted in Sumy, Ukraine, in June, 1996 by Irina Skopina with Alexander Andreevich. These interviews are in the possession of G. L. Nichols and I. N. Skopina.

155. *Istoriya Evangel'skix Xristian-Baptistov*, 169.

156. Ibid., 168.

157. Savinskij, *Istoriya Russko-Ukrainskogo Baptizma*, 297.

158. *Istoriya Evangel'skix Xristian-Baptistov*, 168.

159. Karetnikova, *Almanax po Istorii Russkogo Baptisma, vypusk 4*, 41.

have local training and tried to persuade others to join him in 1907 to establish a seminary in Estonia that could serve both the Russian and German speakers of the region.[160] The suggestion was not acted upon until after the First World War. Some minor changes took place in the Saint Petersburg courses. In 1907 the schedule was moved so that classes began on 15 September rather than in December.[161] This was to enable two sessions to be held in 1907. In the first session, Kargel again taught on sin and sanctification, as well as homiletics.[162] Prokhanov again taught Doctrine of God, the Gospel of John, and History of the Worldwide Evangelical Movement. T. F. Stanberg taught Pneumatology; Nicolay taught the Parables of Jesus; and Straightman taught Holy Life. The classes were held at the Lieven Palace and six graduates are listed from Tsaritsyn, Samara, Yalta, and Rostov-na-Donu. During the second session, which started on 15 November and lasted until 31 December 1907, there were lectures on General Education, Church History, and Bible and Doctrine, taught by Kargel, Nicolay, Maksimovskij, and Prokhanov. Kargel did not stay in the city when he was not teaching in the Gospel Courses. In 1907 he travelled to Ventspilse, Latvia,[163] to teach similar material.[164]

By 1912, the Evangelical Christian Union, as a registered denomination, felt able to put the "Two-month Gospel Courses" on a more formal footing.[165] The ECU leadership approved the start of a Bible College with a two-year training program to be opened in Saint Petersburg.[166] The Saint Petersburg Bible College was opened in 1913, soon after Kargel first served as the vice-chairman of the council of the ECU. The curriculum mirrored what would have been covered in Bible

160. Üxküll, "Hopes and Plans For Russia," 208. In 1909 Baptists began to use a Bible school in Lodz, Poland, which was operated jointly by German and Russian Baptists. It was forced to close in 1911.

161. *Istoriya Evangel'skix Xristian-Baptistov*, 168.

162. He may have also taught on the Book of Revelation. See Savinskij, *Istoriya Evangel'skix Xristian-Baptistov Ukrainy, Rossii, Belorussii*, 297.

163. *Istoriya Evangel'skix Xristian-Baptistov*, 168; Karetnikova, *Almanax po Istorii Russkogo Baptisma, vypusk 4*, 41.

164. Skopina, "Iz Biografii I. V. Kargelya," 696.

165. Prokhanoff, *In the Cauldron of Russia*, 139.

166. The official name of the school was the "Saint Petersburg Bible Courses for Evangelical Christians." For ease of understanding, I will use the name "Saint Petersburg Bible College." Prokhanov allowed this shorter form to be used. See Prokhanoff, *In the Cauldron of Russia*, 167–68.

schools in other countries and had little that would be considered distinctively Russian. The first-year curriculum included: Introduction to the Old Testament, which was a history of the books of the Old Testament, and the proof of their genuineness; Exegetics (expounding the Bible), which was described as a detailed analysis from the historical, philological, and spiritual points of view of the Pentateuch of Moses, the prophetical, and other books of the Bible; Dogmatics, or the statement of Christian teaching; Homiletic Theology, a statement of the rules necessary for drawing up a sermon, pronouncing well, and improving a sermon; the History of the Christian Church; Comparative History of Religions, which was a brief history and description of world religions and an explanation of the superiority of Christianity over them; brief lectures in Philosophy; and the theory of sacred music and singing. The second-year curriculum, which flowed from the first, was composed of: Introduction to the New Testament; Exegetics; Dogmatics; Homiletic Theology, or the Doctrine to be set out in sermons (continuation); History of the Christian Church (continuation); Teaching about Christian Morals, or Christian Ethics; brief lectures in Philosophy; Apologetics or arguments in favor of the truth of Christianity.[167]

The Saint Petersburg Bible College opened in its new form on 14 February 1913 with eighteen students—nine Russians, five Latvians, one Georgian, one German, one Ossetian, and one Ukrainian.[168] Three teachers are listed—Prokhanov, A. A. Reimer (a Mennonite), and K. G. Inkis. Kargel is not listed among the faculty, but he is mentioned in a first-hand account given by a student who attended those classes. The student, J. S. Grachev, described the opening day: on 14 February 1913, at ten o'clock, the first class began, with the opening assembly led by Prokhanov. He spoke of the value of doctrinal preparation. After Prokhanov, each teacher spoke of the material they were to cover and of their personal wishes for the students. V. A. Fetler, who worked with both Latvians and Russians in Saint Petersburg, congratulated Prokhanov on "cutting the first window through to Europe" by opening this evangelical school in Russia. Kargel addressed the students with the example of Ruth, the Moabitess, challenging them to use the

---

167. *Istoriya Evangel'skix Xristian-Baptistov*, 168.
168. Prokhanoff, *In the Cauldron of Russia*, 168.

kernels of truth they would gather. He asked them to reflect on them each evening so as to store them up in the mind and heart.[169]

These students were able to study for a year, but they did not return after the summer break of 1914. The college was closed due to the outbreak of the First World War.[170] With the wider political chaos of the war, the Communist takeover, a famine, and the Civil War, the training of ministers could no longer be accomplished in residential schools but was moved to large local churches and delivered through short-term regional classes.[171] In the 1920s Kargel's ministry as a teacher would emerge again, with even greater authority.

KARGEL'S PUBLISHING EFFORTS[172]

Kargel's concern for spiritual renewal led him to become involved in writing and publishing. His first articles were published in 1895 in North America, in *Zionsbote*, a German-language Mennonite Brethren journal based in Hillsboro, Kansas.[173] Among the titles of his early articles (translated here into English) were "My Friend in the Garden,"[174] "God's Holy Reign in You and His Will,"[175] and "The Important Process of Transformation."[176] From these titles, it is clear that the main focus of Kargel's early writings was the well-being of the individual believer in relation to God. At this point Kargel was well known to quite a number of Russian evangelicals through his preaching, but his writing output was only just beginning. Soon after these initial works came a series of articles in the same journal, such

169. Grachev, "Pervye Biblejskie Kursy Evangel'skix Xristian-Baptistov v Rossii," 73.

170. *Istoriya Evangel'skix Xristian-Baptistov*, 169.

171. See *Istoriya Evangel'skix Xristian-Baptistov*, 214–15 for a list of cities and teachers. Kargel taught in Nizhniy Novgorod Province in 1912 and 1913: see Nikol'skij, "Sektantstvo," 242; Bodyanskiy, "Xronika," 323.

172. In addition to the works noted in the next section, there are several other minor works that appear in Russian in various forms. They are notes from a homiletics course that Kargel taught, sermons attributed to Kargel, and "Lekcii o vtorom Prishestvii Gospoda Iisusa Xrista." These are not discussed in this work.

173. *Zionsbote* also sent 1,000 copies to Russia.

174. Kargel, "Mein Freund in Seinem Garten," 1.

175. Kargel, "Gottes Heilige Regel, Seinen Willen Zu Tun [Part One]," 1; Kargel, "Gottes Heilige Regel, Seinen Willen Zu Tun [Part Two]," 1.

176. Kargel, "Der Grosse Verwandlungsprozess [Part One]," 1; "Der Grosse Verwandlungsprozess [Part Two]," 1.

as a nine-part series significantly entitled simply "Holiness;"[177] an article, "A Good Start but a Sad Ending;"[178] and a fifteen-part series entitled "What is Sin?"[179] All of these show very clearly the influence of Holiness theology. Nearly all of his early written works were first published in German later translated and published in Russian. I will limit my analysis to those works that have been published in Russian, since it was among Russian evangelicals that Kargel's influence was most significant.

In 1896, Kargel published his first book (already referred to) under the title *Light from the Shadows of Future Blessing*.[180] It was a German-language commentary on the typology found in the Tabernacle. The term "shadows" is taken from several New Testament passages which allude to the idea that the components and ceremonies associated with the Old Testament Tabernacle are a shadow of heavenly things including Jesus Christ and His redemption.[181] The book was first printed in Russian in 1908. Kargel stated that "God has shown in the tabernacle a prototype of His drawing near to humankind, and in Christ Jesus we realize the actual fulfillment."[182]

His next work was, similarly, a book based on typology, in which he commented in typological fashion on the Book of Ruth—*Ruth the Moabitess*.[183] In 1897 Kargel published a work on Ruth in *Zionsbote*.[184] In 1928, *Ruth the Moabitess* was published in serial form in Russian in Prokhanov's journal *The Christian*.[185] In the first part of this work, he explained the biblical story of Ruth, chapter by chapter. The end of the

---

177. Kargel, "Die Heiligung [Part One]," 1 through Kargel, "Die Heiligung [Part Nine]," 1.

178. Kargel, "Ein Guter Anfang [part one]," 1; Kargel, "Ein Guter Anfang [part two]," 1.

179. Kargel, "Was ist Die Sünde? [Part One]," 1 through Kargel, "Was ist die Sünde?[Part Fifteen]," 1.

180. The full title is *Svet iz Teni budushhix Blag ili tridcat' dve Besedy o Skinii, Zhertvoprinosheniyax i Svyashhenstve*. The German title is *Licht aus dem Shatten*.

181. For a case study of the hermeneutical principles used by Kargel in *Light from the Shadows of future Blessing* (a. k. a. *The Reflection of Glories to Come*) see Kuznetsova, "Early Russian Evangelicals," 368–77; 523–53.

182. Kargel, *Svet iz Teni budushhix Blag*, 4.

183. Kargel, "Ruf' Moavityanka, ili Mezhi moi proshli po prekrasnym Mestam," 329–77.

184. Kargel, "Buch Ruth," 2.

185. Kargel, "Ruf' Moavityanka" [in *Xristianin*], 27–33.

work seeks to show that Ruth is symbolic of the church: just as Ruth was adopted into the house of Boaz, so the Christian Church has been grafted into the chosen people of Israel.[186]

Kargel's commentary on the book of Revelation, entitled *Commentary on the Revelation of Saint John*,[187] was published in serial form, in German, in *Der Hausfreund*, between the years 1906 and 1911.[188] Although it was only finally published in Russian in 1991, and therefore did not, in its published form, have an impact on Russian evangelicals during Kargel's lifetime, it is likely that the book reflects— at least in part—material that Kargel taught at the Saint Petersburg Bible College. He gave lectures on the Second Coming[189] and his commentary is organized into forty-three lectures that go through the Book of Revelation chapter by chapter. The book uses a fairly literal hermeneutic. A number of important points in Kargel's theology emerge. One is his belief that the Church does not replace Israel in God's plans. There are, he argued, two peoples of God in the divine design—Israel and the Church.[190] In the "end times," God will still deal graciously with the nation of Israel and honor his promises to them. The final resurrection, for Kargel, includes three categories of those who are raised. There are those who will be resurrected before the great tribulation; there are those who will die during the tribulation and who will be raised at the first trumpet; and there are those to be raised who will die during the end of the reign of the anti-Christ.[191] All of this presupposed a literal 1,000-year reign of Christ.[192]

---

186. Kargel, "Ruf' Moavityanka, ili Mezhi moi proshli po prekrasnym Mestam," 374.

187. Kargel, *Tolkovatel' Otkroveniya Svyatogo Ioanna Bogoslova*; Kargel, "Tolkovatel' Otkroveniya Svyatogo Ioanna Bogoslova."

188. Kargel, "Die Offenbarung Johannis [1907]," 17–18; Kargel, "Die Offenbarung Johannis [1912]," 207–9. The starting date of the series is uncertain due to unavailable journal issues.

189. See "Lekcii o vtorom Prishestvii Gospoda Iisusa Xrista" and "O vtorom Prishestvii Gospoda Iisusa Xrista" as an example of notes taken from Kargel's lectures.

190. Kargel, *Tolkovatel' Otkroveniya Svyatogo Ioanna Bogoslova*, 125.

191. Ibid., 231–32.

192. Ibid., 237–42.

The next book from Kargel, *Sin, the Evil of All Evils in this World*,[193] was published in Russian in 1912.[194] In this work, Kargel looked at the world situation and sought to prove that original sin is the root of all the evils in the world.[195] He argued that it is not human ignorance, but rather the sinful nature, that touches every aspect of life and contaminates and corrupts the world. He took the standard evangelical approach, especially the approach characteristic of the Reformed tradition, that sin, the act of rebellion against God, has affected the entire human race as well as all parts of creation. He states: "Therefore, as a physical illness is shown in infinitely various ways, and reveals its all-powerful influence in a body, so it happens with sin. It affects the person in every respect, causing carnal illnesses."[196] Kargel argues that the only way to overcome sin is to abide fully in Christ. He points to a life beyond the initial experience of forgiveness of sin, one in which sin is overcome. "Sadly," said Kargel, many had stopped at the point of receiving forgiveness of sins, and were leading "cold, indifferent, pitiful lives." He urged: "You must not only have forgiveness of your sins but an additional freedom from its power; to be saved from the effects of evil and all the grievances of your daily lives, even as far as your thoughts and convictions. Unless you strive further in your salvation, it is a poor and altogether superficial attempt."[197] He uses the illustration of gravity, a stone, and an airplane. Gravity acts on a stone as sin acts toward a human being. Christ is like an airplane, which is able to overcome the force of gravity, counteracting the ever-present force of sin.[198]

---

193. Kargel, "Grex kak Zlo vsex Zol v ehtom Mire," 5–48.

194. There is a copy of a German version of this book under the title *Die Sünde, das Übel aller Übel in deiser Welt* held at Bethel College in North Newton, Kansas. The library has assigned a date of "190?." There is no publishing information given with the book and the library has estimated that it was printed between 1900 and 1910.

195. For a case study of the hermeneutical principles used by Kargel in *Sin, the Evil of All Evils in this World* (a.k.a. *Sin as the greatest Evil in this World*) see Kuznetsova, "Early Russian Evangelicals," 367–68; 500–522.

196. Kargel, "Grex kak Zlo vsex Zol v ehtom Mire," 14–15.

197. Ibid., 48.

198. Ibid., 39.

Kargel's important book, *What is Your Relationship to the Holy Spirit?*,[199] was published in Russian by 1912[200] and soon was translated and published in Bulgarian.[201] It clearly calls the Christian to progress into a higher Christian life.[202] An Orthodox review of the book was written soon after it was published, praising and quoting the work and calling it "the first serious book of sectarians on repentance."[203] Kargel writes here: "It is an incontestable truth about you and me, when we have been justified in Christ, He can speak to us, as to His disciples, at any time." It seems that Kargel believed what he was saying was a word that needed to be heard—a word from the Holy Spirit. He argued that a disciple of Christ might not possess the "power from on high," an expression that referred back to the command of Jesus to his disciples to wait in Jerusalem until they had received "power from on high." This is what they received at Pentecost. It was an expression often used in Holiness circles. There were believers, said Kargel, who had never made a claim to the promise of this power as their own property, and had never accepted its fullness.[204] Kargel believed that the first step to move beyond forgiveness was that "we must be empty," while the second step was that "we must be ready to give" and be "channels" of the Holy Spirit to others.[205] Kargel also looked at the Holy Spirit's activity throughout the Bible and suggested that the Holy Spirit never filled anyone until after Pentecost.[206]

---

199. Kargel, "V Kakom Ty Otnoshenii k Duxu Svyatomu?" 114–79.

200. The book is advertised in the November 1912 edition of *Gost'*, page 24, as a newly published work which shows that it was first published in or before 1912.

201. Chakalov, "Ivan V. Kargel," 10.

202. For a case study of the hermeneutical principles used by Kargel in *What is your Relationship to the Holy Spirit* (a.k.a. *Where do You stand in your Relationship to the Holy Spirit*) see Kuznetsova, "Early Russian Evangelicals," 340–48; 435–56.

203. Chepurina, "Ispoved' I. V. Kargelya," 509.

204. Kargel, "V Kakom Ty Otnoshenii k Duxu Svyatomu?" 122.

205. Ibid., 132.

206. Ibid., 139.

Sometime near 1928,[207] Kargel produced another book, entitled *Behold, I am Coming Soon*,[208] which looked at world events in the light of some of the prophecies that he saw contained in the Bible. The premillennial views in Kargel's work will be discussed in the next chapter. From 1924 through to 1928, Kargel's work "Old Testament Prototypes,"[209] which uses Old Testament examples of the truths of Christ and the Christian life was published in serial form in Prokhanov's *The Christian*. Kargel dealt with the lives of various Old Testament characters. Abel was fully obedient to God's commands. "The death of Abel speaks to us: suffer affliction, just as your Lord suffered affliction."[210] Enoch walked with God and never grew tired of that intimate relationship.[211] Lot wrongly hesitated and did not obey God's will. Some Christians are, Kargel stated, like Lot. "Angels cannot move them, and even threatening hard blows does not remove them from their Sodom. It seems that only when God applies violence, will it [this removal] be achieved."[212] Moses, by contrast, showed a true conversion. "Today," said Kargel, "all of us meet with people who want to be much cleverer than Moses in this respect." He suggested that these people say: "I can have the belief for myself, I can be quite a good Christian internally—why should I attract attention and act openly?" Kargel continued: "They consider that it is much more desirable to be a Christian and to belong to Christ when it is convenient for them, and if it is not convenient, nobody should know if they are a Christian or not."[213] In looking at the example of Naaman, the point made by Kargel was that Naaman refused to use his own strength but had faith

---

207. It is unclear exactly when this book was written but circa 1928 seems to be the most logical. The year 1919, the end of a great war, and nine years passing since the existence of the Palestine protectorate are all mentioned in the text. M. S. Karetnikova has stated that the original date of the book is 1909. See Karetnikova, *Almanax po Istorii Russkogo Baptisma, vypusk 4*, 58. If she is correct, it must have been rewritten to take into account the events of 1919 and 1920, which is highly unlikely given the nature of the book and its focus on the fulfillment of prophecy. For the mentioning of nine years since the Palestine protectorate see Kargel, "Se, Gryadu Skoro . . . ," 388.

208. Kargel, "Se, Gryadu Skoro . . . ," 378–448.

209. Kargel, "Vetxozavetnye Proobrazy," 255–329.

210. Kargel, "Vetxozavetnye Proobrazy," 262.

211. Ibid., 270.

212. Ibid., 273.

213. Ibid., 284.

in the power of the God of Israel to heal him.[214] Isaiah was "a pliable instrument," used by God.[215] Daniel remained holy and still acted respectfully to an unbelieving authority.[216] All of these Old Testament figures became examples for Russian Baptists.

Where are the Dead according to the Scriptures?[217] was first printed in Russian in serial form in *The Christian* in 1925.[218] It is possible that it was previously written by Kargel in German at an earlier date.[219] Kargel originally wrote this book to counter *Where are the Dead?*,[220] a booklet written in 1908 by an American, John Edgar. In Edgar's view, the dead were asleep, and Kargel opposed what he saw as being a Seventh Day Adventist perspective.[221] Kargel strongly attacked Edgar's work, calling it a "sack cloth over the brightly shining truths of God."[222] In Kargel's opinion, the dead were not asleep but fully conscious, awaiting their resurrection and final judgment in one of two intermediate states—in Christ or in Adam.[223] For Kargel, when Jesus spoke of Lazarus in Abraham's bosom and the rich man in hell[224] he was not offering metaphors for Israel's historical periods, as Edgar contended, but was speaking of actual souls in tangible locations.[225] After Christ's

---

214. Ibid., 292.

215. Ibid., 314.

216. Ibid., 320.

217. Kargel, "Gde, po Pisaniyu, Naxodyatsya Mertvye?" 180–254.

218. Kargel, "Gde, po Pisaniyu, Naxodyatsya Mertvye?" [in *Xristianin*], 17–25. This work continued in serial form from *Xristianin* 7 (1925) 17–25 through to *Xristianin* 12 (1925) 24–32.

219. In the book, Kargel mentioned twice that it he had been "in the faith" approximately fifty years. Considering that he was baptized in 1869, this would indicate that the original writing of this book was circa 1919.

220. Edgar, *Wo sind die Toten?* The second edition in German was printed in 1913. Kargel mentioned that he read the work of Edgar in German. See Kargel, "Gde, po Pisaniyu, Naxodyatsya Mertvye?" 180.

221. Kargel mentions Adventists specifically in this work. See Kargel, "Gde, po Pisaniyu, Naxodyatsya Mertvye?" 202.

222. Kargel, "Gde, po Pisaniyu, Naxodyatsya Mertvye?" 182. In fact, Edgar was a close associate of C. T. Russell, the early leader of the Jehovah's Witnesses.

223. For Kargel, the "dead in Christ" are those who, from the creation of humankind, "searched for God and found him." The "dead in Adam" are those who, "never repented and came to a living faith." Ibid., 225.

224. See Luke 16:19–31.

225. Kargel, "Gde, po Pisaniyu, Naxodyatsya Mertvye?" 209–10.

resurrection, Kargel insisted, all those who died with saving faith (those spoken of as being in Paradise or in Abraham's bosom) actually came into the presence of the resurrected Christ.[226] Those who died without saving faith were in hell, awaiting the final judgment, at which time they would be sentenced to Gehenna or the "second death."[227]

Three years after *Where are the Dead according to the Scriptures?* was published in Russian, Kargel wrote *Zwischen den Enden der Erde: Unter Bruedern in Ketten*.[228] This is a travel log of his 1890 trip to Siberia with Baedeker.[229] The last written work that Ivan Kargel produced was his commentary on the Book of Romans 5–8, published under the title *The Law of the Spirit of Life*.[230] This seems to be material he used in lectures delivered around 1932 while living in Ukraine. These varied publications show Kargel's enduring interest in theology, practice, and experience.

The final book that I will note here is one that encapsulates much of the essence of Kargel's teaching: *Christ—our Sanctification*.[231] This work may have been written as early as 1912[232] but it was eventually published in serial form in the journal *Xristianin* in 1926.[233] Kargel wrote that the reason for producing it was because during his years of teaching in Baptist, Evangelical Christian, and Mennonite circles he had become alarmed that many of the students seemed concerned only with "repentance and belief, justification, and conversion."[234] He wanted to move the believers within the evangelical communities in Russia beyond the simple, basic lessons of the Christian faith, into what he saw as the true essence of the faith—to be sanctified. Sanctification, he argued, is a gift given only to the redeemed. "Justification," he

226. Ibid., 216–17.
227. Ibid., 235–36.
228. Kargel, *Zwischen den Enden*.
229. This book does not look at the detailed accounts of the trip from this book.
230. Kargel, *Zakon Duxa Zhizni*. The only copy of this work was believed to have been confiscated near the end of Kargel's life in 1937. The current version was pieced together from secondary sources and published in 2003.
231. Kargel, "Xristos Osvyashhenie Nashe," 49–113.
232. Karetnikova states that the book was first published in 1912. See Karetnikova, *Almanax po Istorii Russkogo Baptisma, vypusk 4*, 43.
233. For a case study of the hermeneutical principles used by Kargel in *Christ—Our Sanctification* (a.k.a. *Christ is Our Sanctification*) see Kuznetsova, "Early Russian Evangelicals," 350–66; 457–99.
234. Kargel, "Xristos Osvyashhenie Nashe," 49.

wrote, "begins at the point of forgiveness, sanctification is the middle, and perfect sanctification is the end—the glorious redemption."[235] Sanctification is the release from the effects of sin, beginning in this life. "He [Christ] has come to release us from the punishment of sin, from the authority of sin, and finally from the presence of sin. In this very moment, you can be released from the first two—the authority of sin can be broken within your life and, on that basis, you will be on the path to the third—to the removal of the presence of sin."[236] This sanctification, for Kargel, is only possible if someone abides in Christ. It is something that many Christians are unaware of but, he argues, should know. He uses the example of electricity—now commonly known and used, but previously unknown and unused. "So it is with many of the children of God concerning Christ; they cope as though He were not in them."[237]

In this book, Kargel gives his own spiritual testimony, explaining how he was convinced that a deeper relationship with Christ was necessary. The dates that he mentions in the book align with the years when he was in Bulgaria, confirming that he is narrating what happened when, in Anna's words, he was "released from any spiritual narrowness."[238] He speaks of reading two brochures that influenced him.[239] It seems that one of the brochures was written by A. B. Simpson, a Canadian who was the founder (in 1887) of the Christian and Missionary Alliance.[240] The booklet, according to I. V. Karev, was simply entitled, "Himself."[241] Simpson established the Alliance on the basis of a "Four-fold" Gospel: Christ as Savior, Sanctifier, Healer, and Coming King. Among Simpson's range of writings there is one entitled *The Holy Spirit: Power from on High*, and he also wrote on the Tabernacle. The themes developed by Simpson appear in Kargel. When Kargel read first the two brochures he had, he said, been struggling with pride, the inability to forgive, and carnal thoughts. The brochures convinced him that it was possible to overcome these

---

235. Ibid., 51.
236. Ibid., 69.
237. Ibid., 85.
238. Anna Kargel to Vasily Alexandrovich [Pashkov], 1 February 1884, 2/13/022, Pashkov Papers.
239. Kargel, "Xristos Osvyashhenie Nashe," 81.
240. For Simpson see Pitts, "Holiness as Spirituality," 223–48.
241. Karev, "Iz moix Lichnyx Vstrech s I. V. Kargelem," 19.

feelings with a deeper faith. After months of fervent prayer which seemed unanswered, he heard a voice crying, "Crazy man, it is absolutely in vain, you will not receive this!" After he calmed down, he heard these words, "I in them and they in me."[242] For Kargel, this was the turning point in his spiritual life. We know from Anna's account of this period that the months of prayer included prayers by his wife and the Pashkovite circle in Saint Petersburg.

CONCLUSION

When the religious persecution eased in Russia at the end of the nineteenth century, Ivan Kargel returned to Saint Petersburg with his three daughters. After one last itinerant preaching trip to Siberia, he took up the daunting task of rebuilding the Saint Petersburg Evangelicals. Vasily Pashkov died in 1902, and, as a result, Kargel no longer had the financial resources to pursue his former ministry of prison visitations and itinerant preaching. His contact with German Baptists virtually came to an end. He was, by this time, firmly within the Russian-speaking sphere. As he was working with the Saint Petersburg Evangelicals, conflicts again arose over the open Table. Kargel was unwilling to restrict the Table only to those baptized as believers, and as a result several of the group he was leading left. Those who left were soon in contact with Ivan Prokhanov, who developed a church and then a denomination, the Evangelical Christian Union, from this core group. The ECU later became a home for Kargel, as he and his congregation joined the ECU, and he served as ECU vice-chairman and taught in the ECU College. From this new platform, he was involved again in attempts to form a broadly-based Evangelical Alliance in Russia, consistent with his long-held aspirations. These did not succeed and he would not be involved in any further attempts.

The next chapter will examine the way in which Kargel's teaching on the sanctified life was expressed, especially in *Christ—our Sanctification*. In chapter 9 I will look at his last period: the 1920s and the 1930s, up to his death in 1937. This examination will include looking at the *Law of the Spirit of Life*, the last book from Kargel. During the final decades of his life Kargel was the most revered pastoral leader and teacher within the Russian Evangelical Christian and Baptist communities.

242. Kargel, "Xristos Osvyashhenie Nashe," 81–82.

8

Teaching on the Sanctified Life

FROM ABOUT 1909, AS Kargel entered his sixties, his thinking about the sanctified life reached maturity. He taught and wrote extensively on the topic in his sixties and seventies and it was during this time in his life that *Christ—Our Sanctification*, his classic book on the subject, was published. The major thrust of the book is summed up in a passage in which he writes:

> Everything in relation to our growth in sanctification and in our transformation into the image of Christ will depend on the attitude [relationship] in which we stand with our Lord—does He live in us and do we abide in Him—this is unconditional. If everything we do is daily pleasing to Him then the desire of the Apostle Paul to the Thessalonians will be fulfilled, when he wrote: "Now may the God of peace himself sanctify you completely and may your whole spirit and soul and body be kept blameless at the coming of our Lord Jesus Christ."[1]

Here are the themes that had become central to Kargel's spirituality: transformation into the image of Christ, abiding in Christ, and pleasing God in everything. This chapter will seek to make a systematic analysis of Kargel's teaching on the deeper life, using not only *Christ—Our Sanctification* but also work that he published in earlier years. The first part of the analysis will follow the main points made by David Bebbington about Keswick spirituality. Bebbington sees the characteristics of Keswick as including poetic inclinations, the appeal of nature, an element of crisis, the exaltation of faith, an internal sense of peace, repression of the sin nature, and a premillennial view

---

1. Kargel, "Xristos Osvyashhenie Nashe," 113.

of the eschaton.² I will look at each of these, using a sequence that fits Kargel's pattern of thought, and will argue for a remarkable degree of similarity between Kargel and Keswick thinking in these areas. The analysis then focuses on other distinctive aspects of Kargel's teaching.

KARGEL'S EMPHASIS ON SANCTIFICATION

It is important to note, first of all, that Kargel's teaching on sanctification did not derive exclusively from Keswick teaching. He was nurtured in the 1870s in the German Baptist context and the German Baptist Statement of Faith contains an entire section on sanctification.³ It states: "A holy, child-like love for God and His commands is the most important thing in sanctification, and this love, which is produced, maintained, and nourished in the heart, by the Holy Spirit, gradually recreates the person in the image of God. We hold that sanctification should continue throughout our whole lives and that even in the case of the most holy life we still need the forgiving grace of God through the blood of Christ."⁴

This creed was written prior to the rise of the nineteenth-century Holiness movement and the wording here reflects standard Calvinistic thinking about sanctification. It was rare for German Baptists leaders to align themselves with the Holiness movement. Lehmann, one of the most influential of the German Baptist leaders, is quoted in 1876, as the Holiness movement was beginning to have a major impact, as having said that the "first error was sinless perfection; then came antinomianism; then Darbyism . . ."⁵

The Holiness movement did, however, have an impact on some of those within the German Evangelical Alliance. In 1897 F. B. Meyer, Keswick's leading international speaker, who was a Baptist, was the first English speaker at the German Evangelical Alliance's Blankenburg Convention. One of those present in 1897, Pastor Otto Stockmayer, had a strong affinity with Meyer's exposition of deeper spiritual experience. Count Bernstorff, who was also part of this evangelical circle,

---

2. Bebbington, *Holiness in Nineteenth-Century England*, 79–85.
3. Oncken, *Glaubensbekenntnis und Verfassung der Gemeinden Getaufter Christen*, 31–33.
4. Ibid., 32–33.
5. "Mission to the Germans," 270.

arranged conferences for Meyer in Berlin.[6] But German Baptists were little affected.

Surprisingly, Kargel's own Confession of Faith of 1913 does not have a separate section on the Holy Spirit or a section on sanctification. Despite all that he could have said in a section on sanctification, he is silent on the issue, except to say that the "Holy Spirit is accomplishing the sanctification of the born-again."[7] However, in many other writings by Kargel he urged the importance of sanctification. To be sanctified, he argued, requires submission on the part of the believer. The process of personal consecration begins with humility and sincere prayer.[8] God, he says, will not force His children to be holy.

> We have noticed this [that we cannot triumph over a sin] and begged God that He would remove from us that which hinders Him, but it did not happen. Why?—because He does not want to force it against our will. He desires that we would willingly put it on His altar of sacrifice. O, that we would only give ourselves entirely to Him and all that we still possess: and soon, we would receive the fullness of His Holy Ghost! Therefore He is opening, opening wide a place for Him.[9]

The stress is on human action—"putting it on His altar of sacrifice." This language is typical of the nineteenth-century Holiness movement and would not be found in classic examples of Calvinistic spirituality.

Stating the human responsibility in another way, Kargel writes that the word "justification" is only used in reference to a person who is not a believer.[10] The word "sanctification," on the other hand, is only used in relation to the "saved and justified person." The Scriptures never induce the sinner to "live piously or to operate and walk in holiness, but only the righteous person."[11] The first step is for a sinner to be justified. Once that occurs, they are given the responsibility of seeking sanctification.

---

6. For F. B. Meyer at Blankenburg see *The Christian*, 16 April 1925, 6 and Harford, *Keswick Convention*, 162, as cited in Randall, *Spirituality and Social Change*, 98.

7. Kargel, "Confession of Faith of the Evangelical Christians-Baptists," 155.

8. Kargel, "Xristos Osvyashhenie Nashe," 91.

9. Kargel, "V Kakom Ty Otnoshenii k Duxu Svyatomu?" 132.

10. Kargel, "Xristos Osvyashhenie Nashe," 105.

11. Ibid. 50.

Teaching on the Sanctified Life 221

For Kargel, sanctification is the intended outcome of salvation. He calls sanctification "the fulfillment,"[12] or "full salvation." Again the language of "fullness" reflects the Holiness movement. The words of Acts 2:38, to "repent, be baptized, and receive the Holy Spirit" are the only commands of the Lord to "place them into a position to receive the Holy Spirit and His fullness."[13] The same repentance that leads to salvation should be the repentance that further leads to the fullness of the Holy Spirit. Stating it another way, Kargel writes that "justification without sanctification would certainly not be a full salvation." It would "forgive the rebel but would allow him to remain as the enemy of his Lord; it would take away consequences, but miss the purpose."[14] Kargel writes, "I would like to ask each of the readers a serious question. Did you accept the Holy Spirit when you believed?"[15] Saving faith must be accompanied and motivated by the Holy Spirit; otherwise it is the type of faith that achieves nothing. For Kargel, intellectual faith not accompanied by the Holy Spirit was a problem that the church faced in his day. Kargel saw "full salvation" (not just intellectual assent) as bringing many blessings. Anyone knowing the power of the Holy Spirit also has the "Eyes of God," he argued, and can sense when the Holy Spirit is lacking in others.[16] As will be seen later, he was envisaging two classes of Christian: the sanctified and the unsanctified.

In another book, *Sin, the Evil of All Evils in this World*, toward the end Kargel offers an answer to the "sin problem" that reflects the Holiness concept of salvation from the power of sin and the consequences of sin.

> But, maybe you already belong to those that have accepted Christ's salvation; therefore, for that let there be glory and praise to the Lord! Oh, but now watch out that this is not limited only to the satisfaction of escaping hell and the future wrath that you deserve, having received forgiveness for your sins . . . You must have not only forgiveness of your sin but an additional freedom from its power; to be saved from the effects

12. Kargel, "V Kakom Ty Otnoshenii k Duxu Svyatomu?" 158.
13. Kargel, "Xristos Osvyashhenie Nashe," 69.
14. Ibid. Literally, the statement is *"vovse ne bylo by spaseniem."* In the context, Kargel is implying that their salvation is not a full salvation rather than stating clearly that they are not saved.
15. Kargel, "V Kakom Ty Otnoshenii k Duxu Svyatomu?" 115.
16. Ibid.

of evil and all its hindrances in your daily life, even as deep as your thoughts and convictions. Unless you strive further in your salvation, it is a poor and altogether superficial attempt. If you do not expect and do not aspire to a deeper salvation, on a broader scale, it is plain that your understanding is false.[17]

To have "deeper salvation" is to be filled with the Holy Spirit. "The Holy Spirit would like to bring them [believers] into that estate of victory in Christ, their Lord, always giving to them triumph in Him, in a condition in which they would have great pleasure when they encounter various temptations (James 1:2)."[18]

This idea, as Kargel expounded on it, was comparable to what happened to Jesus at His baptism and in His temptation. "The triune God," said Kargel, predetermined the event in which Jesus was filled with the Holy Spirit. Before being filled with the Holy Spirit, Jesus Christ was a "perfect faultless person, carrying the image of God in a human body, glorifying God."[19] But, after he was filled, "the Holy Spirit became the arms and creative force behind the new Person."[20] Kargel used an illustration of an artist who had created a masterpiece, perfect in every respect, with no room for improvement. But the artist makes one final improvement by "uniting himself to his creation, by his own means, giving it its own life, its own wisdom, all power and essence, so that from this instant the creator and creation merge completely."[21]

There was a perceived problem for Kargel in making such a close identification between sanctification and the filling of the Spirit, since Jesus, the one who was "faultless," was filled with the Spirit but did not need to be sanctified. Kargel was able to answer this by saying that the person who is filled with the Holy Spirit is filled with Christ. To be filled with the Holy Spirit in such a way as to know "full salvation" the Christian should be filled with Christ, like a vessel into which not another drop may enter, otherwise the liquid would overflow. Kargel went to some of his favorite pictures in the Old Testament and spoke of the way the Holy Spirit filled the Tabernacle and the Temple in the Old Testament. He then applied this to individual Christian

17. Kargel, "Grex kak Zlo vsex Zol v ehtom Mire," 48.
18. Kargel, "V Kakom Ty Otnoshenii k Duxu Svyatomu?" 139.
19. Ibid., 136.
20. Ibid., 137.
21. Ibid., 136.

believers: "Your body should be the temple of the Holy Spirit . . . And the temple of the Holy Spirit should be filled with Him."[22] Kargel makes a point of stating, in an allegorical way, that when God moved into the Temple with His presence, there was no room for anything else. When God spoke to Moses, the bush was fully filled with fire.[23] For Kargel, sanctification was being filled to the full with the Holy Spirit, fully yielding to God's desires, and giving God full control over all of life. It is in Christ, for Kargel, that victory is found, but connection to that victorious life is linked to obedience to the Holy Spirit.

In his book *Christ—Our Sanctification*, which is the crucial source for Kargel's teaching in this area, he lists eight things that he believes are necessary to comprehend if someone is to make progress in sanctification. The first two points he mentions are related to Christ.[24] First, a believer must understand the deep riches that are in Jesus Christ. "You not only have some of the blessings and gifts from Christ and through Him, but have accepted Him (John 3:16; Col 2:6; John 1:12), and embodied Him so deeply in your soul, that you have become a participator with Him (Heb 3:14), one Body with Him (Eph 3:6), a member of Him, who is the Head (Eph 1:22–23), one with Him, as the branch was one with the Vine (John 15:4–5)."[25] This is a powerful christological statement about sanctification.

Kargel's second point is that the Christian must abide in Christ. "Christ in us, and we in Christ is the unique basis on which the purpose of God can be achieved, to keep us from sin and change us into the image of Christ; this is our unique hope for this present time and for eternal glory (Col 1:27). There is no other way . . ."[26] For Kargel, it was the recognition that all God's will is to be found in Christ that was the secret of sanctification. Abiding in Christ was the central thought in much of Kargel's writings on spirituality.

---

22. Ibid., 131.

23. Kargel, "Xristos Osvyashhenie Nashe," 63.

24. The third was to fully yield to the Holy Spirit. The fourth was to use the Word of God. The fifth was to have true faith. The sixth was to pray. The seventh was to have fellowship with other believers. The eighth was to suffer.

25. Kargel, "Xristos Osvyashhenie Nashe," 78.

26. Ibid., 83.

THE ELEMENT OF CRISIS

Keswick spirituality, according to Bebbington, contained an "element of crisis," related to the Romantic emphasis on dramatic moments.[27] The element of crisis was not meant to be an emotional response from a person but rather came from "the realization of his or her total impotence in the presence of sin's overwhelming power."[28] Kargel was not given to using emotional appeals to produce a spiritual crisis, but he sought to employ powerful logic to bring audiences to a recognition of the need for a response to the gospel, and then, when addressing believers, to advocate the need for sanctification. When he writes of his preaching trips, he tells of spending time with individuals after he preached. He does mention on occasions that there were tears, but he does not seem to have been forcing emotional displays.

Yet, in his own testimony, he describes, and indeed emphasizes, a crisis point in his personal spiritual life. During the first part of his ministry, he considered that he served under the power of what he calls a "first love," which after eight years, he suggests, left him "more carnal, finding it hard to forgive others, becoming proud, swayed by the words of others."[29] He then, as noted above, read two brochures that explained Jesus and the Scriptures in a new way. These brochures called for a new type of faith or trust, which he deeply desired. He prayed fervently for the new experience of faith and eventually received it.[30] The words of Christ that came to him in that moment of crisis were, "I in them and they in me." He later conceived this as "abiding in Christ"—a major theme of his writings on sanctification.

As well as teaching the idea of a believer coming to a crisis in which he or she learns to "abide in Christ," Kargel also taught the need for each believer to be filled with the Holy Spirit. Jesus was baptized by the Holy Spirit at his water baptism, says Kargel, and the presence of the dove was a testimony to the people of a necessary action—of being filled with the Holy Spirit.[31] Kargel recalls his earlier days of being a Christian and writes that he "limited the fullness of the Holy Spirit to the twelve apostles." But later he realized that "[The fullness

---

27. Bebbington, *Holiness in Nineteenth-Century England*, 81.
28. Boyd and Eddy, *Across the Spectrum*, 157.
29. Kargel, "Xristos Osvyashhenie Nashe," 80–81.
30. Ibid., 82.
31. Kargel, "V Kakom Ty Otnoshenii k Duxu Svyatomu?" 135.

of the Holy Spirit] is not for the specially chosen, not only for apostles, evangelists, bishops, pastors, preachers, and teachers, or someone with outstanding ability to direct this affair or that, or those who have reached a sanctified level of redemption; no, it is for every child of God who has come from death to life and it is not based on their spiritual level."[32]

Kargel explains that there has been a lack of teaching regarding the indwelling of the Holy Spirit. It has been wrongly taught, he argues, that the gift of the Holy Spirit "can be received at baptism, in ordination and other ceremonies." Kargel goes on to state that the lack of proper teaching had caused a "sad state which is now an illness within the church at large." Linking this with another central theme of his—spiritual unity—Kargel suggested here that this illness in the church has led to many divisions that can only be healed by "examining one's relationship to the Holy Spirit."[33] Kargel did not explicitly say that the reception of the fullness of the Holy Spirit had to be a crisis experience, but he tended to support that view.

Kargel's teaching on sanctification was—as seen in the material he covered in the classes he taught at the Saint Petersburg Bible College—closely related to his teaching on sin. He believed that "many think that the purpose of God for them was no more and no less than their rescue from eternal death and hell."[34] But he argued for deliverance from the power as well as guilt of sin. If someone is concerned only with justification, he says, they will never leave their "carnal" mindsets. Even though their carnal mindset was removed at the moment of salvation, he contended that they would run back to their carnal views.[35] In describing the carnal life, Kargel uses (in *Christ—our Sanctification* and elsewhere) words such as envy, greed, irreconcilability, anger, passion, slander, gossip, the absence of love, gloating, self-seeking, ambition, vanity, and a grumbling mood.[36] His own crisis point (it seems) was not when he came to the cross of Christ for salvation, but when he came to the cross of Christ for sanctification, or for the death of his "old man." He calls others to move beyond the carnal

32. Ibid., 162.
33. Ibid., 137.
34. Kargel, "Xristos Osvyashhenie Nashe," 66.
35. Ibid., 51.
36. Ibid., 64.

Christian life and to abandon the efforts that come from their own power, and their own work, which will inevitably lead to failure.[37]

Following the crisis, there is a process. Keswick teaching was that once the crisis is recognized, it is "deepened by the awareness that even the believer's striving to be holy is often done in the flesh."[38] The moment of change should occur, Kargel taught, when a person becomes dissatisfied with their present spiritual condition. This will lead to a critical turning point. But the significance is in what follows. Kargel asks believers to "grasp with a childlike faith"[39] that through the sanctification of the Holy Spirit, they have been raised to a higher level of spiritual life in Christ. This childlike faith or trust, which is often associated with conversion, is also the way to sanctification; it allows a believer to yield fully to the Holy Spirit. Sanctification is not acquiring the Holy Spirit for the first time, since "every child of God has received the Holy Spirit,"[40] but what is needed is an ongoing and always developing sensitivity to the commands of the Holy Spirit. The commands of the Holy Spirit will be like "most gentle hints" that need to be obeyed.[41] "Victory [over sin] is only possible if the children of God, by means of a living faith, find themselves in a vital and consistently abiding relationship with Christ."[42] This, for Kargel, is the process issuing from the crisis.

EXALTATION OF FAITH

Another crucial element in Keswick spirituality was the central place given to faith.[43] It is faith that saves and it is also faith that sanctifies. One Keswick figure wrote: "The Keswick position is that in Scripture sanctification comes by faith, and not in any other way."[44] The *Keswick Week* published a query in 1899 about the validity of accepting "holiness by faith in the same way that we accepted justification by

---

37. Ibid., 56.
38. Boyd and Eddy, *Across the Spectrum*, 157.
39. Kargel, "Xristos Osvyashhenie Nashe," 56.
40. Ibid., 90.
41. Ibid., 91.
42. Kargel, "Grex kak Zlo vsex Zol v ehtom Mire," 37.
43. Bebbington, *Holiness in Nineteenth-Century England*, 81.
44. Macfarlane, *Scotland's Keswick*, 13, as cited in Barabas, *So Great Salvation*, 100.

faith."[45] Evan Hopkins, whose work was read by Kargel, responded by stating that "holiness is a gift [received by faith] before sanctification can be worked out in our lives . . . we work *from* holiness, not *to* holiness."[46]

This is also a powerful theme in Kargel's teaching. Kargel writes in stark terms: "Your silence and untroubled rest is an attribute of true faith; on the contrary, your anxiety, your timid crying and struggle, your pursuit, your independent actions, and your use of every possible means are a mark that you do not rely on Him."[47] For a person to seek to use their own strength to overcome sin was not a mark of a genuine desire to please God, but was the mark of a carnal Christian. The results of "the carnal ideas of believers will lead them towards a fleeting contentment with this state or to an elaborate [manufactured] theology."[48] Sin, for Kargel, is such an uncontrollable force that no mere human effort, even by a sincere believer, can overcome it. "It is a craft of Satan to make man believe that he can control sin by doing good."[49] Such a statement would often be made in an evangelistic setting, but for Kargel this was true for the believer as well as the unbeliever. Kargel's ideas were fully in line with Keswick teaching: sanctification, like justification, was by faith.

Kargel used the examples of King David in the Old Testament, Zacchaeus in the Gospels, and the Apostle Paul to show that it was the Holy Spirit's action to convict of sin and to lead to repentance and faith. Again, it is important to see that his primary application of these biblical examples was to believers. King David tried to cover his sin, but only after "the light of the Holy Spirit descends on him do we see him lying prostrate with tears in his eyes and we hear his appeals from a deep grief."[50] Faith, not human effort to do better, is the intended outcome of the work of the Holy Spirit in a believer. "Therefore," Kargel urges, "in temptations, needs, difficulties, illness, loss, struggles, and in all conditions, lean on Him and be still; that

---

45. *The Keswick Week*, 1899, 79–80, as cited in Barabas, *So Great Salvation*, 86.
46. Barabas, *So Great Salvation*, 87.
47. Kargel, "Xristos Osvyashhenie Nashe," 97.
48. Ibid., 105.
49. Kargel, "Grex kak Zlo vsex Zol v ehtom Mire," 35.
50. Kargel, "V Kakom Ty Otnoshenii k Duxu Svyatomu?" 117.

is where faith is found."⁵¹ For Kargel, faith is defined as "leaning on Christ" and is also connected with the ability to "see the promises of God."⁵² When a person has sanctifying faith, that person will "bring to God a full boundless trust; fully relying on Him and what He has said."⁵³ Believers cannot change the old nature by themselves, with their own effort. Many believers attempt to do that, but end up living a pitiful life and complain that they still have much sin. Kargel argued that all human effort to change this old sinful nature "leads us in a false direction and is attempted by a means which actually strengthens the old nature because instead of the old nature being put to death through crucifixion, it becomes stronger."⁵⁴ Kargel sought to make a powerful case for sanctification by faith, not works.

This faith means that a person abides in Christ. Ongoing union with Christ will give the believer victory over the power of sin. This faith is not, however, a passive thing, but must be "recognized and tasted," causing someone "to come to, to live, to walk, and to abide in Jesus the Christ."⁵⁵ This faith will grow over time, allowing someone to withstand more and more the forces of sin. As an individual's faith grows in the process of sanctification, their spiritual "blindness" (a very strong term to use in relation to a believer) gives way to sight, so that they can see God "in us, around us, before us, and behind us."⁵⁶ Not surprisingly, this is connected by Kargel with the Holy Spirit. The fullness of the Spirit is appropriated by faith. Kargel explains that there are two types of faith: "asking faith" and "taking faith."⁵⁷ "Asking faith" is only concerned with asking Jesus for forgiveness. The second type of faith, the one that brings sanctification, is the faith that appropriates or accepts the Holy Spirit. Kargel uses the terms "inhale" and "drink in" the Holy Spirit. This is not a once-and-for-all experience, but a moment-by-moment abiding. "And if you have already appropriated [the Holy Spirit], but again started to thirst, the word pertaining to you is: again and again 'come to me and drink.'"⁵⁸ This relationship

---

51. Kargel, "Xristos Osvyashhenie Nashe," 97.
52. Ibid., 98.
53. Ibid., 96.
54. Ibid., 76.
55. Kargel, "Grex kak Zlo vsex Zol v ehtom Mire," 38.
56. Kargel, "Xristos Osvyashhenie Nashe," 98.
57. Kargel, "V Kakom Ty Otnoshenii k Duxu Svyatomu?" 163–64.
58. Ibid., 164.

with Christ is offered, but must be appropriated. "All purity exists in Christ; but it is valid for us only then when we believe by faith, we take it as our possession, just as we took as our possession our forgiveness, justification and peace with God."[59] As in the Keswick teaching of the period, it is faith that causes the believer to remain in Christ and experience full sanctification.

Kargel often felt frustrated that this teaching was not well-known and in the light of that he regarded it as his special mission to emphasize the possibilities of the life of faith. "Unfortunately, many believers, those who have moved to a life in Christ, have not found out about the life of abiding in Him."[60] They are puzzled, he stated, why they still live as they did before they were converted, in their "feelings, ideas, words, and acts." There were also those who refused to accept this teaching:

> Others, on knowing it, nevertheless do not abide in Him, and this helps us to find the answer to a riddle: why they, as before, continue to live the life of the old man in their feelings, ideas, words and acts. And they cannot live differently because they are not in a condition to rise above their nature, just as a person cannot rise above the ground by pulling themselves up by the hair. Therefore Jesus, the Almighty One, is necessary for us, face-to-face. O if only you might learn that it all depends on whether we abide in Christ.[61]

His frequent use of the phrase "abide in Christ" reflects the influence of Andrew Murray, whose most influential book was called *Abide in Christ* (1895). Kargel stated that it was a "craft of Satan"[62] to try to make believers think that they could overcome sin by doing good works, rather than by faith. Rather than abiding in Christ, a believer who has been deceived tries to do good works in his own strength. Over time he or she becomes frustrated at the lack of success in his or her spiritual growth. At this point there is a need for a crisis point—a crisis that involves the exercise of faith.

---

59. Kargel, "Xristos Osvyashhenie Nashe," 68.
60. Kargel, "Grex kak Zlo vsex Zol v ehtom Mire," 38.
61. Ibid., 38–39.
62. Ibid., 35.

INTERNAL SENSE OF PEACE AND REST

A further mark of Keswick spirituality was "an internal sense of peace and relaxation."[63] In Keswick theology, the believer must cease from striving, to find a "resting-faith."[64] Kargel saw human wisdom and, more broadly, "the flesh," as enemies of the Spirit: they were in constant battle. Only when the Spirit takes control is there peace. Yet Kargel does not present the power of the Holy Spirit as something that can eradicate the sinful nature, as in some strands of Wesleyan theology. Rather, there is power continuously to overcome the sinful nature. This is offered to all believers if they come humbly as a child and "drink" of the Spirit of Christ. In fact, for Kargel, a Christian can lead a moral life and be respected for piety and yet "much of the activity and work that he calls 'fruit' are not really that because it was not accomplished by Christ in him."[65] If the fruit of someone's life is not rooted in abiding in Christ, it is false and not from God. It is from carnal strength. Good intentions are not enough.[66] The reason that human effort could never be appropriate for the sanctification process, in Kargel's view, is that sin is a constant force that will conquer the one who is not abiding in Christ. The believer can be blinded by the thought that "he can fulfill God's will if only he will correctly understand it, or just desire it."[67] Human effort will never accomplish the process of sanctification, for "only an abiding in Christ, connected to His death, destroys all authority of sin in all its forms. The power of the death of Christ, working in us, destroys the power of our old life, just as His death on the cross finished His life on earth."[68] This, as in Keswick teaching, is true rest.

For Kargel, however, sanctification came through yielding to the Lordship of Jesus Christ rather than through relaxation. Kargel wrote in 1912 about the need to "be changed into the image of Christ."[69] This was active. In 1925, he wrote, "Therefore only when Christ becomes truly Lord, above our will and our will power; when His essence

63. Bebbington, *Holiness in Nineteenth-Century England*, 82.
64. Boyd and Eddy, *Across the Spectrum*, 157.
65. Kargel, "Xristos Osvyashhenie Nashe," 72.
66. Kargel, "V Kakom Ty Otnoshenii k Duxu Svyatomu?" 146.
67. Kargel, "Grex kak Zlo vsex Zol v ehtom Mire," 33.
68. Ibid., 34.
69. Kargel, "V Kakom Ty Otnoshenii k Duxu Svyatomu?" 149.

penetrates and takes hold of our essence, our thinking, weighing, deciding, and behavior—only then will holiness be found in action and acts; whether they be on spiritual ground or on the ground of normal daily life."[70] Later he clearly states: "Only true sanctification gives God again the full right to reign over us."[71] When someone yields to God, he or she must "give up fully."[72] In talking about yielding, Kargel mentions believers yielding their lives, past and present, their precious time, and all their property to the purposes of God.[73] These are typical Keswick emphases. There are choices that the believer can—indeed must—make. "If we are not obedient to Him, we impede His activity because His Anointing is a living and active force, aspiring to use us as instruments. If we refuse Him His right to us, we push Him from ourselves."[74]

It may be significant that Kargel's stress in the 1920s on a more active dedication, favoring the idea of Christ reigning as Lord in the life of the believer, was being taught at Keswick in that period. As Keswick celebrated its Jubilee in 1925, Graham Scroggie, who became the minister of Scotland's largest Baptist church (Charlotte Chapel, Edinburgh) and was the most influential Keswick teacher of that era, directed the audience at the Convention towards "contemplating the greatest of all Objects—the Lord Jesus Christ."[75] For Scroggie, Keswick needed to move from a passive "rest of faith," which had been its traditional stance, and embrace a more vigorous activism. As Scroggie saw it, to "make Christ Lord" was the "single post-conversion act."[76] People could and should accept the evangelistic message that Jesus Christ died for their sins, but as believers they needed to accept the message that Jesus Christ was also their Lord. "Abandonment to the Lordship of Jesus Christ,"[77] as it was termed, became crucial at Keswick, as it was in Kargel's teaching.

---

70. Kargel, "Xristos Osvyashhenie Nashe," 63.
71. Ibid., 70.
72. Ibid., 91.
73. Ibid., 70–71.
74. Kargel, "V Kakom Ty Otnoshenii k Duxu Svyatomu?" 146.
75. *Keswick Week*, 1925, 275, as cited in Randall, *Evangelical Experiences*, 27.
76. *Keswick Week*, 1922, 109, as cited in Randall, *Evangelical Experiences*, 28.
77. Randall, *Evangelical Experiences*, 28.

For Kargel, an individual's prayer life, which should be active, was intended at the same time to be a mark of the peace and rest that accompany sanctification. "Consistent prayer,"[78] he stated, is a sign that someone has fully yielded to Christ and given up the "I" in exchange for "The Source." Prayers should not be undertaken as a duty. Prayers should become "for us a delight and pleasure—only then will prayers sanctify us."[79] If prayers consist only of expressions such as "my God, give me," they are a mark of "a poor soul," even if they are accompanied with tears. These kinds of prayers, for Kargel, were like a thirsty person lying next to a stream and asking someone for a drink, instead of taking the refreshing water.[80] Kargel goes on, in typical fashion, to instruct his hearers and readers that the true purpose of prayer is not to be calmed, soothed, or granted wishes. The meaning of prayer can be found in Christ and his prayers. Prayer, for Christ and for us, according to Kargel, is intended to "give a deeper taste of the Father."[81] This "deeper taste" will cause prayer to cease to be a chore; it will become an "inexpressible joy . . . delight and pleasure," and in that context it will be "prayer that consecrates us."[82] Again, rest is not the final purpose of the spiritual life but is a mark of a relationship with God. In 1925, Kargel clearly stated that sanctification "does not happen at all without us; it can only take place through our own will and personal decision."[83] Action was necessary—and true rest followed.

REPRESSIONISM

Repressionism is the idea that through sanctification sin is repressed, held back, and kept under control. This view was promulgated at Keswick and was considered a defining trait, although the word was rarely used.[84] In Keswick terms, "Victory over sin, therefore, is not a matter of suppression, eradication, or the ability to perform virtuous deeds; rather, it lies in the counteraction of the Spirit, who controls the

---

78. Kargel, "Xristos Osvyashhenie Nashe," 100.
79. Ibid., 99.
80. Ibid., 100.
81. Ibid., 101.
82. Ibid., 99.
83. Ibid., 58.
84. Bebbington, *Holiness in Nineteenth-Century England*, 83.

surrendered believer."[85] The main Convention teachers, such as Evan Hopkins, opposed Wesleyan ideas of "eradication"—meaning that the old sin nature is abolished, completely destroyed, and removed from the believer who has been sanctified. Keswick, from its beginning, regarded the idea of eradication as being "both unscriptural and dangerous."[86]

Kargel saw sin as an unstoppable force that is constantly active, affecting all creation, including the soil and plants.[87] It is like gravity, pulling everything down. Sin affected the angels, "bringing a change to their essence, character" and in "their attitude towards God,"[88] which resulted in Satan and the fallen angels being expelled forever from heaven. Humankind entered into sin along with all creation. Kargel writes of humankind created in God's image. "But, as sin penetrated heaven, it also penetrated into paradise, and caused it to be a place of death" and humans have "sadly become the carrier and the root of a sinful seed."[89] Kargel writes in his commentary on Romans 6:12: "This principle of sin also remains in the children of God. God has not destroyed it, because in itself it [the principle of sin] is not the misfortune, but we experience misfortune when we submit to its domination. If we stand in faith regarding our 'old man' and 'sinful body' (Romans 6:6), and together with Christ we are on the cross, then the sinful principle remains dead, completely paralyzed, and cannot harm us."[90] These quotations are good examples of the way in which Kargel promoted the Keswick idea of the repression of the sinful nature. When the believer is abiding in Christ, the power of sin is paralyzed. But the sinful nature is still powerful, more powerful than the ability of believers. This sinful nature cannot be eradicated. The only answer is abiding in Christ, but if someone ceases to abide in Christ, sin will gain authority and eventually induce the believer to return to a defiled life.

---

85. Boyd and Eddy, *Across the Spectrum*, 157.
86. Barabas, *So Great Salvation*, 72.
87. Kargel, "Grex kak Zlo vsex Zol v ehtom Mire," 42.
88. Ibid., 43.
89. Ibid., 42.
90. Kargel, *Zakon Duxa Zhizni*, 72.

For Kargel, sin is a sickness that carries the germ of death.[91] It "paralyzes the believer's vitality."[92] Sin is also a "despotic authority" that taints everything human, including the ability to reason properly.[93] The Holy Spirit must move upon a person's mind, first of all to open up to the person the knowledge of the immensity of sin. Only after this occurs can someone fully comprehend the cross. At the point of salvation past sins are forgiven, but the force of sin remains constantly present. Kargel believed that people and even people groups had habitual sins that caused them to react to God in different ways. He wrote: "All of us are born with a bent toward sin, but we came into the world without formed habits."[94] Habitual sins, as he saw it, are due to actions that are reinforced from people's exposure to a specific environment. Kargel believed that a person could leave a habit in the same way in which they formed it—gradually. Kargel explained again and again that it is only possible to break sin, even habitual sin, through Jesus Christ and his power.[95] Habits, although they are related to culture and environment, are rooted in sin and the victory over sin is found in Christ only. Through Christ's work, through the Spirit and through faith, sin is counteracted.

ROMANTIC AFFINITIES

A striking feature of many aspects of the Keswick expression of evangelical spirituality was that they were in part shaped by Romantic sensibilities.[96] This was seen, for example, in Keswick speakers' use of Romantic poetry and in their appeals to nature. Romanticism, as a broader cultural phenomenon, was a reaction to the Enlightenment stress on reason. Romanticism preferred to laud the individual will and human feelings, and encouraged a "'natural supernaturalism' . . . to discern spiritual significance in the everyday world."[97] It is significant that, in common with a number of Keswick Convention

---

91. Kargel, "Grex kak Zlo vsex Zol v ehtom Mire," 14.
92. Ibid., 16.
93. Ibid., 28.
94. Ibid., 26.
95. Ibid., 28.
96. Bebbington, *Evangelicalism in Modern Britain*, 167–69.
97. Abrams, *Natural Supernaturalism*, 32, as cited in Bebbington, *Evangelicalism in Modern Britain*, 81.

speakers, Kargel quoted poetry.[98] Few details of the poetry he quoted have survived, but Kargel did include one poetic work immediately following his account of his spiritual empowering in *Christ—Our Sanctification*. He spoke about how he realized that Revelation 3:20, where Jesus Christ is standing at the door and knocking, was meant for him as a believer to "supply me with the gifts."[99] He used this same explanation of the verse in his last written work.[100] It is clear that the understanding embodied in this poem was deeply felt.

> Only in Christ is there the freedom from sin (I John 3:6; Romans 8:2–10);
>
> Only in HIM is the end of the old life and the old "I" (Galatians 2:19–20);
>
> Only in HIM is the end of the life within the world (Galatians 6:14–15);
>
> Only in HIM is there always victory (II Corinthians 2:14);
>
> Only in HIM is strength and fortification (I Corinthians 1:24; Ephesians 6:10; Isaiah 45:24; Jeremiah 6:19);
>
> Only in HIM are we enriched with all (I Corinthians 1:5–7, 29–30);
>
> Only in HIM are all the Divine promises "Yes" and "Amen" (II Corinthians 1:20);
>
> Only in HIM is there unity with all God's children (Ephesians 4:16; John 17:21–23);
>
> Only in HIM is all new (II Corinthians 5:17);
>
> Only in HIM is it possible to reign in life (Romans 5:17, 21);
>
> Only in HIM is completeness (Colossians 2:10);
>
> Only in HIM can we pray and be heard (John 15:7).[101]

The Russian Baptist tradition took up the use of such poetry in worship in a way that was not true of Baptist worship in Western countries.

It is also the case that the writings of Kargel contain many expressions of personal feelings, although he never suggests that there should

98. Kargel, *Zakon Duxa Zhizni*, 173; Kargel, *Svet iz Teni budushhix Blag*, 20–21.
99. Kargel, "Xristos Osvyashhenie Nashe," 82.
100. Kargel, *Zakon Duxa Zhizni*, 156.
101. Kargel, "Xristos Osvyashhenie Nashe," 83–84.

be a reliance on feelings. When he first encountered the Pashkovites, he described the "thrilling feeling" as he heard "a prayer by such a person in high standing."[102] This is a classic Romantic expression. Kargel also spoke about the importance of "feelings, ideas, words, and acts" being transformed by abiding in Christ.[103] In terms of direct encounter with God, for instance in prayer, Kargel's language had Romantic overtones, as he stressed the possibilities of prayer. Kargel, however, in contrast to many Keswick speakers, did not have the kind of education that would have introduced him to a wide range of literature, and so his range of allusions was more limited.[104] Nonetheless, when he came to interpret Scripture, Kargel was concerned that the Word of God should not be approached in an overly rational way. He recognized that it was divine literature that spoke to the whole person, as created by God. He also urged looking at the biblical text afresh every time it was opened. He wrote: "If we seriously desire to receive all the new blessings and new forces from Scripture, we should awaken afresh to [the passage], coming to it as if we had never read or listened to it before and are reading it for the first time. Only in this way does God speak the word which is and gives life."[105] These sentiments reflect the Romantic perspective in his hermeneutics.

When speaking of being filled with the Holy Spirit, as he often did, Kargel frequently used Jesus' baptism as an example. The dove rested on Jesus. For the believer, sanctification comes as the result of "emptying ourselves for the heavenly Dove, so that He will find a quiet resting place for His feet."[106] The dove at Jesus' baptism came upon him because the Holy Spirit had finally found a resting place on earth that was "truly pure and holy."[107] Kargel here painted a powerful and

---

102. "Russland. St. Petersburg. Nachrichten Von Br. Kargel," 184.

103. Kargel, "Grex kak Zlo vsex Zol v ehtom Mire," 38.

104. Of the works of Kargel to which I am referring, many were originally written in German. I am using the Russian translations. If there was Romantic phraseology in the original German it may have been lost in the translations. Additionally, Kargel may not have been exposed to the Romantic language style to the same degree as some of the Keswick figures. For Romantic language among Keswick figures see Bebbington, *Holiness in Nineteenth-Century England*, 79–80.

105. Kargel, "Xristos Osvyashhenie Nashe," 94.

106. Kargel, "V Kakom Ty Otnoshenii k Duxu Svyatomu?" 158.

107. Ibid. 160.

dramatic picture. Jesus was the access point into creation for God's Spirit. To abide in Christ was to be filled with the same Holy Spirit.

Although Kargel was concerned to apply this to believers who were part of the Church in which the Holy Spirit was at work, he found dramatic power in Old Testament examples, as did a number of Keswick teachers such as F. B. Meyer. The example of Enoch who "walked with God" fascinated Kargel, and he challenged his readers: "Think about it, three hundred long years, never hiding from God, never leaving His eyes, to live a continuous life with Him and in Him! It cannot be anything other than the blessed life of spiritual triumph!" Kargel linked this with the teaching he found in the New Testament, suggesting that this "was something of what the apostle [Paul] tasted." Kargel quoted Paul, "Thanks be to God who always gives us triumph in Christ" (2 Cor 2:14). The idea of "tasting" highlights the senses. Kargel also applied this kind of metaphor to Jesus, saying that, "our Lord thirsted" for this experience for his disciples; and Kargel, almost inevitably, linked this with Jesus' words: "Abide in me, and I in you; he who abides in me, and I in them will bear much fruit" (John 15:4–5).[108]

The Keswick meetings were located in an area of England noted for pleasant and calm surroundings. Ivan Kargel and his family enjoyed the months they resided in the quiet seaside town of Hapsal as well as the days spent on the Pashkov Estate in Krekshino. But for much of Kargel's life he resided in Saint Petersburg, the Russian capital city, and also in Vyborg, which was a relatively large city, while often travelling to remote German and Russian villages. It was not possible to have a permanent convention center in Russia in Kargel's period. Many of the venues where Kargel preached were located in the natural beauty of raw nature. This was due to the persecution against Baptists, Mennonite Brethren, and Evangelical Christians during the Pobedonostsev era (1880–1905) which forced the preaching venues to be purposely held in a rural environment to avoid the surveillance of the state. But Kargel was thrilled when he could leave his activities for a time and rest with the family at the Pashkov Estate in Krekshino, south of Moscow.[109] In 1890, when Anna Kargel spent time in Krekshino, she felt "ten or eleven years younger."[110] The fresh

108. Kargel, "Vetxozavetnye Proobrazy," 270.

109. Kargel, *Zwischen den Enden*, 178.

110. Anna Kargel to Vasily Alexandrovich [Pashkov], 14 July 1890, 2/13/084, Pashkov Papers.

air and the quiet setting of the countryside estate appealed to both the Kargels. Towards the end of his life, it is clearly evident that nature appealed to Kargel in a significant way. He was renowned for his daily walks in the forest, where he would go for thought and prayer.[111] It does seem that Kargel was attracted by nature, drawn to the quiet forests where he spent more time during his last years of reflection and contemplation.

Yet at the same time as he valued spiritual experience, Kargel warned against those who did not place equal stress on the importance of authentic practice of the faith. He wrote sternly about such people:

> They believe that the life of true Christianity will consist of sweet feelings, edifications, spiritual pleasures, singing beautiful songs, and hearing inspired sermons, etc. When these things are offered to them, they are pleased. If words appear about the fruit of the Holy Spirit, about holy living, or about a change of their entire being, all this seems to be legalism and meanness to them. And yet, the intentions of God in our redemption are those very things; that we become a likeness of the image of His only-begotten Son: this is the only reason why He does not take us immediately to glory after our conversion.[112]

In his overall approach, Kargel urged those to whom he spoke to seek a Spirit-filled life which meant, for him, constant renewal. Life in the Holy Spirit, for him, caused, "all the directions of the heart to be new, a new life opens before us, always pressing forward . . . new ideas, new language, and even the most ordinary acts become fresh because they are renewed by God."[113] He asks the readers of his books to use "spiritual eyes," "inner eyes," and "spiritual ears" to sense what God is saying and not to rely on minds damaged by sin.[114]

Perhaps in all of this he was unknowingly shaped by Romanticism, but for him the key was a spirituality shaped by the New Testament. In his book, *What is Your Relationship to the Holy Spirit?*, as he discusses the fruit of the Spirit, Kargel speaks about this fruit as a "cluster of many berries. The same juice flows into each of them; the same powerful and wonderful force that flows through Christ our Vine will

---

111. Mickevich, "Poslednie Zemnye Obiteli I. V. Kargel," 24.
112. Ibid., 149.
113. Kargel, "V Kakom Ty Otnoshenii k Duxu Svyatomu?" 119–20.
114. Kargel, "Grex kak Zlo vsex Zol v ehtom Mire," 17–19.

keep us in unbroken communication with Him." With this power, he continues, everything is transformed: "your acts, your words, and all your ideas."[115] The concept is Romantic, but for Kargel it was strictly biblical.

PREMILLENNIALISM

Kargel's view of the Second Advent of Christ became more explicitly premillennial over time, showing the influence of Brethren and Keswick thinking. Premillennialism is a school of thought that has its antecedents in the early church[116] and that was elaborated in the works of the early Brethren figure, John Nelson Darby.[117] It holds that "the second coming of Christ will precede the millennium and is therefore imminent."[118] It is often coupled with a pessimistic outlook on the future.[119] In England its appeal was "chiefly to the well-to-do"[120] in the mid-nineteenth century where it had grown in popularity within the more conservative evangelical circles. The eschatology of the Brethren was premillennial, with strong Romantic overtones,[121] and at Keswick this teaching was also accepted.[122] Brethren were a significant presence at Keswick by the 1920s.[123]

By contrast, the German Baptist position on eschatology, which Kargel would initially have held, was not clearly defined. The German Baptist statement of faith affirmed the physical return of Christ as the "culmination of redemption" in such a way that "the eyes of the whole world" will see him. It also affirmed that the dead will "physically rise." There is no reference to a present or future millennium, a tribulation period, or to a particular sequence of events.[124] This allowed the early

115. Kargel, "V Kakom Ty Otnoshenii k Duxu Svyatomu?" 150–51.

116. Bebbington, *The Dominance of Evangelicalism*, 179.

117. For the development of premillennialism see Bebbington, *Evangelicalism in Modern Britain*, 81–86.

118. Bebbington, "Evangelicalism in Modern Britain and America," 192.

119. Grass, *Gathering to His Name*, 102–3.

120. Bebbington, *The Dominance of Evangelicalism*, 181.

121. Grass, *Gathering to His Name*, 168. For the Romantic elements in the Brethren see Bebbington, "The Place of the Brethren Movement in International Evangelicalism," 248–56.

122. Bebbington, *Holiness in Nineteenth-Century England*, 83.

123. Shuff, *Searching for the True Church*, 16.

124. Oncken, *Glaubensbekenntnis und Verfassung der Gemeinden Getaufter Christen*, 44–46.

German Baptists to embrace a variety of views about the eschaton. Kargel's 1913 Confession of Faith marks his departure from these German Baptist ideas, and clearly indicates a premillennial stance on eschatology:

> Christ is coming for His Own, invisible to the world (1 Corinthians 15:51–52), like a thief in the night (Matthew 24:42–44; 1 Thessalonians 5:2), but those who are watching for Him will not be caught by surprise (1 Thessalonians 5:4–10) and those who are ready will enter with Him into Glory (Matthew 25:10); [but] those who are not ready will be left with the unfaithful for the great tribulation (Matthew 24:40–41; 25:11–13; Luke 12:45–46). Those who have died in Him, He will [resurrect] from death; those and the others living [in Him] will be gathered up together to Himself (1 Thessalonians 4:16–17) so as to be [forever with the Lord].
>
> [But after that, Christ will come] with His Own and with His heavenly angels (Matthew 16:27; 25:31; Jude 14; Revelation 19:11–14) and every eye will see Him (Matthew 24:30; John 19:37; Revelation 1:7). Then the judgment will begin, but only for those who [are living] on the earth (Matthew 25:31–46; Revelation 19:15–19); from the unjust no one will [be resurrected] (Revelation 20:5) until the passing of the thousand years reign [of] Christ with His Own (Revelation 20:4).[125] When the thousand years have ended, [there will be a short interval of the hostility of Satan's people] (Revelation 20:7–10), then the unjust will [be resurrected] (Revelation 20:13) and the final judgment will take place (Revelation 20:11–15).[126]

This statement is clearly premillennial, asserting that Christ will return for his own, not seen by this world (the rapture), before a period of great tribulation, and that Christ will rule on earth for a thousand years.

This premillennial view was not the only eschatological view held among the Evangelical Christians of Russia. Although they accepted Kargel's Confession of Faith, it seems that Prokhanov himself espoused a post-millennial view, believing that Christ's kingdom was gradually expanding and that the church was preparing the world for the return of the Messiah. He had probably learned about this perspective during his time at Bristol Baptist College. Puzynin suggests

---

125. See Kargel, "Gde, po Pisaniyu, Naxodyatsya Mertvye?" 246ff.
126. Kargel, "Confession of Faith of the Evangelical Christians-Baptists," 158.

that the theology of post-millennialism "was well harmonized with the modernistic tendencies of [Prokhanov's] theology" and that it served as an engine for his social and political activity.[127] Provided "modernistic" is understood as "forward-looking," this argument is persuasive. Kargel, on the other hand, was exposed to premillennialism through his reading of Brethren authors. Premillennialism was a defining point of the Brethren and it undergirded their interpretation of Scripture.[128] Most Keswick leaders also came to espouse this theology.[129] Although both Radstock[130] and Pashkov[131] held to premillennial views, for a time Prokhanov's alternative approach was attractive within Evangelical Christian circles.[132] The tension between these two perspectives of millennialism was also experienced in English evangelicalism at approximately the same time.[133] However, under Stalin's leadership, when Russian evangelicals could not perceive that the world was becoming a better place, Kargel's premillennial view, rather than Prokhanov's post-millennialism, gained adherents.

Kargel's premillennial views are also shown in his *Where are the Dead according to the Scriptures?* In this book, as noted earlier, he discusses the condition of the human soul after death, attacking the view of "soul sleep," arguing that at the end all humankind will be divided into two groups, those who have died in Christ and those who have died in Adam.[134] Hell (and sheol), as understood by Kargel, is the realm where those who are "dead in Adam" reside until the final judgment, and is a place of suffering. Gehenna, he argues, is different from hell, and will be created at the end of time as a literal place, in which there is eternal suffering and the second death. In Kargel's opinion, it was unfortunate that Martin Luther had mistranslated "Gehenna" as "hell."[135] Those who die "in Christ"[136] before the final judgment

127. Puzynin, "The Tradition of the Gospel Christians," 189–90.
128. Shuff, *Searching for the True Church*, 1.
129. Randall, "A Christian Cosmopolitan," 179.
130. Puzynin, "The Tradition of the Gospel Christians," 56.
131. Ibid., 128.
132. Ibid., 202.
133. See Randall, *Evangelical Experiences*, 160–61.
134. Kargel, "Gde, po Pisaniyu, Naxodyatsya Mertvye?" 225.
135. Ibid., 246.
136. For Kargel, this would include those who died before Christ's first coming and had "saving faith," and therefore found themselves in Paradise or Abraham's

reside under "the table of oblation" with Christ.[137] During the time "under the table," the souls do not sleep: they can "see, hear, speak ... feel, remember ... have needs, and care for others."[138] These souls are in a state of rest, comfort, and fellowship with Christ, yet are able to make supplications.[139] The actual period of time spent like this is uncertain, because they will remain there until Christ returns to earth. According to Kargel, there will be two resurrections. The first resurrection will include "all those who belong to Christ and follow Him."[140] The second resurrection will occur after the destruction of the earth and will include all those who are "wicked" and have "died in Adam."[141]

Kargel's chronology of the eschaton is unmistakably laid out in this book: there is to be the first resurrection at Christ's first (secret) coming, the tribulation, the millennium, the destruction of the earth, the second resurrection, judgment, and finally the new heavens and the new earth.[142] This scheme is also detailed in his later book *Behold, I am Coming Soon*. Some of Kargel's work reflects pre-tribulation futurism, with the idea that Christ could return secretly at any moment, but there are also elements of historicist premillennialism, which approaches the book of Revelation and the prophecies of Daniel as narratives that can be "decoded by pairing symbols such as vials of wrath with remarkable historical events."[143] Throughout *Behold, I am Coming Soon* Kargel couples contemporary events with Scripture. He ends the book with warnings from three parables—the ten virgins (Matt 25:1–13), the ten talents (Matt 25:14–30), and the wicked servant (Luke 12:41–48)—which for him serve to highlight the truth that Christ will come when the time is ready.[144] As to the events of history, he tries to prove that the gospel has been preached to all the

---

bosom, as well as those who died after Christ's first coming and had "saving faith" in Christ. See ibid., 225.

137. Ibid., 217.
138. Ibid., 209.
139. Ibid., 217.
140. Ibid., 226.
141. Ibid., 231.
142. Ibid., 226–49.
143. Bebbington, *Evangelicalism in Modern Britain*, 85.
144. Kargel, "Se, Gryadu Skoro ... ," 425–30.

nations,[145] the church has reached its goal,[146] and the nation of Israel has been gathered.[147] All of these factors, for Kargel, pointed to the imminent return of Christ, signaling the start of the tribulation and then the millennium.[148] The Second Advent of Jesus Christ is affirmed in all the statements of faith of Russian evangelicals mentioned in *The History of Evangelical Christians–Baptists in the USSR* (*HEC-B*), but Kargel is identified in *HEC-B* as teaching that Christ will come for the redeemed, a coming "unseen by the world"—the secret rapture—and that Christ will finally come at the end of time and that this "will be seen by the eyes of all humankind."[149]

EVANGELICAL UNITY

Kargel's desire for unity and oneness among evangelical Christians strongly reflects an underlying principle in both the Evangelical Alliance and Keswick. The motto of the Keswick Convention was "All one in Christ Jesus."[150] Kargel's affirmation of the motto was evident when he wrote: "In Christ, the Head, there is a new unity between all members which must be recognized even though we are each members of different Christian streams."[151] The Evangelical Alliance, by its very name, sought to bring about evangelical cooperation. This vision influenced Pashkov, Baedeker, Wieler, Kargel, and others to start a similar organization in their context. Although the attempt to found an organization across the Russian Empire failed, there were fresh attempts at unity in the 1920s. In Britain, during the 1920s, the Evangelical Alliance was able to consolidate various traditions within evangelicalism by holding conferences with "Fundamentalists, centrists, and progressives [who spoke] together in defense of the gospel."[152] Although these precise divisions did not exist in Kargel's context, there were similar tensions between the Evangelical Christians and Russian Baptists. During the 1924 attempt at unity, for example, Kargel was

---

145. Ibid., 402.
146. Ibid., 403.
147. Ibid., 388, 404.
148. Ibid., 397–401.
149. Ibid., 446.
150. Randall and Hilborn, *One Body in Christ*, 152.
151. Kargel, "Xristos Osvyashhenie Nashe," 104.
152. Bebbington, *Evangelicalism in Modern Britain*, 221.

sent on behalf of the Evangelical Christians to seek to foster constructive dialogue with the Russian Baptists.[153]

Kargel viewed evangelical unity in spiritual terms. He constantly struggled, from the mid-1880s onwards, to promote unity within the Russian evangelical constituency, and his travels took him across denominational lines. He was often frustrated by a focus on the external aspects of Christianity. He wrote in 1912: "Concerning you, God's beloved, who are persistently demanding that water baptism should not be by means of sprinkling, you who do not recognize that our brother has been truly baptized if he has not been immersed, when will you start insisting that everyone be filled with the Holy Spirit, immersed in Him, because only that is a true baptism of the Holy Spirit?"[154] Kargel believed that evangelical theology was defective if it did not focus on the "sanctification of the heart and the realization of the unity of the Body, which was created by Christ."[155] For Kargel, the Holy Spirit was needed to bring unity within the body of Christ. He wrote to encourage believers to see the Holy Spirit as the key to fellowship. True fellowship was not based on "similarity of characteristics, gifts, position, education, opinions and views, position in society," or even membership of the same spiritual group; but "it is Christ, the Great Head of the Body, who connects all of them."[156]

As Kargel discussed the early church, for him a model to be followed, he pointed to their radical community life. Few people were prepared to take radical steps, said Kargel. "And this experience of the Holy Spirit has not been repeated since the first Church. O, if only [the Holy Spirit] would come through the Church today, it would clear the way for the same recurrence in her and in each separate living body, as the Body of Christ."[157] He writes: "The early believers also sold their houses and property and divided everything in accordance with the need of everyone (Acts 2:44–45). How could all this be undertaken? We read nothing about meetings and decisions of the church in this account. That was not the reason for such self-sacrifice; no they [self-sacrificing actions] will never accomplish similar things. There were

---

153. *Istoriya Evangel'skix Xristian-Baptistov*, 192.
154. Kargel, "V Kakom Ty Otnoshenii k Duxu Svyatomu?" 162.
155. Kargel, "Xristos Osvyashhenie Nashe," 105.
156. Ibid., 103.
157. Kargel, "V Kakom Ty Otnoshenii k Duxu Svyatomu?" 130.

no previous examples of this kind of activity. There can be only one explanation for this phenomenon; a higher power brought it forth. Why don't we insist on such things from the newly repentant?"[158]

Kargel's ability to bridge over divisions was noted by some Orthodox writers. One of these stated that Kargel's book, *What is Your Relationship to the Holy Spirit?*, "shows that sectarians, if they want, can create a climate within which, instead of sectarian egotism and intolerance towards people of other Christian denominations, there are the seeds of brotherly unity of all believers in Christ."[159] Just as Keswick "helped glue together Evangelicals from different denominations,"[160] so throughout his life Kargel applied that type of "glue" to the Russian-speaking evangelical context.

THE WORK OF THE HOLY SPIRIT

Kargel, in his writing about the Spirit, spoke of the "Higher Power" (from Russian, "power from on high").[161] The idea of "power from on high" for sanctification was common in Holiness circles. But there are unusual characteristics of Kargel's understanding. He writes concerning Christians who have been justified by faith: "[Christ] can speak to us, as to His disciples, at any time, 'You are pure,' but we may not possess this power from above because we have never declared a claim to the promise of it as our own property, and we also have never accepted its fullness."[162] This reference to "claiming the promise" of power comes from a fairly early period in his development and eventually gave way to the understanding that the "higher power" resulted from personal consecration and not a personal decision to make a claim upon it. Later he argued that sanctification involved the engagement of the human will or rather the submission of the will in "full consent with the will of God."[163] The power was also explained by Kargel in traditional Holiness terms as the power of Pentecost.[164] After Pentecost, the disciples were radically changed; they were children of God, filled

158. Ibid., 127.
159. Chepurina, "Ispoved' I. V. Kargelya," 509.
160. Bebbington, *Evangelicalism in Modern Britain*, 258.
161. *sila svyshe* [power from above].
162. Kargel, "V Kakom Ty Otnoshenii k Duxu Svyatomu?" 122.
163. Kargel, "Xristos Osvyashhenie Nashe," 58.
164. Kargel, "V Kakom Ty Otnoshenii k Duxu Svyatomu?" 121.

with his Spirit, speaking his words, and doing his deeds.[165] Elsewhere he states that they did not understand the process of sanctification even though they had spent three-and-a-half years with Christ.[166]

For Kargel, the "power from on high" was needed for holiness, true ministry, and ultimately to enable the believer to be Christ-like. A crucial reason to seek the higher power for Kargel was to please God and as part of that to stop sinning.[167] He viewed "cruelty, the absence of love, a carnal mind, and a desire to be praised" as signals that one was not living in harmony with the Holy Spirit and in need to "seize for yourself the force from above" and to "be filled with the higher power."[168] Kargel stated that God's power allows the believer to "give all we have back to the Lord."[169] When believers are filled with the Holy Spirit, they are enabled to be the Lord's property. Kargel reminds readers that every breath and every heartbeat are from God. "Not one day, not one hour, not one half hour belongs to you, but to the One who gave up his life to redeem your life and all you possess."[170] This power was also needed for ministry. Many are empty, Kargel argued, because they are not willing to give to others. The process of sanctification and being filled with power is not an end in itself to enjoy; it is intended for acts of service. He writes about why believers should be "filled," and insists that "it was not intended for them only, but also for others . . . self denying channels that are filling others, willingly giving each drop that is filling us."[171]

The final reason to seek power is to be like Christ. "Sanctification is necessary to separate us from sin and to make us Christ-like."[172] Kargel suggests that God's purpose is not that people become morally good. There are morally good people in this world but they do good deeds in their own strength and this is never enough to please God.[173] The higher purpose of God is "no more and no less than being in the

165. Ibid., 125.
166. Kargel, "Xristos Osvyashhenie Nashe," 87–88.
167. Ibid., 68.
168. Kargel, "V Kakom Ty Otnoshenii k Duxu Svyatomu?" 124.
169. Ibid., 70.
170. Ibid., 71.
171. Kargel, "V Kakom Ty Otnoshenii k Duxu Svyatomu?" 133.
172. Kargel, "Xristos Osvyashhenie Nashe," 71.
173. Ibid., 71–72.

image of the Lord."[174] This means that believers are similar to Jesus "in His life and actions, similar to Christ in his joys and sufferings, similar to Christ in his speech and being, and similar to Christ in his thoughts and emotions."[175]

Another characteristic of Kargel's view of the work of the Spirit is his thinking about "the anointing." He believed that "anointing" is a state of being. It was more than being filled with the Holy Spirit; it was a state of existence. "Thus, a great question is not whether we have accepted, reached, and taken hold of Him [the Holy Spirit] but whether He, at last, has received, reached and taken hold of us."[176] For Kargel, the anointing is "when the He [Holy Spirit] has seized them and their souls in every way, they came under His domination, only after He was breathed on them. This sacred heavenly consecration must seize our essence so that it belongs to Him."[177] He warns: "It is not a frantic triumph or frantic feeling . . . it is more like a silent state, a sober conscience."[178] The anointing "gently impregnates all of our essence up to the last fibers of the heart and dominates over it by means of promptings that bring happiness or promptings that bring prohibitions. But these prohibitions, prompted by the Holy Spirit in the state of anointing, do not feel slavish; they are promptings that bring unbounded pleasure as you abandon yourself to them, and you would never forfeit them, not for anything in the world."[179] This work of the Spirit will keep the believer away from unhealthy things.[180] For Kargel, however, this anointing is not connected to the idea of being sinless or perfect; rather than any talk of perfection he refers to the anointing as being like a gentle balm by which "our meekness will be known to all people."[181]

It is only possible for a person to receive the anointing, according to Kargel, when that person is fully yielded to the Holy Spirit; no

---

174. Ibid., 72.
175. Ibid., 73.
176. Kargel, "V Kakom Ty Otnoshenii k Duxu Svyatomu?" 146.
177. Ibid., 141–42.
178. Ibid., 142.
179. Ibid.
180. Ibid., 143.
181. Ibid., 144.

unconverted person can be anointed.[182] Kargel's view was that "the main stipulation to receive the anointing is that you have selflessly obeyed the Holy Spirit."[183] There are two conditions that must be met to receive and maintain the anointing. First of all, one must pay full attention to the Holy Spirit and encounter him in awe and worship. This is described by Kargel in exalted Trinitarian terms: "Think now of the Holy Spirit as the Creator of your new life, the Keeper of it, think of Him as the Third person of the Godhead who has undertaken supervision over you entirely, to change you into the image of the Christ."[184] Second, to maintain the anointing a person must continue in "selfless obedience to the Holy Spirit." Kargel states: "If you want to be under the anointing and abide in Him . . . there can be no yielding to the counsel of flesh and blood, or of human philosophizing."[185] In much of Kargel's writings in the area of pneumatology there is a certain dualism: the Spirit is contrasted with the flesh in a way that seems to undermine the unity of the whole person as a person renewed by the Holy Spirit.

A final distinctive element in Kargel's theology of the Holy Spirit is the idea of a Double Portion of the Spirit.[186] This theology is outlined in his work, *What is Your Relationship to the Holy Spirit?*, where he discusses the differences between Elisha and Elijah. Kargel notes the many things that are common to both the prophets, showing that they both proclaimed God's truth and exhibited full trust in the Lord. For him, however, Elisha is the prophet who always paid back evil with good.[187] Also, the ministry of Elisha reached outside Israel's

---

182. Ibid., 145.

183. Ibid., 146.

184. Ibid., 145–46.

185. Ibid., 146.

186. The Russian and English versions of 2 Kings 2:9 differ in that the Russian states "to me would be double," whereas the English uses the term "a double portion." Kargel reflects the Russian translation and calls this the "Spirit Double." I will use the more common phrase in English, "Double Portion."

187. Kargel, "V Kakom Ty Otnoshenii k Duxu Svyatomu?" 173. Kargel does deal with two difficult events in the life of Elisha that seem to contradict his view. The story of the forty-two children who were attacked by two bears is examined, as well as the leprosy that was inflicted on Gehazi. Both instances, explains Kargel, were not the result of Elisha's vengeance, but show his jealous protection of the name of the Lord and his commands. See Kargel, "V Kakom Ty Otnoshenii k Duxu Svyatomu?" 167–68.

realm and healed Naaman, an idolater and the commander of an army that represented a power opposed to Israel. Elisha, too, showed a concern for the ordinary person and everyday needs, for example when he rescued an axe head that had fallen into a stream.[188] Above all, in his work and ministry Elisha showed a love for his enemies by not calling down fire to destroy them.[189] The Double Portion of the Spirit on Elisha was for Kargel "the Spirit of Christ in which He shows His glory."[190] It was a Spirit that was "self-denying and loving, open to the poor, needy, and unfortunate ones."[191] It is a blessing that all God's children should seek.[192]

Kargel lists the things that are necessary to receive a Double Portion of the Spirit. First, it is necessary to remove any complacency that the Christian might have, making them willing to give all they have to gain the fullness of the Holy Spirit.[193] Second, a person needs to learn to believe as Elisha believed; to "seize God's hand" and go wherever God leads.[194] Third, the Spirit of Christ must be received in full.[195] Finally, it is necessary to die to self, offer self on the altar, and be finished with the old man.[196] The Holiness terminology could not have been more explicit.

THE SUFFERING OF GOD'S CHILDREN

The final aspect of Kargel's understanding of the sanctified life is the place of suffering. For Kargel it was suffering that united the believer more deeply with Christ. Toivo Pilli, writing of Baptist churches in Eastern Europe, states, "experiencing suffering for Christ, as well as living with an inward-looking view, were all an inseparable part of

---

188. Kargel, "V Kakom Ty Otnoshenii k Duxu Svyatomu?" 172.
189. Ibid., 173.
190. Ibid., 171.
191. Ibid. Kargel goes on in this paragraph to make reference to the early twentieth century in Russia, stating that "Soon the spirit of denial and the spirit of the antiChrist, which claim that they also care about the destiny of the unfortunate and the poor, will not be able continue their proud claims and appearance of righteousness."
192. Ibid., 179.
193. Ibid., 174.
194. Ibid., 176.
195. Ibid., 177.
196. Ibid., 178.

[Eastern European Baptist] self-understanding."[197] Suffering was the common language among the evangelical Christians in Kargel's *Sitz im Leben* and Kargel brought God into that conversation. In his book *Christ—Our Sanctification,* suffering is included as one of the crucial ways of achieving sanctification, being listed alongside the standard evangelical means of fostering the devotional life such as daily Bible reading and prayer.[198] It is the topic with which he chooses to conclude the book.

For Kargel, suffering not only identifies the believer with Christ and his sufferings; it also removes sin and its temptation by showing that the Christian cannot hold on to anything as a right—neither safety, nor possessions, nor health. Suffering also confirms that the believer is on the true and narrow way of Christ. It allows the believer to participate in Christ's holiness. Further, only on the journey of suffering can patience be born and developed.[199]

Suffering is often related to the struggle against sin. The suffering that a believer feels should be welcomed as the fire that refines gold, since it points to the reality that the Holy Spirit is committed to the believer. Suffering is proof of "perfect fidelity"; and it is a "test of obedience that should be accomplished all the more seriously and despite its difficulty."[200] However, not all suffering produces the intended result. Kargel states that there are two inappropriate responses. A person can ignore suffering, "never thinking that it is of the Lord," or can feel "despair under it," never looking to the Lord for strength and wisdom.[201] For Kargel, the purpose of suffering is not to produce grief or pain, but rather to direct the child of God into the will of the Father—to sanctification. He writes: "Certainly, illness, sufferings, losses, hard blows, or any grief in us, do not make us better if we do not look through them to the Father and find what He wants to tell us through them. Yet, even if we allow them to speak to us and we understand the will of the Father, but do not agree to go in His way, there will be no sanctification."[202]

    197. Pilli, "Baptist Identities in Eastern Europe," 97.

    198. Kargel, "Xristos Osvyashhenie Nashe," 105–13. He spoke of counting the cost, abiding in Christ, yielding to the Spirit, reading the Bible, faith, prayer, and fellowship.

    199. Ibid., 107.

    200. Ibid.

    201. Ibid., 108.

    202. Ibid., 106.

Kargel acknowledges that sometimes Christians suffer because of their own bad behavior. He mentions being in the Caucasus, bringing support and comfort to the banned brothers and sisters, when he heard of certain brothers who had not shown proper respect to the authorities and were sarcastic in their attitudes. He writes: "I should have told them, 'Dear friends, you are not suffering affliction at all for your Lord or because of your righteousness, but you suffer affliction for your language and for your bad behavior.'"[203] Perhaps the "should" indicates that Kargel thought of this response only later.

The theme of following Christ was central to Kargel's thinking about the Christian and suffering. For Kargel, suffering reminds believers that they are in the true way and that they have, as did Christ, laid their "lives on the sacrificial altar."[204] It confirms that they are on the true path, following Christ in his journey to the cross, and that their lives are in harmony with what Peter and Paul wrote—that all Christians must suffer. Kargel states that "there is no other outcome. Suffering is necessary for us to enter the kingdom of God."[205] Suffering is a means to sanctification because it reminds an individual that he or she is "a child of God."[206] Further, suffering allows a believer to "take part in His holiness."[207] God is at work creating those who are sanctified, who are being made in the image of his Son. Suffering is used by God "only because in the ordinary way He did not manage to achieve it [sanctification]."[208] It "removes all the roughnesses[209] from human nature and allows "spiritual fruit to ripen."[210] Kargel writes that only through suffering "can patience be birthed and allowed to achieve maturity and essentially only through patience will one achieve perfection."[211] Yet Kargel points out that "thousands upon thousands have not learned from suffering." Times of suffering are lessons and those who do not attend the lectures will never be able to

---

203. Kargel, "Vetxozavetnye Proobrazy," 321.
204. Kargel, "Xristos Osvyashhenie Nashe," 106.
205. Ibid., 107.
206. Ibid., 108.
207. Ibid., 110.
208. Ibid., 111.
209. Ibid.
210. Ibid., 112.
211. Ibid., 107.

pass the final exam,[212] by which he means the final judgment. Finally, concluding his discussion of suffering in *Christ—Our Sanctification*, Kargel suggests that suffering promotes expectation of the return of Christ, restores the habit of prayer and fasting, allows a person to hear Scripture's "fine melody" and affirms that faith is sufficient in all things and at all times.[213]

CONCLUSION

Ivan Kargel work, *Christ—Our Sanctification*, is a systematic explanation of his views concerning sanctification in the life of a believer. When Kargel's book is examined against the grid provided by David Bebbington in *Holiness in Nineteenth-Century England*, as he explains Keswick Holiness theology, the similarities are striking. This alignment with Keswick thinking is not only found in this book of Kargel's but is also evident in others written by him. It is remarkable to note the resemblance, considering that Kargel never travelled to Keswick nor participated in any of the major Holiness conferences in Europe. What he learned was gained through personal study and reflection on Scripture, through reading Holiness literature, and through spending extensive time with Baedeker and others who were shaped by the movement.[214] There are many allusions in Kargel's writings that point to the Keswick influence on his view of spirituality, including an element of crisis, the exaltation of faith, an internal sense of peace and rest, repressionism, Romantic ideas, Premillennialism, and the theme of "All one in Christ Jesus." Kargel in turn adapted the ideas to fit his unique situation, which was the evangelical movement in Russia in the late nineteenth and early twentieth century. Each of these elements was expressed by him in a distinct form and not simply translated into Russian or German. They were molded to fit the real life situations of Kargel's audiences. Additionally, Kargel added further dimensions to his expression of evangelical spirituality. He emphasized the work of the Holy Spirit and suffering. I would argue that the most significant feature of Kargel's expression of holiness is his work on suffering in the life of the believer and its direct relationship to "Christ-likeness."

212. Ibid., 111.
213. Ibid., 113.
214. Kargel quotes C. H. Spurgeon and D. L. Moody in this book. See "Xristos Osvyashhenie Nashe," 69, 98.

9

Kargel as a Spiritual Guide

Having looked at Kargel's teaching on holiness, a theme that became central to his distinctive understanding of evangelical spirituality, this chapter, which looks at the final part of his life, examines his wider role as a pastor and teacher within the Russian evangelical community. In 1919 Kargel reached seventy years of age and from this point until his death in 1937, at the age of eighty-eight, he held an undisputed position in the Russian evangelical community as a pastor and wise teacher—a spiritual guide. The period 1917 to 1925 is seen as a time of remarkable growth of Protestant evangelicalism in Russia.[1] Kargel lived through and beyond this period. His contacts with wealthy evangelicals continued. From 1919 until 1921 he was protected by Prince Gagarin during the period of terrible famines.[2] In 1920 he and his daughters moved to Kursk Province and travelled to Sumy Province on teaching trips.[3] In 1922 he returned to Saint Petersburg to teach at the Bible College. Some of the tensions between the Baptists and the Evangelical Christians, which Kargel had experienced since the 1870s, boiled up again in the mid-1920s. From 1928, the situation in Russia became very hard for evangelical groups, as Stalin instituted severe persecution. Despite all these hardships and difficulties, Kargel continued to work, and at the age of eighty-eight he produced a verse-by-verse commentary on the book of Romans. Between 1920 and 1928, six of Kargel's works, which have been mentioned previously, were published as books or in serial form.[4] His work on Romans is

---

1. Sawatsky, *Soviet Evangelicals*, 38.
2. Miller, *In the Midst of Wolves*, 66.
3. Skopina, "Iz Biografii I. V. Kargelya," 696.
4 The titles are: *Behold, I am Coming Soon*; *Old Testament Prototypes*; *Lectures*

generally more academic than his other works. For example, he cites commentaries by other authors.

The Russian Revolution and its consequent ramifications have been "one of the biggest events in world history."[5] The Russian Empire changed in 1905 to a constitutional monarchy with the implementation of the October Manifesto. The changes satisfied some, but not all, and the socialists pressed for further concessions, causing sporadic strikes and fuelling radical ideologies of dissent. Russia's political situation continued to deteriorate due to food shortages and a lack of fuel, which caused wide-spread strikes across the country. Tsar Nicholas II opposed the strikers and ordered the State Duma to dissolve in 1917. His actions triggered the February Revolution when his soldiers rebelled and sided with the strikers. Following this, Nicholas II abdicated his throne and the Provisional Government was established. The socialists, who were dissatisfied with the *bourgeois* Provisional Government, organized elections, causing the government to disband.

This situation allowed Vladimir Lenin and the Bolsheviks to seize control of the capital city in 1917 in what is known as the October Revolution, or the Bolshevik Revolution. Lenin then led the country into civil war as he and the Bolsheviks (the Red Army) asserted control. The opposition (White Army) included those still loyal to the monarchy, those in other political parties including elements of the Socialist party who opposed Marxist ideology, and many peasants. By 1921, Lenin's Soviet Communist Party had secured control of Russia. One year later, the Tenth All-Russian Congress was converted into the First All-Union Congress marking the early foundation of the Union of Soviet Socialist Republics (USSR).[6] Following the death of Lenin in 1924, Joseph Stalin gained control of the government and eventually set out immense plans for the industrialization and collectivization of the Soviet Union. As a result of his sweeping changes there were famine, deteriorating living conditions, and the implementation of a massive penal system. The penal system relied on internal exile, labor camps (*Gulag*) and executions. It categorized prisoners into

---

on the Second Coming of Christ; Where are the Dead According to the Scriptures?; Christ—Our Sanctification; and Ruth the Moabitess.

5. Figes, *A People's Tragedy*, xvii. This book is useful for its coverage of the Russian Revolution.

6. The constitution of the Union of Soviet Socialist Republics was ratified on 31 January 1924, ten days after Lenin's death. See Clarkson, *History of Russia*, 569–70.

three groups, those "involved in politics," "counter-revolutionaries," and "common criminals."[7] Those who opposed industrialization and collectivization as well as those who held religious beliefs were categorized as counter-revolutionaries and were imprisoned with common criminals. It is against this backdrop that Kargel lived his last years. This chapter will place this last period in Kargel's life in context, examine the commentary on Romans, and deal with the years prior to his death.

KARGEL AND THE STATE

The years following the Russian Revolution were shaped by two factors: Marxist ideology, as it created a new Russian society emerging from their Civil War, and the 1921 famine, which resulted from a drought and a lack of agricultural preparation due to the Civil War. Leninist interpretations of Marxist ideology established a framework for religious policy that continued throughout the Soviet period. The reality of Russian society was linked with a new ideology. The first editorial of the new Russian journal, *Revolution and Church*, in 1919, stated, "The short-range objective of the Soviet government is to establish a secular state by implementing the law 'On the separation of the church from the state and the school from the church'; the long range objective is to secure an atheistic society by transforming Russia's economic substructure and by indoctrinating its citizenry with the outlook of materialism."[8]

For the evangelicals in the Russian, Ukrainian, Belorussian and Transcaucasian regions, the dominant issue following the formation of the Union of Soviet Socialist Republic (USSR) was their relationship with the victorious political regime. At first, the Bolsheviks wooed the evangelicals.[9] In the years following the Civil War, the government exerted tremendous pressure on the Russian Orthodox Church, while leaving the evangelicals in relative peace. In 1912, the Ministry of Internal Affairs reported that there were 66,788 Baptists of Russian extraction in the Empire.[10] These numbers do not include the

---

7. Courtois et al., *The Black Book of Communism*, 137.

8. *Revoliutsiia i Tserkov* (No.1, 1919), 1–5, as cited in Blane, "The Relations between the Russian Protestant Sects and the State," 193.

9. Brandenburg, *The Meek and the Mighty*, 168.

10. "Statisticheskie svedenii o sektantax k l Ivanaria 1912" (St. Petersburg, 1912),

Evangelical Christian Union but do indicate that the Russian Baptist Union had tripled their numbers in seven years. The decade following the collapse of the Russian aristocracy could be referred to as a "Golden Age" for Russian religious dissidents.[11]

The Russian Orthodox Church suffered a significant set-back in this period. The Bolsheviks attempted to "modernize" the worldview of those they ruled by replacing religion with a science. They tried to disestablish the Russian Orthodox Church through political means, the confiscation of church property and controlling church-related schools. Patriarch Tikhon openly opposed the Bolsheviks and was arrested in 1922. Following Tikhon's death in 1925, the official relationship between Russian Orthodox Church and Soviet state remained undefined until 1943.[12] Prokhanov, in the midst of these changes within the Russian Orthodox Church, launched *The Gospel Call*, a journal aimed at influencing Orthodox believers in a Protestant direction. He submitted it to the censors and was granted permission to print 100,000 copies.[13] Prokhanov and the Evangelical Christian Union successfully reached out to many Orthodox Christians through conferences and personal meetings.[14] Part of the reason why the decade following the Russian Civil War was such a fruitful time for the Russian evangelicals was that they were led by the energetic Prokhanov and guided by the wisdom offered by Kargel. The Russian Baptist Union also experienced an increase in their numbers in this period, although they did not have such high profile leaders as did the ECU. J. H. Rushbrooke, the Secretary of the Baptist World Alliance, declared that the events in Russia in the mid-1920s constituted "a spiritual awakening which is unique in our time."[15] These spiritual awakenings in Russia were

---

in Klibanov, 224, as cited in Steeves, "The Russian Baptist Union," 89. For a discussion on Baptist population figures see Steeves, "The Russian Baptist Union," 89 n. 2.

11. Prokhorov, "The Golden Age of the Soviet Baptists in the 1920s," 88–101; Coleman, *Russian Baptists and Spiritual Revolution*, 154.

12. Without a state-recognized Patriarch to lead and unite the Russian Orthodox Church, Stalin intensified his religious persecution. In 1943, as a concession to gain the support of the Russian Orthodox Church, Stalin permitted the church to hold an ecclesiastical council to elect a Patriarch and recognized Sergius as Patriarch. For more on Russian Orthodox leadership between 1925 and 1943 see Shubin, *A History of Russian Christianity*, vol. IV, 107–54.

13. Prokhanoff, *In the Cauldron of Russia*, 210–12.

14. Ibid., 212–14.

15. J. H. Rushbrooke, "Baptisty v raznych staranakh," reprinted in *Baptist*, Nos. 1–2, 1926: 11, as cited in Steeves, "The Russian Baptist Union," 208.

dependent on freedom for the evangelicals and were cut short in 1928 with the implementation of Stalin's Five-Year Plan.[16]

Kargel lived through this time of enormous change in Russian society. There were new issues about church and state. Pacifism was one issue that caused considerable tension among evangelicals. It was not a position that was either advocated or opposed by the Pashkovites or the Saint Petersburg Evangelicals, although it was never a position Kargel espoused. It was not until the formation of the ECU that the question of military service was brought to the fore. During the life of the ECU, the attitude to military service moved back and forth, depending on the political climate. By 1920, pacifism was the dominant position of both the Evangelical Christian Union and the Russian Baptist Union.[17] In 1922, Prokhanov wrote an appeal calling on all Christians in the world to take concrete steps so that every Christian would refuse involvement in war.[18] In the following year, he was imprisoned for his alleged anti-Soviet statements. In 1923, in Stockholm, both the Russian Baptist Union and the Evangelical Christian Union appealed to the Baptist World Alliance to support a resolution declaring that Baptists throughout the entire world should refuse to participate in military service.[19] During his 1923 imprisonment, however, Prokhanov abandoned his pacifistic stance, and was then released from prison.[20]

The appeal from the two Russian communities was rejected by the BWA, which stated that the issue of military service was to be left to the individual conscience. Both groups returned to Russia from Stockholm to be told by the Soviet authorities that they would need to produce a statement at their next congresses in support of military service. It seemed that only after such a statement was made would freedom for their activities be considered. The Evangelical Christians held their next congress in September 1923, with Prokhanov as chair and Kargel as vice-chair. They discussed the issue of military service

---

16. There were two Five-Year Plans developed by Stalin: 1928–32 and 1933–38. They were designed to transform all of Russia into one socialized and industrialized state. For further reading on the industrialization of Russia and the Five-Year Plans see Boobbyer, *The Stalin Era*, 48–64.

17. Sawatsky, *Soviet Evangelicals*, 116.

18. Ibid.

19. Ibid., 117.

20. Ibid., 116–17.

and agreed to honor the Baptist World Alliance's request to leave the issue to individual conscience and "to ask members of churches to pray worldwide."[21] As a result of this statement which implied that individuals may submit to the government's desire regarding service in the military, nearly 400 members left the ECU.[22] The Russian Baptist Union, which held its next conference in December 1923, produced a statement that echoed the government's desire for peace and disarmament, but left the choice of military obligations to the individual conscience of each Baptist. Even with its diluted pacifistic statement, sufficient votes for its approval were only possible after the secret police arrested twelve conference members who staunchly supported pacifism.[23]

As well as the statements made at the congresses of the two Unions, Prokhanov and four other Evangelical Christian Union leaders wrote a letter declaring their loyalty to the government. In October 1923, the leadership of the Evangelical Christian Union accepted military service but left the manner of service (taking up weapons, medical service, or alternative labor) up to the personal discretion of each Christian,[24] with Kargel being quoted as supportive of "full recognition of military service."[25] Prokhanov was forced publicly to retract his previous support of pacifism and to agree that his followers in the ECU should fulfill their duty to the government and serve when asked. Kargel never changed his views on the duties of a citizen to be loyal to the State, which included military duty when this was required. Over the next three years, the Soviets applied pressure to the evangelicals to produce resolutions opposing pacifism. Military service was becoming a litmus test of Soviet citizenship. Depending on the climate, the ECU would use the writings of Kargel to support military service or some of Prokhanov's to oppose it.[26]

Kargel was called upon at various congresses to field questions concerning his support of military service. In a 1932 letter to Ya. I. Zhidkov, then the leader of the Evangelical Christians, Kargel

21. *Istoriya Evangel'skix Xristian-Baptistov*, 205.
22. Ibid., 178.
23. Ibid., 205
24. Brandenburg, *The Meek and the Mighty*, 184–85.
25. Ibid., 185.
26. *Istoriya Evangel'skix Xristian-Baptistov*, 205.

complained about the badgering he was receiving.²⁷ In responding to questions on military service, he showed a desire to avoid splits over the issue.²⁸ But he consistently echoed the German Baptist Statement, which stated that it was a "Christian's duty" to serve the government the Lord had placed over them, even if that meant that they were to "bear the obligation of military duty."²⁹ Late in his life, during the Soviet period, Kargel was asked by the Evangelical Christian Union to reconsider his views. At the age of eighty-two, he was not prepared to change his stance on military service and he was much more concerned about wider political pressure. ECU members were being issued with "membership cards" to show they were "true believers."³⁰ In a letter to Zhidkov (who had lost three sons in war),³¹ he argued that the heart of the problem was not pacifism but rather subservience to the political powers. He writes:

> If your father was a casual trader or you yourself were a businessman, already your [ECU] membership is called into question [due to anti-capitalist Soviet ideology]. And more terrible it is for you if your son or father was an officer in the previous armies; but on the contrary, you may be blessed if your relative was in the Red Army. But still another mountain to climb is the possibility that you or your parents were landowners. That would be an inexcusable sin. The politics that you are involved with are worldly and have no place in Christ's kingdom and the work of the Union.³²

Despite the fact that Kargel was in close contact for many decades with Russian Baptists, Evangelical Christians, and Mennonites who held to a pacifistic stance, the views he held on church and state when he was with the German Baptists remained with him

---

27. Kargel, *Tolkovatel' Otkroveniya Svyatogo Ioanna Bogoslova*, 263. The full text of this letter was published as an appendix to Kargel's commentary. For further discussion of the letter see "Reshenie Orgkomiteta po voprosu protivocerkovnoj deyatel'nosti VSEXB."

28. Kargel, *Tolkovatel' Otkroveniya Svyatogo Ioanna Bogoslova*, 262–66.

29. Oncken, *Glaubensbekenntnis und Verfassung der Gemeinden Getaufter Christen*, 42–43.

30. Kargel, *Tolkovatel' Otkroveniya Svyatogo Ioanna Bogoslova*, 265. For further discussion of the letter see Kuznetsova, "Early Russian Evangelicals," 310.

31. Sawatsky, *Soviet Evangelicals*, 119.

32. Kargel, *Tolkovatel' Otkroveniya Svyatogo Ioanna Bogoslova*, 264–65.

throughout his life. He considered that it was the Christian's duty to support and obey the government. This view became the one officially held by the Russian Baptist Union and the Evangelical Christian Union.[33] Kargel's guidance was influential in this area.

PASTOR AND TEACHER

Ivan Kargel and his three unmarried daughters moved to Ukraine in August 1920.[34] At this point Elena was thirty-seven years of age, Maria was thirty-four, and Elizaveta was thirty-two. He was invited there by the Evangelical Christian Union leaders in the Sumy Region of Ukraine who recognized that their preachers needed training, but who were not able to send them to the college in Saint Petersburg. The Russian famine of 1921 was also a factor in the move.

The local Evangelical Christian congregation of Nikolaevka welcomed the Kargel family. At first the Kargels lived with the Zaxarchenko family, but they later moved into their own house, which the church members built for them near the home of a presbyter of the church. Amidst the difficulties of life during the famine, Elena and Maria held reading classes for illiterate people. Elizaveta assisted her father as he taught and sometimes helped him to express his thoughts in Russian. Elizaveta at times preached to the congregation and she also organized circles for the women and taught Bible classes.[35] Elena eventually returned to Saint Petersburg. Maria stayed with her father to oversee the family's domestic situation and Elizaveta continued her teaching ministry with her father.

From 1920 until 1923, Kargel taught two-week and six-week courses in a variety of villages in the Sumy Region. The six-week courses in Nikolaevka (in Sumy Province) were attended by up to fifty-five students.[36] Kargel also taught at eight-week classes on the Book of Revelation, the Second Coming of Christ, and Homiletics and Theology, with approximately fifty-five students in attendance.[37] In the period 1920 to 1922, Kargel served the small congregation in Nikolaevka. In 1922, a scandal broke out when a member of the church,

---

33. For a broader discussion see Steeves, "The Russian Baptist Union," 505–10.
34. Turchaninov, "Vospominanie o Zhizni i Sluzhenii Kargelya," para. 4–5.
35. Skopina, "Iz Biografii I. V. Kargelya," 697.
36. Reshetnikov and Sannikov, *Obzor Istorii Evangel'sko-Baptistskogo*, 172.
37. Skopina, "Iz Biografii I. V. Kargelya," 696–97.

Victor Mikhailovich Ternovenko, attempted (unsuccessfully) to influence the church in Nikolaevka to stop giving money and food to the Kargel family. It is possible that he had become jealous of the support and attention that was being given to Ivan Kargel and his daughters. Later that year, while the Kargels were on an extended trip to Saint Petersburg, Ternovenko sold the Kargels' house in Nikolaevka.[38] It seems that the church had built the house on Ternovenko's property and that the Kargels never received official government permission to live within the house. The Kargel family learned of the situation and viewed the loss of the house as a sign from the Lord. They did not return to Nikolaevka.[39] Their household goods were shipped to the smaller village of Tokara, seven kilometers from Lebedin, by A. F. Savenko, a member of the Tokara congregation.[40]

The village of Tokara is located on the small Psyol River (a tributary of the Dnieper River) in the heart of a large pine forest. When Ivan, Maria, and Elizaveta Kargel[41] returned from Saint Petersburg to the Sumy Region later in 1922, they settled in Tokara, which had a quieter pace of life than Nikolaevka and beautiful natural surroundings that suited them well. Tokara was still relatively close to the circles of believers they had been serving over the previous two years, and by the time the Kargels moved to the smaller village Ivan Kargel's reputation had spread throughout the region. People began to travel to Tokara from as far away as Romania to discuss spiritual questions and receive guidance from Kargel, who had by now come to be regarded as a sage.[42] At nine o'clock each morning, he held a family prayer meeting. He read from the Scriptures and expounded on the passages to his daughters and any visitors. Then they would pray and have breakfast. The time from ten o'clock until twelve o'clock was taken up with talking to visitors, who often lined up outside his door. At twelve o'clock he took his daily walk in the forest where he carried out his personal devotions and prayer. After twelve o'clock, his

---

38. Turchaninov, "Vospominanie o Zhizni i Sluzhenii Kargelya," para. 7.

39. The story is told in the village that when a wall was removed from the former Kargel house, a beam fell, crushing one of the Ternovenko brothers and that Victor Ternovenko was killed by "his own comrades" while leading the village police force during wartime. See Turchaninov, "Vospominanie o Zhizni i Sluzhenii Kargelya," para. 7.

40. Turchaninov, "Vospominanie o Zhizni i Sluzhenii Kargelya," para. 8.

41. Elena stayed in Saint Petersburg.

42. Skopina, "Iz Biografii I. V. Kargelya," 699.

daughters would continue to receive visitors, counseling and teaching in place of their father.⁴³

Despite Ivan Kargel being in his mid-seventies, he persisted in his itinerant preaching and teaching. Within the Sumy Region, he travelled to various churches to preach, teach, and counsel individuals.⁴⁴ There are many stories that speak about how he unexpectedly arrived at a church where his help was needed at that precise time.⁴⁵ It is also often said that he would pray for those who were sick and they were healed. This seems to have been a more prominent aspect of his work in this later period. Ivan Andreevich Koplik, who was involved in pastoral ministry along with Kargel in the village of Nikolaevka, related several stories of miracles associated with Kargel, including the healing of Koplik's daughter.⁴⁶ It is recorded that on one occasion Kargel prayed for a family that needed kerosene and, apparently miraculously, it arrived from abroad.⁴⁷

As well as engaging in local ministries, Kargel also kept in touch with wider ECU affairs. In 1923 Kargel served his final term as vice-chair of the Evangelical Christian Union with Prokhanov as chair.⁴⁸ He continued to teach in the various ECU extension campuses in Sumy and Poltava. He also served on the advisory board of the First All-Ukrainian Congress of Evangelical Christians held in Kharkov in 1926.⁴⁹

In 1923 the ECU was able to reopen the Bible College in Saint Petersburg and Kargel returned to teach in the college. The first course was a nine-month training program organized together with the Baptist Union.⁵⁰ The classes were held in *Dom Evangelia* [Gospel

---

43. Ibid. The daily habits of Kargel's life in Tokara were still well known to the believers when I visited in 2000 to interview people there who remembered him. I also visited his final home at the edge of the forest.

44. Reshetnikov and Sannikov, *Obzor Istorii Evangel'sko-Baptistskogo*, 172.

45. Turchaninov, "Vospominanie o Zhizni i Sluzhenii Kargelya," para. 6; Karetnikova, *Al'manax po Istorii Russkogo Baptisma, vypusk 4*, 289–98.

46. Personal interviews conducted in Sumy, Ukraine in June, 1996 by Irina Skopina with Alexander Andreevich, These interviews are in the possession of G. L. Nichols and I. N. Skopina.

47. Skopina, "Iz Biografii I. V. Kargelya," 697.

48. Ibid. In 1928, following the Baptist World Alliance meetings in Toronto, Prokhanov defected to Canada. He died in 1935 in Berlin.

49. "Pervyj Vseukrainskij S"ezd Evangel'skix Xristian," section 16.

50. *Istoriya Evangel'skix Xristian-Baptistov*, 215.

House], a building that had been built by Fetler and was now owned by the Russian Baptist Union. Fifty students graduated at the end of the first year.[51] Kargel taught in the nine-month programs in the city during most of the 1920s.[52] He seems to have continued his teaching outside the college, since in 1924, writing from Kharkov Province, he thanked a group in America for sending him ten dollars and mentioned that "The Lord allowed me to hold four Bible Courses here for the workers of God."[53] His teaching in the Saint Petersburg Bible College in 1924 included courses covering the Book of Revelation and the Second Coming of Christ, Dogmatics, and Homiletics. Other teachers included Ivan Prokhanov, V. I. Bykov, N. A. Kazakov, and V. I. Prokhanov (the son of Ivan Prokhanov). The Saint Petersburg College continued to operate until 1929, training pastors and missionaries.[54]

Kargel was given certain topics to cover, but it is clear that his influence in the college went beyond his set topics. One student during the mid-1920s recalled an evening at the college during which Kargel gave a talk on healing. He spoke from his own experience and also about those for whom he had prayed. The central point which Kargel taught on that occasion—the student recalled—was that the students should be in constant communication with the Holy Spirit through prayer, for it was only then that the Holy Spirit could begin to control and heal. The students should be in full submission to God's will and then there would be an anointing by Spirit, the vessels of their hearts would burn, and they would be consecrated to minister to the Lord and his people.[55] These concerns are fully consistent with Kargel's approach to evangelical spirituality as a whole, and the stress on healing indicates that as well as teaching the themes to which he had long been committed, he was introducing new emphases. In 1929 Kargel was arrested by the police while he was lecturing. This happened a few months after the initiation of Stalin's first Five-Year Plan. Following the arrest, Kargel was permanently banished from Saint Petersburg

---

51. Ibid., 204.

52. Class photos from this period feature Kargel and Prokhanov seated in the middle among their students. These were printed in *The Christian*. For examples of these photos see *Xristianin*, 4 (1924) 17; *Xristianin* 4 (1925) 67; *Xristianin* 4 (1927) 68; *Xristianin*, 6 (1927) 4.

53. "Svedeniya o Dele Bozhiem," 15.

54. Ibid.

55. Karetnikova, "Ivan Veniaminovich Kargel," 686–87.

and the college was closed.⁵⁶ Kargel returned to Tokara, Ukraine, and never returned to Saint Petersburg.

The Saint Petersburg College received funding from the Baptist World Alliance in 1923.⁵⁷ The origin of these funds may have been the Southern Baptist Convention. In 1924 the Convention reported: "Then, there is Russia filling the whole horizon. Up to this time we have been confining our endeavors to relieving the physical suffering of the people. It is only this year that we made a small beginning in a missionary way, and that was assisting the modest seminary of the 'Evangelical Christians' in Petrograd [Saint Petersburg]. They are staunch Baptists. It is indeed a humble start. At the earliest possible moment we must have in Russia at least one great seminary."⁵⁸ Five years later, the Saint Petersburg College had, since its initiation, produced nearly 400 graduates. Many graduates of the college looked back on those days with appreciation for the education they received.⁵⁹ The college was used by both the Evangelical Christians and the Baptists until 1927, when the Russian Baptist Union started their own Bible school in Moscow.⁶⁰

Prokhanov was in America from May 1925 until November 1926.⁶¹ He returned to Russia in late 1926 to teach and to lead the Tenth All-Russian Evangelical Christian Conference, and he remained until May 1928.⁶² He travelled to Toronto to attend the BWA meetings in 1928 and while he was there defected from the Soviet Union to Canada. Despite Prokhanov's great gifts, it was Kargel, rather than Prokhanov, who was the principal shaper of Russian evangelical spirituality.

---

56. Karetnikova, *Al'manax po Istorii Russkogo Baptisma, vypusk 4*, 59.

57. *Istoriya Evangel'skix Xristian-Baptistov*, 196. In 1911, the BWA had raised $75,000 for the establishment of a seminary in Russia. See Popov, "Vasilii Gurevich Pavlov and the Early Years of the Baptist World Alliance," 17. For an explanation of how that money was ultimately used see Jones, *The European Baptist Federation*, 109–11.

58. Gill, "Foreign Mission Board Report," 275.

59. Koval'kov and Chernopyatov, "Ivan Veniaminovich Kargel," 48–49.

60. *Istoriya Evangel'skix Xristian-Baptistov*, 215.

61. Prokhanoff, *In the Cauldron of Russia*, 227.

62. Ibid., 239.

KARGEL'S THEOLOGICAL INFLUENCE

One important way in which Kargel exercised a lasting theological influence on the evangelicals of Russia was through his 1913 Confession of Faith, which he originally wrote for his Saint Petersburg congregation. It was used throughout the ECU in parallel with other statements of faith, including one written by Prokhanov.[63] In 1944, when the Evangelical Christian Union merged with the Russian Baptist Union to form the All-Union Council of Evangelical Christians-Baptists (AUCEC-B), one of the ways in which unity was sought was through a common statement of faith. This became even more important later, when the AUCEC-B included the Mennonites[64] and Pentecostals. Kargel's 1913 Confession of Faith was officially adopted in 1966.[65] The fact that Kargel's confession was chosen over other statements, for example by Oncken, and Prokhanov,[66] shows how Kargel's views were seen as expressing a theology that was able to unite all the evangelicals of the USSR.[67]

In 1980, the AUCEC-B began to revise Kargel's Confession of Faith and a new statement was accepted in 1984 at the 43rd All-Union Congress.[68] Although Kargel's confession became the official AUCEC-B doctrinal statement, a variety of statements of faith circulated among evangelicals in Russia. Ten are mentioned in *The History of Evangelical Christians—Baptists in the USSR (HEC-B)*.[69] Of the ten,

---

63. Prokhanov's statement of faith grew to approximately sixty pages. For his section on the church see Lumpkin, *Baptist Confessions of Faith*, 423–35.

64. For more information on the incorporation of the Mennonites into the AUCEC-B see Sawatsky, "A Call for Union of Baptists and Mennonites Issued by a Russian Baptist Leader," 230–39.

65. Karev, "Doklad General'nogo Sekretarya VSEXB A. V. Kareva o Zhizni i Deyatel'nosti Soyuza Evangel'skix Xristian Baptistov v SSSR," 23; Sawatsky, *Soviet Evangelicals*, 344. Prior to this, the AUCEC-B did not have an official statement of faith other than the Apostles' Creed. See Puzynin, "The Tradition of the Gospel Christians," 226.

66. Karev, "Postanovlenie Vsesoyuznogo S"ezda Evangel'skix Xristian Baptistov Po Dokladu General'nogo Sekretarya VSEXB A. V. Kareva," 48.

67. Hebly suggests that Kargel's 1913 Confession of Faith may have been selected to appease the Communist government who did not like modern statements of faith as these could be a sign of living faith. See Hebly, "A New Confession of the Evangelical Christian Baptists in the Soviet Union," 6–7.

68. *Istoriya Evangel'skix Xristian-Baptistov*, 449.

69. Ibid., 438–39.

three are based on the 1847 Hamburg Statement of Faith,[70] three are related to the Evangelical Christian Union,[71] one is a Stundo-baptist confession from Kherson Province,[72] one is the Mennonite Brethren confession,[73] one belongs to the Pentecostals,[74] and the final statement is Kargel's 1913 Confession of Faith.

The authors of *HEC-B* compare these statements, and Kargel's Confession of Faith is frequently mentioned.[75] On the subject of the Word of God, *HEC-B* shows that the statements of faith by both Kargel and Friesen (also from the ECU) assert that the Word of God is "indispensable" for salvation.[76] On the subject of salvation, *HEC-B* states that Kargel believed in a two-step process of salvation: the first step was to move from unbelief to faith in Christ, which occurs by grace, whereas the second step, for further blessing, occurs through co-operation with the Holy Spirit. Kargel's view of the atonement is directly quoted in *HEC-B*. "I. V. Kargel, in his doctrinal confession states that salvation is 'by means of the death of Christ for all people, God offers propitiation, reconciliation, and pardon . . . of sins, justification and life eternal.'"[77] On the church, *HEC-B* draws attention to Kargel's

---

70. The "Confession of Faith of a Catechumen of the Russian Brotherhood" (1871), a statement of faith copied by M. Ratushnyi and presumably given to him by Johann Wieler; the "Hamburg Statement of Faith" (1847), translated into Russian in 1876 by Pavlov and used in the Caucasus Region; the "Confession of the Christian Faith of the Baptists" (1928), Pavlov's translation of the Hamburg Statement, republished by N. V. Odintsov in 1928.

71. The "Symbol of Evangelical Faith of the Petersburg Believers" (1897), used among the Saint Petersburg congregations (author unknown); the "Brief Doctrinal Statement of the Christians of the Evangelical Confession" (1903), written by P. M. Friesen, revised by Prokhanov in 1908, and accepted by a congress of the Evangelical Christian Union in 1909; the "Doctrinal Statement of the Evangelical Christians" (1910), written by Prokhanov, who later revised and republished it in 1924.

72. The "Confession of Faith of the Russian Baptists" (1879), written by I. G. Riaboshapka and submitted to the Ministry of Internal Affairs of Kherson Province.

73. The "Confession of Faith of the Mennonite Brethren of Russia" (1902).

74. The "Doctrinal Statement of the Christians of Evangelical Faith" (1925), probably written by Ivan E. Voronaev, one of the early leaders of the Pentecostal movement in Russia and a former Baptist.

75. Kargel's 1913 Confession of Faith is not explicitly mentioned with regard to statements on humankind, election, the means of salvation, conversion, the law in the Christian life, foot washing, oaths, dealing with enemies and proper church order between congregations.

76. *Istoriya Evangel'skix Xristian-Baptistov*, 440.

77. Ibid., 442.

distinction between the universal and the local church. Kargel makes clear that there is one universal Body of Christ.[78] The local church is the community that is "watching the purity and holiness of its members [and] removes the unclean [from her] midst."[79] It is also noted that Kargel's section on the church places importance "on interdependency and on *koinonia*" among the evangelical communities.[80] *HEC-B* notes that Kargel does not mention presbyters and deacons directly, as all the other confessions do, but rather uses Paul's list of "apostles, prophets, evangelists, pastors, and teachers."[81] In Kargel's section on baptism, he wrote, "the significance of baptism is diverse," but it "cannot be [administered] to children."[82] On the Lord's Supper, Kargel wrote: "The Lord's Supper was given to us by the Lord as a remembrance ... not only of His return for us but also that He is our spiritual and heavenly food."[83] Kargel does not mention the need for baptism or church membership to partake in the meal. This openness reflects the practice of the Pashkovites, which he had imbibed. He does state that baptism and the Lord's Supper are "entrusted only to the disciples of Christ."[84] Kargel's stance affirms evangelical unity and also diversity.

Ethical and societal issues are also covered in his 1913 Confession of Faith. On marriage, *HEC-B* states that when comparing all the confessions it is only Kargel's that does not permit remarriage and "considers that the divorcee should remain celibate."[85] He stated that "only death [can release] one from marriage" and that divorce is only permitted in the case of adultery.[86] The author's of *HEC-B* have actually constructed an argument from silence regarding Kargel's views of remarriage, because in his 1913 confession Kargel does not state that the divorcee should remain celibate. On questions of the Christian's duty to the government, *HEC-B* places Kargel's belief that Christians are to be obedient citizens alongside Prokhanov's argument for

---

78. Ibid., 443.
79. Kargel, "Confession of Faith of the Evangelical Christians-Baptists," 156.
80. Jones, *The European Baptist Federation*, 16.
81. *Istoriya Evangel'skix Xristian-Baptistov*, 443.
82. Kargel, "Confession of Faith of the Evangelical Christians-Baptists," 157.
83. *Istoriya Evangel'skix Xristian-Baptistov*, 444.
84. Kargel, "Confession of Faith of the Evangelical Christians-Baptists," 157.
85. *Istoriya Evangel'skix Xristian-Baptistov*, 445.
86. Kargel, "Confession of Faith of the Evangelical Christians-Baptists," 157.

alternative service rather than bearing arms. Kargel is shown to be in line with the Hamburg Statement. *HEC-B* quotes the Hamburg Statement as evidence that Kargel was not alone in his stance that governments are "empowered and vested with authority" from God and that the Christian is obliged to show "absolute obedience to laws of the country if those do not limit free discharge of duties of our Christian belief." The Hamburg Statement is unequivocal in stating that "we consider ourselves obliged to bear the arms of military service to the government when they will demand it from us."[87] Kargel, although he moved away from the German Baptists in many areas, retained their view of the state.[88]

Finally, on the all-important (for Kargel) topic of sanctification, *HEC-B* notes that the subject is covered only in two of the influential German and Russian Statements of Faith.[89] Only Kargel's and Friesen's statements contain references to sanctification. Despite all that Kargel could have said in a section on sanctification, he is virtually silent on the issue, except to say that, the "Holy Spirit is accomplishing the sanctification of the born-again." This is under his heading concerning the Redemption of Man.[90] *HEC-B* additionally makes reference to Kargel's book, *Christ—Our Sanctification*, as evidence of the importance for him of this aspect of evangelical faith. Kargel's book is the only book mentioned in this section of *HEC-B*, pointing to the influence of his writings for later Russian evangelicals. The lack of a separate section on sanctification in the 1913 Confession of Faith suggests that although this was a crucial matter for Kargel, he considered that it was not a question that should divide evangelicals. However, he places characteristic emphasis on the Holy Spirit in *What is Your Relationship to the Holy Spirit?*, which was written one year previously, in 1912. He refers to Acts 2:42, which states that the early Christians "devoted themselves to the apostles' teaching and fellowship, to the breaking of bread, and the prayers," and states that this form of community life could not have happened apart from the Holy Spirit's powerful presence.[91] For Kargel, all theology is pneumatological.

---

87. *Istoriya Evangel'skix Xristian-Baptistov*, 445.
88. Kargel, "Confession of Faith of the Evangelical Christians-Baptists," 157–58.
89. *Istoriya Evangel'skix Xristian-Baptistov*, 447.
90. Kargel, "Confession of Faith of the Evangelical Christians-Baptists," 155.
91. Kargel, "V Kakom Ty Otnoshenii k Duxu Svyatomu?" 127.

KARGEL ON ROMANS: THE HOPE OF SALVATION

It was during the final years of Ivan Kargel's life that he wrote a commentary on the Book of Romans. It is probably material he gave in lectures in Sumy Province in the 1920s. Only the sections on chapters 5 to 8 of Romans have survived, and they were published under the title, *Law of the Spirit of Life*. This book is almost certainly only a portion of the original work. There is no introduction or conclusion to the book and there are references throughout the work to thoughts developed in earlier chapters. Kargel makes his way through these four chapters of Romans verse by verse (and at times, word by word), expounding the meanings of the verses with a particular emphasis on their spiritual application.

He begins his commentary on Romans 5:1 by reminding readers that they have already explored the topic of justification in previous studies and that the Apostle Paul,[92] in this section, explores the consequences of justification. I will highlight key points in the theology of Kargel as found in his final book, seeking to show that in this last period of his life he emphasized certain distinctive aspects of evangelical spirituality.

Kargel writes in classically evangelical terms, telling readers that the moment a person believes in Jesus Christ as his or her personal Savior a peace arises within, confirming a real relationship with God. Writing on the evangelical tradition, Kenneth Collins states that this tradition highlights "the reality of the *personal* dimension of the gospel, that the saving faith in Jesus Christ is not a superficial work but a work of great depth in the life of the soul, one that touches believers deeply in terms of their hearts, dispositions, and affections."[93] Bebbington highlights assurance: "Once a person has received salvation as a gift of God, he may be assured, according to evangelicals, that he possesses it."[94]

This relationship, for Kargel, overcomes the "enmity that exhausted the heart and poisoned the life."[95] The antagonism of the past

---

92. Kargel clearly assumes Paul to be the author of Romans despite its place in the Russian Bible between the book of Jude and I Corinthians which could allow for some speculation.
93. Collins, *The Evangelical Moment*, 53.
94. Bebbington, *Evangelicalism in Modern Britain*, 6.
95. Kargel, *Zakon Duxa Zhizni*, 9.

has been forgotten, but unlike former enemies who are reconciled in limited ways, God as Heavenly Father opens all the treasures of his favors and "they become ours through our Lord Jesus Christ."[96] The believer enters this new condition through justification. It is a condition that is not static. Kargel argues in typical fashion that a believer "must enter all the more deeply"[97] into the state of peace with God. Many believers still live a "meager life." They have faith but no hope. "Faith always owns today but hope, in a sense, purchases the future . . . hope owns the future as definitely and truly as faith owns the here and now; it is therefore necessary to expect the arrival of the possession."[98] In Kargel's view, the possessions of the future are present in Christ: they are all the riches listed in Ephesians 1:3, 2 Peter 1:3 and 1 Corinthians 1:5–7. It is this hope in future blessings that allows someone to go through suffering, knowing that it is God's will. Kargel quotes David Brown[99] to suggest that patience means quietly waiting in adverse conditions, something which is only possible if someone has a sure hope in the things promised by God.[100]

Kargel makes a point of emphasizing the Holy Spirit in Romans 5:5. In familiar terms, Kargel states that without the Holy Spirit, nobody could press on in knowledge of God the Father or Jesus the Son. "The Holy Spirit pours light onto everything,"[101] he says, and is the first cause of someone turning to God. Without the Holy Spirit's promptings it is impossible for the heart to sense God's love. In Kargel's commentary on verse 5:6 he seeks to show that Jesus died for all humankind, but that there is a unique relationship for believers: "The Father saw us as being in the life of Christ and, in that sense, with Him when He died."[102] Sanctification is described as a "continuation of salvation."[103] Biblical salvation is the kind of progression that requires an abiding in Christ, which will result in the

---

96. Ibid.

97. Ibid., 10.

98. Ibid., 12.

99. This is probably David Brown of the Jamieson-Fausset-Brown commentaries (1871). Kargel quotes David Brown several times in this work.

100. Kargel, *Zakon Duxa Zhizni*, 14.

101. Ibid., 18.

102. Ibid., 19.

103. Ibid., 24.

ongoing removal of sin's force in one's life. Keswick theology taught that sanctification did not proceed automatically but that there were "grave responsibilities resting upon Christians" to walk in the Spirit.[104] Kargel echoes these thoughts in his introduction to Romans 5:12–21, stating that these verses show the transition from sin to forgiveness, and from "justifying faith to true sanctification."[105] Sin, like a poison, has come into the world through Adam.[106] Kargel quotes Godet,[107] who pictured sin in Adam as being like a spark that caused a wild fire; but Christ is the fire extinguisher who can put the fire out. Kargel goes on to say that Godet's illustration does not explain the text fully, because in addition to dealing with sin, Christ also gives peace with God, open communication with the Holy Spirit, and eternal life. Sin does not have the last word; God, through Jesus Christ, will dwell with humankind in an environment free from sin.[108]

Throughout the rest of his commentary on the fifth chapter of Romans, Kargel vividly contrasts the life of the first and second Adam, especially drawing attention to the devastating effects of sin on all creation. Life in the sphere of the first Adam is "as a dead fish floating in a stream, it does not have an opportunity to resist what happens."[109] Being in the sphere of the first Adam is to live "under the authority of the one who has the power of death, which is the devil."[110] However, for a person to have and to live a life in the sphere of Christ, the second Adam, is to have Christ as the captain. Life in the sphere of the second Adam also means to "receive full favor and gifts that lead to [submission to Christ's] lordship."[111] With Christ as the source of life, the atmosphere of life changes: "the atmosphere that surrounds them [the believer], which they inhale and exhale," is Christ himself.[112] Kargel is concerned here to point to the futility of trusting in anything

---

104. Barabas, *So Great Salvation*, 105.

105. Kargel, *Zakon Duxa Zhizni*, 27.

106. Ibid., 29.

107. Most likely Dr. Frederic Louis Godet, the Swiss-born New Testament scholar.

108. Kargel, *Zakon Duxa Zhizni*, 36.

109. Ibid., 39–40.

110. Ibid., 40.

111. Ibid.

112. Ibid.

connected with the life that has been shaped and is shaped by the sin of the first Adam. It is life in Christ that represents full salvation.

ROMANS CHAPTER 6: UNION WITH CHRIST

Kargel explains that in the sixth chapter of Romans, Paul will "speak about sanctification, which necessarily and certainly should follow justification if we participate in the salvation and redemption of Christ."[113] Kargel makes the case that, according to Romans 6, when people become Christians they are dead to sin. It is impossible, he argues, for them to live with—to abide in—sin; he categorically asserts that it is "absurd to think that one can still sin."[114] Yet human responsibility is involved. When Kargel examines Romans 6:2, he looks at the issue from another perspective. He asks his readers if they have truly come to the treasury of God's grace and seized, through his mercy, the kind of faith that will put all sin to death. This can only happen, he continues, when someone is willing to go further in their relationship with Christ by fully identifying themselves with the "the Great Head" [Christ]. Many poor believers "do not believe God and His Word and all that He speaks because they do not experience that they have died to sin."[115] These thoughts are similar to those of Andrew Murray, who wrote that, "Obedience is the path to holiness."[116] For Murray and Kargel, holiness was the result not simply of knowing what God has done, or being aware of God's will, or even wanting to obey it. What is needed is the actual "doing of it."[117]

Commenting on the question of baptism, as outlined in this part of Romans, Kargel argues that the baptism of believers, by immersion, is a unique, external, and visible sign for Christians that marks the "beginning of a life of faith and the death of sin."[118] It represents the certainty of a believer's union with Christ in his life, but particularly union with Christ in his death. Being placed under the water is a sign that the believer has died to sin; Christ's death becomes the believer's death to sin. Being raised from the water shows that Christ's

---

113. Ibid., 53.
114. Ibid., 55.
115. Ibid.
116. Murray, *The Believer's Secret of Holiness*, 52.
117. Ibid.
118. Kargel, *Zakon Duxa Zhizni*, 56.

righteousness has become the believer's righteousness, and Christ's obedience has become the believer's obedience. These conditions become active, Kargel suggests, not in the physical act of baptism, but through "knowledge and acceptance [of the gospel] through faith."[119] Just as a funeral is only given for someone who has died, Kargel states, baptism should only be given to someone who has died to sin. But, according to Kargel, many have been physically baptized who have no understanding of the essence of the meaning of what has taken place; they have the symbol but fail to comprehend the meaning of the symbol.[120]

Within evangelicalism, one of the issues most debated regarding baptism is whether a child of believing parents can be baptized.[121] Kargel denied the possibility of children receiving baptism, believing that "only those who heard [and] accepted the Word of God and believed in Him" could be baptized.[122] He does not argue explicitly for a sacramental view of baptism, for baptism as a means of grace, but he portrays baptism in exalted terms. He points to the three features of redemption that are explained in Romans and which are seen in baptism. The first feature is the sacrifice of the Son of God, which brings the believer justification. Everything that occurred before is forgiven and the person receives justification through Christ. The second feature of redemption is identification with the death of Christ, which leads to sanctification. For Kargel, the cross is the mark of a substitutionary sacrifice that takes away the guilt of sin. From the cross comes power, but to receive this power the believer must take his or her place with Christ on the cross. The third feature of redemption, for Kargel, is to abide in Christ. This abiding leads to all blessings being received by the believer.[123] Just as Christ truly died a full physical death and was raised to new life, so too the believer must die to sin and be raised to new life in Christ. This new life is explained by Kargel using the illustration of engrafting, in which "the cultivated sapling absorbs into

---

119. Ibid., 57.
120. Ibid.
121. Boyd and Eddy, *Across the Spectrum*, 202.
122. Kargel, "Confession of Faith of the Evangelical Christians-Baptists," 157.
123. Kargel, *Zakon Duxa Zhizni*, 58–59.

itself the life of the tree and rises up."[124] Spiritually, this is the life that comes from union with Christ and for this faith is essential.

This new life is not without conflicts, because the flesh is still connected to the first Adam. This might seem to contradict the idea of being "dead to sin." For Kargel, however, it is extremely important to understand that despite union with Christ and renewal by the Holy Spirit, a person does not break the relationship that all human beings have with the first Adam. "It [the old man] is to be found in the body, which means that until our old man is crucified with Christ, the sinful body will not cease to exist or be removed from us."[125] Being "crucified with Christ," for Kargel, is an ongoing process. The struggle reflects Keswick's position on the repression of sin: a "constant struggle going on inside the consecrated believer, but one in which God, if he was allowed, would always defeat the enemies of the soul."[126] A believer can be released from the power of sin, but a connection between the old man and the first Adam remains. It is constantly necessary to remember that the old man has been crucified with Christ. The believer must act in a way that shows that the "old man" is dead, because it was crucified with Christ; this is the life of faith. This is what Kargel means when he speaks of being united with Christ in his death, burial, and resurrection.

Kargel elaborates on Paul's comments on slavery and freedom in Romans 6:6–7 by stating rather starkly:

> The slave, while he was still alive, could not be released from slavery; he could try to refuse to work; he could complain bitterly, but that would not release him. Only when he was laid dead on a stretcher was his slavery terminated. Likewise, we are not released from sin except when we are crucified with Christ and remain so through faith in His death; only then will all the guilt of sin cease. We answer the requirements of sin as a dead person answers, and then we learn that sin, with all its temptations, has no power over us. Here, and nowhere else, are we rescued from the "old man" and the "sinful body."[127]

---

124. Ibid., 61.
125. Ibid., 63.
126. Bebbington, *Holiness in Nineteenth-Century England*, 83.
127. Kargel, *Zakon Duxa Zhizni*, 65.

For Kargel, Jesus overcame death through the cross and now holds the keys to death. Sin means that death has dominion over humankind. A sinless Christ chose to submit to the dominion of death in our place as the sacrificial Lamb of God. Using dramatic, Romantic language, Kargel wrote: "At that moment, when death had seized Him, its destruction reached its extreme limit . . . in the face of this One, death overflowed its cup and therefore had to return its force and supremacy to Him."[128] When Jesus died for sin he broke the power of sin; death lost its authority over humankind. True to his christological vision, Kargel describes how Jesus was raised from the dead by God the Father and how, since his resurrection, he has been in the presence of the Father. While on earth, Jesus rejected all sin, and now he has a resurrected body, which cannot sin. The application from Kargel is that "we by the power of our union with him in his death, we should be free from sin."[129] The believer's union with Christ is the source of the power to defeat sin.

Although Kargel believed that Christians should be free from sin, he acknowledged that as human beings they had freedom either to submit to sin or to overcome it. The struggle is lost when believers ignore the Holy Spirit, who speaks to Christians, reminding them of the death of the "old man." The sanctification process can be interrupted by human choice. The Holiness teacher, Jessie Penn-Lewis, who spoke at the Pashkovite meetings in Saint Petersburg, wrote:

> the believer needs to have a steady grasp of his standing in Christ as identified with Him in His death on the Cross, and his union with Him in spirit in His place on the Throne (Ephesians 2:19–23; 2:6), and he must "hold fast" with steady faith-grip, the "Head" (Colossians 2:19) as the One Who is, by His Spirit, giving him grace (Hebrews 4:16) and strength to recover the ground which he has ignorantly yielded to the foe. For the man himself must ACT to get rid of passivity.[130]

Kargel follows this approach, stating: "Do not stop your condition of being united with Christ's death, because if that happens you will lose all authority over the sin remaining in you and you will be seduced to follow what is harmful." He warns against the way in which

---

128. Ibid., 67.
129. Ibid., 71.
130. Penn-Lewis and Evans, *War on the Saints*, 92–93.

"the sinful principle dominates, raising unclean ideas, representations, imaginations and feelings, and together with them causes all kinds of lust."[131] Kargel clearly articulates the belief that the ultimate purpose of union with Christ is sanctification, a deeper walk with God. The desire for sin is to be counteracted. Kargel echoed the Keswick perspective that sanctification is not "a summons to inactivity but a call to duty."[132]

TWO KINDS OF CHRISTIANS

In his commentary on Romans 6:12–13, Kargel reaffirms his belief that there are only two kinds of Christians: either a Christian "absolutely rules over sin through unity with Jesus Christ or he is enslaved to it."[133] In the first condition, grace rules, leading to life; while in the second condition, sin rules, leading to death. There is no middle ground for Kargel. Anything other than union with Christ in the face of sin means that a believer will collapse against sin's overpowering force. Even if the person has been redeemed, sin will overpower that person, causing them to live a defeated, albeit redeemed, life. For Kargel, there is the dreadful possibility that a person can be saved but that sin is not crucified in the person's life. Kargel refers to the teaching of Jesus about cutting off sin. "These unfortunate souls look with their eyes and in due course consider with pleasure that which they should not see . . . the eyes were not pulled out, the ear, the hand, the leg, etc., were not cut off."[134] In Kargel's teaching, a life that has been redeemed, to serve and glorify God through the death and resurrection of Christ, may become so distorted that it gives up the struggle against sin and submits to sin's power.

Kargel's view of the Lordship of Christ comes through in his comments on these verses. The call is to complete submission to Christ. This is how he comments on Romans 6:13: "Give yourself absolutely, not partly, do not hold anything back; release your hands from yourself in such a way that you are no longer the owner, but the only true owner is God. Every kind of double-minded behavior must be put to an end. Our God has redeemed us completely and wants to

---

131. Kargel, *Zakon Duxa Zhizni*, 72.
132. Boyd and Eddy, *Across the Spectrum*, 159.
133. Kargel, *Zakon Duxa Zhizni*, 73.
134. Ibid., 74.

completely own us."¹³⁵ For Kargel, the Christian believer has a free choice: to sin or not to sin. Jesus, he argued, has released the believer from the power of sin and caused grace to reign over law.¹³⁶ To choose to be obedient to Christ is to be "walking with God" in righteousness.¹³⁷

When dealing with Romans 6:17, Kargel uses Greek and English commentaries and by pointing to the various translations argues that the word translated as "image" refers directly to Jesus Christ. "He [Christ] and no one else is the true prototype of the doctrine; in Him it was embodied."¹³⁸ This idea is important to Kargel's overall theology because what matters is commitment to Christ, not to a creed or a system of theology. This commitment must be wholehearted. Kargel is quick to point out that "without sanctification nobody can see the Lord." He supports this by showing that the new life of sanctification is unknown to "many 'Christians' who constantly bargain to see how much sin they can retain." This type of "Christians," he writes, has never yielded themselves to the Lord and therefore He does not know them and they do not know His new life. Kargel continues to show that it is as if they work on their own strengthen trying to reach the first rung of a ladder which will lead them to eternal life. But, they never comprehend that the "new life [sanctified life] is also eternal life" which is to be experienced in the here and now by knowing Jesus Christ.¹³⁹ By virtue of the pursuit of sanctification, believers can experience eternal life in the present, are free from sin and live in God's holiness.

Kargel quotes here from someone he simply calls "a theologian." It is significant that the quotation includes a standard phrase within the Holiness movement, "the blessed life." Kargel applies the quotation to his discussion of freedom from sin. "The blessed life is not only full freedom from original sin and the consequences of the fall but also a perfect life, pleasing to the Lord, similar to His, with freedom to approach Him in honest dialogue for all eternity."¹⁴⁰ The expression "full freedom from original sin" seems close to Methodist eradica-

135. Ibid.
136. Ibid., 78.
137. Ibid., 79.
138. Ibid., 80.
139. Ibid., 87.
140. Ibid., 88.

tionism. There is no evidence that Kargel read Methodists such as Phoebe Palmer, who placed great emphasis on instantaneous deliverance from sin.[141] But for Kargel, as for many in the Holiness camp, Christians could be divided into two categories: those dominated by sin and those overcoming sin through Christ.

THE NEW RELATIONSHIP

Moving to chapter 7 of Romans, Kargel emphasizes Paul's illustration of marriage as referring to the relationship that humankind has with the law. Adam is the "first husband." Jesus is the "second husband." But, some Christians, Kargel argues, wrongly think that they are still under the first husband's rules. The first marriage was under the law while the second is based on grace and is lived out in freedom.[142] In the first marriage, humanity is under the domination of death and assigned death's yoke. In the second marriage, humankind is released so that people can voluntarily, with all their hearts, fulfill the will of God. This abundant life can only be known through Jesus; it is the product of the fullness of life of Christ.[143]

It is possible, according to Kargel, for the believer to move between these conditions. Sin, as he repeats so often, is an ever present force in the Christian's life. The life under the law produces patterns and scars that cannot be ignored. If believers do not heed the promptings of the Holy Spirit, they will again find themselves "facing the deep abyss of destruction."[144] Kargel suggested that even St. Paul may have returned to a life under the law after he experienced conversion. When Paul speaks about his life under the law in Romans 7:9, Kargel writes that some theologians try to show that Paul was referring to the time before he was converted. But, Kargel—unusually among commentators—thinks that Paul may have been referring to his three years in Arabia, when he may have slipped back into a life under the law.[145]

It is the new and abiding relationship with Christ that brings about, for Kargel, a new "I." It is the new "I" that responds with the words, "I have died," when sin comes to tempt. This response is only

141. White, *The Beauty of Holiness*, 129–30.
142. Kargel, *Zakon Duxa Zhizni*, 95–96.
143. Ibid., 101.
144. Ibid., 104.
145. Ibid., 111.

possible because of union with Christ through faith. "If there is union through faith with the crucified and resurrected Christ, sin has neither life, nor power, nor domination; there is only the existence of powerlessness; sin cannot control; on the contrary, it is controlled from above."[146] This was widely accepted teaching at Keswick. The old "I" must be silenced, said Kargel, and the new "I," which is in Christ, must speak. Kargel emphasizes the differences between Paul's actions and his desires as stated in Romans 7:15. He stresses that there will always be a great chasm between human desires and godly action. "I am like a weak bow that does not possess what is necessary to shoot an arrow."[147] The ongoing struggle between the two "I"s will be constant. Only Christ can overcome the habits of sin. In a sermon preached at Keswick on this same chapter of Romans, Evan Hopkins illustrated this point of the two "I"s by referring to a cork tied to a piece of lead. The cork represents the power to float and the struggle is with the lead, which pulls it down.[148] It is likely that Kargel's ideas were derived from Hopkins.

Kargel strongly opposed the idea that the old nature would grow weak over time. This idea for Kargel is a terrible self-deception. He writes of the "powerlessness" of the "new man" without guidance from Christ.[149] On the positive side, Kargel highlights Romans 7:22 to show that it is possible to take pleasure in the law of God. Yet this pleasure in the law is opposed by the sinful nature. Kargel believes that the "law of sin is stronger than our spirit and our spirit by itself cannot stand against it."[150] The only hope is to terminate all connections with the past life. But this does not terminate the sinful nature. Kargel restated the Keswick interpretation of the struggling Apostle Paul in Romans 7, which opposed the idea that "Paul is describing the normal experience of every Christian."[151] Kargel considered that Paul was referring to his own attempts to live by human strength. For Paul, and all Christians, evil will remain the victor until the believer has come to the point that

---

146. Ibid., 119.
147. Ibid., 120.
148. Stevenson, *Keswick's Authentic Voice*, 161.
149. Kargel, *Zakon Duxa Zhizni*, 125.
150. Ibid., 128.
151. Barabas, *So Great Salvation*, 76.

he or she can truly take pleasure in the "heavenly law" of God.[152] For Kargel, pleasure in the law of God is a state in which believers find themselves freely walking in the way of God, accomplishing all things through Christ. In this state, he believes, when temptations or fears arise, the believer will be dead to them through the death of Christ. As Kargel ends his commentary on the seventh chapter of Romans, he makes the point again that if a believer takes pleasure in the law of God, he or she will be "more than a conqueror; the resurrection life will fill him and develop within him. Yes, he will overcome in life through his union with Jesus Christ!"[153] It would be difficult to match or surpass these clear words as a sustained elucidation of Holiness teaching.

VICTORY THROUGH ABIDING IN CHRIST

In the last section of his commentary on Romans chapter 5 to 8, Kargel takes up a very familiar theme—abiding in Christ. The words of Paul in Romans 8:1, "in Christ Jesus," have two meanings for Kargel. First of all, there is the reality of being justified through Christ. Second, there is the experiential truth of abiding with Christ. They are distinct, yet inseparable.[154] Using an example from the forest around him, Kargel argues that to be in Adam is like being connected to a dead tree, where any attempt to revitalize that life would be futile. To be in Christ means to abide ceaselessly with him and in him. "Where there is an abiding in Christ, there is no condemnation. It is very necessary to add to this that union with Christ is not something that gradually arises [is generated, formed]—no, let no one wait for that to happen. Nor is it something that we should create our own version of: we cannot create it by our prayers or our work. In fact, from God's perspective we are in Christ as soon as we believe in Him."[155] This truth of being in Christ is understood and experienced only with the assistance of the Holy Spirit. The "law of the spirit of life," as Paul puts it in Romans 8:2, is the Holy Spirit, who creates in the believer the ability to comprehend the redeemed life of freedom in Christ. "Really, the opportunity to live in

---

152. Kargel, *Zakon Duxa Zhizni*, 130–31.
153. Ibid., 133.
154. Ibid., 136.
155. Ibid., 138.

Christ Jesus is given to us thanks to the mediation of the Holy Spirit."[156] It is this relationship that is crucial. Kargel quotes a story from Evan Hopkins, to show this relationship.

> If the piece of iron could speak, what could it tell about itself? I am black, cold and rigid. But carry me to a fire and what change then will be made! The iron does not stop being iron, but the blackness soon disappears, the cold ceases, the hardness and rigidity too disappear. The metal has entered a new experience. Fire and iron—their substances are unique but as soon as they are connected, they become one. And if the metal could speak, it could not praise itself; it could only praise the fire which has made it a brightly shining object in the likeness of itself.[157]

Barabas notes that this illustration was "one used by [Evan H. Hopkins] in many of his addresses."[158]

When a person accepts the truths of Christ's redemption, it is possible that he or she still remains under the force of sin, never comprehending the words of the Holy Spirit. Kargel's high view of the Holy Spirit leads him to suggest that the promptings of the Holy Spirit may be aided by the Word of God but that "even if we cannot recall one of God's precepts" the leading of the Holy Spirit can be followed and there will be a fulfilling of the Word of God.[159]

Although Kargel's theology is clearly Christological and pneumatological, he also draws, as has been noted, from the Old Testament. He suggests that just as Israel was released from the bondage of slavery in Egypt, the spiritual Christian is released from the bondage to sin. Israel was condemned to wander in the wilderness because they did not trust God to bring them into the Promised Land, and the carnal person is condemned to wander in a wilderness of despair and death.[160] Yet the Israelites who left Egypt and those who wandered in the wilderness were all children of God. Kargel argues that all Christians share the same eternal destiny, yet the relationship to the Holy Spirit varies: the Holy Spirit abides within the spiritual Christian but in the case of

---

156. Ibid., 139.
157. Ibid., 141.
158. Barabas, *So Great Salvation*, 79–80.
159. Kargel, *Zakon Duxa Zhizni*, 148.
160. Ibid., 155.

the carnal Christian the Holy Spirit is seeking to "release him from his carnal estate."[161] Here Kargel quotes Revelation 3:20 to show that Jesus is standing at the door of the heart of the carnal believer, requesting entrance. In the case of the spiritual Christian, through the Holy Spirit Christ abides and there is victory. For Kargel, it is impossible to separate the indwelling of the Holy Spirit from abiding in Christ.

This has implications in the area of victory over temptation. The spiritual Christian, in Kargel's thinking, will cease to pay attention to temptation: such a person is a "dead corpse" when it comes to sin, and is "spiritually alive to righteousness."[162] In his commentary on Romans 8:11, Kargel spends considerable time looking at the idea of the resurrection of Christ and the believer being given new life through the resurrection and pointing to the differences in the Russian and German translations.[163] He concludes by stating that the resurrection life in Christ is not meant to be understood as a future state, but is for the believer a present state of victory. "But he [Paul] speaks about the resurrection as something in the present, achievable now, yes, which he probably has already achieved."[164] For Kargel, to live the sanctified life was to live in the present moment in the resurrection of Christ. If this does not occur, the converted person will lose the struggle against the flesh. Their life of "crying, struggling, praying, listening to sermons, and doing good works will not help if the life in the flesh has not ended."[165] Such believers have been deceived; they have reached the erroneous conclusion that their diligent religious activity will produce spiritual results. Kargel believes that the life of the Spirit that Paul expresses in Romans 8:13 is "not only a passive disregard for the desires of the flesh, but a conscious dynamic action by means of the Holy Spirit that lives in us."[166]

This dynamic relationship with the Holy Spirit occurs when someone concentrates all attention on Christ. This is expressed by Kargel in terms that suggest the kind of "nature mysticism" popular

---

161. Ibid., 156.

162. Ibid., 159.

163. Ibid., 163. He points to the German word *Auferstehung*, suggesting a broader meaning of resurrection than the Russian word for resurrection, which is limited to life after death.

164. Ibid., 164.

165. Ibid., 166.

166. Ibid.

at Keswick. F. B. Meyer recalled vividly how, in 1887, he climbed the hill beside Keswick and as he did so he received the Holy Spirit like the breath of the wind.[167] Kargel writes: "Our gaze must be directed on Him and our heart must be open to Him so that it will notice the slightest hint of Him; because He comes and speaks with a gentle and quiet whisper. His conversation is like a quiet and gentle breeze, which is clear only to those who are intimately close to Him."[168] Kargel, having spoken in such a significant way about contemplating Christ, then continues with his other major theme: the work of the Spirit.

> He does not drive and does not force, but involves and leads as one would lead children (Psalms 31:8–9). We should concentrate with all our being and watch closely to ensure that the Holy Spirit fills us entirely and guides our thoughts and deeds. It is all the same, whether we bear witness to the Lord, or talk about earthly affairs; whether we are talking with friends and brothers, or we find ourselves among strangers; whether we are happy or suffering; whether we are deeply struggling with temptation, or our path is taking us far above this earth—yes, in even the slightest trifles of our daily life the Holy Spirit must direct and have dominion.[169]

Beginning with comments on Romans 8:15 and on through to the end of the chapter, Kargel presents an understanding of the terms "Abba Father" and "sons and daughters of God." He believes that the term "children of God" refers to all of God's children, whereas the term "sons and daughters of God" refers exclusively to those who have matured. For Kargel, the term "child" or "children" implies someone who is young or immature. The terms "son" or "daughter," he argues, imply maturity.[170] The son and daughter also have a relationship with a parent. Someone could be a child and not know his or her parents while no one could be considered a son or daughter without knowing them. In a rather strange allusion, Kargel points to the exclusion of some from the priesthood in Nehemiah 7:63–65 because they could

---

167. Meyer, *A Keswick Experience*, 2–3, as cited in Randall, *Spirituality and Social Change*, 88.
168. Kargel, *Zakon Duxa Zhizni*, 169.
169. Ibid.
170. Ibid., 173.

not prove their genealogical record.[171] He uses the term "Sonship,"[172] a unique word in Russian, which he employs to refer to the mature followers of God, remarking that it better expresses the Greek. The term "Abba," when addressing God, is an intimate term. The use of "Abba Father" is significant for Kargel. The believer who addresses God as Abba "owns the right to stand face to face and eye to eye with our Lord, without any coercion from His side and without a shudder from ours."[173] Although Kargel stressed the believer's relationship with Christ and the Spirit, the relationship with God the Father was also crucial to his spirituality.

From Romans 8:23 onwards, Kargel builds on the idea of Sonship and brings in the idea of a "Double Sonship." The first Sonship is that of the spirit—the human spirit. This occurs when the Holy Spirit permeates the inner being of the believer. The second Sonship is that of the flesh, when the physical body of the believer is fully redeemed.

> This Sonship by which we have entered into the glorious redemption of Christ is double. We already have the first but the second is still necessary. The two are: the Sonship of the spirit, which we entered when we receive the Holy Spirit (Romans 8:9, 15), and the Sonship of the flesh, which will occur when it is fully redeemed. The first should lead into the second. The freedom of the glory of the children of God (Romans 8:21) does not exist when the spirit is released from the flesh and is saved, but when the bodies of the sons of God are freed from corruption and are redeemed. If we all exist in such a way that we are in the Sonship of the spirit then we shall sigh together with all creation waiting for the Sonship of the flesh, which is the redemption of our body.[174]

All of creation, including humankind's physical bodies, is still infected with the poison of sin, but one day all of creation will be restored to the creator and the effects of the fall will be eliminated. This is the final victory. The Double Sonship idea seems rather dualistic, but for Kargel it was a way to show that the sanctification process

171. Ibid., 175.

172. The Russian word he uses is *synovstvo*. It is not a word typically used in religious discussions, but rather a term which refers to the relationship between a biological son and his father.

173. Ibid., 173.

174. Ibid., 185.

starts in the inner person at salvation but will not be complete until it transforms the entire person, spiritual and physical.

The future state of liberation was of interest to Kargel, but the present state of the believer was of greater interest. For Kargel, it is the Holy Spirit who subdues the power of sin in the flesh and because of that the believer must live under his continuous guidance. The believer should be able to stand firm against doubts, fully alive and walking with Christ. There can, he argues, be a healing or sanctification of the spirit, soul, and body.[175] Yet, humankind (with all creation) is affected by sin and there is a constant pull away from Christ, producing—as Romans 8 puts it so graphically—sighs and groaning, longings for full redemption, or sanctification. Kargel notes that the human body and soul are joined to the universe "for they were at one time taken as a piece from it."[176] Sonship concerns the physical body as well as the spirit, since the body may begin to glorify God. The second Sonship has to do with the future, but in the process of sanctification it starts to be expressed while the believer is alive on earth. But the believer must wait patiently for the culmination of creation. Life on earth is like the school of patience, Kargel comments, preparing believers for the higher ways of God. He quotes Otto Stockmayer, a German evangelical leader who spoke at Keswick, to prove that patience means to "abide under something," implying that we are to develop patience as we live within, or even under, the suffering of the creation.[177]

When dealing with Romans 8:26, a verse used by some in the Pentecostal tradition to explain the phenomenon of *glossolalia*, Kargel is silent on the issue. He neither condemns nor supports the interpretation that the groaning here is speaking in tongues. He does state that there are times, mostly under difficulty and suffering, when one does not know what to pray. The options before a person in that situation are confusing: maybe they should pray that the trial be removed; maybe they should seek wisdom to find a way around the trial; or maybe they should seek more grace. Kargel suggests that the Holy Spirit acts in such times like an older brother who intercedes with the Father on behalf of the younger brother. The picture is a vivid one. The younger brother [the believer] lacks the "concepts and vocabulary"

175. Ibid., 187.
176. Ibid., 185.
177. Ibid., 188.

to address the Father. If the older brother [the Holy Spirit] is close enough to the younger brother, he can perfectly interpret the needs of the younger brother and "lamentations arise one by one, without words, as in a concentrated form, for their power is endlessly greater than words and is able to carry all our difficulties and needs upward to the Father's heart!"[178] Kargel does not state that the words are audible, but indicates that in his view the laments carried by the Spirit are beyond words. Later he clearly states that "we must know that our unspoken laments are heard,"[179] again showing that the groanings that are too deep for words are not spoken audibly. For Kargel there is victory through abiding in Christ, but it is not an easy victory.

CALVINISM AND ARMINIANISM[180]

The Calvinist-Arminian debate does not seem to have been one in which Kargel was deeply engaged. His early grounding in the German Baptist environment was Calvinistic. *HEC-B* states that the Hamburg Baptist Statement was "Calvinistic" because "one of its authors, I. G. Oncken [J. G. Oncken] was from his youth under the strong influence of Calvin."[181] This is a rather vague statement that does not do justice to Oncken's theological journey. As he became much closer to the evangelical movements in Russia than to the German Baptists, it seems that Kargel's views about Calvinism probably changed. However, he never speaks about how this happened. It is impossible to force Kargel into one of the classic systems of theology. Others have recognized this and called his 1913 Confession of Faith "a brief masterpiece," which has solved the issue of Calvinism or Arminianism for Russian evangelicals.[182] As he dealt with biblical passages he made

---

178. Ibid., 190.

179. Ibid., 191.

180. I am using the terms Calvinism and Arminianism in a popular sense. I am fully aware that there is much more involved in understanding these systems of Christian theology than "five points" on each side. However, my purpose is not to explore in detail these systems of theology but to show that Kargel was not a systematic theologian. He did not fit fully into either of these broad understandings of the Christian faith, choosing to operate outside these systems.

181. *Istoriya Evangel'skix Xristian-Baptistov*, 446.

182. Kouznetsov, "A View on Russian Evangelical Soteriology," 68. Kouznetsov and Peter Penner (co-promoter of the thesis) are native Russian-speakers who have a wealth of experience within the Russian context. This thesis seeks to take the discus-

little attempt to reconcile conflicting verses. In Kargel's Confession of Faith of 1913, he affirms the perseverance of the saints, meaning that someone cannot lose their salvation, by stating "the same Holy Spirit is accomplishing the sanctification of the born-again (2 Corinthians 3:18; 2 Thessalonians 2:13) and [protecting] them for eternal life (1 Peter 1:5; Jude 24; Romans 6:22)."[183]

Kargel's view of sin is very much in agreement with a classic Calvinistic approach, with its assertion of "the depravity of man." He affirms that sin has affected every area of creation, is passed on from parents to children, and even gathers strength through the generations.[184] Humans do not become sinful, but rather are born sinners. He states that the human mind and human reason are tainted by sin, and describes this experience as being like a fog. The power of reason, for Kargel, could not achieve spiritual results. It is confined to the "lower levels" of solving mechanical problems. The power of reason is affected by sin in such a way as to block all understanding of the divine and spiritual realm.[185] Sin has affected the human tongue,[186] heart,[187] and will,[188] rendering them spiritually incapable of comprehending God. Also in line with a Calvinistic viewpoint is Kargel's belief that the Holy Spirit must first act to open an individual's mind to the gospel. He states that, "no sinner will ever be released from sin and its power until Jesus Christ frees him."[189] It is, says Kargel, "the Voice of the Lord, which revives [believers] and bestows [on them] the power to live a spiritual life."[190] It is sin that "seals the mouths of sinners from praise and prayer . . . and causes them to be deaf to God's words."[191]

In *Christ—Our Sanctification*, Kargel affirms that believers were elected in Christ before the creation of the world, predestined

---

sion further, affirming that the Russian evangelical perspective on soteriology was deeply influenced by Ivan Kargel.

183. Kargel, "Confession of Faith of the Evangelical Christians-Baptists," 155.
184. Kargel, "Grex kak Zlo vsex Zol v ehtom Mire," 15.
185. Ibid., 30.
186. Ibid., 31.
187. Ibid., 32.
188. Ibid., 33.
189. Ibid., 34.
190. Ibid., 17.
191. Ibid., 19.

in Christ by the Father, and are new creatures in Christ.[192] This has Calvinistic echoes. But at the end of his life, in the *Law of the Spirit of Life*, he writes:

> On the question of faith, a person has the right of free choice; he can choose to believe if he wants and he can receive by faith the mercy of God, and likewise, he can reject faith and therefore reject salvation. Thus God, in eternity [before time], as He was predetermining and deciding, did not take away man's freedom and according to that he now directs His appeal [call] to the human will. If God had not taken the human will into consideration, it would have been impossible to accuse a person for remaining in faithlessness and hold him accountable. God's foreknowledge[193] of His elected ones leads them to being predestined;[194] so that they would be similar to the image of His Son.[195]

In the progress of salvation, Kargel believed that election is based on foreknowledge.[196] He does not teach unconditional election, but an election based on what God found when he "searched for something that was in alignment with His will."[197] For Kargel, election is not based on the decrees of God, or, as he puts it, an "arbitrary act accomplished by God with His eyes closed."[198] Kargel does not fit perfectly into either a Calvinistic or Arminian systematic theological framework. He is consistent with Calvinistic thought in his view of the depravity of humanity and the idea of the perseverance of the saints. But at the same time he is consistent with Arminian thought in believing that election is not to be understood as unconditional, simply a decree of God, but rather as based on God's foreknowledge. Predestination for

---

192. Kargel, "Xristos Osvyashhenie Nashe," 84–85.

193. *preduznanie* [foreknowledge].

194. *predopredelenie* [being predestined].

195. Kargel, *Zakon Duxa Zhizni*, 194–95.

196. Kargel's *Ordo Salutis* seems to be Predestination (Image of Christ), Foreknowledge, Election, Evangelism, Faith, Repentance, Conversion, Justification, Regeneration, Perseverance, Sanctification (first Sonship), Glorification (Second Sonship).

197. Kargel, *Zakon Duxa Zhizni*, 193. This is a paraphrase. In his original thoughts concerning God's will, Kargel wrote that it was an alignment with God's earlier decree that Christ's incarnation would be the standard by which humankind was to be judged.

198. Ibid., 194.

Kargel is a result of God seeing a future trust in Christ. It would also appear that Kargel held to an unlimited rather than a limited atonement, given his various statements that Jesus died for all sins but the application of salvation is based on being in Christ.[199]

Kargel's comments on Romans 8:30 show that he did not try to construct a systematic interpretation of Scripture to synthesize two opposing views. Kargel discusses God's calling to humankind. He writes that, "all whom God foreknew and predestined in eternity, now, here in time, He calls them."[200] In this calling, individuals understand that God is speaking individually and particularly to them. "This appeal is usually connected to two circumstances: God gives an open heart and an attentive ear (John 6:43–45; Luke 10:22–24; Matthew 11:25–30) so that the call will penetrate to the depths and become an irresistible call."[201] Thus, Kargel suggests that everyone has free will and yet the special calling of God is irresistible. He makes no attempt to reconcile these views.

Kargel ends his commentary on Romans 8 with a description of the love of God, likening it to an ocean.[202] All the elect are fully protected by the love of God, demonstrated in the death and resurrection of Jesus Christ. The love of God in Christ Jesus is also focused upon the redemption of creation. Kargel quotes Andrew Murray's statement that the only definition of God given in Scripture is that "He is Spirit and He is Love."[203] If someone has entered into the ocean of God's love in Jesus Christ, they will be hidden in that love forever.[204] This approach to the subject of election, one which cannot properly be labeled Calvinistic or Arminian, became a trademark of the Russian evangelicals.

In a 1966 report by A. V. Karev, the General Secretary of the All-Union Council of Evangelical Christians-Baptists, Karev stated that "we [the AUCEC-B] know nothing of the controversy between

---

199. Kargel, *Zakon Duxa Zhizni*, 19, 67–69; Kargel, *Svet iz Teni budushhix Blag*, 191–92.

200. Kargel, *Zakon Duxa Zhizni*, 196.

201. Ibid.

202. Ibid., 213.

203. Ibid., 206.

204. Ibid., 213.

Calvinistic and Arminian Baptists."[205] This is not entirely true. The Evangelical Christian Union and, to a lesser degree, the Russian Baptist Union had both been influenced by Ivan Kargel. It is true that Kargel did not subscribe to either Calvinism or Arminianism as systematic formulations, but he was aware of the debates. Kargel affirmed the free will of humankind and saw election as based on the foreknowledge of God. But, at the same time, he believed in a special calling that is irresistible for the elect, who have been given an open heart and sensitive ears.[206] The terms are those taken from soteriological discussions.

Toivo Pilli draws attention to the christocentric theology of Ivan Kargel, implying that it echoed Orthodoxy within the Slavic context.[207] The christocentric theology of Kargel has parallels with the Orthodox tradition, which sees "humanity reach[ing] its maximal realization" through Christ.[208] However, it is clear that Kargel's formation was within evangelical theology, with powerful Keswick overtones, and that his concern was for biblical rather than systematic presentations of doctrine. The position of the Evangelical Christians was that "the grace of God is offered . . . to all people, not just those predestined to be saved. God's predestination . . . is based on foreknowledge."[209] The All-Union Council of Evangelical Christians-Baptists followed Kargel and the ECU in refusing to be bound by established systems of theology in this area.

KARGEL'S LAST DAYS

Following Kargel's banishment from St. Petersburg in 1929, he and two of his daughters returned to Tokara in Sumy Province. In 1936 someone by the name of Morgunov arrived in Sumy Province and claimed to be from the Evangelical Christian Union. He visited many local congregations.[210] It is suspected that he was working for the government and that he took down the names of active evangelical work-

---

205. Karev, "Report of the Life and Activity," 8.
206. Kargel, *Zakon Duxa Zhizni,* 196.
207. Pilli, "Baptist Identities in Eastern Europe," 98.
208. Bunaciu, "The Meaning of Tradition in Orthodox Theology," 44.
209. *Istoriya Evangel'skix Xristian-Baptistov,* 447.
210. Skopina, "Iz Biografii I. V. Kargelya," 700.

ers and reported them. Certainly many arrests in the villages of Sumy Province followed Morgunov's visit.[211]

In August 1936 Elizaveta and Maria Kargel were arrested after a search of the Kargel home. They were imprisoned for nearly one year before being sentenced to a five-year exile in Siberia on 15 September 1937.[212] When Kargel's daughters were taken from him, he was moved to the village of Lebedin by the Tokara believers. One month before his daughters' sentences, on 5 August 1937, at the age of eighty-eight, Ivan Kargel was arrested by the police who also confiscated eight boxes of literature from his home in Lebedin. He had been in prisons all across the Russian Empire, but never as a prisoner. He and the other evangelical Christians were confined in Sumy Province's prison,[213] which was quite possibly one of the prisons he had visited in the late 1890s. His oldest surviving daughter, Elena, arrived in Sumy from Saint Petersburg while her father was still in prison but soon went into hiding.[214] He was confined for several days before being released due to his frailty.[215]

After his release, Kargel had nowhere to go. Many of the believers in the area had been arrested. Two of his daughters were now in prison and the third was in hiding to avoid arrest. After several days, a small apartment was found for him on the edge of Lebedin in an area called Bezymovke. A woman by the name of Ekaterina Ivanovna Vasilec took responsibility for him.[216] The story is recorded of the day before Kargel's death. He told Ekaterina Ivanovna, "Tomorrow, when you come, I will not be here, I shall be with the Father."[217] She suggested that she stay with him through the night, but he insisted that this was not necessary. "I want to be with my Father," Kargel insisted, and

---

211. Skopina says that there is no record of Morgunov in the archives of the Sumy churches and therefore infers that he was a Soviet informant. There was a Christian worker with the Evangelical Christian Union named Nikolay Georgievich Morgunov who first worked in Odessa and later moved to Kiev. He was put under Soviet pressure in 1937. See *Istoriya Evangel'skix Xristian-Baptistov*, 537–38. In 1926 he visited the various churches in Kharkov Province, which is next to Sumy Province. See *Istoriya Evangel'skix Xristian-Baptistov*, 491.

212. Skopina, "Iz Biografii I. V. Kargelya," 700.

213. This prison was built in 1650.

214. "Rossiya," 19.

215. Skopina, "Iz Biografii I. V. Kargelya," 701.

216. Ibid.

217. *Mickevich*, "Poslednie Zemnye Obiteli I. V. Kargelya," 22–23.

"when I shall leave to go to the Heavenly Father, do not search for me in a cemetery; and there is no need for any monument. I will not be here anymore."[218] Ekaterina Ivanovna returned the next morning (23 November 1937) to find that Ivan Kargel had died during the night.[219] His spiritual life had sustained him right to the end. Mrs. Sololova presided over his funeral, which was attended by ten women. All his remaining personal items were collected by the militia and his room was sealed by the police who, records show, even locked his cat inside.[220]

Days after Ivan Kargel's death, on 5 December 1937, his daughter Elena was arrested. She was accused of spreading counter-revolutionary propaganda among the Evangelical Christians and of protesting against the organization of collective farms. On 9 December 1937, in Kharkov, she was found guilty and sentenced to be executed.[221] On 16 January 1938, Elena, at the age of fifty-four, was shot and was buried in the east sector of Sumy's central cemetery. In 1989 she was rehabilitated posthumously.[222] Elizaveta and Maria Kargel served their ten-year sentences in Siberia. They both chose to stay in Siberia and with the assistance of friends, bought the house in the city of Jashkino, in Kemerovskoj Province.[223] The Kargel sisters continued their Christian ministry and corresponded with many evangelical believers in Ukraine and Russia. Their letters have been collected and were published in 1997[224] and 2009.[225] Despite the fact that they grew their own food, they were forced in their old age to live off the good will of others. The sisters were often invited to move from Siberia but never felt this was right. Elizaveta Kargel died of pneumonia in 1956

---

218. Skopina, "Iz Biografii I. V. Kargelya," 701. These words are not recorded by Mickevich.

219. There was no monument on his grave until 1982, when the All-Union Council of Evangelical Christians-Baptists celebrated his life and opened a new church in Tokara.

220. Skopina, "Iz Biografii I. V. Kargelya," 701.

221. The document has been published in Karetnikova, *Al'manax po Istorii Russkogo Baptisma, vypusk 4*, 299–301.

222. Skopina, "Iz Biografii I. V. Kargelya," 701. This is the process of acquittal or the restoration of a person who was prosecuted and sentenced without due basis in the period of the Soviet Union. The Russian word is *reabilitatsiya*.

223. Karetnikova, *Al'manax po Istorii Russkogo Baptisma, vypusk 4*, 288.

224. "Iz Pisem E. I. Kargel' o Razdelenii Cerkvej," 680–83.

225. Karetnikova, *Al'manax po Istorii Russkogo Baptisma, vypusk 4*, 231–88.

at the age of seventy. The last letter from Maria Kargel is dated 12 July 1961. Sometime after that letter, her neighbor wrote to Ekaterina Ivanovna Vasilec explaining that Maria had died at the age of seventy-five, shortly after a fire had destroyed all her possessions.[226]

CONCLUSION

This chapter has explored the final period of Kargel's life and in particular his role as a teacher and spiritual guide within the Russian evangelical context. His influence was unparalleled. Detailed attention has been given to his evangelical theology as expressed in his commentary on Romans. This work brings out all his major themes. There is his characteristic stress on full salvation from sin. "Through Adam, sin has come into the world and has come to the center [of humankind] to distribute all its vicious effects, its faults, its crimes, and its penalties. Sin, like a poison, like the cause of an illness, has come into the world through one person and become an epidemic, infecting all of humankind."[227] But there is redemption. The focus, as always, is on Christ. Redemption is full-orbed: "Here everything is given to us, related to life and abiding in Christ."[228] There are, for Kargel, immense possibilities related to union with Christ. However, many Christians fail to realize these possibilities. Kargel, in line with typical Holiness teaching, argues for two categories of Christians, carnal and spiritual: "Two completely opposite conditions, as different as night and day, occur in the life of faith for the children of God . . . So different are these two states that they make the difference both in the life and activity of the believer, depending on which condition they are found to be in."[229] Kargel also outlined the idea of a Double Sonship. This is the belief that there is a "Sonship of the spirit" and a "Sonship of the flesh." This chapter has shown that Ivan Kargel continued to influence Russian evangelicals through his teaching and writing. The *Law of the Spirit of Life* offers a summary of Kargel's distinctive expression of evangelical spirituality: to "abide in Christ," in his death, burial and resurrection, is the heart of the Christian life.

226. Ibid., 288.
227. Kargel, *Zakon Duxa Zhizni*, 28–29.
228. Ibid., 59.
229. Ibid., 149.

10

Conclusion

THIS BOOK HAS EXAMINED the life and work of Johann G. Kargel (1849–1937), who was later known as Ivan Veniaminovich Kargel within the Russian setting. The focus has been on Kargel's personal development and ministry, first within the German Baptist context and then as a leader among Russian evangelicals. He had an enormous influence within the Russian evangelical milieu of his time, particularly through his approach to spirituality. I have argued that from the 1880s onwards much of his thinking was derived from the Holiness movements that affected evangelicalism in the 1870s, and especially from the spirituality of the Keswick Convention, which began in 1875. A year before Keswick began, one of the advocates of the new views referred to a "mighty struggle going on in the Church of God between two doctrines"—"sanctification by works and sanctification by faith." The speaker advocated the second.[1] Kargel saw that choice clearly and also committed himself, from the early 1880s, to "sanctification by faith." The phases in his developing ministry are indicated in chapters 2 to 7 of this book, which take the study up to 1909. Chapters 8 and 9 are not delineated by dates. However, the focus of these chapters is on the last decades of Kargel's life and in particular on his contribution as one who commended the teaching of the inner life and who acted as a spiritual guide. The book has been organized mainly as a chronological study, since there are clear phases in Kargel's spiritual development. In this book I have relied heavily upon a primary source of personal letters between V. A. Pashkov and Ivan and Anna Kargel, particularly in chapters 4 and 5. This source has not previously been used and has

---

1. D. B. Hankin, *Account of the Union Meeting for the Promotion of Scriptural Holiness, held at Oxford, August 29 to September 7, 1874* (London, n.d.), 84, as cited in Bebbington, *Evangelicalism in Modern Britain*, 151.

yielded significant details in the understanding of Russian-speaking evangelicalism.

THE GERMAN BAPTIST PERIOD

Although there are few details of Kargel's evangelical conversion, it appears that it took place in 1869, and in the same year, on 6 October, he was baptized and joined the Baptist congregation in Tiflis, Georgia. This church owed its beginnings to Martin Kalweit, a German Baptist who found himself in Tiflis in 1862.[2] The small congregation attracted Germans and Russians. A number of future Russian Baptist leaders would come from this church, notably V. G. Pavlov and V. V. Ivanov.[3] Services were in Russian and German, but the stronger influence was German, since by this time the wider German Baptist movement across a number of parts of Europe was well organized and was expanding. It was this movement that gave Kargel his early spiritual nurture. The German Baptist vision, mirroring the wider Baptist vision of the period in Britain and North America, was strongly evangelical, emphasizing conversion, the cross, the Bible, and activism.[4] Each of these emphases was absorbed by Kargel and each was evident in Kargel's thinking throughout his life. In this period German rather than Russian ways appeared more impressive to the new believers joining the Tiflis church, as the Germans promoted organized forms of Baptist church life. V. V. Ivanov, from Tiflis, though critical of the "cold formality" and orderliness that he experienced among the German Baptist congregations, was also discouraged by the Russian believers' inability to achieve the efficient organization of the Germans.[5]

In the early 1870s Kargel also made contacts among another group of Germans—the Mennonite Brethren. His closest relationship was with Johann Wieler. This friendship was to last until Wieler's death, and Kargel and Wieler were to form an influential partnership. As has been seen, Johann Kargel lived with the Wieler family for several months in 1872,[6] and it was through the contact that was

---

2. Byford, *Peasants and Prophets*, 79.
3. Brandenburg, *The Meek and the Mighty*, 100.
4. Bebbington, *Evangelicalism in Modern Britain*, 2–17.
5. Gosudarstvennyi muzei istorii reigii, Koll. I, op.8, folder 1, l. 287, as cited in Coleman, *Russian Baptists and Spiritual Revolution*, 97.
6. Martens, "Grossmutter's Brief," 4.

established at that time with the Mennonite Brethren that Kargel attended a Mennonite Brethren conference in Southern Russia in 1873. He later referred to this conference as the setting in which he received his call into the pastoral ministry. In his short autobiography he wrote: "In 1873 I went to the conference in Klippenfeld (Molotschna) from which I began my ministry in the Word, which commenced in Volhynia."[7] This first ministry, in Sorotschin, in the far western part of the Russian Empire (in present-day Ukraine), was in a German Baptist church. From there Kargel went to Hamburg to train at the German Baptist Mission School, set up and led by Johann G. Oncken, the powerful leader of the German Baptists. Kargel did have some wider links, through Wieler, but his spiritual grounding up to the mid-1870s was firmly within the Baptist camp.

In early 1875 Kargel felt called to Saint Petersburg to be involved in the German Baptist church there. This move was to prove decisive in his spiritual development. From 1875 to 1880, as the (first) German Baptist minister in the capital city of the Russian Empire, Kargel had a high profile within the German Baptist community. He was excited at the progress in Saint Petersburg, writing in the German Baptist Union's *Missionsblatt* in 1877 about conversions and baptisms taking place.[8] But Kargel was also making new contacts outside Baptist life. A remarkable evangelical movement was taking root and growing in this period among a number of Russians from aristocratic circles. The origins of this movement lay in the influence of the English evangelical, Lord Radstock, and through his preaching in Saint Petersburg a number of leading Russian figures were converted to evangelical faith, including Colonel Vasily Pashkov and Count Modest Korff. In 1878 Kargel wrote enthusiastically in *Missionsblatt* about a meeting he had been to at Count Korff's house.[9] This was highly significant. Kargel's contacts with this stream of evangelicalism, which owed a great deal, through Radstock, to interdenominational British evangelical thinking and also to the Brethren movement, were to challenge Kargel's strictly Baptist views and also open up new spiritual possibilities.

A major turning point in Johann Kargel's life was his marriage, in 1880, to Anna Semenova, who (although not from an aristocratic

---

7. Kargel, *Zwischen den Enden*, viii.
8. Kargel, "Russia, Further News," 4–6.
9. "Russland. St. Petersburg. Nachrichten Von Br. Kargel," 183.

background) was a member of the Pashkovite circle, as it came to be termed. Kargel wrote about how "God gave me a helper" in 1880 and how, in the same year, he was called to Bulgaria.[10] It was at the 1879 German Baptist Conference in Hamburg that Kargel heard the news about a group in Bulgaria that wanted someone from the German Baptist movement to come and baptize them and establish a Baptist church. Kargel was already considering his future. He spoke in 1880 about how the weather in Saint Petersburg had been causing his health to suffer.[11] Johann and Anna Kargel, as a newly married couple, began their life and ministry together in Bulgaria in late 1880. Kargel conducted baptisms in Kazanluk and in Rustchuk, where the couple settled.

The time in Bulgaria was hard for Anna, who missed the Pashkovite meetings and the close fellowship she had known with Pashkov and his wife. Increasingly she began to pray that her husband would embrace broader evangelical views and would open himself to a deeper work of the Holy Spirit in his life. She wrote to Mrs. Pashkov in 1882 in forthright terms about how she had prayed that God remove Johann's resistance.[12] One issue about which Anna felt strongly was the question of who could be admitted to the Lord's Table. German Baptists restricted admittance to those baptized as believers while the Pashkovite approach, which Anna followed, was an open Table. Anna's hopes for change in her husband were realized. Writing much later, Kargel spoke of how in 1883 he found the sanctification he had been seeking.[13]

EVANGELICAL SPIRITUALITY AND EVANGELICAL MINISTRY

The Kargels, now with young daughters, returned to Saint Petersburg in 1884, to take up new work among the Pashkovites. From this point on, Kargel's ministry was to be primarily among Russian speakers. Pashkov was exiled from Russia in 1884 and Ivan Kargel took on major responsibility for the Evangelical Christian community in the

10. Kargel, *Zwischen den Enden*, x.
11. "St. Petersburg," 9.
12. Anna Kargel to Alexandra Ivanovna [Pashkov], 12 January 1882, 2/13/006, Pashkov Papers.
13. Kargel, "Xristos Osvyashhenie Nashe," 80–82.

capital. Kargel also developed a close association with Friedrich Baedeker, whose own evangelical faith had been shaped by Lord Radstock and who (like Radstock) was associated with the Brethren. Baedeker was involved in Holiness gatherings,[14] and as Kargel worked closely with Baedeker he imbibed more of the Holiness spirituality that was by then being mediated in Britain through the Keswick Convention. Baedeker was granted a unique authorization by the Russian government to visit the prisons of Russia. From the mid-1880s Kargel and Baedeker were freely able to travel together, speak, and distribute literature in normally inaccessible areas because of the authorization. The use of Christian literature was evident throughout Kargel's ministry, both as a form of evangelism and as resources for Christian believers. Through Baedeker, Kargel began to read publications such as *The Christian*, which would have confirmed him in his increasingly interdenominational evangelical approach, and Brethren literature such as *The Golden Lamp*.[15] An experiential evangelical faith was becoming central to Kargel's theological vision.

It is not that Kargel cut himself off from the Baptist world. In the period from 1884 to the late 1880s he was involved in wider events that included Baptists, not least a conference in 1884 in Novo-Vasilievka (which he co-chaired with Wieler) out of which came the Russian Baptist Union. But Kargel was less and less interested in the German Baptist approach, which laid great stress on the distinctiveness of the Baptist movement. Kargel followed the direction set by Pashkov, which was to seek to bring evangelicals in Russia together under the umbrella of an Evangelical Alliance, with denominational perspectives being played down. This approach can be termed "non-creedal," in the sense that what was primary was experience of Christ rather than assent to written confessions of faith, although the Evangelical Alliance did have a basis of faith and Kargel penned the longest-lasting Confession of Faith used by the Russian Baptists. However, the crucial issue for Kargel, as he put it in a letter to Pashkov in 1885, was not denominational but was about whether "the works of the Lord" were seen in the Russian Empire.[16] The nurturing of genuine spiritual

---

14. Dieter, *The Holiness Revival of the Nineteenth Century*, 171.

15. J. G. Kargel to "Dear brother in the Lord" [possibly Baedeker], 28 October 1885, 2/13/047, Pashkov Papers.

16. J. G. Kargel to "Dear brother in the Christ" [V. A. Pashkov], 4 June 1885, 2/13/016, Pashkov Papers.

experience, regardless of denominational affiliation, became Kargel's primary goal.

Increasingly, Kargel began to express his emphases in explicitly Holiness terms, using language employed at Keswick. By 1886 Kargel was holding what can be termed mini-Keswick meetings with Baedeker in different parts of the Russian Empire. He found the spiritual atmosphere of these meetings much more attractive than that which he had encountered in German Baptist gatherings. Thus in 1886, as he was sharing in one of these type meetings, Kargel wrote letters to Pashkov that were full of language denoting the influence of Keswick spirituality—"total dying to sin," "power in and through Him [Christ] to withstand temptation," and "full joy and full peace in a childlike faith in his personal presence."[17] Two years earlier, Evan Hopkins, the most influential thinker within the early Keswick movement, whose work Kargel read, wrote in *The Law of Liberty in the Spiritual Life* that when believers see that they are "identified with Christ in his death," what follows is that the believer "is also delivered from sin as a ruling principle. Its power is broken. He is in that sense free from sin." However, Hopkins also wanted to stress that there was progress in sanctification.[18] Kargel was by now the foremost teacher within the Russian evangelical community echoing this Keswick teaching.

In the 1890s, along with his promulgation of Keswick spirituality, Kargel was also very active in a variety of evangelistic and humanitarian ministries. His travels to prisons across the Russian Empire took up a great deal of his time and energy, and he also became involved in seeking to help exiled believers, not least through his emigration assistance plan. Kargel remained an evangelist who carried the message of conversion, the cross, and the Bible, and was also, throughout his life, an evangelical activist. There were many struggles, disappointments, and tensions in this period. His wife died and the emigration scheme failed. The Saint Petersburg evangelical circle had been experiencing intermittent tensions. In the 1880s Kargel had tried to deal with these by seeking to convince them to follow the New Testament in

---

17. J. G. Kargel to "Dear friend and brother in Christ Jesus" [V. A. Pashkov], 12 May 1886, 2/13/049, Pashkov Papers.

18. Hopkins, *The Law of Liberty in the Spiritual Life*, 92–102, as cited in Price and Randall, *Transforming Keswick*, 48, 223.

their community life.[19] As the Evangelical Christian movement that had started in a relatively informal way in Saint Petersburg spread more widely across Russia, especially under the leadership of Ivan Prokhanov, it experienced leadership difficulties and divisions. It was not always obvious that Kargel's hope that a deeper spirituality would be the ultimate answer to the problems of the time was being fulfilled.

RUSSIAN EVANGELICAL THEOLOGIAN

From the beginning of the twentieth century, Kargel began to be acknowledged as the most significant Russian evangelical theologian of his generation. His contribution was seen increasingly in his teaching, his writings, and in the leadership he gave to wider evangelical initiatives. Kargel's vision was that Russian evangelicals could unite around evangelical distinctives. The idea was developing from 1906 onwards, among some in Russia, of a new body drawing evangelicals together. Prokhanov, the most dynamic of the younger Russian evangelical leaders, circulated a letter about this—a letter signed by Kargel, among others. One possibility was to form an Evangelical Alliance that would unite disparate groups and individuals who wished to see a spiritual awakening in Russia. Pashkov, Kargel, and other evangelicals saw the opportunity to propagate their ideas of spiritual renewal.[20] The idea of broader unity was not accepted by all, however, and was emphatically rejected by the Baptists. From this failed attempt, a group was organized that became known as the Evangelical Christian Union (ECU). The Evangelical Christian Union was comprised of Russian evangelical congregations and was led by Prokhanov for over twenty years. It was the body with which Kargel identified for the remainder of his life.

Through his teaching at the ECU's Bible College in Saint Petersburg, through his preaching in many other places, and through his prolific writings, Kargel had an enormous influence on evangelicals in the Russian-speaking world in the first three decades of the twentieth century and beyond. His ability as a teacher of the Word of God caused him to be considered "the greatest spiritual tutor" of the

---

19. J. G. Kargel to "Dear brother in the Lord Jesus Christ" [V. A. Pashkov], 24 January 1885, 2/13/035, Pashkov Papers.

20. *Istoriya Evangel'skix Xristian-Baptistov*, 152.

Russian evangelical movement.[21] His relationship with the Baptists—within the wider evangelical community in Russia—was not as close in the later as in the earlier period of his ministry, since he was a strong advocate of the open Table. But he did not see the Russian Baptists and the Evangelical Christian Union as competitors. Indeed, he sought to use his influence within the Evangelical Christian Union to bring these two evangelical organizations in Russia closer together. In his teaching in the Bible College, his favored topics were sin and sanctification, homiletics, and the Book of Revelation. These topics reflect the earlier influences he had received from the German Baptists, but more particularly from the Keswick movement and the Brethren.

Kargel's highly significant book, *What is your Relationship to the Holy Spirit?*, was first printed in Russian in 1912 and reprinted in 1945. In the press release for the 1945 reprint, N. J. Poysti recalled from his childhood memories of Kargel that "he [Kargel] emphasized the necessity of being baptized in the Spirit."[22] But the term "baptism of/by the Holy Spirit" was actually rarely used by Kargel in his writings. When Kargel did use the term, it was limited to either the actual Day of Pentecost or to Jesus' baptism. Kargel preferred to use the term "being filled with the Holy Spirit." He believed that being filled with the Holy Spirit was the experience that should be sought.[23] There is a parallel between Kargel and the Keswick teacher Graham Scroggie, who urged caution about the language of being baptized by the Holy Spirit and encouraged those at Keswick to be obedient to the "unambiguous command [of Scripture] to be filled with the Spirit."[24] For Kargel, to have the true fruit of the Spirit's filling was not a matter of "your works, even prayers and supplications." Only one thing was necessary: "give yourself to Him to fill you, to supervise you all day long, and submit to Him everything that you are, that you have, and that you create: your acts, your words, and all your ideas. Give Him all authority over you and all freedom to act within you, give Him the ability to execute His will above your will and soon you will become

---

21. Karev, "Tropa moej Zhizni," 61.

22. Poysti, "We Publish a Very Important Book," 24 and Kargel, *V Kakom Ty Otnoshenii k Duxu Svyatomu?* 7.

23. Kargel, "V Kakom Ty Otnoshenii k Duxu Svyatomu?" 162.

24. Randall, *Evangelical Experiences*, 32.

His field where His fruit will visibly grow."[25] The notion of "all day long" is intended to speak of continuous filling.

In his commentary on Romans, Kargel spoke of the need for the Christian to live in the Spirit, not in the flesh. These two were as "different as night and day," yet every child of God is in one or the other. "If they live by the flesh, though they never would think of themselves as such, they are poor, destitute, blind, and naked: but if they are led by the Spirit of God and controlled by Him, they will walk in happiness and blessings."[26] But the central issue for a believer is to understand his or her position in Christ. Either an individual has full faith, which is demonstrated by a new life in Christ, or they have a partial faith, which is demonstrated by the lack of change in their life.[27] The effects of sin can only be counteracted by a Christian constantly identifying with the death of the "old man" on the cross of Christ. If the child of God is not "crucified," sin will remain. The "carnal believer" refuses to consent to the Holy Spirit and Christ, thinking that they can submit to the will of God on their own. Kargel believed that it was impossible to direct a carnal Christian toward a life of submission to God, that it was a lie to think that a carnal mind could submit to the will of God. A Christian operating by means of the flesh will, he argued, remain defeated until they are "co-crucified with the resurrected Christ."[28] This is classic Holiness theology.

While emphasizing the Spirit, Kargel was also determinedly Christological. The "image of the Son" is a critical key to understanding Kargel's theology. In his commentary on Romans 8:29 he wrote that God "before the creation of humankind" was involved in predetermining. But in Kargel's thinking, God predetermined[29] humankind's image; humankind can become the image of Christ through divine foreknowledge and election. The focus, for Kargel, is on Christ, the "only begotten Son in whom [God] elected and destined humankind for Sonship" (Eph 1:4–5). This, states Kargel, is the image to which we—Christian believers—must rise.[30] Union with, and conformity

---

25. Kargel, "V Kakom Ty Otnoshenii k Duxu Svyatomu?" 150.
26. Kargel, *Zakon Duxa Zhizni*, 149.
27. Ibid, 136–38.
28. Ibid, 154.
29. *predreshil* [predetermined].
30. Ibid, 195.

to, Christ were central themes in much of Kargel's writings, and this is indicative of a Keswick perspective. "Union with Christ," Barabas comments, has been the doctrine that "Keswick called to the attention of the world [in 1877] and has been stressed ever since."[31]

Yet at the same time Kargel added his own perspectives. He wrote a great deal about suffering as integral to the holiness experience. In his last letter to Pashkov, Kargel tells of the benefits of suffering. In June 1901, as Kargel was preparing to embark on another trip to Siberia, he wrote to Pashkov speaking of suffering as being the language that God used to talk with his family, with believers. Kargel placed this in the context of deeper spiritual experience. He spoke with some confidence, as well as with desire:

> O, thanks be to Him, that I have understood His language. I know that He wants to go to the source of my being, and that He wants to own everything. He does not want anything of my old self to be left over and truly wants to be my all in all. I also know that this is my only peace in time and in eternity. In this living belief I have given Him every corner of my heart; it is now up to Him to save that which is totally committed to Him. He will do this.[32]

Although Kargel saw suffering in broad terms as part of spiritual experience, here there was a focus on physical suffering. He was sensitive to the sufferings in his own family, as well as in those around him.[33] Thus, Kargel took the evangelical message and, in particular, a Keswick understanding of holiness, and adjusted it so that it would touch the needs of the Russian soul. He added unique ideas to the classic expressions of Keswick, most notably by placing primary emphasis on the role of suffering in the sanctification process. Additionally, he redefined the ideas of anointing and higher power to include the imagery of a Double Sonship and a Double Portion of the Spirit.

KARGEL'S CONTINUING INFLUENCE

After Ivan Kargel died in 1937, *Bratsky Vestnik*, the official journal of the All-Union Council of Evangelical Christians-Baptists (AUCEC-B),

---

31. Barabas, *So Great Salvation*, 103.
32. J. G. Kargel to "My honored, beloved friend and brother in Christ" [V. A. Pashkov], 7 June 1901, 2/13/111, Pashkov Papers.
33. Ibid.

continued to print material by Kargel on a regular basis. Nearly 25 percent of the all the issues of *Bratsky Vestnik* published between its beginnings in 1945 and 1988 (when Russian Baptist organizations changed) contained an article from or a reference to Ivan Kargel. *Bratsky Vestnik* was circulated and copied throughout the Russian-speaking evangelical world to more than 25,000 pastors and leaders.[34] In 1946, Alexander Karev, then General Secretary of the AUCEC-B, acknowledged Kargel as being a major influence in his spiritual formation.[35] Alexander Karev led the Evangelical Christian Union after Prokhanov's departure from Russia and was the first General Secretary of the merged Union formed in 1944. He remained as General Secretary until 1971 and exercised strong leadership. In 1955 Karev again acknowledged the spiritual effect of the life, writings, and lectures of Kargel on him and others.[36] In an article that celebrated Karev's ninetieth birthday, the author states that Kargel was the central force that shaped Karev's theological training[37] and his understanding of Scripture.[38]

Others echoed Alexander Karev's praise of Kargel. In 1947, I. Motorin urged young evangelicals to honor their legacy and study their Bibles deeply so that they could interpret it as highly gifted preachers such as "Spurgeon, Moody, Torrey, Kargel, and Prokhanov."[39] In 1954, future preachers were told to use Kargel as an example in their preaching.[40] Also in that year, Zhidkov, then President of the AUCEC-B, spoke about the sermon preached by Ivan Kargel in 1902 that brought about his conversion.[41] In 1966, a speaker at the AUCEC-B annual conference stated, "I was at the congress in Leningrad [Saint Petersburg] in 1920; I heard brothers I. S. Prokhanov and I. V. Kargel, and I want the God who was with them to be with us."[42] In 1972, Alexei M. Bychkov, then the General Secretary of the AUCEC-B, stated that the writings of Kargel were some of the first spiritual works he read

---

34. de Chalandeau, *The Christians in the USSR*, 33.
35. Karev, "Iz moix Lichnyx Vstrech s I. V. Kargelem," 19–20.
36. Karev, "Tropa moej Zhizni," 61.
37. C., "Aleksandr Vasil'evich Karev," 59.
38. Ibid, 63.
39. Motorin, "Kak Izuchat' Bibliyu," 60.
40. Motorin, "Sluzhenie Propovednika," 46.
41. Zhidkov, "Nemnogo o Sebe," 29.
42. "Vtoroj Den' S"ezda, Utrennee Zasedanie 5 Oktyabrya," 43.

and were foundational in his understanding of the Christian faith.[43] During the 100th year jubilee of the Saint Petersburg [Leningrad] Baptist church, held in 1974,[44] Kargel's name was listed as one of six influential people in the history of the Russian evangelical movement.[45]

Bratsky Vestnik reported in 1983 that their readers were requesting that more works by Kargel be printed.[46] Earlier the magazine had printed sections of *What is Your Relationship to the Holy Spirit?* and *Light from the Shadows of Future Blessing*.[47] Following the 1983 request, Bratsky Vestnik printed more of Kargel's works in serial form: *Christ—Our Sanctification* in 1982, *Ruth the Moabitess* from 1983 to 1984, and more from *Light from the Shadows of Future Blessing* from 1984 to 1988. After the fall of Communism, the hunger for Kargel's works continued and in 1997 Marina Sergeevna Karetnikova gathered many of the writings of Ivan Kargel and produced *The Collected Works*. *Light from the Shadows of Future Blessing*, in its entirety, was published in 1998. In addition to Kargel's continuing influence among the Evangelical Christians-Baptists, the Pentecostal Union of Russia and Ukraine considers the writings and personal ministry of Kargel as an essential factor in the formation of their stream of Christianity.[48] Walter Sawatsky claims that among the Reform Baptists in Russia (Council of Churches of Evangelical Christians-Baptists), who broke away from the AUCEC-B in 1961, Kargel has been the most quoted author.[49] Through his books and teaching, Kargel had an unparalleled influence on Russian evangelical life. In a letter written in 1947

---

43. K., "Vnov' Izbrannyj General'nyj Sekretar' Vsesoyuznogo Soveta Evangel'skix Xristian-Baptistov," 67.

44. This celebration marked the establishment of the first Evangelical Christians-Baptists Union church in Saint Petersburg by the start of Radstock's preaching in 1874. See K., "100-letnij Yubilej Leningradskoj Cerkvi EXB," 71.

45. K., "100-letnij Yubilej Leningradskoj Cerkvi EXB," 69.

46. Bychkov, "Soobshhenie Prezidiuma VSEXB o Rabote Mezhdu Plenumami," 37.

47. Bratsky Vestnik did not reprint all of Kargel's works and Bratsky Vestnik was not the only source of his writings. During the Communist era, some original prints survived the searches while other texts were preservesed through handwritten copies. There were also smaller local journals and private printing activity (*samizdat*) that reproduced his writings in serial form.

48. Franchuk, "Prosila Rossiya Dozhdya u Gospoda," D:\files\books\book_02\f_008.html.

49. Sawatsky, *Soviet Evangelicals*, 278.

in which senior leaders of the AUCEC-B set out the views and principles they held, "Preaching Sanctification" is listed as one of the "five distinctive features of the Christian Baptists of the USSR."[50] Kargel's commitments lived on.

FURTHER RESEARCH

My study has revealed several areas where further and wider research could prove fruitful. The Pashkov Papers are a rich source of primary material, a source which is easily accessible and relatively untouched. There are many details within the correspondence of Pashkov that shed considerable light on the situation of evangelicals within the Russian Empire. More research is needed in the area of Orthodox and evangelical relationships in Russia. The theology of Kargel, especially his theological thinking about sanctification and about union with Christ, has some parallels in the Orthodoxy theology of deification. This deserves further study, which may result in fresh understandings of the commonalities of spirituality among the evangelicals and the Orthodox in the Russian-speaking world.

Also, this research has indicated a strong connection between Pashkov and the Sakharov brothers in Astrakhanka area. Daniel H. Shubin has noted that the Sakharovs (Zakharovs) were associated with the Novo-Molokans. This was, as noted, a movement that contained a mixture of Molokan, Baptist, and Mennonite elements.[51] Further research needs to be done on this group, especially in the light of the complex developments within early Russian evangelicalism, particularly in the case of the Mennonite Brethren. This research could yield new ideas regarding the indigenous Russian roots of the Mennonite Brethren. It may also prove useful in showing the ecumenical nature of both the Pashkovites and the Molokans.

---

50. *Religion and the People*, Birmingham, April 1947, as cited by Bolshakoff, *Russian Nonconformity*, 126. The letter was sent to the American Baptists and is signed by the Presidium of the All-Union Council which at that time was Yakov Zhidkov (Chairman), M. Goliaev, (vice-chairman), M. Orlov (vice-chairman), P. Malin (treasurer) and A. Karev (General Secretary). The entire is letter was reprinted in this work by Bolshakoff. The five points were: the principle of unity, the preaching of the pure gospel, the preaching of sanctification, the spirit of early Christianity, and the desire to carry on God's work in our country with our own means.

51. See Shubin, *A History of Russian Christianity*, vol. III, 138–39.

Another area of research that deserves to be mentioned is the early theology of Kargel as expressed in his German writings. I limited the scope of this project primarily to his writings in Russian, since my purpose has been to argue for the Keswick influence, through Kargel, on the shaping of Russian evangelical spirituality. Exploration of Kargel's German writings, however, might yield further understanding of the process by which his theology changed to a more Keswick perspective. This would also shed light on important aspects of German and Russian Baptist connections. Another related aspect for further investigation would be connections between the Holiness movement centered in Blankenburg, Germany, and Kargel. Further study might uncover new links within the wider Holiness movement across Europe.

Finally, I suggest that further research could be done on the influence of Kargel not only on the groups that today make up the AUCEC-B, but also on other Russian Baptists and on other evangelicals in Russia, and perhaps beyond. This would include looking at primary sources from the Council of Churches of Evangelical Christians-Baptists (Reform Baptists) and also from the Union of Christians of Evangelical Faith-Pentecostals. It is clear from secondary sources that these Russian-speaking groups acknowledge Kargel's influence on their development and theology, but I have not used primary sources from either group. This further research would add to the understanding of the varied ways in which Holiness teaching was spread throughout the Russian-speaking evangelical world.

CONCLUSION

Ivan Kargel's unique expression of evangelical spirituality, with a strong tendency toward the tenets of Holiness theology as found in Keswick teaching, shaped in a decisive way the spirituality of the evangelicals of the Russian-speaking world. Born as a German in the Russian Empire, he eventually found himself at the heart of the growing Baptist movement on the continent of Europe. As a result, he was given the opportunity to exercise ministry in Saint Petersburg, where he attracted the attention of Baptists both in Europe and North America as he registered the first Baptist congregation in Orthodox Russia. At an early stage in his ministry Kargel developed a lasting friendship with a significant early shaper of the Mennonite Brethren,

Johann Wieler, and then with Vasily Pashkov in Saint Petersburg, the wealthy evangelical who supported his work. These relationships were highly significant. Even more significant was his wife's encouragement to embrace a spirituality that was reflective of the Holiness movement, which he did while in Bulgaria.

In many ways, as he came to a mature understanding of evangelical spirituality, Kargel echoed all the themes present in Keswick teaching. Through the journeys that he undertook across the Russian Empire with Friedrich Baedeker, he became more and more committed to passing on a message about trust in Christ for full salvation— for justification as well as sanctification—and urging consecration to Christ, abiding in Christ, and the necessity of the filling and power of the Holy Spirit. He also underlined suffering as an integral part of the way of Christ-likeness. Here Kargel was taking the wider Holiness expression of spirituality and applying it to the context in which he found himself. His context involved restrictions on evangelicals, the banning of believers, war, revolution, and death. He concluded that suffering was at the core of authentic spirituality.

Ivan Kargel advocated the centrality of sanctification and he transmitted this message not only in capital cities, villages, prisons, and classrooms, but also through his writings, which were enormously influential. He refused, in his teaching, to adopt a systematic approach to theology, but instead urged believers to go to Scripture and draw from the riches of Christian experience found there. In this way he provided Russian-speaking evangelicals with a theological and spiritual perspective that was both deeply biblical and robustly experiential, and which allowed them to sustain their Christian communities within the anti-religious climate of a totalitarian state. The threads that go into forming the diverse tapestry of the evangelicals of the Russian-speaking world have various origins, some indigenous and others related to worldwide movements. Kargel, as a German who adapted to Russian ways, played a major part in shaping evangelical identity in the Russian context by transmitting the spirituality of Keswick to Russia, and by weaving some of the colors of the tapestry of wider evangelical spirituality into the tapestry of Russian evangelical life.

APPENDIX ONE

1913 Confession of Faith by Ivan V. Kargel

I. CONCERNING GOD

We believe in the only true God, revealing Himself in three persons: Father, Son and Holy Spirit, which are in oneness everlasting (Psalms 90:3), perfect (Matthew 5:48), holy (Revelation 15:4; Isaiah 6:3), mighty (Genesis 17:1), all-wise (Psalms 139:2–4; Acts 15:18), righteous (Psalms 11:7; Romans 3:26), good (Psalms 119:68; Matthew 19:17) and love (1 John 4:8, 16).

God the Father we confess as Creator of heaven and earth and of all things, visible and invisible (Genesis 1:1; Colossians 1:16); God the Son is the one born by the Father in eternity (Psalms 3:7; John 3:16) and by the favored, blessed Virgin Mary (Luke 1:28, 31, 35); He is our Savior and Savior of all the world (John 3:16–17; Romans 3:24); God the Holy Spirit is the Comforter, coming from the Father, glorifying the Son (John 16:14), convicting the world (John 16:8), giving new birth to man (John 3:5), guiding the disciples of Christ (John 16:13).

II. CONCERNING THE WORD OF GOD

We believe that all canonical books of the Old and New Testament as represented in the entire Bible, or the Holy Scripture (excluding the Apocrypha), are inspired by the Holy Spirit (2 Peter 1:21) and given by the Lord (Psalms 148:8–9), as indispensable, unique (Proverbs 30:6; Mark 7:13), and a completely su
God of our salvation (Hebrews 1:1–2; John 5:39; 20:31) and His will concerning our faith (Philippians 1:27) and life (Acts 20:32; 2 Timothy 3:15–17).

III. CONCERNING MAN

We believe that God created man after His image (Genesis 1:27), but that he, tempted by Satan, fell into sin and came short of the glory of God (Romans 3:23). By the sin of one man all were infected (Romans 5:12, 19), became the children of wrath (Ephesians 2:3), and came under punishment for sin which is death (Romans 6:23), spiritually (Genesis 2:17; Luke 15:32; Ephesians 2:1), physically (Romans 5:14) and eternally—or a second death which is death after the physical death (Matthew 25:41; Revelation 20:12-15).

IV. CONCERNING THE REDEMPTION OF MAN

In the question concerning the redemption of man, we believe that man cannot save himself (Matthew 16:26), not by his own righteousness (Isaiah 64:6; Romans 10:3), not by any work (Galatians 2:16; 3:10; Romans 3:20) and not by the help of any other man (Psalms 49:8-9; Hebrews 10:11).

In the only salvation accomplished by God Himself in Jesus Christ (Acts 4:12; 2 Corinthians 5:18-19; 1 Timothy 2:5-6) by means of Christ's death for all men (Matthew 20:28; 1 Peter 1:18-19; 1 John 2:2; Hebrews 2:9), the Lord is offering righteousness (Romans 3:25), reconciliation (2 Corinthians 5:19-20; Colossians 1:20), forgiveness of sins (Colossians 1:14; 2:13, 14; Hebrews 9:22), justification (Romans 3:24; 4:5; 2 Corinthians 5:21), and eternal life (John 3:16; 5:24; 1 John 5:11-12; Romans 6:23).

This work of redemption is *accomplished* by God for man but it remains ineffective for him, unless the work of God is *fulfilled* in man. The first has been accomplished by Christ without our help (Romans 5:6-8); the second has been accomplished by the Holy Spirit with the consent of man. The Holy Spirit creates in man an inner upheaval or repentance (Psalms 32:3-5; 51:3-9), faith in the sacrifice of Christ, and trust in the accomplished atonement (Isaiah 53:5; Romans 4:24-25; Ephesians 2:8; Hebrews 10:10-14), the new birth or new life (John 1:12-13; 3:3-8; James 1:18; 1 Peter 1:23) as well as the adoption as sons (Romans 8:14-16; Galatians 4:4-6). Also the same Holy Spirit is accomplishing the sanctification of the born-again (2 Corinthians 3:18; 2 Thessalonians 2:13) and protecting them for eternal life (1 Peter 1:5; Jude 24; Romans 6:22).

V. CONCERNING THE CHURCH OF CHRIST

The universal Church of Christ is built upon the foundation of the apostles and prophets, Christ Jesus Himself being the cornerstone (Ephesians 2:20). She consists of those who are saved (Acts 2:47), who believe (Acts 4:4; 5:14; 6:7), who are called to be saints (Romans 1:7; 1 Corinthians 1:2; 2 Corinthians 1:1; Ephesians 1:1), and those who are in this world as well as those who are saved but who have gone to be with the Lord (Hebrews 12:22–23). Those and these are constituting one body whose head is Christ (Romans 12:5; 1 Corinthians 12:27; Ephesians 1:22–23). And although the members of this church are from different nations (Revelation 5:9–10), different social conditions (Galatians 3:28; Colossians 3:11), and have different gifts (1 Corinthians 12:14–18), they all are one in Christ (John 17:11, 21–23; Acts 4:32; Ephesians 2:15; 4:4) and individually members one with another (Romans 12:5).

The individual local churches (communities) are only part of the one universal Church; they are formed by the Lord in different countries, cities, and local places for the uniting of the saved children of God on earth (John 10:16; 11:52), for the joint glorification of God (Romans 15:6; 1 Corinthians 14:26; Colossians 3:16), for the growth of the members in the knowledge of God and Christ (Colossians 2:2; Ephesians 3:18–19), for the perfection of the life of faith according to the image of Christ (Ephesians 4:12–15), for the mutual participation in all these things (1 Peter 4:10; Jude 20; Romans 15:14; Ephesians 4:16), and for the spreading of the Kingdom of God on earth (Acts 13:1–3; Romans 10:15; Philippians 1:5).

On the other hand, the Church separates from this world (Acts 2:40; 5:13) and, watching the purity and holiness of its members, removes the unclean from her midst (Acts 5:1–11; 1 Corinthians 5:1:13).

VI. CONCERNING THE SERVANTS OF CHRIST AND OF THE CHURCH

We believe that Jesus Christ, as He gave to His Church from the beginning apostles, prophets, evangelists, pastors, and teachers (Ephesians 4:11), so He is continuing to give those in the measure of necessity until this present time. And as the Holy Spirit is granting His gifts to them [servants] (1 Corinthians 12:4–10), He Himself is putting them forward for service (Acts 13:1–2) so the Church must acknowledge them and accept them (Acts 13:3; 3 John 8–10), but at the same time she must break with evil doers [false teachers] (Philippians 3:2; Revelation 2:2). In the Word of God is found a description of their moral qualities (1 Timothy 3:1–12; Titus 1:5–9; 2:7–8), their service (Matthew 20:25–28; Acts 20:28; 1 Peter 5:1–3; Romans 12:7–8), and their reward (1 Peter 5:4).

VII. CONCERNING CHRIST'S INSTITUTIONS FOR THE CHURCH

The Lord Jesus Christ left to His disciples two institutions: baptism and the Lord's Supper, which the Church must observe as long as she exists in this world. Both baptism and the Lord's Supper are entrusted only to the disciples of Christ (Luke 22:14–15; Acts 20:7).

1. Baptism must be preceded by the message or teaching about salvation in Christ (Matthew 28:19; Acts 2:29, 36, 41; 10:47–48), repentance (Matthew 3:7–8; Acts 2:37–38), faith (Mark 16:16; Acts 8:36–37), and the acceptance of the Holy Spirit (Acts 10:47; 19:2–3). The significance of baptism is diverse: it is the symbol of the washing away of sins (Acts 22:16), the promise to God of a clear conscience (1 Peter 3:21), obedience to the Lord (Matthew 3:14–15; Luke 7:29–30), and the sign of burial and resurrection with Christ (Romans 6:2–4). From all this, it follows that it cannot be administered to children, just as the first disciples (Acts 8:12) only baptized those who heard and accepted the Word of God and believed in Him.

2. The Lord's Supper has been given by the Lord Himself in remembrance of Him (Luke 22:19; 1 Corinthians 11:24–25), especially His suffering and death paid as the price for ransom (1 Peter 1:18–19; 1 Corinthians 11:26), in remembrance of His love reaching to the uttermost (John 13:1; 15:13; Romans 5:8), and of the giving of Himself not only for us, but also to provide for our spiritual, heavenly food (John 6:51; 1 Corinthians 10:16). Received with living faith it makes us partakers of fellowship with Him, as well as with all members of His Church (1 Corinthians 10:16–17).

VIII. CONCERNING MARRIAGE

The Word of God teaches that marriage was already instituted in paradise [Garden of Eden] by the Lord (Genesis 1:27–28) and confirmed by Jesus Christ and the apostles (Matthew 19:4–6; 1 Corinthians 7:1–40; Hebrews 13:4). Concerning divorce, the Lord says from the beginning that it does not exist (Matthew 19:6–8) and only death can release one from marriage (Romans 7:2). The only exception which the Lord permits is in the case of adultery (Matthew 5:32; 19:9).

IX. CONCERNING GOVERNMENT AUTHORITY

We believe and confess, that every true Christian must be a most faithful citizen of his government and a submissive subject to the authorities, "not only to avoid God's wrath but also for the sake of conscience" (Romans 13:5). We confess with the apostle: "Let every person be subject to the governing authorities. For there is no authority except from God, and those that exist have been instituted by God" (Rom. 13: 1). So we count it a privilege to pay them all of their dues (Romans 13:7), not to resist them (Romans 13:2) or do evil, but on the contrary, to do what is good (Romans 13:3–4), and to make prayers of supplications, intercessions, and thanksgivings for all men, for kings and all who are in high positions (1 Timothy 2:1–4).

In relationship to God, however, we state that one cannot suffer any human interference, having Christ Jesus as the only mediator (1 Timothy 2:5), the only teacher (Matthew 23:8), and the only High Priest (Hebrews 4:14); it was He who ordered us to render to Caesar those things that are Caesar's and to render to God the things that are God's (Matthew 22:21).

X. CONCERNING THE SECOND COMING OF THE LORD AND HIS JUDGMENT

Christ is coming for His Own, invisible to the world (1 Corinthians 15:51–52), like a thief in the night (Matthew 24:42–44; 1 Thessalonians 5:2), but those who are watching for Him will not be caught by surprise (1 Thessalonians 5: 4–10) and those who are ready will enter with Him into Glory (Matthew 25:10); but those who are not ready will be left with the unfaithful for the great tribulation (Matthew 24:40–41; 25:11–13; Luke 12:45–46). Those who have died in Him, He will resurrect from death; those and the others living in Him will be gathered up together to Himself (1 Thessalonians 4:16–17) so as to be forever with the Lord.

But after that, Christ will come with His Own and with His heavenly angels (Matthew 16:27; 25:31; Jude 14; Revelation 19:11–14) and every eye will see Him (Matthew 24:30; John 19:37; Revelation 1:7). Then the judgment will begin, but only for those who are living on the earth (Matthew 25:31–46; Revelation 19:15–19); from the unjust no one will be resurrected (Revelation 20:5) until the passing of the thousand-year reign of Christ with His Own (Revelation 20:4). When the thousand years have ended, there will be a short interval of the hostility of Satan's people (Revelation 20: 7–10), then the unjust will be resurrected (Revelation 20:13) and the final judgment will take place (Revelation 20:11–15).[1]

---

1. This translation is based on the work of Maria Vogel as found in Parker, *Baptists in Europe*, 154–58. I have made a few modifications of my own to her work, seeking to improve the accuracy and style of the translation. I have chosen not to apply contemporary gender-neutral language wishing to retain the original language pattern which should not be assumed to be gender-specific. For a Russian version of Kargel's 1913 Statement of Faith see "Verouchenie Evangel'skix Xristian-Baptistov," 15–18. For an additional English translation of Kargel's 1913 Statement of Faith see de Chalandeau, *The Christians in the USSR*, 59–62.

APPENDIX TWO

Timeline

THE SHAPING OF A BAPTIST LEADER, 1849–1874

Year (month)	
1849	I. V. Kargel born (presumably to an Armenian mother and German father)
1855	Granville Waldegrave (Lord Radstock) visited battlefields of the Crimean War
1855	C. Plonus started a German Baptist work in Saint Petersburg
1855–1881	Alexander II reigned in the Russian Empire
1858	Russian Bible Society revived
1858	William Boardman published *The Higher Christian Life*
1860	Mennonite Brethren formed
1860	Gottfried Alf baptized Matthew Kelm
1861	Emancipation of Russian peasants
1861	The First Baptist church founded in Russian territory (Adamov, Poland)
1863 (9)	Matthew Kelm baptized Karl Ondra
1866	Friedrich Baedeker dedicated his life to Christ under Radstock's influence
1867	Nikita Voronin became the first Russian to be baptized by immersion (Kura River in Tiflis by Martin Kalweit)

Year (month)	
1868–1872	Lord Radstock travelled occasionally to Paris to met with Russian nobles
1869	Johann Oncken visited the Molotschna region in the Russian Empire
1869	Ivan Stepanovich Prokhanov born
1869	Abraham Unger baptized Efim Tsymbal, a Russian
1869	Ivan Kargel was baptized by Martin Kalweit in the Kura River in Tiflis
1870	Stundo-baptism began in Ukraine
1871	Nikita Voronin baptized Vasily Pavlov
1872 (5)	First Mennonite Brethren Conference (Andreasfeld)
1872 (11)	Kargel preached in Odessa and stayed with Johann Wieler and visited the Molotschna region
1873 (5)	Second Mennonite Brethren Conference (Klippenfeld) where Kargel was called into ministry
1873	Kargel began a pastorate in the German Baptist church in Sorotschin, Volhynia
1874 (3–8)	Kargel attended the Hamburg Mission School and was ordained by Oncken
1874	Radstock visited Saint Petersburg
1874	Vasily Pashkov dedicated his life to Christ under Radstock's influence
1874 (6)	Karl Ondra visited Saint Petersburg
1874 (8)	Kargel designated to travel to Saint Petersburg to petition the government for Baptist freedom

EXPOSED TO EVANGELICALISM 1874–1880

1875	Kargel resided in Saint Petersburg to serve as pastor to the German Baptists
1875	Hannah Whitall Smith wrote *The Christian's Secret of a Happy Life*
1875	The First Keswick Convention held
1875	Vasily Pavlov attended the Hamburg Mission School and was ordained by Oncken

Year (month)	
1875–1876	Radstock and his family resided in Saint Petersburg
1876	Society for the Encouragement of Spiritual and Ethical Reading was founded
1876	Kargel attended the Triennial Conference in Hamburg
1876 (7)	Kargel's ministry began to be funded by the American Baptist Missionary Union
1877	Kargel became a naturalized Russian citizen
1877 (5)	Karl Ondra and Adam Schiewe forcibly removed from the Volhynia Province
1877–1878	Russo Turkish War
1878 (5)	Kargel's first contact with Pashkovites
1879 (11)	Kargel registered the first Baptist Congregation in Orthodox Russia and took an oath of allegiance to the Tsar
1880s	George Müller, Friedrich Baedeker and Otto Stockmayer visited Russia as itinerant evangelists
1880	Kargel's church moved to Serpuchiowska Street with nearly 100 members
1880	Konstantin Pobedonostsev became General Director of the Holy Synod
1880	Kargel travelled to Tiflis to oversee the opening of the first Russian Baptist Church there
1880	Ivan Kargel married Anna Alexandrovna Semenova

BULGARIA PERIOD, 1880–1884

1880 (9)	Kargel baptized the first Bulgarian Baptists
1880 (11)	Anna Kargel arrived Rustchuk, Bulgaria where the family would reside
1881	Alexander II assassinated in a bombing
1881–1894	Alexander III reigned in the Russian Empire
1882 (4)	The Kargels' first daughter Natasha was born in Rustchuk, Bulgaria

Year (month)	
1882	Pobedonostsev advised Alexander III of the dangers of Pashkov
1882 (5)	The Kargels visited Balta after a pogrom
1882 (7)	Kargel officiated in the opening of a new Baptist church Bucharest
1883	Pashkov forbidden to enter his Moscow estate
1883	George Müller baptized Pashkov in Saint Petersburg
1883	Alexander III issued a proclamation forbidding non-Orthodox teaching
1883 (7)	The Kargels' second daughter Elena was born (most likely in Rustchuk)
1883	Ivan Kargel experienced a personal revival
1884 (3)	The Kargel family left Bulgaria to reside in Saint Petersburg
1884 (4)	Pashkov held a conference in Saint Petersburg for all evangelicals in the Russian Empire but the gathering was disbanded by federal police soon after it began
1884 (5)	Johann Wieler and Ivan Kargel were elected as president and vice-president of the seminal Russian Baptist Union during the Novo Vasilievka Conference
1884	Dei Mazaev baptized
1884 (5)	Society for the Encouragement of Spiritual and Ethical Reading was forced to close
1884	Vasily Pashkov and Modest Korff exiled from Russian Empire
1884 (6)	Kargel on an eight week trip through the Volga region
1884	Oncken died

PART OF THE PASHKOVITE CIRCLE, 1884–1887

1884	Kargel family was residing in Pashkov's apartment on Vyborskaya in Saint Petersburg

Year (month)	
1885	Kargel started to use "Higher Life" language and explicitly embraced an open Lord's Supper
1885 (1)	Tensions developed in the Saint Petersburg Evangelicals over the election of elders
1885 (5–6)	Kargel visited Volhynia and Molotschna for ten weeks
1885	Baedeker visited Saint Petersburg
1885	Kargel visited Poland for five weeks
1885	Kargel visited Poland and Volhynia
1886	Prokhanov converted to evangelical Christianity and was baptized one year later
1886	Kargel visited Moscow, Orel, Novo-Vasilievka and the Kherson Province
1886 (4–5)	Kargel travelled with Baedeker to Tiflis and held "mini-Keswick Conferences"
1886 (5)	The Kargels' third daughter, Maria is born in Gansel, Estonia (Hapsal, Estonia)
1886	Kargel visiting Lithuania and Estonia
1886 (9)	The Kargel family returned to Saint Petersburg to provide leadership for the German Baptist Church while Schiewe, the pastor of the congregation, travelled to America to raise funds
1887	Mazaev elected as president of the Russian Baptists
1887	Pashkov returned briefly to Russia
1887 (6–7)	The Kargel family spent the summer in Hapsal, Ivan Kargel preached among the Estonian islands
1887 (11)	The Kargels' fourth daughter, Elizaveta is born in Saint Petersburg
1887 (12)	The Kargel family was residing in Saint Petersburg on Bolshoi Morskaya # 43
1888 (1)	Kargel was in Rückenau teaching in the Mennonite Brethren Training Seminar
1888 (10–11)	Kargel travelled to Rustchuk, Bucharest, Odessa and Wieler's home in the Molotschna region

Year (month)	
REACHING THE RUSSIAN EMPIRE, 1887–1898	
1887	The Kargel family briefly resided in Hapsal, Estonia
1888	Governmental pressure increased against evangelicals in Saint Petersburg
1888	Plans started for the "Emigration Assistance Program" by Pashkov and Kargel
1888 (1)	Kargel was in Rückenau teaching in a Mennonite Brethren Training Seminar
1888–1893	Prokhanov was a student in Saint Petersburg
1889	Prokhanov started the journal *Beseda*
1889 (1)	Kargel was in Friedensfeld teaching in a Mennonite Brethren Training Seminar
1889 (3–5)	Kargel travelled to Israel and returned to Saint Petersburg through Bulgaria and Germany
1889	Wieler died
1890 (1)	Kargel was in the Molotschna region teaching in a Mennonite Brethren Training Seminar
1890 (4–8)	Kargel took his first trip to Siberia with Baedeker
1890 (7)	Anna Kargel and four girls resided in Pashkov's settlement of Krekshino in the Moscow Province
1890 (9)	Kargel was in Tokyo, Japan, on his return trip from Siberia
1890 (10)	Kargel was in Port Said, Egypt, on his return trip from Siberia
1891	Trans-Siberian Railroad started
1891 (6)	Anna Kargel was reported to be in poor health
1891 (7–8)	Ivan Kargel took medical treatments in Kissingen, Bavaria
1891 (11)	The Kargel family was residing in the Finnish city of Vyborg
1892 (5–6)	Kargel made a ten week trip through the Volga region and Orenburg
1894–1917	Nicholas II reigned in the Russian Empire

Year (month)	
1894 (1)	I. V. Kargel was Andreasfeld teaching in a Mennonite Brethren Training Seminar and then travelled on to Astrakhanka and Kharkov
1894 (2)	The last known letter written from Anna Kargel to the Pashkovs
1894 (4–6)	Ivan Kargel took medical treatments in Woerishofen, Bavaria
1894 (9–10)	Kargel travelled to the Caucasus through Odessa and Batum
1895–1898	Prokhanov travelled in England, Germany and France for study after being forced to leave Russia
1895	Kargel began to publish articles on holiness in German journals
1895	Kargel was in the south of Russia teaching in a Mennonite Brethren Training Seminar
1895 (3)	Kargel travelled to the South (Volhynia) and Helsinki, Finland
1895 (6)	Emigration Assistance Program of Pashkov and Kargel abandoned
1895 (7)	Ivan Kargel mentioned his wife Anna's poor health in a letter
1895 (7–9)	Kargel took his second Siberian trip
1895 (9)	Kargel mentioned that his wife's face was burnt in a cooking accident in a letter to Pashkov
1895 (12)	Kargel received the governmental authorization to visit prisons previously held by Baedeker
1896 (1)	Kargel visited prisons in Poland
1896 (4)	Kargel visited prisons in Smolensk and Minsk Provinces
1896 (5)	Kargel visited prisons in the Smolensk, Vitebsk, Kaluga, Orel, Kursk, and Kharkov
1896 (5)	Ivan Kargel's last known mention of his wife Anna in letters to Pashkov
1896	*Light from the Shadows of Future Blessing* was published in German
1897	*Ruth the Moabitess* was published in German

Year (month)	
EVANGELICAL CHRISTIAN ENDEAVORS, 1898–1909	
1898	The Kargel family returned to reside in Saint Petersburg
1898	Prokhanov returned to Saint Petersburg
1901 (6–7)	Kargel took his third trip to Siberia to visit prisoners
1902	Yakov Zhidkov came to Christ after hearing Kargel preach in Saint Petersburg
1902	Pashkov died in exile from Russia in Rome
1903	Russian Baptist Union legally registered
1903	Several youth left Kargel's Saint Petersburg congregation and met independently
1905	Trans-Siberian Railroad completed
1905	Kargel held six-week courses on Holiness topics in the Lieven estate
1905	Prokhanov began the journal *Xristianin*
1905 (1)	Prokhanov began to develop the "Russian Christian Youth Movement"
1905 (4)	Nicholas II declared the "Act of Tolerance" granting religious freedom for all citizens of Russia
1905 (5)	Pobedonostsev resigned from all his positions
1905	Baptist World Alliance founded in London
1905 (10)	Imperial Manifesto granted sweeping changes for freedom within the Russian Empire
1905 (12)	Prokhanov started the "Two-month Gospel Courses" in Saint Petersburg with Kargel teaching
1906	*Commentary on the Book of Revelation* was published in German in serial form
1906 (12)	Kargel, Prokhanov and others sign a letter of intent to initiate the Russian Evangelical Alliance
1906 (12)	Prokhanov held the second "Two-month Gospel Courses" in Saint Petersburg with Kargel teaching on the book of Revelation and sin and sanctification

Year (month)	
190?	*Sin, the Evil of all Evils in this World* was published in German
1907	Kargel credited with helping start the "Russian Fellowship of Evangelical Christians in Finland"
1907 (1)	Kargel elected as chair of the Integrated Congress, attempting to bring unity to evangelicals
1907 (6)	Russian Evangelical Alliance charter signed by 20 persons
1907 (10)	Prokhanov reorganized the "Two-Month Gospel Courses" and offered two sessions per year at the Lieven estate with Kargel teaching on sin and sanctification and homiletics
1908	*Light from the Shadows of Future Blessing* was published in Russian
1908 (4)	The first Congress of the "Evangelical Union of Christian Youth" held in Moscow and led by Prokhanov with 18 attendees
1908 (11)	Prokhanov registered the "First Saint Petersburg Community of Evangelical Christians" leaving Kargel to register the "Second Saint Petersburg Community of Evangelical Christians" soon after
1909 (1)	Russian Evangelical Alliance elected N. F. Lieven and Paul Nicolay as chair and vice-chair but the Baptists refused to take part
1909	Prokhanov and Kargel registered the All-Russian Evangelical Christian Union
1909	The first All-Russian Congress of Evangelical Christians met in Saint Petersburg
1909–1911	Vasily Pavlov was president of the Russian Baptist Union

THE TEACHING YEARS (1909–1928)

1910 (12)	The second All-Russian Congress of Evangelical Christians met in Saint Petersburg

Year (month)	
1911	Prokhanov became a vice-president in the Baptist World Alliance
1911	The All-Russian Union of Evangelical Christians and the Russian Baptist Union officially became members in the Baptist World Alliance
1911	Mazaev again became president of the Russian Baptist Union
1911 (12)	The third All-Russian Congress of Evangelical Christians met in Saint Petersburg and Kargel was elected as vice-chair for the first time
1912	*Sin, the Evil of All Evils in this World* was published in Russian
1912	*What is your relationship to the Holy Spirit?* was published in Russian
1912	*Christ—Our Sanctification* was published in Russian
1913	Kargel wrote a confession of faith for his Saint Petersburg congregation
1914	World War I began
1917	Russia's February Revolution occurred and caused widespread labor strikes across Russia
1917–1925	Rapid growth of evangelicalism in Russia
1917 (4)	The All-Russian Congress of Baptists met in Vladikavkaz after a six year break
1917 (5)	The fourth All-Russian Congress of Evangelical Christians met in Saint Petersburg
1917 (12)	The fifth All-Russian Congress of Evangelical Christians met in Moscow and Kargel was again elected as vice-chair
1918	Armistice was declared ending World War I
1918	Vladimir Lenin took control of Russia
1918	Civil war began in Russia
1919	*Where are the Dead according to the Scriptures?* was published in German

Timeline

Year (month)	
1919 (10)	The sixth All-Russian Congress of Evangelical Christians met in Saint Petersburg together with the sixth Congress of the Evangelical Union of Christian Youth, both chaired by Prokhanov
1920	Famine struck Russia in the midst of the civil war producing cholera and typhoid epidemics
1920	Mazaev and the position of president was replaced with a council which provided leadership to the Russian Baptist Union
1920 (4)	Kargel with his two daughters, Elizaveta and Maria, were residing in Nikolaevka, Ukraine
1920 (5)	Evangelical Christian Union and Baptist Union congresses were jointly held in Moscow where they briefly merged and took the name "All-Russian Council of Evangelical Christians–Baptists"
1920–1923	Kargel taught occasionally in the Sumy Province on the book of Revelation and Homiletics
1921	The "All-Russian Council of Evangelical Christians–Baptists" dissolved
1921	Russian law prohibited children from being in worship services or being taught in churches
1921 (4–6)	Prokhanov was in prison due to his evangelical activities
1921 (12)	The eighth All-Russian Congress of Evangelical Christians met in Saint Petersburg
1922	Kargel with his two daughters, Elizaveta and Maria, were residing in Tokara, Ukraine and he taught in the Sumy Province
1922 (10)	Russian Civil War ended in Vladivostok and the USSR was founded
1923	The Saint Petersburg Bible College reopened with Kargel again teaching in the city but travelling frequently to Tokara, Ukraine

Year (month)	
1923	The third BWA Conference was held in Stockholm where the Evangelical Christian Union and the Russian Baptist Union were advised not to merge but work co-operatively
1923	A joint Bible school was created between the Evangelical Christian Union and the Russian Baptist Union
1923 (10)	The ninth All-Union Congress of Evangelical Christians (name changed from All-Russian Congress) met in Saint Petersburg and Kargel was elected as vice-president at the age of 74
1924–1928	*Old Testament Prototypes* was published in Russian in serial form
1924–1929	*Lectures on the Second Coming of Christ* was published in Russian in serial form
1925	Russian Baptist Union ceased all cooperation with the Evangelical Christian Union
1925	*Where are the Dead according to the Scriptures?* was published in Russian in serial form
1926	Evangelicals began to experience increased persecution from the communist government
1926 (5)	The first All-Ukrainian Congress of Evangelical Christians held in Kharkov with Kargel serving on the advisory council
1926 (11)	The tenth All-Union Congress of Evangelical Christians met in Saint Petersburg where Kargel and Prokhanov discussed the issues involved with military service and pacifism
1926	*Christ—Our Sanctification* was published in serial form in Russian

UKRAINE PERIOD, 1928–1937

1923–1929	Kargel travelled often between Saint Petersburg and Tokara, Ukraine

Year (month)	
1926–1927	Kargel made several teaching trips to Kharkov, Ukraine
1928	*Ruth the Moabitess* was published in Russian
1928	*Behold, I am Coming Soon* was published in Russian sometime near 1928
1928	Prokhanov failed to return to Russia following the fourth BWA meeting held in Toronto
1928	*To the Ends of the Earth: Among the Brothers in Chains* was published in German
1928–1932	Joseph Stalin's first Five-Year Plan to transform Russian society and eliminate religion
1929	Kargel was arrested while lecturing at the Saint Petersburg Bible College, the school was closed and he was banished from Saint Petersburg and returned permanently to Ukraine
1929	Russian Baptist Union organized their own Bible school in Moscow
1932	*Law of the Spirit of Life* was written near to this date but was not published until 2003
1933–1938	Joseph Stalin's second Five-Year Plan to transform Russian society and eliminate religion
1935	Prokhanov died in Berlin, Germany
1936 (8)	Elizaveta and Maria Kargel were arrested and exiled to Siberia after spending one year in prison
1936	Ivan Kargel was moved from Tokara to Lebedin, Ukraine
1937 (11)	Ivan Veniaminovich Kargel died at the age of 88 after being arrested and released
1938	Elena Kargel was arrested and executed in Sumy, Ukraine
1944	The All-Union Council of Evangelical Christians–Baptists (AUCEC-B) was formed
1945	AUCEC-B started the journal *Bratsky Vestnik*
1957	Elizaveta Kargel died in Siberia at the age of 70
1961	Maria Kargel died in Siberia at the age of 75

Year (month)	
1966	Kargel's 1913 Confession of Faith was officially adopted as the doctrinal statement of the AUCEC-B
1984	Kargel's 1913 Confession of Faith was replaced as the official doctrinal statement of the AUCEC-B
1991	*Commentary on the Revelation of Saint John the Theologian* was published in Russian
1997	*The Collected Works* of I. V. Kargel were published
1998	*Light from the Shadows of Future Blessing* was republished in Russian

APPENDIX THREE

Map of German Baptist Churches in Eastern Volhynia

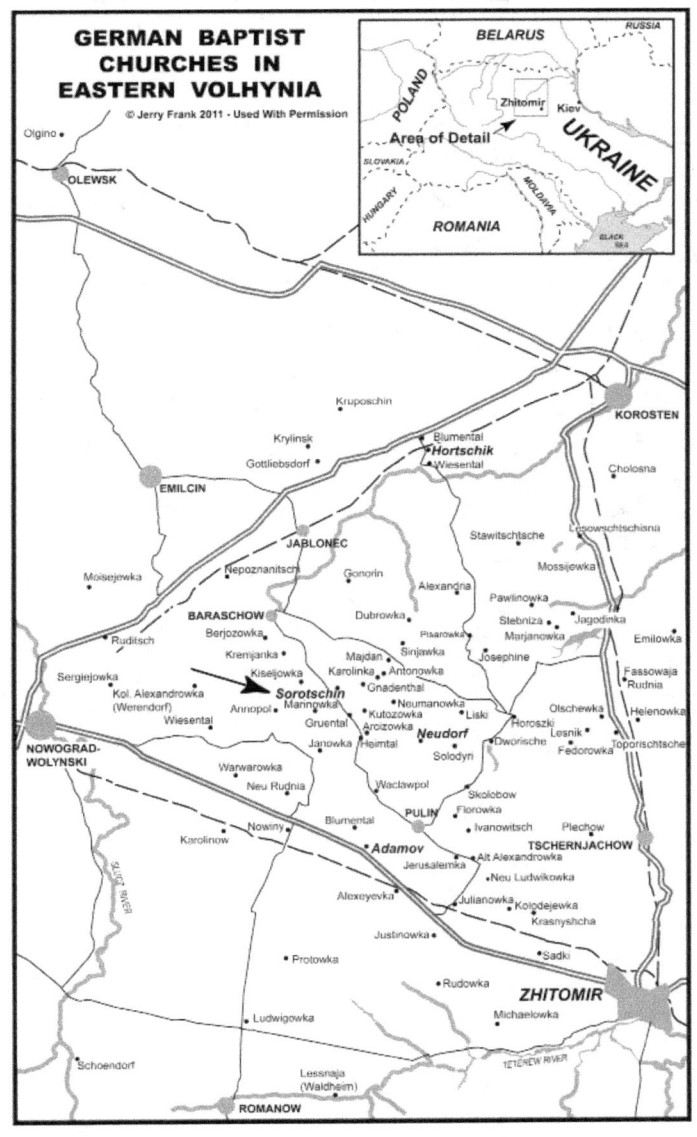

APPENDIX FOUR

Kargel's Map of his Trip to Siberia in 1890 from *Zwischen den Ended der Erde*

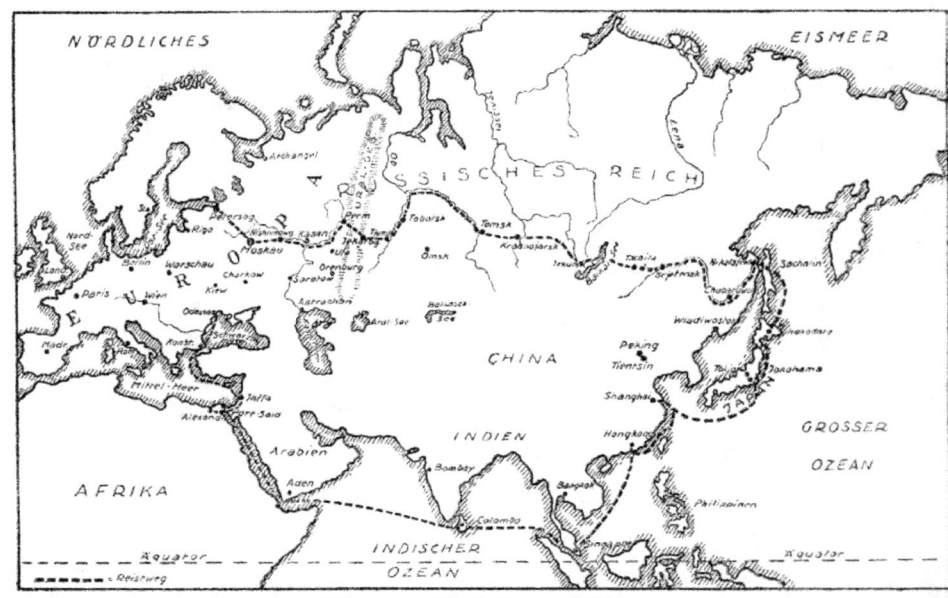

Skizze zur Reise durch Sibirien

APPENDIX FIVE

Map of the Caucasus Region

APPENDIX SIX

Map of the Provinces of Western (European) Russia, c. 1900

APPENDIX SEVEN

Map of the Historic Russian Provinces in Modern-day Ukraine

APPENDIX EIGHT

Photograph of Ivan Kargel

APPENDIX NINE

Sketching of Ivan Kargel

Bibliography

"Annual Report." *Quarterly Reporter of the German Baptist Mission* 77 (July 1877) 2–6.
Auszug aus dem Protocoll der Achten Bundes-Conferenz. Hamburg: Oncken, 1870. Oncken Archives, Elstal, Germany.
Auszug aus dem Protocoll der Elften Bundes-Conferenz. Hamburg: Oncken, 1879. Oncken Archives, Elstal, Germany.
Auszug aus dem Protocoll der Zehnten Bundes-Conferenz. Hamburg: Oncken, 1876. Oncken Archives, Elstal, Germany.
Baptist World Congress, London, July 11–19, 1905: Record of Proceedings. London: Baptist Union, 1905.
Baptist World Congress, Philadelphia, June 19–25, 1911: Record of Proceedings. Philadelphia: Harper and Brother, 1911.
"Bulgaria." *Quarterly Reporter of the German Baptist Mission* 92 (April 1881) 11–13.
"Clenskij Kalendar' Russkoj Evangel'skoj Svobodnoj Cerkvi v Finlandii" [Calendar of the Members of the Russian Evangelical Free Church in Finland]. International Baptist Theological Seminary Library, Prague, Czech Republic.
Christliches Jahrbuch zur Belehrung und Unterhaltung. Simferopol: Spat, 1902.
Documents of Moscow 1966 All-Union Conference of Evangelical Christian-Baptists. Moscow: VSEXB, 1966.
"Donesenie o sezde nemeckih menonitov i baptistov" [Report of the Meeting of the German Mennonites and Baptists]. In *Istoriya Evangel'skogo Dvizheniya v Evrazii, Disk 1.0* [The History of the Evangelical Movement in Eurasia, disk 1.0]. Odessa, Ukraine: EAAA, 2001. D:\files\texts\2\0155a.html.
"Ein macedonischer Ruf an die Gemeinden des Bundes aus der Bulgarei." *Wahrheitszeuge* 2.18 (15 September, 1880) 142–43.
"Eine Reise nach Kasanlik [part one]." *Wahrheitszeuge* 3.10 (15 May 1881) 94.
"Eine Reise nach Kasanlik [part two]." *Wahrheitszeuge* 3.11 (1 June 1881) 104.
"Erste Fruechte der Neuen Freiheit in Russland." *Wahrheitszeuge* 2.7 (1 April 1880) 54.
"Extension of the German Baptist Mission into Asia and Africa." *Quarterly Reporter of the German Baptist Mission* 47 (October 1869) 381–84.
"Germany, Reports from the Mission." *The Baptist Missionary Magazine* 66.11 (November 1886) 428–30.
Istoriya Evangel'skix Xristian-Baptistov v SSSR [History of Evangelical Christians-Baptists in the USSR]. Moscow: VSEXB, 1989.
Istoriya Evangel'skogo Dvizheniya v Evrazii, disk 1.0 [The History of the Evangelical Movement in Eurasia, disk 1.0]. Odessa, Ukraine: EAAA, 2001.
Istoriya Evangel'skogo Dvizheniya v Evrazii, disk 2.0 [The History of the Evangelical Movement in Eurasia, disk 2.0]. Odessa, Ukraine: EAAA, 2002.

Istoriya Evangel'skogo Dvizheniya v Evrazii, disk 3.0. [The History of the Evangelical Movement in Eurasia, disk 3.0]. Odessa, Ukraine: EAAA, 2003.

Istoriya Evangel'skogo Dvizheniya v Evrazii, disk 4.0. [The History of the Evangelical Movement in Eurasia, disk 4.0]. Odessa, Ukraine: EAAA, 2005.

"Ivan Benjaminovitsh Kargell." On-line: http://wwnet.fi/users/veijone/kargel.html [accessed 15 March 2011].

"Iz Pisem E. I. Kargel' o Razdelenii Cerkvej" [From the Letters of E. I. Kargel about the Separation of Churches]. In *Sobranie Sochinenij*, 680–83. St. Petersburg: Bibliya Dlya Bsex, 1997.

"Izliyanie Duxa Svyatogo i Pyatidesyatnicheskoe Dvizhenie" [The Outpouring of the Holy Spirit and the Pentecostal Movement]. International Baptist Theological Seminary Library, Prague.

"Letters from Mr. Oncken in Russia." *Quarterly Reporter of the German Baptist Mission* 48 (January 1870) 797–806.

"Livonia and Esthonia." *Quarterly Reporter of the German Baptist Mission* 32 (January 1866) 149–51.

"The Macedonian Cry Re-echoed from Macedonia Itself." *Quarterly Reporter of the German Baptist Mission* 90 (October 1880) 1–2.

"Mission to Germany." *The Missionary Magazine* 49.7 (July 1869) 276–82.

"Mission to Germany." *The Baptist Missionary Magazine* 52.7 (July 1872) 282–88.

"Mission to Germany; Appeal from the German Committee." *The Baptist Missionary Magazine* 56.3 (March 1876) 77–80.

"Mission to the Germans." *The Baptist Missionary* Magazine 56.7 (July 1876) 270–73.

"Ot Vsesoyuznogo Soveta Evangel'skix Xristian-baptistov" [From the All-Union Council of Evangelical Christians-Baptists]. *Bratsky Vestnik* 3 (1957) 4.

Pashkov Paper. University of Birmingham, Birmingham, England. (microfiche, International Baptist Theological Seminary, Prague).

"Pervyj Vseukrainskij S'ezd Evangel'skix Xristian" [The first All-Ukrainian Meeting of the Evangelical Christians]. In *Istoriya Evangel'skogo Dvizheniya v Evrazii, Disk 1.0* [The History of the Evangelical Movement in Eurasia, disk 1.0]. Odessa, Ukraine: EAAA, 2001. D:\files\texts\5\0015a.html.

"Recognition of the Church at St. Petersburg." *The Baptist Missionary Magazine* 60.5 (May 1880) 124–25.

"Reshenie Orgkomiteta po voprosu protivocerkovnoj deyatel'nosti VSEXB" [Decisions of the State Committee concerning the religious Activities of the AUCEC-B]. In *Istoriya Evangel'skogo Dvizheniya v Evrazii, Disk 1.0* [The History of the Evangelical Movement in Eurasia, disk 1.0]. Odessa, Ukraine: EAAA, 2001. D:\files\texts\8\0073a.html.

"Rossiya" [Russia]. In *Evangel'skaya Vera* 8.7–9 (July-September 1939) 19.

"Russia, St. Petersburg." *Quarterly Reporter of the German Baptist Mission* 81 (July 1878) 7–8.

"Russland. St. Petersburg. Nachrichten von Br. Kargel." *Missionsblatt* 36.10 (October 1878) 183–88.

"Statistics of Continental Baptist Churches." *Quarterly Reporter of the German Baptist Mission* 63 (October 1873) 61–62.

"Statistics of Continental Baptist Churches." *Quarterly Reporter of the German Baptist Mission* 69 (July 1875) 15–16.

"Statistik 1882 der vereinigten Gemeinden Getaufter Christen (Baptisten) in Deutschland, Dänemark, Holland, der Schweiz, Polen, Russland, der Türkei, Afrika and Australien." Oncken Archives, Elstal, Germany.

"Statistik 1883 der vereinigten Gemeinden Getaufter Christen (Baptisten) in Deutschland, Dänemark, Holland, der Schweiz, Polen, Russland, der Türkei, Afrika and Australien." Oncken Archives, Elstal, Germany.

"Statistik 1886 der vereinigten Gemeinden Getaufter Christen (Baptisten) in Deutschland und den umliegenden Ländern." Oncken Archives, Elstal, Germany.

"Statistik 1887 der vereinigten Gemeinden Getaufter Christen (Baptisten) in Deutschland und den umliegenden Ländern." Oncken Archives, Elstal, Germany.

"St. Petersburg." *Quarterly Reporter of the German Baptist Mission* 87 (January 1880) 9.

"Svedeniya o Dele Bozhiem" [Information on God's Work]. *Seyatel' Istiny* 1 (January 1924) 14–15.

"Sweden. The First Baptist in Finland." *Quarterly Reporter of the German Baptist Mission* 46 (July 1869) 374–75.

"Verouchenie Evangel'skix Xristian-Baptistov" [The Statement of Faith of the Evangelical Christians-Baptists]. *Bratsky Vestnik* 4 (1966) 15–18.

"Vtoroj Den' S"ezda, Utrennee Zasedanie 5 Oktyabrya" [The Second Day of the Congress, Morning Session, 5 October]. *Bratsky Vestnik* 6 (1966) 43–45.

"Work in St. Petersburg." *Quarterly Reporter of the German Baptist Mission* 89 (July 1880) 8–9.

Aaltio, Teuvo. "A History of the National Baptists in Finland." BD thesis, Baptist Theological Seminary, Rueschlikon, Switzerland, 1958.

Abrams, M. H. *Natural Supernaturalism: Tradition and Revolution in Romantic Literature*. London: Norton, 1971.

Adams, Theodore F. *Baptists around the World*. Nashville, TN: Broadman, 1967.

Aitken, Tom. *Blood and Fire, Tsar and Commissar: The Salvation Army in Russia, 1907–1923*. Milton Keynes, UK: Paternoster, 2007.

Amburger, Eric. *Geshichte des Protestanismus in Russland*. Stuttgart: Evangelisches, 1961.

Angelov, Theo. "The Baptist Movement in Bulgaria." *Journal of European Baptist Studies* 1.3 (May 2001) 8–18.

Armstrong, Anthony. *The Church of England, the Methodists and Society 1700–1850*. London: University of London Press, 1973.

Baechtold, Theodor. "Johann Gerhard Oncken and Baptist Beginnings in Switzerland." B.D. thesis, Baptist Seminary, Rueschlikon, Switzerland, 1970.

Balders, Günter. *Theurer Bruder Oncken, das Leben Johann Gerhard Onckens in Bildern und Dokumenten*. Kassel, Germany: Oncken, 1978.

Balousov, S. V. "Pervyj Nazidatel'nyj S"ezd Baptistov v Omske Sibir" [The First Supportive Congress in Baptist in Omsk, Siberia]. *Baptist* 6–7 (December 1925) 35–39.

Barabas, Steven. *So Great Salvation: The History and Message of the Keswick Convention*. Grand Rapids. 1952. Reprint. Eugene, OR: Wipf & Stock, 2005.

Barnes, I. *Truth is Immortal: The Story of Baptists in Europe*. London: Kingsgate, 1955.

Bebbington, D. W. "Baptists and Fundamentalism in Inter-War Britain." In *Protestant Evangelicalism: Britain, Ireland, Germany and America c.1750–c.1950: Essays in Honor of W. R. Ward*, edited by Keith Robbins, 297–326. New York: Blackwell, 1990.

———. *The Dominance of Evangelicalism: The Age of Spurgeon and Moody.* Downers Grove, IL: InterVarsity, 2005.

———. "Evangelicalism in Modern Britain and America: A Comparison." In *Amazing Grace,* edited by George A. Rawlyk and Mark A. Noll, 183–212. Grand Rapids: Baker, 1993.

———. *Evangelicalism in Modern Britain: A History from the 1730s to the 1980s.* London: Unwin Hyman, 1989.

———. *Holiness in Nineteenth-Century England.* Carlisle, UK: Paternoster, 2000.

———. "The Place of the Brethren Movement in International Evangelicalism." In *The Growth of the Brethren Movement,* edited by N. Dickson and T. Grass, 241–260. Milton Keynes, UK: Paternoster, 2006.

Beeson, Trevor. *Discretion and Valor.* Philadelphia: Fortress, 1974.

Belkov, Pavel. "Unity and Leadership in the Evangelical-Baptist Movement in Russia through the Mid-1920s." B.D. thesis, International Baptist Theological Seminary, Prague, 1998.

Belousov, A. "Tri Kolybeli Bratstva Evangel'skix Xristian-Baptistov v SSSR" [The Three Cradles of the Brotherhood of the Evangelical Christians-Baptists in the USSR]. *Bratsky Vestnik* 4 (1967) 9–19.

Bender, Harold Stauffer. "Kargel, Johann." In *The Mennonite Encyclopedia,* edited by Harold Stauffer Bender et al., 4:1099. Scottdale, PA: Mennonite, 1956–1990.

Bender, Harold Stauffer, Cornelius Krahn, Melvin Gingerich, Cornelius J. Dyck, and Dennis D. Martin. *The Mennonite Encyclopedia.* 5 vols. Scottdale, PA: Mennonite, 1956–1990.

Billington, Anthony, Tony Lane, and Max Turner, eds. *Mission and Meaning: Essays Presented to Peter Cotterell.* Carlisle, UK: Paternoster, 1995.

Blane, Andrew Q. "The Relations between the Russian Protestant Sects and the State." Ph.D. diss., Duke University, 1964.

Blumit, Oswald A., and Oswald J. Smith. *Sentenced to Siberia.* Wheaton, IL: Mayflower, 1943.

Bodyanskiy, N. "Xronika" [The Chronicle]. *Missionerskoe Obozrenie* 18.10 (October 1913) 313–26.

Bolshakoff, Serge. *Russian Nonconformity.* Philadelphia: Westminster, 1950.

Boobbyer, Philip. *Conscience, Dissent and Reform in Soviet Russia.* BASEES/Routledge series on Russian and East European Studies 21. London: Routledge, 2005.

———. *The Stalin Era.* London: Routledge, 2000.

Bourdeaux, Michael. *Faith on Trial in Russia.* London: Hodder and Stoughton, 1971.

Boyd, Gregory A., and Paul R. Eddy. *Across the Spectrum: Understanding Issues in Evangelical Theology.* Grand Rapids: Baker Academic, 2002.

Brandenburg, Hans. *The Meek and the Mighty: The Emergence of the Evangelical Movement in Russia.* New York: Oxford University Press, 1977.

Breyfogle, Nicholas B. *Heretics and Colonizers: Forging Russia's Empire in the South Caucasus.* New York: Cornell University Press, 2005.

Briggs, John H. Y. The *English Baptists of the Nineteenth Century: A History of the English Baptist,* Volume III, edited by Roger Hayden. Didcot, UK: The Baptist Historical Society, 1994.

———. "Evangelical Ecumenism: The Amalgamation of General and Particular Baptists in 1891 (Part Two)." *The Baptist Quarterly* 34.3 (July 1991) 160–79.

———. "From 1905 to the End of the First World War." In *Baptists Together in Christ 1905–2005*, edited by Richard V. Pierard, 20–46. Falls Church, VA: Baptist World Alliance, 2005.

Broadbent, E. H. *The Pilgrim Church*. London: Pickering & Inglis, 1950.

Bunaciu, Otniel Ioan. "The Meaning of Tradition in Orthodox Theology." In *Baptists and the Orthodox Church: On the Way to Understanding*, edited by Ian Randall, 30–45. Prague: International Baptist Theological Seminary, 2003.

Bundy, David D. *Keswick: A Bibliographic Introduction to the Higher Life Movements*. Wilmore, KY: Asbury Theological Seminary, 1975.

Burgess, Stanley M., ed. *The New International Dictionary of Pentecostal and Charismatic Movements*. Grand Rapids: Zondervan, 2002.

Buss, Gerald. *The Bear's Hug: Religious Believers in the Soviet Union, 1917–86*. London: Hodder and Stoughton, 1987.

Butkevich T. I., *Obzor Russkix Sekt i ix Tolkov, s izlozheniem ix Proisxozhdeniya i Veroucheniya i s Oproverzheniem Poslednego* [Review of Russian Sects and Persuasions, Outlining their Origin and Doctrine with a Denial the Latter]. Petrograd: Tuzov, 1915.

Bychkov, A. M. "Soobshhenie Prezidiuma VSEXB o Rabote Mezhdu Plenumami" [Report of the Presidium of the AUCEC-B concerning Work between Plenums]. *Bratsky Vestnik* 1 (1983) 35–42.

Byford, Charles Taylor. *Baptist Pioneers in Russia and South Eastern Europe*. 2nd ed. London: James Clarke, 1912.

———. "The Movement in Russia." In *The Baptist Movement in the Continent of Europe: A Contribution to Modern History*, edited by J. H. Rushbrooke, 69–98. London: Carey, 1915.

———. *Peasants and Prophets*. 3rd ed. London: Kingsgate, 1914.

———. *The Soul of Russia*. London: Kingsgate, 1914.

C., E. I. "Aleksandr Vasil'evich Karev (K devyanostoletiyu so dnya rozhdeniya)" [Alexander Vasil'evich Karev (on his ninetieth Birthday)]. *Bratsky Vestnik* 6 (1984) 56–70.

Casey, Robert P. *Religion in Russia*. London: Harper & Brothers, 1946.

Chakalov, V. "Ivan V. Kargel." *Xristiyanski Priyatel* (Bulgaria) 1.6 (June 1939) 10.

Chepurina, N. "Ispoved' I. V. Kargelya" [The Confession of I. V. Kargel]. *Obzor' Sektantskoj Literatury* 19.3 (March 1914) 507–12.

Chomonev, G. M. "Poyavyavaneto na Baptizma v Bulgariya" [The Appearance of Baptist in Bulgaria]. *Evangelist* (Bulgaria) 1 (January-March 1920) 2–5.

Chulos, Chris J. *Converging Worlds*. DeKalb, IL: Northern Illinois University Press, 2003.

Clarkson, Jesse D. *A History of Russia*. New York: Random House, 1968.

Coleman, Heather J. "Baptist Beginnings in Russia and Ukraine." *Baptist History and Heritage* 42.1 (2007) 24–36.

———. *Russian Baptists and Spiritual Revolution, 1905–1929*. Indiana-Michigan series in Russian and East European studies. Bloomington, IN: Indiana University Press, 2005.

Collins, Kenneth J. *The Evangelical Moment*. Grand Rapids: Baker Academic, 2005.

Conybeare, Frederick C. *Russian Dissenters*. New York: Russell and Russell, 1962.

Cooke, John Hunt. *Johann Gerhard Oncken: His Life and Work*. London: Partridge, 1908.

Corley, Felix. *Religion in the Soviet Union: An Archival Reader*. New York: New York Press, 1996.
Corrado, Sharyl. "Introduction: In Search of an Eastern European Identity." In *Eastern European Baptist History: New Perspectives*, edited by Sharyl Corrado and Toivo Pilli, 7–13. Prague: International Baptist Theological Seminary, 2007.
———. "The Philosophy of Ministry of Colonel Vasiliy Pashkov." M.A. thesis, Wheaton College, 2000.
Corrado, Sharyl, and Toivo Pilli, eds. *Eastern European Baptist History: New Perspectives*. Prague: International Baptist Theological Seminary, 2007.
Courtois, Stâephane, Nicolas Werth, Jean-Louis Panne, Andrzej Paczkowski, Karel Bartosek, and Jean-Louise Margolin. *The Black Book of Communism*. Translated by Jonathon Murphy. Cambridge: Harvard University Press, 1999.
Crampton, R. J. *A Concise History of Bulgaria*. Cambridge: Cambridge University Press, 2005.
Crankshaw, Edward. *The Shadow of the Winter Palace: Russia's Drift to Revolution, 1825–1917*. New York: Viking, 1976.
Cross, Anthony, and Philip Thompson, eds. *Baptist Sacramentalism*. Studies in Baptist History and Thought 5. Carlisle, UK: Paternoster, 2003.
Dayton, Donald. *The American Holiness Movement: A Bibliographic Introduction*. Wilmore, KY: Asbury Theological Seminary, 1971.
———. *Theological Roots of Pentecostalism*. Grand Rapids: Zondervan, 1987.
de Chalandeau, Alexander. *The Christians in the USSR*. Chicago: Harper, 1978.
———. "The Theology of the Evangelical Christians-Baptists in the USSR as Reflected in the Bratskii Vestnik." Ph.D. diss., Universite des Sciences Humaines de Strasbourg, 1978.
Dickson, Neil, and Tim Grass, eds. *The Growth of the Brethren Movement: National and International Experiences*. Studies in Evangelical History and Thought. Milton Keynes, UK: Paternoster, 2006.
Diedrich, Hans-Christian. *Urspruenge und Anfaenge Russischen Freikirchentums*. Erlangen: Lilienfeld, 1985.
Dieter, Melvin Easterday. *The Holiness Revival of the Nineteenth Century*. Metuchen, New Jersey: Scarecrow, 1980.
Dilakoff, Jacob. "The Autobiography of Jacob Dilakoff, Independent Missionary in Russia." Translated by Labaree and Shedd. *The European Harvest Field* (September 1935) 11–13, 18.
Ditchfield, G. M. *The Evangelical Revival*. London: UCL Press, 1998.
Donat, Rudolf. *Das Waschsende Werk: Ausbreitung der Deutschen Baptistengemeinde durch Sechzig Jahre (1849–1909)*. Kassel, Germany: Oncken, 1960.
Doerksen, Ben. "Mennonite Brethren Missions: Historical Development, Philosophy, and Policies." Ph.D. diss., Fuller Theological Seminary, 1986.
Dorodnicyn, Aleksijj [Episkop Aleksijj]. *Yuzhno- Russkij Neobaptizm, Izvestnyj pod Imenem Shtundisty po Oficial'nym Dokumentam* [South Russia Neobaptistism, known by the Name of Stundists according to Official Documents]. Stavropol: n.p., 1903. Southern Baptist Historical Library and Archives, Nashville, Tennessee.
———. *Religiozno-racionalisticheskoe Dvizhenie na Yuge Rossii vo Vtoroj Polovine 19-go stoletiya* [The Religious-Rationalistic Movement in South Russia in the Second-Half of the Nineteenth Century]. Kazan: n.p., 1909. Southern Baptist Historical Library and Archives, Nashville, TN.

Dostoevsky, F. M. *Polnoe Sobranie Sochinenij* [The Full Collected Works]. 30 volumes. Leningrad: Nauka, 1972-1990.
Dubnow, Simon. *History of the Jews in Russia and Poland*. Translated by Israel Friedlaender. 1918. Reprint. Bergenfield, NJ: Avotaynu, 2000.
Dueck, Abe J. *Moving Beyond Secession: Defining Russian Mennonite Brethren Mission and Identity 1872-1922*. Winnipeg, Canada: Kindred, 1997.
Durasoff, Steve. "The All Union Council of Evangelical Christians-Baptists." Ph.D. diss., New York University, 1968.
———. *Bright Wind of the Spirit: Pentecostalism Today*. Englewood Cliffs, NJ: Prentice-Hall, 1972.
———. *The Russian Protestants: Evangelicals in the Soviet Union, 1944-1964*. Rutherford, NJ: Fairleigh Dickinson University Press, 1969.
Dyck, Johannes. "Moulding the Brotherhood: Johann Wieler (1839-1889) and the Communities of the Early Evangelicals in Russia." M.Th. thesis, International Baptist Theological Seminary, University of Wales, 2007.
Easton, P. Z. "Baptist Work in Russia and the Caucasus." *The Baptist Missionary Magazine* 63.2 (February 1883) 34-36.
Edgar, John. *Wo sind die Toten?: Eine religiös-psychologische Studie auf positiv biblischer Grundlage*. Elberfeld-Sonnenborn, Germany: Haendeler, 1913.
Eisenach, George. *Pietism and the Russian Germans in the United States*. Berne, IN: Berne, 1948.
Endelman, Todd M., ed. *Jewish Apostasy in the Modern World*. New York: Holmes & Meier, 1987.
Ewing, John W. *Goodly Fellowship: A Centenary Tribute to the Life and Work of the World's Evangelical Alliance*. London: Marshall, Morgan, and Scott, 1946.
Fairbairn, Donald. *Eastern Orthodoxy through Western Eyes*. Louisville: Westminster John Knox, 2002.
Figes, Orlando. *A People's Tragedy: The Russian Revolution 1891-1924*. London: Pimlico, 1996.
Findlay, James F. *Dwight L. Moody: American Evangelist, 1837-1899*. Chicago: University of Chicago Press, 1969.
Fletcher, William C. *Soviet Charismatics: The Pentecostals in the USSR*. New York: Lang, 1985.
Flugge, C. A. *Notschreie aus Russland*. Kassel, Germany: Christliche Traktatgesellschaft, 1930.
Franchuk V. I. "Prosila Rossiya Dozhdya u Gospoda" [Russia Begged the Lord for Rain]. In *Istoriya Evangel'skogo Dvizheniya v Evrazii, Disk 2.0* [The History of the Evangelical Movement in Eurasia, disk 2.0.]. Odessa, Ukraine: EAAA, 2002. D:\files\books\book_02\f_000.html-D:\files\books\book_02\f_015.html.
Franz, J. J. "A Brief History of the Prussian-Russian Mennonites." B.D. thesis, Northern Baptist Theological Seminary, 1928.
Freeman, Curtis W., James W. McClendon Jr., and C. Roselee Velloso Da Silva, eds. *Baptist Roots: A Reader in the Theology of a Christian People*. Valley Forge, PA: Judson, 1999.
Freidmann, Robert. *Mennonite Piety through the Centuries: Its Genius and its Literature*. Goshen College, IN: The Mennonite Historical Society, 1949.
Friesen, Abraham. *In Defense of Privilege: Russian Mennonites and the State Before and During World War II*. Winnipeg, Canada: Kindred, 2006.

Friesen, Peter M. *The Mennonite Brotherhood in Russia (1789–1910)*. Fresno, CA: Board of Christian Literature, 1978.

Geldbach, Erich. "Julius Köbner's Contribution to Baptist Identity." In *Baptist Identities: International Studies from the Seventeenth to the Twentieth Centuries*, Studies in Baptist History and Thought 19, edited by Ian Randall, Toivo Pilli, and Anthony Cross, 63–76. Carlisle, UK: Paternoster, 2006.

Gill, Everett. "Foreign Mission Board Report." In *Annual of the Southern Baptist Convention 1924*, 275. Nashville: Marshall & Bruce, 1924.

Golobashhenko, S. I. *Istoriya Evangel'sko–Baptistskogo Dvizheniya v Ukraine* [History of the Evangelical-Baptist movement in Ukraine]. Odessa, Ukraine: Bogomyslie, 1998.

———. "Istoriya Evangel'sko–Baptistskogo Dvizheniya v Ukraine" [The History of the Evangelical-Baptist Movement in Ukraine]. In *Istoriya Evangel'skogo Dvizheniya v Evrazii, disk 1.0* [The History of the Evangelical Movement in Eurasia, disk 1.0]. Odessa, Ukraine: EAAA, 2001. D:/files/books/book_002/0045_t.html-D:/files/books/book_002/0061_t.html.

Gorodetzky, Nadejda. *The Humiliated Christ in Modern Russian Thought*. London: Society for Promoting Christian Knowledge, 1938.

Grachev, Yu. S. "Pervye Biblejskie Kursy Evangel'skix Xristian-Baptistov v Rossii" [The First Bible Course of the Evangelical Christians-Baptists in Russia]. *Bratsky Vestnik* 3 (1971) 72–73.

Grass, Tim. *Gathering to His Name: The Story of the Open Brethren in Britain and Ireland*. Milton Keynes, UK: Paternoster, 2006.

Green, Bernard. *Crossing the Boundaries: A History of the European Baptist Federation*. Didcot, UK: Baptist Historical Society, 1999.

Gutsche, Waldemar. *Westliche Quellen des russischen Stundismus: Anfänge der evngelischen Bewegung in Russland*. Kassel, Germany: Oncken, 1956.

———. *Religion und Evangelium in Sowjetrussland zwichen Zwei Weltkriegen (1917–1944)*. Kassel, Germany: Oncken, 1959.

Hanson, Bradley, ed. *Modern Christian Spirituality: Methodological and Historical Essays*. AAR Studies in Religion 62. Atlanta, GA: Scholars, 1990.

Harford, Charles F., ed. *Keswick Convention: Its Message, Its Methods and Its Men*. London: Marshall Brothers, 1907.

Harms, John F. *Geschichte der Mennoniten Bruedergemeinde: 1860–1924*. Hillsboro, KS: Mennonite Brethren, 1926.

Hauptmann, Peter. *Kirche im Osten: Studien zur Osteuropaischen Kirchengeschiehte und Kirchenkunde*. Goettingen: Vandenhoeck & Ruprecht, 1982.

Hebly, J. A. "A New Confession of the Evangelical Christian Baptists in the Soviet Union." *Occasional Papers on Religion in Eastern Europe* 4.1 (January 1984) 1–14.

———. *Protestants in Russia*. Belfast: Christian Journals, 1976.

Heier, Edmund. *Religious Schism in the Russian Aristocracy 1860–1900: Radstockism and Pashkovism*. The Hague: Nijhoff, 1970.

Heretz, Leonid. *Russia on the Eve of Modernity: Popular Religion and Traditional Culture under the Last Tsars*. Cambridge: Cambridge University Press, 2008.

Hill, Kent R. *The Puzzle of the Soviet Church*. Portland, OR: Multnomah, 1989.

———. *Turbulent Times for the Soviet Church: The Inside Story*. Portland, OR: Multnomah, 1991.

Holmio, Armas K. E. *The Finnish Missionary Society 1859–1950*. Hancock, MI: Finnish Lutheran, 1950.

Hopkins, Charles Howard. *John R. Mott*. Grand Rapids: Eerdmans, 1979.
Hopkins, Evan. *The Law of Liberty in the Spiritual Life*. London: Marshall Bros., 1884.
Hornbacker, Eduard A. "Hundert Jahre Deutscher Baptismus in Russland." Typed manuscript, 1969. Southern Baptist Historical Library and Archives, Nashville, TN.
Hovey, Alvah. *Barnas Sears: A Christian Educator*. New York: Silver, Burdett, 1902.
Howard, David M. *The Dream That Would Not Die: The Birth and Growth of the World Evangelical Fellowship*. Exeter, UK: Paternoster, 1986.
Hunter, Leslie S. *Scandinavian Churches: A Picture of the Development and Life of the Churches of Denmark, Finland, Iceland, Norway, and Sweden*. London: Faber and Faber, 1965.
Hutten, Kurt. *Iron Curtain Christians*. Minneapolis: Augsburg, 1967.
Hutton, J. E. *A History of the Moravian Church*. London: Moravian, 1909.
Ignat'ev, R. S. "Pashkovcy-Baptisty v' Peterburg" [Pashkovites-Baptists in Petersburg]. *Istoricheskij Vestnik* 4 (1909) 184–92.
Iswolsky, Helen. *Soul of Russia*. New York: Sheed and Ward, 1943.
Iwanow, Boris. *In Religion in the USSR*. Munich: Institute for the Study of the USSR, 1960.
Jack, Walter L. *Evangelische Strömungen im Russischen Volke*. Wernigerode, Germany: Licht dem Osten, 1920.
Jansson, E. "Finland." *The Baptist Missionary Magazine* 69.8 (August 1889) 348.
Jones, Keith G. *The European Baptist Federation: A Case Study in European Baptist Interdependency 1950–2006*. Studies in Baptist History and Thought 18. Milton Keynes: Paternoster, 2009.
Jones, Malcolm V., and James Y. Muckle. "Marginalia: Three Letters from V. D. Bonch-Bruyevich in the Pashkov Papers." *Slavonic and East European Review* 60.1 (January 1982) 75–84.
Jordan, Philip D. *The Evangelical Alliance for the United States of America, 1847–1900: Ecumenism, Identity and the Religion of the Republic*. New York: Mellen, 1982.
K., A. A. "100-letnij Yubilej Leningradskoj Cerkvi EXB" [The Hundredth Anniversary of the Evangelical Christians-Baptist in Leningrad]. *Bratsky Vestnik* 2 (1975) 69–72.
K., P. "Vnov' Izbrannyj General'nyj Sekretar' Vsesoyuznogo Soveta Evangel'skix Xristian-Baptistov" [The Newly Elected General Secretary of the All-Union Council of Evangelical Christians-Baptists]. *Bratsky Vestnik* 2 (1972) 64–67.
Kahle, Wilhelm. *Evangelische Christen in Russland und der Sowjetunion*. Wuppertal, Germany: Oncken, 1978.
Kalweit, Martin. "Letter from Mr. Kalweit." *The Missionary Magazine* 50.1 (January 1870) 19–21.
Karetnikova, Marina S. "Ivan Veniaminovich Kargel." In *Sobranie Sochinenij*, 684–88. St. Petersburg: Bibliya Dlya Bsex, 1997.
———, ed. *Almanax po Istorii Russkogo Baptisma, vypusk 1* [Almanac of the History of the Russian Baptists, volume 1]. St. Petersburg: Biblia Dlya Bsex, 1997.
———, ed. *Almanax po Istorii Russkogo Baptisma, vypusk 2* [Almanac of the History of the Russian Baptists, volume 2]. St. Petersburg: Biblia Dlya Bsex, 2001.
———, ed. *Almanax po Istorii Russkogo Baptisma, vypusk 3* [Almanac of the History of the Russian Baptists, volume 3]. St. Petersburg: Biblia Dlya Bsex, 2004.
———, ed. *Almanax po Istorii Russkogo Baptisma, vypusk 4* [Almanac of the History of the Russian Baptists, volume 4]. St. Petersburg: Biblia Dlya Bsex, 2009.

———. "Biografiya I. V. Kargelya: K 70-letiyu so dnya ego konchiny" [Biography of I. V. Kargel: On the 70th Anniversary of the Day of his Death]. On-line: http://www.rosbaptist.ru/index.php?Itemid=221&id=137&option=com_content&task=view [accessed 15 March 2011].

———. "Velikij Duxovnyj Uchitel': K 150-letiyu so dnya rozhdeniya I. V. Kargelya (1849–1937)" [The Great Spiritual Teacher: On the 150 Anniversary of the Birth of I. V. Kargel (1849–1937)]. On-line: http://www.krotov.info/spravki/persons/20person/kargel.html [accessed 15 March 2011].

Karev, A. V. "Doklad General'nogo Sekretarya VSEXB A. V. Kareva o Zhizni i Deyatel'nosti Soyuza Evangel'skix Xristian-Baptistov v SSSR" [The Report of the Secretary-General of the AUCEC-B A. V. Karev on the Life and Work of the Union of Evangelical Christians-Baptists in the USSR]. *Bratsky Vestnik* 6 (1966) 15–36.

———. "Iz moix Lichnyx Vstrech s I. V. Kargelem" [From My Personal Meetings with I. V. Kargel]. *Bratsky Vestnik* 3 (1946) 19–20.

———. "Postanovlenie Vsesoyuznogo S"ezda Evangel'skix Xristian-Baptistov po Dokladu General'nogo Sekretarya VSEXB A. V. Kareva" [The Resolution of the All-Union Congress of Evangelical Christians-Baptists according to the Report from General-Secretary of the AUCEC-B, A. V. Karev]. *Bratsky Vestnik* 6 (1966) 47–48.

———. "Report of the Life and Activity of the Union of Evangelical Christian-Baptists in the USSR." In *Documents of Moscow 1966 All-Union Conference of Evangelical Christian-Baptists*, 5–47. Moscow: VSEXB, 1966.

———. "The Russian Evangelical Baptist Movement: Under His Cross in Soviet Russia." Typed manuscript translated by Fredrick P. Leman, 1960. Centre for Mennonite Brethren Studies, Winnipeg, Canada.

———. "Russkoe Evangel'sko-Baptistskoe Dvizhenie" [The Russian Evangelical-Baptist Movement]. *Bratsky Vestnik* 3 (1957) 5–51.

———. "Tropa Moej Zhizni" [The Path of my Life]. *Bratsky Vestnik* 1 (1955) 57–63.

Karev, A. V. and K. V. Somov. *Istoriya Xristianstva* [The History of Christianity]. Moscow: SEXB, 1990.

Kargel, Ivan (Johann) G. "Buch Ruth." *Zionsbote* (Kansas) 12, 41 (20 October 1897) 2.

———. "Bulgarei. Bruder Kargel's Besuch Beiden Bruedern in Kasanlyk." *Wahrheitszeuge* 3.6 (15 March 1881) 59–61.

———. "Confession of Faith of the Evangelical Christians-Baptists." In *Baptists in Europe: History and Confessions of Faith*, edited by Keith Parker, 154. Nashville: Broadman, 1982.

———. "Conflicts in Bulgaria (continued)." *Quarterly Reporter of the German Baptist Mission* 101 (July 1883) 5–7.

———. "Der grosse Verwandlungsprozess. [Part One]." *Zionsbote* (Kansas) 11.45 (11 November 1896) 1.

———. "Der grosse Verwandlungsprozess [Part Two]." *Zionsbote* (Kansas) 11.46 (18 November 1896) 1.

———. "Die Heiligung [Part One]." *Zionsbote* (Kansas) 13.28 (13 July 1898) 1.

———. "Die Heiligung [Part Nine]." *Zionsbote* (Kansas) 13.36 (7 September 1898) 1.

———. "Die Offenbarung Johannis [1907]." *Der Hausfreund* 18.3 (17 January 1907) 17–18.

———. "Die Offenbarung Johannis [1912]." *Der Hausfreund* 23.26 (27 June 1912) 207–9.

---. *Die Sünde, das Übel aller Übel in deiser Welt.* Aleksandrovska, Ekaterinoslav Gub: Knizhnyj Magazin' D. Isaask, Shenvize, [circa 1908].

---. "Ein Besuch in Jeruselem und Umgegend." In *Christliches Jahrbuch zur Belehrung und Unterhaltung,* 3–126. Spat near Simferopol, Ukraine: Selbstverlag, 1902.

---. "Ein Guter Anfang mit Traurigem Ende [part one]." *Zionsbote* (Kansas) 20, 40 (5 October 1904) 1.

---. "Ein Guter Anfang mit Traurigem Ende [part two]." *Zionsbote* (Kansas) 20.41 (12 October 1904) 1.

---. "Eine Auslegung des Buches der Offenbarung" [An Interpretation of the Book of Revelation]. Canadian Mennonite University Library, Winnipeg, Canada.

---. "Gde, po Pisaniyu, Naxodyatsya Mertvye" [Where are the Dead according to the Scriptures]. *Xristianin* 7 (1925) 17–25.

---. "Gde, po Pisaniyu, Naxodyatsya Mertvye" [Where are the Dead according to the Scriptures]. *Xristianin* 12 (1925) 24–32.

---. "Gde, po Pisaniyu, Naxodyatsya Mertvye?" [Where are the Dead according to the Scriptures?]. In *Sobranie Sochinenij,* 180–254. St. Petersburg: Bibliya Dlya Bsex, 1997.

---. "Gottes Heilige Regel, Seinen Willen zu Tun [Part One]." *Zionsbote* (Kansas) 20.16 (20 April 1904) 1.

---. "Gottes Heilige Regel, Seinen Willen zu Tun [Part Two]." *Zionsbote* (Kansas) 20.17 (27 April 1904) 1.

---. "Grex kak Zlo vsex Zol v ehtom Mire" [Sin, the Evil of all Evils in this World]. In *Sobranie Sochinenij,* 5–48. St. Petersburg: Bibliya Dlya Bsex, 1997.

---. "Iz Pisem I. V. Kargelya" [From the Letters of I. V. Kargel]. In *Sobranie Sochinenij,* 671–79. St. Petersburg: Bibliya Dlya Bsex, 1997.

---. "Izliyanie Duxa Svyatogo i Pyatidesyatnicheskoe Dvizhenie" [The Outpouring of the Holy Spirit and the Pentecostal Movement]. In *Almanax po Istorii Russkogo Baptisma, vypusk 3,* edited by Marina S. Karetnikova, 11–61. St. Petersburg: Biblia Dlya Bsex, 2004.

---. *Klagen und Fragen.* Spat, Crimea: Zeugnisse von Christo, 1901.

---. "Lekcii o vtorom Prishestvii Gospoda Iisusa Xrista" [Lectures on the Second Coming of the Lord Jesus Christ]. On-line: http://blagovestnik.org/books/00417.htm#a01 [accessed 15 March 2011].

---. *Licht aus dem Shatten.* Danzig: Dannermann, 1896.

---. "Mein Freund in seinem Garten." *Zionsbote* (Kansas) 11.49 (11 December 1895) 1.

---. "O vtorom Prishestvii Gospoda Iisusa Xrista" [On the Second Coming of the Lord Jesus Christ]. Columbia University, Rare Book and Manuscript Library, Bakhmeteff Archive of Russian and East European History and Culture, General Manuscript Collection, I. V. Kargel Manuscript, New York.

---. "Pura." *Zionsbote* (Kansas) 11.28 (10 July 1895) 1.

---. "Ruf' Moavityanka" [Ruth the Moabitess]. *Xristianin* 4 (1928) 27–33.

---. "Ruf' Moavityanka, ili Mezhi Moi Proshli po Prekrasnym Mestam" [Ruth the Moabitess, or the Lines Have Fallen for Me in Pleasant Places]. In *Sobranie Sochinenij,* 329–377. St. Petersburg: Bibliya Dlya Bsex, 1997.

---. "Russia, Further News from St. Petersburg." *Quarterly Reporter of the German Baptist* Mission 76 (April 1877) 4–6.

———. "Russia, St. Petersburg." *Quarterly Reporter of the German Baptist Mission* 73 (April 1876) 7–9.

———. "Russia, St. Petersburg." *Quarterly Reporter of the German Baptist Mission* 79 (January 1878) 8.

———. "Russland. St. Petersburg." *Missionsblatt* 36.7 (July 1878) 126.

———. "Se, Gryadu Skoro . . ." [Behold I am Coming Soon . . .]. In *Sobranie Sochinenij*, 378–448. St. Petersburg: Bibliya Dlya Bsex, 1997.

———. *Sobranie Sochinenij* [The Collected Works]. St. Petersburg: Bibliya Dlya Bsex, 1997.

———. "Soroczin. Missionsreisen des Br. Kargel." *Missionsblatt* 32.5 (May 1874) 83–88.

———. *Svet iz Teni budushhix Blag ili tridcat' dve Besedy o Skinij, Zhertvoprinosheniyax' i Svyashenstvyo* [Light from the Shadow of Future Blessing, or Thirty-Two Conversations about the Tabernacle, Sacrificial System, and the Priesthood]. Saint Petersburg: Mansfel'd, 1908.

———. *Svet iz Teni budushhix Blag ili tridcat' dve Besedy o Skinij, Zhertvoprinosheniyax' i Svyashenstvyo* [Light from the Shadow of Future Blessing, or Thirty-Two Conversations about the Tabernacle, Sacrificial System and the Priesthood]. St. Petersburg: Bibliya Dlya Bsex, 1998.

———. *Tolkovatel' Otkroveniya Svyatogo Ioanna Bogoslova* [Commentary on the Revelation of Saint John the Theologian]. St Petersburg: Xudozhestvennaya, 1991.

———. "Tolkovatel' Otkroveniya Svyatogo Ioanna Bogoslova" [Commentary on the Revelation of Saint John the Theologian]. In *Sobranie Sochinenij*, 449–670. St. Petersburg: Bibliya Dlya Bsex, 1997.

———. *V Kakom Ty Otnoshenii k Duxu Svyatomu?* [What is Your Relationship to the Holy Spirit?]. n.p, n.d. Wheaton College's Special Collections, Wheaton, IL. This archive holds an early Russian copy of this book with a four-page introduction in Russian written by N. I. Pejsti (N. I. Poysti).

———. "V Kakom Ty Otnoshenii k Duxu Svyatomu?" [What is Your Relationship to the Holy Spirit?]. In *Sobranie Sochinenij*, 114–79. St. Petersburg: Bibliya Dlya Bsex, 1997.

———. "Vetxozavetnye Proobrazy" [Old Testament Prototypes]. In *Sobranie Sochinenij*, 255–329. St. Petersburg: Bibliya Dlya Bsex, 1997.

———. "Was ist die Sünde? [Part One]." *Zionsbote* (Kansas) 16.10 (7 March 1900) 1.

———. "Was ist die Sünde? [Part Fifteen]." *Zionsbote* (Kansas) 16.29 (18 July 1900) 1.

———. "Xristos Osvyashhenie Nashe" [Christ–Our Sanctification]. In *Sobranie Sochinenij*, 49–113. St. Petersburg: Bibliya Dlya Bsex, 1997.

———. *Zakon Duxa Zhizni*. [The Law of the Spirit of Life]. St. Petersburg: Bibliya Dlya Bsex, 2003.

———. *Zwischen den Enden der Erde: Unter Bruedern in Ketten*. Weinigerode , Germany: Licht im Osten, 1928.

Kelm, Matthew. "Russia, Letter from the Polish Emigrants." *Quarterly Reporter of the German Baptist Mission* 24 (January 1864) 13.

Kerr, Russell Neil. "Christianity in the Soviet Union." M.Th. thesis, Northern Baptist Theological Seminary, 1960.

Kiparsky, Valentin. *English and American Characters in Russian Fiction*. Berlin: Saladruck Steinkopf and Sohn, 1964.

Klibanov, A. I. *History of Religious Sectarianism in Russia (1860s–1917)*. New York: Pergamon, 1982.

Klippenstein, Lawrence. "Johann Wieler (1839–1889) among Russian Evangelicals: A New Source of Mennonites and Evangelicalism in Imperial Russia." *Journal of Mennonite Studies* 5 (1987) 44–60.

———. "Religion and Dissent in the Era of Reform: The Russian Stundobaptists, 1858–1884." M.A. thesis, University of Minnesota, 1971.

———. "Russian Evangelicalism Revisited: Ivan Kargel and the Founding of the Russian Baptist Union." *Baptist History and Heritage* 27.2 (April 1992) 42–48.

———. Salvation on the Steppe: Missioner Johann Wieler and the Nineteenth Century Stundo-Baptist Movement. Unpublished paper, 2003. Mennonite Heritage Center Archives, Winnipeg, Canada.

Kolarz, Walter. *Religion in the Soviet Union*. London: Macmillan, 1962.

Korff, Modest M. *Am Zarenhof: Erinnerungen aus der Geistlichen Erweckungsbewegung in Russland*. Translated by Maria Kroeker. Wernigerobe, Germany: Licht im Osten, 1927.

Kouznetsov, Victor. "A View on Russian Evangelical Soteriology: Scripture or Tradition." M.Th. thesis, University of South Africa, 2001.

Koval'kov, V. M., and P. M. Chernopyatov. "Ivan Veniaminovich Kargel." *Bratsky Vestnik* 6 (1979) 47–49.

Krapohl, Robert H., and Charles H. Lippy. *The Evangelicals: A Historical, Thematic, and Biographical Guide*. Westport, CT: Greenwood, 1999.

Kraus, C. Norman. *Evangelicalism and Anabaptism*. Scottdale, PA: Herald, 1979.

Kroeker, A. *Pfarrer Eduard Wuest*. Spat near Simferopol, Ukraine: Selbstverlag, 1903.

Kupsch, Eduard. "Geschichte der Baptisten in Polen, 1852–1932." Lodz, Poland: Self-published, 1932. Mennonite Heritage Centre Archives, Winnipeg, Canada.

Kuznetsova, Miriam. "Early Russian Evangelicals (1874–1929): Historical Background and Hermeneutical Tendencies Based on I. V. Kargel's Written Heritage." Ph.D. diss., University of Pretoria, 2009.

Lane, Christel. *Christian Religion in the Soviet Union*. Albany, NY: State University of New York Press, 1978.

Latimer, Robert Sloan. *Dr. Baedeker and His Apostolic Work in Russia*. London: Morgan and Scott, 1907.

———. *Ein Bote des Koenigs*. Barmen, Germany: Muller, 1907.

———. *Under Three Tsars: Liberty of Conscience in Russia*. New York: Revell, 1909.

———. *With Christ in Russia*. London: Hodder and Stoughton, 1910.

Lawrence, John. *Russians Observed*. London: Hodder and Stoughton, 1969.

Lehmann, Joseph. "Letter from Rev. Joseph Lehmann." *The Baptist Missionary Magazine* 57.11 (November 1877) 376–78.

Leskov, N. S. *Schism in High Society*. Nottingham, UK: Bramcote, 1995.

Letkemann, Peter. "The First Mennonite Sangerfest in Russia." *Mennonite Historian* 32.1 (March 2006) 4–5.

Lewis, A. J. *Zinzendorf: The Ecumenical Pioneer*. London: SCM, 1962.

Lieven, Sophia. *Duxovnoe Probuzhdenie V Rossii* [Spiritual Awakening in Russia]. 4th ed. Korntal, Germany: Svet na Vostoke, 1990.

———. *Eine Saat, die Reiche Fruchte Brachte*. Basel, Switzerland: Brunnen, 1952.

———. "Kolybel' Evangel'skogo Dvizheniya v Peterburge" [The Cradle of the Evangelical Movement in Petersburg]. *Bratsky Vestnik* 4 (1970) 70–73.

———. "Kratkij Ocherk Zhizni i Deyatel'nosti Brata I. V. Kargelya" [A Brief Sketch of the Life and Work of Brother I. V. Kargel]. *Evangel'skaya Vera* 9.1 (March 1940) 8–10.

Lyobashchenko, V. I. *Istoriya Protestantizmu v Ukaini* [The History of Protestantism in Ukraine]. Kiev, Ukraine: Polis, 1996.

Loewen, Harry. "Echoes of Drumbeats: The Movement of Exuberance among the Mennonite Brethren." *Journal of Mennonite Studies* 3 (1985) 118–27.

Loewen, Heinrich. *In Vergessenheit Geratene Beziehungen*. Bielefeld, Germany: Logos, 1989.

Lotz, Denton, ed. *Baptist Witness in the USSR*. Valley Forge, PA: International Ministries, 1987.

Luckey, H. *Gerhard Oncken und die Anfang des Deutschen Baptismus*. Kassel, Germany: Oncken, 1958.

Lumpkin, William Latane. *Baptist Confessions of Faith*. Valley Forge, PA: Judson, 1969.

Lysenkaite, Ruta. "Baptist Beginnings in the Baltic Countries: The Case of the Church in Memel." M.Th. thesis, International Baptist Theological Seminary, University of Wales, 2002.

M. "Missionary Students in Hamburg." *Quarterly Reporter of the German Baptist Mission* 29 (April 1865) 89–93.

Macfarlane, Norman C. *Scotland's Keswick: Sketches and Reminiscences*. London: Marshall, 1916.

Marsden, George M. *Understanding Fundamentalism and Evangelicalism*. Grand Rapids: Eerdmans, 1991.

Martens, H. "Grossmutter's Brief: An Autobiography by Helena (Wieler) Martens nee Thielmann (1851–1928)." Volume 3749:11. Mennonite Heritage Center Archives, Winnipeg, Canada.

Mason, J. C. S. *The Moravian Church and the Missionary Awakening in England, 1760–1800*. Royal Historical Society Studies in History. Woodbridge, UK: Boydell, 2001.

Masters, Peter. *Remember the Prisoners*. Chicago: Moody, 1986.

Maynard, John Sir. *The Russian Peasant*. New York: Collier, 1942.

McBeth, Leon H. *The Baptist Heritage*. Nashville: Broadman, 1987.

McGrath, Alister E. *Christian Theology*. 3rd ed. Oxford: Blackwell, 2001.

Meyendorff, John. *Byzantine Theology*. New York: Fordham University Press, 1979.

Meyer, F. B. *A Keswick Experience*. London: n.p, n.d.

Miller, Donald. *In the Midst of Wolves: History of the German Baptists in Volhynia, Russia 1863–1943*. Portland, OR: Multnomah, 2000.

Mickevich, A. I. "Poslednie Zemnye obiteli I. V. Kargelya" [The Last Earthly Abode of I. V. Kargel]. *Bratsky Vestnik* 5 (1946) 22–24.

Mojzes, Paul Benjamin. "A History of the Congregational and Methodist Churches in Bulgaria and Yugoslavia." Ph.D. diss., Boston University Graduate School, 1965.

Moon, Norman S. *Education for Ministry: Bristol Baptist College 1679–1979*. Bristol, UK: Bristol Baptist College, 1979.

Motel, Hans Beat. *Glieder an Einem Leib: Die Freikirchen in Selbstdarstellungen*. Konstanz, Germany: Christliche Verlagsanstalt, 1975.

Motorin, I. "Kak Izuchat' Bibliyu" [How to study the Bible]. *Bratsky Vestnik* 1 (1947) 56–60.

———. "Sluzhenie Propovednika" [The Ministry of a Preacher]. *Bratsky Vestnik* 1 (1954) 43–46.

Murray, Andrew. *The Believer's Secret of Holiness*. Minneapolis: Bethany House, 1984.
Murray, Iain H., ed. *C. H. Spurgeon: The Early Years 1834-1859*. London: Banner of Truth, 1962.
Nesdoly, Samuel John. *Among the Soviet Evangelicals*. Carlisle, PA: Banner of Truth, 1986.
———. "Baptists in Tsarist Russia." In *Modern Encyclopedia of Religions in Russia and the Soviet Union*, edited by Paul D. Steeves, 3:202-11. Gulf Breeze, Florida: Academic International Press, 1991.
———. "Evangelical Sectarianism in Russia: A Study of the Stundists, Baptists, Pashkovites, and Evangelical Christians, 1855-1917." Ph.D. diss., Queen's University, Kingston, Ontario, 1977.
Neuschaefer, F. "Schlußfeier der Missionsschule." *Missionsblatt* 32.10 (October 1874) 170-71.
Nichols, Gregory L. "Ivan Kargel and the Pietistic Community of Late Imperial Russia." In *Eastern European Baptist History: New Perspectives*, edited by Sharyl Corrado and Toivo Pilli, 71-87. Prague: International Baptist Theological Seminary, 2007.
———. "Ivan Kargel and the Fulfillment of Revival: The Fullness of Salvation which leads to Sanctification." *Baptistic Theologies* 1.1 (Spring 2009) 23-39.
Nikolaevskij, P. "K" Istorii Russkogo Sektanstva" [On the History of Russian Sectarianism]. *Strannik"* 9 (1892) 42-59.
Nikol'skij, A. "Sektantstvo" [Sectarianism]. *Missionerskoe Obozrenie* 17.9 (September 1912) 240-42.
Noll, Mark A. *The Rise of Evangelicalism*. Downers Grove, IL: InterVarsity, 2003.
Oncken, J. G. *Glaubensbekenntnis und Verfassung der Gemeinden Getaufter Christen*. 8th ed. Hamburg: Oncken Nachfolger, 1889.
Ondra. "Poland and Russia." *Quarterly Reporter of the German Baptist Mission* 63 (October 1873) 58-60.
———. "Polen und Russland." *Missionsblatt* 32.10 (October 1874) 175-78.
———. "Russland and Polen." *Missionsblatt* 32.11 (November 1874) 192-95.
Oprenov, Teodor B. "The Origins and Early Development of Baptists in Bulgaria." *Baptist History and Heritage* 42.1 (Winter 2007) 8-23.
Otfinoski, Steven. *Bulgaria*. 2nd ed. New York: Facts on File, 1999.
Parker, G. Keith. *Baptists in Europe: History and Confessions of Faith*. Nashville: Broadman, 1982.
Parsons, Howard L. *Christianity Today in the USSR*. New York: International, 1987.
Pavlof, Vasilia. "An Autobiography." In *Modern Baptist Heroes and Martyrs*, edited by J. N. Prestridge, 95-103. Louisville, KY: World, 1911.
Payne, Ernest A. *The Baptist Union: A Short History*. London: Kingsgate, 1959.
———. *Out of Great Tribulation*. London: Baptist Union of Great Britain and Ireland, 1972.
Penn-Lewis, Jessie, and Robert Evans. *War on the Saints*. 2nd ed. London: Marshall Bros., 1916.
———. *War on the Saints*. Abridged ed. Fort Washington, PA: The Christian Literature Crusade, 1977.
Pierard, Richard V., ed. *Baptists Together in Christ, 1905-2005*. Falls Church, VA: Baptist World Alliance, 2005.
Pilli, Toivo. "Baptists in Estonia, 1884-1940." *The Baptist Quarterly* 39.1 (January 2001) 27-34.

———. "Baptist Identities in Eastern Europe." In *Baptist Identities: International Studies from the Seventeenth to the Twentieth Centuries,* Studies in Baptist History and Thought 19, edited by Ian Randall, Toivo Pilli, and Anthony Cross, 92–108. Carlisle, UK: Paternoster, 2006.

Pitts, Bill. "Holiness as Spirituality: The Religious Quest of A. B. Simpson." In *Modern Christian Spirituality: Methodological and Historical Essays,* edited by Bradley C. Hanson, 223–48. Atlanta: Scholars, 1990.

Podmore, Colin. *The Moravian Church in England, 1728–1760.* Oxford Historical Monographs. Oxford: Clarendon, 1998.

Pollock, J. C. *The Faith of the Russian Evangelicals.* New York: McGraw-Hill, 1964.

———. *The Keswick Story.* London: Hodder and Stoughton, 1964.

Popov, V. A. *I. S. Prokhanov Stranicy Zhizni* [Pages from the Life of I. S. Prokhanov]. St. Petersburg: Bibliya Dlya Vsex, 1996.

———. "Iz Istorii nashego Bratstva: V. G. Pavlov v Germanii pervye Gody Truda na Nive Gospodnej" [From the History of our Brotherhood: V. G. Pavlov in Germany the First Years of Labor on the Field of the Lord]. *Bratsky Vestnik* 5 (1991) 62–69.

———. "Vasilii Gurevich Pavlov and the Early Years of the Baptist World Alliance." Translated by Zacharov, Alexander. *The Baptist Quarterly* 36.1 (January 1995) 4–20.

Pospielovsky, Demitry. *The Russian Church under the Soviet Regime, 1917–1982.* 2 vols. Crestwood, NY: St Vladimir Seminary, 1984.

Poysti, N. J. "We Publish a Very Important Book." *The Gospel Call* (August 1945) 23–24.

Pöysti, Osmo. "Ivan Veniaminovitsh Kargel." On-line: http://opsti.japo.fi/whozwho/kargel.htm [accessed 15 March 2011].

Prestridge, J. N. *Modern Baptist Heroes and Martyrs.* Louisville: World, 1911.

Price, Charles, and Ian Randall. *Transforming Keswick.* Carlisle, UK: OM, 2000.

Prokhorov, Konstantin. "The Golden Age of the Soviet Baptists in the 1920s." In *Eastern European Baptist History: New Perspectives,* edited by Sharyl Corrado and Toivo Pilli, 88–101. Prague: International Baptist Theological Seminary, 2007.

Prokhanoff, I. S. *In the Cauldron of Russia, 1869–1933.* New York: All Russian Evangelical Christian Union, 1933.

———. "Na rodine Yana Gusa i Petra Hel'chickogo" [In the Homeland of Jan Huss and Peter [hacek over the second c and an acute accent mark over the y] Chelčický]. *Xristianin* 5 (1924) 23–24.

Puzynin, Andrei. "The Tradition of the Gospel Christians: A Study of their Identity and Theology during the Russian, Soviet and Post-Soviet Periods." Ph.D. diss., University of Wales, 2008.

Randall, Ian, ed. *Baptists and the Orthodox Church: On the Way to Understanding.* Prague: International Baptist Theological Seminary, 2003.

———. *Communities of Conviction: Baptist Beginnings in Europe.* Schwarzenfield, Germany: Neufeld, 2009.

———. "Eastern European Baptists and the Evangelical Alliance, 1846–1896." In *Eastern European Baptist History: New Perspectives,* edited by Sharyl Corrado and Toivo Pilli, 14–33. Prague: International Baptist Theological Seminary, 2007.

———. "The Evangelical Alliance and Europe." *Journal of European Baptist Studies* 1.3 (May, 2001) 39–49.

———. "'Every Apostolic Church a Mission Society': European Baptist Origins and Identity." In *Ecumenism and History: Studies in Honour of John H. Y. Briggs*, edited by Anthony R. Cross, 281–301. Carlisle, UK: Paternoster, 2002.

———. *Evangelical Experiences: A Study of the Spirituality of English Evangelicalism 1918–1939*. Carlisle, UK: Paternoster, 1999.

———. "F. B. Meyer: Baptist Ambassador for Keswick Holiness." *Baptist History and Heritage* 37.2 (Spring 2002) 44–60.

———. *Spirituality and Social Change: The Contribution of F. B. Meyer (1847–1929)*, Studies in Evangelical History and Thought. Carlisle, UK: Paternoster, 2003.

———. *What a Friend We Have in Jesus: The Evangelical Tradition*. Traditions of Christian Spirituality. London: Darton, Longman & Todd, 2005.

———. "The World is Our Parish: Spurgeon's College and World Mission, 1856–1892." In *Baptists and Mission: Papers from the Fourth International Conference on Baptist Studies*, Studies in Baptist History and Thought 29, edited by Ian M. Randall and Anthony Cross, 64–77. Carlisle, UK: Paternoster, 2007.

———. "A Christian Cosmopolitan: F. B. Meyers in Britain and America." In *Amazing Grace*, edited by George A. Rawlyk and Mark A. Noll, 157–82. Grand Rapids: Baker, 1993.

Randall, Ian, and Anthony Cross, eds. *Baptists and Mission*. Studies in Baptist History and Thought 29. Carlisle, UK: Paternoster, 2007.

Randall, Ian, and Tim Grass. "Spurgeon and the Sacraments." In *Baptist Sacramentalism*, Studies in Baptist History and Thought 5, edited by Anthony Cross and Philip Thompson, 55–75. Carlisle, UK: Paternoster, 2003.

Randall, Ian, and David Hilborn. *One Body in Christ: The Historical Significance of the Evangelical Alliance*. Carlisle, UK: Paternoster, 2001.

Randall, Ian, Toivo Pilli, and Anthony R. Cross, eds. *Baptist Identities: International Studies from the Seventeenth to the Twentieth Centuries*. Studies in Baptist History and Thought 19. Carlisle, UK: Paternoster, 2006.

Rawlyk, George A, and Mark A. Noll, eds. *Amazing Grace: Evangelicalism in Australia, Britain, Canada and the United States*. Grand Rapids: Baker, 1993.

Redekopp, Alfred H. *Jacob Thielmann and Helen Kroeker*. Winnipeg, Canada: Redekopp, 1992.

Reshetnikov, Yu., and S. Sannikov. *Obzor Istorii Evangel'sko-Baptistskogo Bratstva na Ukraine* [Overview of the History of the Evangelical-Baptist Brotherhood in Ukraine]. Odessa, Ukraine: Bogomyslie, 2000.

Riasanovsky, Nicholas V. and Mark D. Steinberg. *A History of Russia*. New York: Oxford University Press, 2005.

Richards, Ruben R. "Religious Liberty in the USSR: The Baptist Experience." B.D. thesis, Baptist Theological Seminary, Rueschlikon, Switzerland, 1991.

Robbins, Keith, ed. *Protestant Evangelicalism: Britain, Ireland, Germany, and America c.1750–c.1950: Essays in Honour of W. R. Ward*. Oxford: Blackwell, 1990.

Rouse, Ruth. *The World's Student Christian Federation: The World's Student Christian Federation: A History of the First Thirty Years*. London: SCM, 1948.

Rowdon, H. H. "The Concept of 'Living by Faith.'" In *Mission and Meaning: Essays Presented to Peter Cotterell*, edited by A. Billington, A. N. Lane and M. Turner, 339–56. Carlisle, UK: Paternoster, 1995.

Rowe, Michael. *The Russian Resurrection*. London: Marshall Pickering, 1994.

Rushbrooke, J. H. *Baptists in the USSR*. Nashville: Broadman, 1943.

———. *The Baptist Movement in the Continent of Europe*. London: Kingsgate, 1923.

———. *Some Chapters of European Baptist History*. London: Kingsgate, 1929.

———, ed. *The Baptist Movement in the Continent of Europe: A Contribution to Modern History*. London: Carey, 1915.

Ryle, J. C. *Holiness: Its Nature, Hindrances, Difficulties, and Roots*. 1879. Reprint. Moscow, Idaho: Nolan, 2001.

Saloff-Astakhaff, N. I. *Christianity in Russia*. New York: Loizeaux Brothers, 1941.

———. *Interesting Facts of the Russian Revolution*. New York: Saloff-Astakhoff, 1931.

Sandeen, Ernest Robert. *The Roots of Fundamentalism*. Chicago: University of Chicago Press, 1970.

Sannikov, S. V., ed. *Istoria Baptizma* [The History of the Baptists]. Odessa: Bogomislie, 1996.

Savinskij, S. N. *Istoriya Russko-Ukrainskogo Baptizma* [The History of the Russian-Ukrainian Baptists]. Odessa, Ukraine: Bogomyslie, 1995.

———. *Istoriya Evangel'skix Xristian-Baptistov Ukrainy, Rossii, Belorussii* [The History of the Evangelical Christians-Baptists of Ukraine, Russia and Belorussia]. Bibliya Dlya Bsex: St. Petersburg, 1999.

Sawatsky, Walter. "A Call for Union of Baptists and Mennonites Issued by a Russian Baptist Leader." *The Mennonite Quarterly Review* 50.3 (July 1976) 230–39.

———. "Russian Mennonites and Baptists (1930–1990)." In *Mennonites and Baptists: A Continuing Conversation*, edited by Paul Toews, 113–31. Hillsboro, KS: Kindred, 1993.

———. *Soviet Evangelicals since World War II*. Scottdale, PA: Herald, 1981.

Scheffbuch, Winrich. *Christians under the Hammer and Sickle*. Translated by Mark A. Noll. Grand Rapids: Zondervan, 1972.

Schroeder, William. *Mennonite Historical Atlas*. Winnipeg, Canada: Springfield, 1996.

Sheldrake, Philip. *Spirituality and History*. London: SPCK, 1991.

Shubin, Daniel H. *A History of Russian Christianity*. 4 Vols. New York: Algora, 2004.

Shuff, Roger. *Searching for the True Church: Brethren and Evangelicals in Mid-Twentieth-Century England*. Studies in Evangelical History and Thought. Carlisle, UK: Paternoster, 2005.

Simon, Gerhard. *Church, State, and Opposition in the USSR*. Berkeley: University of California Press, 1974.

Skopina, I. N. "Iz Biografii I. V. Kargelya i ego Docherej" [From the Biography of I. V. Kargel and his Daughters]. In *Sobranie Sochinenij*, 689–701. St. Petersburg: Bibliya Dlya Bsex, 1997.

Smith, C. Henry. *The Coming of the Russian Mennonites*. Berne, IN: Mennonite, 1927.

———. *The Story of the Russian Mennonites*. 4th ed. Newton, Kansas: Mennonite, 1957.

Spener, Philip Jacob. *Pia Desideria*. Translated, edited, and introduced by Theodore G. Tappert. 2nd ed. Philadelphia: Fortress, 1964.

Spurgeon, C. H. "Baptismal Regeneration." *Metropolitan Tabernacle Pulpit* 10:573 (5 June 1864). On-line: http://www.scribd.com/doc/16094014/Baptismal-Regeneration-Charles-H-Spurgeon [accessed 22 September 2009].

Stassen, Glen H. "Anabaptist Influence in the Origin of the Particular Baptists." *The Mennonite Quarterly Review* 36 (October, 1962) 322–48.

Stead, W. T. *Truth about Russia*. London: Cassell, 1888.

Steeves, Paul D. "Baptists, Union of Russian (1884–1935)." In *Modern Encyclopedia of Religions in Russia and the Soviet Union*, edited by Paul D. Steeves, 3:211–17. Gulf Breeze, Florida: Academic International Press, 1991.

———. "The Russian Baptist Union 1917–1935: Evangelical Awakening in Russia." PhD diss., University of Kansas, 1976.
Stevenson, Herbert, ed. *Keswick's Authentic Voice*. London: Marshall, Morgan and Scott, 1959.
Stewart, Kenneth J. *Restoring the Reformation*. Studies in Evangelical History and Thought. Milton Keynes, UK: Paternoster, 2006.
Stoeffler, F. Ernest. *German Pietism during the Eighteenth Century*. Leiden: Brill, 1973.
Struve, Nikita. *Christians in Contemporary Russia*. London: Harvill, 1967.
———. "Other Christian Denominations." In *Religion in the USSR*, edited by Boris Iwanow, 131–42. Munich: Institute for the Study of the USSR, 1960.
Stumpp, Karl. *The Emigration from Germany to Russia in the Years 1763–1862*. Lincoln, NE: American Historical Society of Germans from Russia, 1982.
Stunt, Timothy C. F. *From Awakening to Secession: Radical Evangelicals in Switzerland and Britain*. Edinburgh: T. & T. Clark, 2000.
Suyarko, A. V. "Vospominanie o Zhizni i Sluzhenii Kargelya" [Memories of the Life and Ministry of Kargel]. *Istoriya Evangel'skogo Dvizheniya v Evrazii, disk 1.0* [The History of the Evangelical Movement in Eurasia, disk 1.0]. Odessa, Ukraine: EAAA, 2001. D:\files\texts\2\0122a.html.
Summerton, N. "George Müller and the Financing of the Scriptural Knowledge Institution." In *The Growth of the Brethren Movement*, Studies in Evangelical History and Thought, edited by N. Dickson and T. Grass, 49–79. Milton Keynes, UK: Paternoster, 2006.
Synan, Vinson. *The Holiness-Pentecostal Tradition: Charismatic Movements in the Twentieth Century*. Grand Rapids: Eerdmans, 1997.
———. *The Century of the Holy Spirit: 100 Years of Pentecostal and Charismatic Renewal 1901–2001*. Nashville: Nelson, 2001.
Thompson, A. E. *The Life of A. B. Simpson*. Brooklyn, NY: Christian Alliance, 1920.
Thompson, Donald C. *Donald Thompson in Russia*. New York: Century, 1918.
Toews, John B. "Baptists and Mennonite Brethren in Russia (1790–1930)." In *Mennonites and Baptists: A Continuing Conversation*, edited by Paul Toews, 81–96. Hillsboro, KS: Kindred, 1993.
———. *Czars, Soviets, and Mennonites*. Newton, KS: Faith and Life, 1982.
———. "Early Mennonite Brethren and Evangelism in Russia." *Direction* 28.2 (1999) 187–200.
———. "The Mennonite Brethren in Russia during the 1890s." *Direction* 30.2 (Fall 2001) 139–52.
———. *A Pilgrimage of Faith: The Mennonite Brethren Church in Russia and North America 1860–1990*. Winnipeg, Canada: Kindred, 1990.
Toews, Paul, ed. *Mennonites and Baptists: A Continuing Conversation*. Winnipeg, Canada: Kindred, 1993.
Torrey, R. A. *How to Obtain Fullness of Power*. Wheaton, IL: Sword of the Lord, 1897.
Treadgold, Donald W. *Twentieth Century Russia*. Chicago: McNally, 1959.
Trotter, A. *Lord Radstock: An Interpretation and a Record*. London: Hodder and Stoughton, 1914.
Troyanovsky, Igor, editor. *Religion in the Soviet Republics*. San Francisco: HarperSanFrancisco, 1991.
Turchaninov, Dimitri. "Vospominanie o Zhizni i Sluzhenii Kargelya" [Memories of the Life and Ministry of Kargel]. *Istoriya Evangel'skogo Dvizheniya V Evrazii,*

Disk 3.0 [The History of the Evangelical Movement in Eurasia, disk 3.0]. Odessa, Ukraine: EAAA, 2003. D:\files\articles\5\02781.html.
Üxküll, Baron Woldemar. "Hopes and Plans for Russia." *The Baptist Missionary Magazine* 87.6 (June 1907) 208–9.
Val'kevich, V. L. *Zapiska o Propagande Protestantskix" Sekt" v" Rossii i, v" Osobennosti na Kavkaze* [Notes on the Protestant Sects in Russia Particularly in the Caucasus]. Tiflis: Kancelyarij Glavnonachal'stvuyushhago Grazhdanskoyu Chast'yu na Kavkaze, 1900.
Vehkaoja, Markku E. H. "A Comparative Study of Selected Finnish Free Churches and their Leadership." B.D. thesis, Baptist Theological Seminary, Rueschlikon, Switzerland, 1973.
Vins, Georgij. *Tropoyu Vernosti* [On the Path of Faith]. St. Petersburg: Bibliya Dlya Bsex, 1997.
Vital, David. *The Origins of Zionism*. Oxford: Clarendon, 1975.
Voronaeff, Paul. *Christians under the Hammer and Sickle*. Wichita, KS: Defender, 1939.
W, C. A. *The Stundists: The Persecution of Believers in Russia at the Close of the Last Century*. Oak Park, IL: Bible Truth, 1976.
Wagner, William L. *New Move Forward in Europe: Growth Patterns of German Speaking Baptists in Europe*. South Pasadena, CA: William Carey Library, 1978.
Ward, W. R. *The Protestant Evangelical Awakening*. Cambridge: Cambridge University Press, 1992.
Wardin, Albert W. "The Baptists in Bulgaria." *The Baptist Quarterly* 34.4 (October 1991) 148–59.
———. "Baptists (German) in Russia and USSR." In *Modern Encyclopedia of Religions in Russia and the Soviet Union*, edited by Paul D. Steeves, 3:192–202. Gulf Breeze, FL: Academic International Press, 1991.
———. *Evangelical Sectarianism in the Russian Empire and the USSR: A Bibliographical Guide*. London: Scarecrow, 1995.
———. *Gottfried F. Alf: Pioneer of the Baptist Movement in Poland*. Brentwood, TN: Baptist History and Heritage Society, 2003.
———. "How Indigenous Was the Baptist Movement in the Russian Empire?" *Journal of European Baptist Studies* 9.2 (January 2009) 29–37.
———. "Mennonite Brethren and German Baptists in Russia." In *Mennonites and Baptists: A Continuing Conversation*, edited by Paul Toews, 97–112. Hillsboro, KS: Kindred, 1993.
———. "Pentecostal Beginnings among the Russians in Finland and Northern Russia (1911–1921)." *Fides et Historia* 26.2 (Summer 1994) 50–61.
———, ed. *Baptists around the World*. Nashville: Broadman & Holman, 1995.
Ware, Kallistos. *The Orthodox Way*. Crestwood, NY: St. Vladimir's Seminary, 1979.
Warns, Johannes. *Russland und das Evangelium*. Kassel, Germany: Oncken, 1920.
Westin, Gunnar. *The Free Church through the Ages*. Nashville: Broadman, 1958.
White, Charles Edward. *The Beauty of Holiness: Phoebe Palmer as Theologian, Revivalist, Feminist, and Humanitarian*. Grand Rapids: Asbury, 1986.
Wieler, J. "Tagebuch vom ersten Januar 1872 bis 1883." Centre for Mennonite Brethren Studies, Volume 1108, Winnipeg, Canada.
Windolf, Emil. "Verschiedenes zur Geschichte des Seminars." Blatt 9–10, 1874. Oncken Archives, Elstal, Germany.
Wirth, Günter, ed. *Evangelische Christen in der Sowjetunion*. Berlin: Union, 1955.

Whitall-Smith, Hannah. *The Christian's Secret of a Happy Life*. Pittsburgh, PA: Whitaker House, 1983.

Whitley, W. T., ed. *Baptist World Congress, Stockholm, July 21-27 1923: Record of Proceedings*. London: Kingsgate, 1923.

———, ed. *Baptist World Congress, Toronto, June 23-29, 1928: Record of Proceedings*. Toronto: Stewart, 1928.

Wood, John. *Born in the Fire: The Story of William Fetler alias Basil Malof (1883-1957)*. Stanway: self-published, 1998.

Zernov, Nicolas. *The Russians and their Church*. New York: Macmillan, 1945.

Zhidkov, Ya. I. "Na Putyax Edinstva" [On the Paths to Unity]. *Bratsky Vestnik* 3 (1957) 52-69.

———. "Nemnogo o Sebe" [A little about Myself]. *Bratsky Vestnik* 5-6 (1954) 22-32.

Zhuk, Sergei I. *Russia's Lost Reformation*. Washington, DC: Woodrow Wilson Center Press, 2004.

———. "'A Separate Nation' of 'Those Who Imitate Germans': Ukrainian Evangelical Peasants and Problems of Cultural Identification in the Ukrainian Provinces of Late Imperial Russia." *Ab Imperio* (March 2006) 139-60.

Index

Abide in Christ, 11, 229
"Act of Tolerance," 194
Activism, Kargel's view of, 184–85
Adamov German Baptist church, 30
Akimovich, Mixail, ordination of, 199
Åland, Baptist beginnings in, 144
Alexander II
    assassination of, 69
    friend of Pashkov, 67
Alexander III
    death of, 169
    grants religious freedom, 69
Alexandrovich, Alexander, 67
Alexandrowoski-Sarood, Kargel visits, 163
Alf, Gottfried, 30
    August Meereis baptized by, 38
    Matthew Kelm baptized by, 38
"All Union Council of Evangelical Christians-Baptists" (AUCEC-B), 198–99
    formation of, 265
    Kargel's Confession of Faith and, 265–67
All-Russian Conference, converted into First All-Union Congress, 254
All-Russian Conferences of the Evangelical Christian Union, 196
All-Russian Evangelical Christian Conference, Prokhanov leads tenth, 264
"All-Russian Evangelical Christian Union" (ECU), 195, 196–98, 300
    ordination of members, 199
    pacifism and, 257
    problems of, 203–4
    registration of, 195
    temporary Council, 203
    view of Second Advent of Christ, 240–41
    See also Evangelical Christian Union
All-Union Congress, 254
All-Union Council of Evangelical Christians-Baptists (AUCEC-B), 198–99
    formation of, 265
    Kargel's Confession of Faith and, 265–67
    Zhidkov served as first president of, 198–99
Alt Danzig Baptist Church, 49
Altona Baptist church, 40
American Baptist Missionary Union
    begins support of Kargel, 62
    Lehmann's appeal for financial help, 62
    lists Baptist churches in Russia, 48–49
    sponsors Erik Jansson, 145
American Bible Society, Stephen Kurdov becomes a colporteur for, 83
Andreevska Church, 146
Anointing, 247–48

Anti-Pashkovism movement, 69
Arminianism, Calvinism and, 286–90
Arndt, Johann, 7
Aschendorf, Eduard
   Hamburg Mission School and, 42
Astrakhanka, 125, 149
   Kargel's and, 98, 130
   meeting in Rückenau attended by Christians from, 119
AUCEC-B ("All Union Council of Evangelical Christians-Baptists"), 198–99
   formation of, 265
   Kargel's Confession of Faith and, 265–67
   Zhidkov served as first president of, 198–99

Bad Blankenburg, conference at, 189
Baedeker, Friedrich, 109, 133
   Dagö Island (Estonia), 141–43
   evangelical unity and, 243
   in Hapsal, Estonia, 141–42
   Kargel and, 297
   translator for Robert P. Smith, 111
   travels published, 169
   visits Kargel in St. Petersburg, 110–11
Baedeker, Karl, 109
   pioneer in guide books, 110
Baku
   emigration assistance plan and, 161
   Kargel preaches to prisoners in, 168
Balihin, F. P., 189
Balta
   humanitarian aid to, 91
   pogrom in, 90–91

Baptism
   Believers baptism, 50
   children and, 273–74
   emphasis on immersion, 31
   German Baptist belief in, 31
   symbolism of, 272–73
"Baptism of the Holy Spirit," 10
Baptist meetings, described by Martin Kalweit, 25–26
Baptist Mission School, in Hamburg, 3
The Baptist Missionary Magazine, 3–4, 64
Baptist Union
   Bulgarian established, 116
   Prokhanov supports unity among, 191
Baptist World Alliance (BWA), 188–89
   adopts military service stance, 257–58
   declares events in Russia a spiritual awakening, 256
   helps fund St. Petersburg Bible College, 264
   Orlov a delegate to, 199
   Prokhanov elected vice-president of, 198
   Russian Baptist become members in, 198
Baptist World Congress, Kargel attends, 188–89
Baptists
   believers baptism and, 31
   Bulgarian
      resistance to, 81
      view of, 91–92
   Caucasus, 15
   development of German, 26–32
   evangelical Christian connections, 188–93
   jailing of in Bulgaria, 88
   Kargel's
      beginning with, 23–32

Baptists, Kargel's (*cont.*)
    disappointment with spirituality of, 133–35
    Mennonites and, 32–36
    of South Russia and Caucasus, 6, 124, 130
    See also German Baptist; Russian Baptist
Bebbington, David, 20
    on characteristics of the Keswick Convention, 10
    Evangelicalism in Modern Britain, 8
    Keswick
        spirituality, 218, 224
        view of sin, 11
    marks of evangelicalism, 179
Behold, I am Coming Soon, 76, 213, 242
Beseda, 151–52
Bessarabia Province, meeting in Rückenau attended by Christians from, 119
Bezzubov, P. S., 151
    criticizes Kargel, 191
Bible, Kargel's view of, 9, 184
Bible College
    Bristol, 192
    Hamburg, 3
    St. Petersburg, 178, 204–8
        BWA helps fund, 264
        reopens, 262–63
Bible Depot, 89
    closed, 149
Bobrinsky, Alexis Pavlovich (Count), as Kargel's translator, 26, 190
Bolshevik Revolution, 254
Bolsheviks
    October Revolution and, 254
    Russian Orthodox Church and, 256
Bond, Lewis, 82
    discussion with Kargel, 86–87

Bonekemper, Karl, 16
Bratsky Vestnik, 189, 190
    on the Integrated Congress, 202–3
Brethren. *See* Mennonite Brethren
Bristol Baptist College, 192
British and Foreign Bible Society, 85
    Martyin Herring in Bulgaria and, 82
    Yakov Deliakovich Deliakov and, 25
Broadman, W. E., *The Higher Christian Life*, 10
Brown, David, 187, 270
Bulgaria
    Anna Kargel's view of, 87
    Baptists in, 81–84
        persecuted of, 88
    Kargel
        description of, 85–86
        and his family leave, 99–104
        ministry in with Anna, 72–73, 80–104, 296
    description of, 85–86
    on his call to, 84
    continued contact with, 116–18
    rebellion against the Ottomans, 82
    Russian troops help liberate, 82
Bulgarian Baptists, Kargel's returning to Russia and, 99–100
Bulgarian Evangelical Society, 82
Bulgarians
    massacred by Ottomans, 68
    view of Protestants, 91–92
BWA (Baptist World Alliance), 188–89
    adopts military service stance, 257–58
    declares events in Russia a spiritual awakening, 256

BWA (*cont.*)
   helps fund St. Petersburg Bible College, 264
   Orlov a deligate to, 199
   Prokhanov elected vice-president of, 198
   Russian Baptist become members in, 198

Calvinism, Arminianism and, 286–90
Catherine II, 32
Caucasus
   Ivanov organizes Baptists in, 15
   Kargel and, 22
   Baedeker travel to, 112
Chanin, Minai, attends meeting in Rückenau attended, 119
Chernopyatov, M.P., 189
Chertkova, Elizaveta, assumes leadership role in St. Petersburg, 107
Children of God, 283–84
   view of Holy Spirit, 180
Chomonev, Georgi M., 72, 100
Christ,
   Kargel's view of death on the cross of, 181–82
   second advent of, 185–86
   premillennialism and, 239–43
   significance of death/resurrection of, 275
   victory through abiding in, 280–86
The Christian, 111–12, 298
   Old Testament Prototypes published in, 213
   Ruth the Moabitess published in, 209
Christians, types of, 276–78
The Christian's Secret of a Happy Life, 10
Christ—Our Sanctification, 181, 215, 218, 235, 268, 287

Citizenship, dual, 64
Closed communion, German Baptist belief in, 31
Collegia pietatis, 7
Commentary on the Revelation of St. John, 182–83, 210
Communal meals, in place of Holy Communion, 14
Communion, 127–28
   communal meals in place of, 14
   disagreement concerning, 122
   German Baptist belief in closed, 31
   Kargel's view of, 267
   on open, 135–36
Communist Revolution, 254
   Finnish Methodist Church and, 146
   Russian Orthodox Church and, 256
Confession of Faith
   Friesen's, 266
   German Baptist, 31
   Hamburg, 266
   Kargel and, 268
   view on Calvinism and Arminianism, 286
   Kargel's, 9, 183–84, 265, 286
   mentioned in *The History of Evangelical Christians-Baptists in the USSR*, 265–66
   Oncken's, 265
   Prokhanov's, 265
   Russian, 268, 298
Congregationalists
   Bulgarian resistance to, 81
   establish first protestant church in Bulgaria, 81
Congress of Evangelical Christians, 196–98
Conversion experience
   emphasis on, 31
   Kargel on the importance of, 179

Count Sievers, Oncken defends German evangelicals to, 48, 50
Crimean Peninsula, Kargel and Baedeker travel through, 112
Crisis, element of, sanctified life and, 224–26
Crucified with Christ, 274
Czechoslovak Baptist Union, Prokhanov ordained by, 199

Dagö Island (Estonia)
　Baedeker visits, 141–43
　Kargel visits, 114, 141–43
Darby, John Nelson, premillennialism and, 239–43
Deacons, pastor's authority over questioned, 41
Deliakov, Yakov Deliakovich
　introduced to Kalweit, 25
　Voronin, Nikita Isaevich and, 25
Depravity of man, 287
Der Hausfreund, Commentary on the Revelation of St. John published in, 210
Der Wahrheitszeuge, Kargel described his trip to Bulgaria in, 85
Dieter, M. E., *The Holiness Revival of the Nineteenth Century*, 6
Dilakoff, Jacob. *See* Deliakov, Yakov Deliakovich
Divorce, Kargel's view of, 267
Dnepropetrovsk, 199
Domashnyaya Uchitel'nice, Anna Semenova and, 72
Don (region), meeting in Rückenau attended by Christians from, 119
Dostoyevsky, F. M., *Mirages: Stunda and Radstockists*, 34
Double Portion of the Spirit, 248
Double Sonship, 284–85

Drumnikov, Grigor B., 82–83
　baptized by Kargel, 87
　Kargel's arrival in Kazanluk and, 84
　letter to the German Baptist Union, 83
　meets Kargel and Heringer at Kazanluk, 86
Dueck, Abe J., 34, 117
Duff, Mildred, 109
　visits Kargel in St. Petersburg, 110
Dukhobors, 14, 122

East London Missionary Training Institute, 123
Easton, P. Z., meets Kargel in St. Petersburg, 84
Edgar, John, *Where are the Dead?*, 214
Edwards, Jonathan, 8
Egypt, Kargel visits, 163
Einlage, meeting in Rückenau attended by Christians from, 119–20
Einlage Mennonite Church, 31, 119
Ekaterinoslav, emigration assistance plan, 160
Ekatherinburg, Kargel visits, 163
Ekatherinin Institute, Anna Semenova and, 72
Elbe River, baptisms in, 28
Elders, elected or appointed, 108
Elizabethpol, 150
　emigration assistance plan and, 161
　Kargel visits, 168
Emigration assistance plan, 158, 158–62
English Reformed Church, Johann Oncken and, 27
Esikuvat Puhuvat (eli Messias Vanhassa Testamentissa), 147

Estonia
    Kargel's move to Hapsal, 114
    ministry to, 140–43
Estonian Baptist, theology influenced by Schiewe, 109
Eucharist, 127–28
    communal meal in place of, 14
    disagreement concerning, 94, 122
    Kargel's view of, 267
    on open, 135–36
    Pashkovites and, 71
European Baptist Conference, Kargel attends, 188–89
Evangelical Alliance, 10, 109, 178
    Baedeker works with, 111
    conference in Geneva 1861, 47
    evangelical unity and, 243–45
    Pashkov and the evangelical alliance, 121–24
    reasons for founding of, 48
Evangelical Alliance conference, Balihan Russian representative to, 189
Evangelical Christians
    Baptist connections to, 188–93
    registration of St. Petersburg, 195
    secret meetings of, 147
    unity of, 200–204, 243–45
Evangelical Christian Union
    accepts idea of military service, 258
    asks Kargel to reconsider his views on military service, 259
    established, 178
    merged with Russian Baptist Union, 265
    pacifism and, 257–58
    Prokhanov supports unity with Baptist Union, 191
    reaches out to Orthodox Christians, 256
    Sumy Province, invites Kargel to come to, 260
    "Two Month Gospel Courses" and, 206
    view on Calvinism and Arminianism, 290
    Zhidkov takes leadership of, 191
Evangelical movements, 7–9
Evangelical Revival in Britain, 8
"Evangelical Union of Christian Youth," 194
Evangelicalism in Modern Britain, 8
Evangelicalism, four marks of, 179
Exiled believers, 166–71

Faith
    exaltation of, 226–29
    Kargel's view of, 228–29
Famine, 1921, 255
Fast, H. I., 159
Felter, V. A.
    approves of the Russian Evangelical Alliance, 201
    teacher at St. Petersburg Bible College, 207
Finland
    first Free Church founded in, 143
    Kargel's work in, 140, 143–47
Finnish Methodist Church, 146
Fisher, August, 82
Foot washing, 126–27
Friedensfeld
    Kargel's and, 98
    MB Training Seminar in, 157
    meeting in Rückenau attended by Christians from, 119
Friesen, P. M., 121
    approves of the Russian Evangelical Alliance, 201
    statement of faith, 266

Gagarin, Prince, protects Kargel during famines, 253
Gagarina, Vera, assumes leadership role in St. Petersburg, 107
Galka, 148
Geldbach, Erich, 48
German Baptist
  adopted the confession of faith, 31
  belief in closed communion, 31
  developments of, 26–32
  influence on Mennonites, 34
  Kargel's time with, 295–97
  breaks with, 105–6
  life in St. Petersburg, 48–53
  military service as litmus test, 259
  Odessa Baptist Church, Johann Kargel and, 97
  premillennial stance, 240
  registered with Russian government, 64–65
  statement of faith, second advent of Christ, 239–40
  See also Baptists
German Baptist Mission, 1876 annual report, reports on Kargel, 62–63
German Baptist Triennial Conference (*Bundes Conferenz*), 31, 40, 84
  Kargel attends, 83
German Baptist Union
  beginning of, 29
  conference, 41
  disassociate from Russian Baptist, 131
  Drumnidov's letter to, 83
  Kargel and, 61–66
Gerusi
  emigration assistance plan and, 161
  Kargel visits, 168–69
  Martin Kalweit exiled to, 25

Glossolalia, 186
Godet, Frédéric Louis, 187
  view of sin, 271
"God's Holy Reign in You and His Will," 208
Gojer, N. A., signatory of Russian Evangelical Alliance, 200
The Golden Lamp, 111–12, 298
The Gospel Call, 256
Grachev, J. S., on first day at St. Petersburg Bible College, 207
Grand Duchy of Finland. *See* Finland
Guinness, Fanny, Harley House and, 123
Guinness, H. Grattan, 109
  Harley House and, 123
  visits Kargel in St. Petersburg, 110
Gülzau, Johann Andreas
  Ondra consults with, 51
  teaches at Hamburg Mission School, 42

Hamburg Baptist Church
  fire of 1842 and, 29
  gains legal status, 29
  Oncken and, 27
Hamburg Mission School, 3, 30, 41–45
  class schedule, 43
  commissioning by, 31–32
  training provided at, 41–45
  Vasil Khristov Marchev attends, 101
  war with France and, 36
Hamburg Statement of Faith, 266
  Kargel and, 268
  view on Calvinism and Arminianism, 286
"Hamburg Struggle," 41
Hapsal, Estonia
  Kargel's ministry to, 114, 139, 140–43

Helenendorf, Kargel visits, 168
Helsinki
    Andreevska Church, 146
    Lord Radstock preaches in, 67
Herb, Joseph C., studies at Hamburg Mission School, 42
Heringer, Martin, 82
    arrives at Kazanluk, 86
    meets Kargel in Rustchuk, 85
Herrnhut community, 8
The Higher Christian Life, 10
"Higher Life" movement, 9
The History of Evangelical Christians-Baptist in the USSR (HEC-B), 188, 190, 242, 265–66
Holiness
    Kargel's emphasis on, 9–12
    Keswick Convention on, 11
"Holiness," nine part series on, 209
Holiness movement, 96, 109
    presented to St. Petersburg Germans, 111
    visits Kargel in St. Petersburg, 110
The Holiness Revival of the Nineteenth Century, 6
Holiness stream, 1–2
Holy Spirit
    Christ given through mediation of, 281
    heeding promptings of, 278
    infilling of, 185–86
    Kargel on, 180
    fullness of, 224–25
    knowledge of God through, 270
    obedience to, 272–73
    sanctified life and, 245–49
    work of, 283
Homiletics
    Gülzau teaches, 42
    Kargel teaches, 205–6, 260, 263, 301
    Oncken teaches, 42

Hopkins, Evan, 187
Horssazik Baptist Church, 49
Humanitarian aid, to Balta Jews, 91

"Imperial Manifesto," 194–95
Inkis, K. G., teacher at St. Petersburg Bible College, 207
Integrated Congress, held in St. Petersburg, 201–3
Irkutsk, Kargel visits, 163
Ischl, Austria, Kargel meets Pashkov in, 173
Israel, Johann G. Kargel travels to, 153–54
Ivanov, Vasily V., 190, 295
    compared Russian Baptists to the Tiflis church, 37–38
    organizes Baptists in the Caucasus, 15
Ivanovna, Alexandra, 171
Ivanovna, Ekaterinia, takes responsibility for care of Kargel, 291–92

Jakobstad, 144
Jamieson-Fausset-Brown commentaries, 187
Jansson, Erik, 144–45
Jesus Christ
    Kargel's view of death on the cross of, 181–82
    second advent of, 185–86
    premillennialism and, 239–43
    significance of death/resurrection of, 275
    victory through abiding in, 280–286
"Jumpers," 126
Justification
    Keswick Convention and, 136
    sanctification follows, 272

Kalweit, Karl, baptism of, 26
Kalweit, Martin K., 14–15, 148
  Baptist meetings described by, 25–26
  Deliakov introduced to, 25
  exiled to Gerusi, 25
  Kargel assists at ordination of, 113
  letter to Johann Oncken, 24
  sent out from Memel church, 23
  Triflis Baptist church begun by, 295
Kamyshin, 148
Karetnikova, Marina Sergeevna, 2, 3, 76, 186, 189, 305
Karev, A. V., view on Calvinism and Arminianism, 288–89
Kargel, Anna
  in Bulgaria, 72–73, 80–104, 296
  Bulgarians view of, 91–92
  correspondence to Pashkov from Bulgaria, 93–94
  daughters of, 70–78. *See also* specific daughter
  death of, 77–78, 175
  desire for peace in St. Petersburg church, 99
  effect of Pashkovs exile on, 171
  letter on husband's release from spiritual narrowness, 96
  longs for St. Petersburg, 88
  move to Krekshino, 172
  sanctification experience, 94–96
  spiritual anguish of, 93–95
  suffers severe burn, 175
  translates Bulgarian letters to Pashkov, 100–101
  view of Bulgarians, 87
  view of the Lord's Supper, 94
  writes about Balta trip, 91
Kargel, Elena, 74–75
  arrested and executed, 292
  goes into hiding, 291
  holds reading classes for the illiterate, 260
Kargel, Elizaveta, 75
  arrested, imprisoned and exiled, 291–92
  death of, 292–93
  preaches and teaches, 260
Kargel, Johann G. (Ivan Veniaminovich), 63–64, 129
  1876 German Baptist Mission report, 62–63
  American Baptist Missionary Union begins support of, 62
  Anna Semenova and, 71–72
  arrested and imprisoned, 291
  arrives at Kazanluk, 86
  assists work in St. Petersburg, 40, 110–11
  Baedeker and, 297
  banished from St. Petersburg, 290
  baptism of, 23, 295
  Baptist and evangelical connections of, 188–93
  Baptist beginnings of, 23–32
  becomes a naturalized Russian, 64
  as biblical expositor, 44
  birth/childhood of, 21–22
  breaks with German Baptist, 105–6
  in Bulgaria, 72–73, 80–104, 116–18, 296
  Bulgarians view of, 91–92
  christocentric theology of, 290
  Christ's death on the cross and, 181–82
  commentary on
    Revelation, 183, 210
    Romans, 183, 215, 233, 253, 269–76
  committed to full-time Christian ministry, 3

Kargel, Johann G. (*cont.*)
  Confession of Faith, 9, 183–84, 265–67, 286
    premillennialism and, 240
  continuing influence of, 303–6
  daughters of, 70–78. *See also* specific daughter
  death of, 291–92
  describes impression of Bulgarians, 85–86
  on difficulties of uniting Russian and German Baptists, 131
  disappointed with Baptist spirituality, 133–35
  discussion with Lewis Bond, 86–87
  drawn into Pashkovite inner circle, 68
  emigration assistance plan, 158–62
  emphasis
    on holiness by, 9–12
    on sanctification, 219–23
  Estonian ministry of, 140–43
  evangelical
    Christians and, 147–58
    distinctives, 185
    ministry of, 297–300
    spirituality, 297–300
    theology, 179–88
  exiled believers and, 166–71
  expresses importance of friendship of Pashkov, 173–74
  financial concerns vs. ministry, 61–62
  first pastorate of, 36–41
  on the fullness of the Holy Spirit, 224–25
  German Baptist period, 295–97
  German Baptist Triennial Conference and, 83
  German Baptist Union and, 61–66
  graduate of Hamburg Mission School, 42
  health problems, 84, 99–100, 139, 174
  on his call to Bulgaria, 84
  on the Holy Spirit, 180
  on importance of conversion, 179
  influenced of Keswick beliefs on, 136
  Johann Wieler and, 35–36
  joins Russian Baptist, 15
  Kargel's commentary on Romans, 269–76
    chapter 6, 272–76
  last days of, 290–93
  leaves Bulgaria, 99–104
  letter on work in Triflis, 113
  life in Tokara, 261–62
  lives with the Wieler family, 33
  on Luther's salvation, 8–9
  marriage of, 72–73, 296
  on the May Mennonite Brethren conference, 39
  meetings become international, 69
  Mennonite Brethren's 1873 conference and, 36–37
  ministry of in St. Petersburg, 106–10
  ministry to Mennonite Brethren, 155–58
  moves to
    Hapsal, Estonia, 114, 139
    Lebedin, 291
    Rustchuk, 87
    St. Petersburg, 77
    Tokara, 291
    Ukraine, 260
    Vyborg, Finland, 140
  Nove-Vasilevka conference and, 124–28
    outcome of, 128–33

Index 369

Kargel, Johann G. *(cont.)*
  officiated opening of Bucharest Baptist Church, 98
  on an open communion table, 135–36
  Pashkov and the Evangelical Alliance, 121–24
  Pashkovites and, 66–70
  as pastor and teacher, 260–64
  on political powers, 259
  prison ministry, 162–66
  publishing efforts, 208–217
  registers German Baptist church with Russian government, 64–65
  new freedom, 65
  on repentance, 179–80
  on Revelation, 183, 205, 210, 260, 263, 301
    writes commentary on, 183, 210
  reports to Pashkov on Bulgarian work, 89
  on Romans, 183, 215, 233, 253, 269–76
    chapter 6, 272–76
  Russian Baptist and, 2–7
  as Russian evangelical theologian, 300–303
  Russian Orthodox church and, 12–17
  sanctification experience, 94–96
  seeks medical advice, 173
  selected as chair of Integrated Conference, 202
  signatory of Russian Evangelical Alliance, 200
  significance of death/resurrection of Jesus, 275
  signs registration documents, 195
  as a spiritual guide, 253–93
  in St. Petersburg, 295–96
  1875–80, 47–79
  1884–1887, 105–38
  1898-1909, 178–217
  attempts at unity, 118–21
  German Baptist life, 48–53
  Pashkov and the evangelical alliance, 121–24
  St. Petersburg Bible College and, 204–8
  the State and, 255–94
  studies at Hamburg Mission School, 42
  takes a wider interdenominational view, 96
  teaches
    homiletics, 205–6, 260, 263, 301
    Revelation, 205, 260, 263, 301
  theological influence of, 265–68
  Tiflis Baptist church and, 26
  travels in the Russian Empire, 139–77
  travels to Israel, 153–54
  view of
    anointing, 247–48
    faith, 228–29
    Holy Spirit, 224–25, 283
    loyalty to the State, 258
    marriage and divorce, 267
    prayer life, 232
    resurrection, 242, 282
    sanctification, 230, 246, 268
    Second Advent of Christ, 239–43
    sin, 227–28, 233–34, 271–78, 287
    the Bible, 184
    the Lords Supper, 94
    Calvinism and Arminianism, 286–90
    military service, 258–59
  vision of evangelical unity, 200–204
  visit to Siberia, 192
  Volhynia trip, 37

Kargel, Johann G., (cont.)
  Vyborg, Finland, 143–47
  wider ministry of, 110–15
  work in Rustchuk by, 89–92
  works with Jews in Balta, 90
Kargel, Maria, 75
  arrested, imprisoned and exiled, 291–92
  born in Estonia, 114
  death of, 293
  holds reading classes for the illiterate, 260
Kargel, Natasha, 74
  death of, 76–77, 176
Katharsis, in Orthodoxy and, 12
Kazanluk
  Baptist congregation begins in, 87
  Kargel and Heninger arrive at, 86
  Kargel travels to, 84–85
  ministry of Kargel in, 80–81
Kazanluk Baptist church
  congregation, 82
  founding church of the Baptist Union of Bulgaria, 116
  Kargel and, 116–17
Kelm, Matthew, Sorotschin German Baptist Church and, 38
Keswick Convention, 2
  emphasis on holiness, 9
  evangelical unity and, 243–45
  on holiness, 11
  Kargel influenced by, 136
  launching of, 10
  Pentecostalism and, 186
  premillennialism belief and, 11
  repressionism and, 232–34
  romanticism and, 234–39
  sanctification and, 11, 136, 271
  sin, 11
  view on sanctification, 271
Kharkov, Kargel and Baedeker travel through, 112

Klippenfeld, Mennonite conference at, 36
Klippenstein, Lawrence, 34
Klundt, Jacob, 82
Köbner, Julius, 28
  crafted German Baptist confession of faith, 31
  seeks reconciliation in Hamburg, 41
Korff, Modest (Count), 59, 60, 69, 102, 121, 122, 296
Korff, Modest Modestovich (Count), 190
  approves of the Russian Evangelical Alliance, 201
  exiled, 102, 123
Koval'kov, V. M., 189
Kovno, Lithuania
  conversions in, 148
  tracks distributed in, 133
Krasnojarsk, Kargel visits, 163
Krekshino, Anna Kargel moves to, 172
Kruzeinas, Natalie Nikolaevna, Pashkov's St. Petersburg administrator, 123
Kuban (region), meeting in Rückenau attended by Christians from, 119
Kuntze, Eduard, active in the Evangelical Alliance, 48
Kura River, baptisms in, 23, 26
Kurdov, Stephen, 83
Kursk, Kargel visits, 164
  Kargels move to, 253
Kushnerenko, Grigorii, attends meeting in Rückenau attended, 119
Kuznetsova, Miriam, 3, 71, 183, 186

The Law of Liberty in the Spiritual Life, 299
The Law of the Spirit of Life, 181, 182–83, 186, 215, 269, 288

Lebedin, Kargel moves to, 291
Lehmann, Gottfried W.
  active in the Evangelical
    Alliance, 48
  appointed pastor in Berlin, 29
  letter to American Baptist
    Missionary Union, 62
  report on Kargel's work, 63–64
  revised the German Baptist
    confession of faith, 31
Lehmann, Samuel, 155
  graduate of Hamburg Mission
    School, 42
Liban (Poland), Kargel visits, 114
Liebig, August
  German Baptist Triennial
    Conference and, 83
  works with Jews in Balta, 90
Lieven, A. P., elected chair of
    Russian Evangelical
    Alliance, 200
Lieven, Natalia, assumes leadership role in St. Petersburg,
    107
Lieven, Sophia (Princess), 21, 107
  on the conversion of Kargel, 23
  Integrated Congress held in
    home of, 201–2
  Kargel's daughters and, 76
  Kargel's reside with, 77
Lieven Palace, Kargel's live in, 107
Light from the Shadows of Future Blessing, 147, 180, 182–83, 188, 209
Lodz, Kargel preaches in, 166
Lompalanka Baptist church
  established, 116
  founding church of the Baptist
    Union of Bulgaria, 116
London, East London Missionary
    Institute, 123
Lord Radstock, 109, 298
  influence of, 57–61
  Orthodox curtail activities of,
    69
  Pashkov and, 66–67
  peaches in,
    Copenhagen, 67
    Helsinki, 146
  premillennialism and, 241
Lord's Supper, 127–28
  communal meal in place of, 14
  disagreement concerning, 94
  Kargel's view of, 267
  on open, 135–36
  Pashkovites and, 71
Luther, Martin, 187
Lutheran Church of Finland, 143
Lutherans
  Johann Oncken report on
    Russian, 33–34
  persecuted Baptists in
    Sorotschin, 38
  Pietist, 143
Lyubomirovka, meeting in
    Rückenau attended by
    Christians from, 119

"The Macedonian Cry Re-Echoed
    from Macedonia Itself", 83
Mackintosh, C. H., 183, 187
Maksimovskij, A. M., 206
Marchev, Vasil Khristov
  commended by Kargel, 116
  critical of aspects of Bulgarian
    Baptists, 116
  Hamburg Mission School, 101
  returns to Bulgaria, 104, 116
Marriage, Kargel's view of, 267
Mazaev, Andrej Markovich, 148
  attends meeting in Rückenau
    attended, 119
  critical of the Russian
    Evangelical Alliance, 201
  Kargel assists at ordination of,
    113
Mazaev, Dei Ivanovich, 151, 189,
    190
  addresses BWA in 1905, 198

Mazaev, Dei Ivanovich (*cont.*)
   critical of the Russian Evangelical Alliance, 201
   elected Baptist Russian president, 131
   selected as vice-chair of Integrated Conference, 202
"Mazaev Reform," 151
McCall Mission, 123
Meereis, August, 38
Memel Baptist Church, 49
   Lithuania Baptist mother church, 23–24
Mennonite Brethren, 30, 37
   1872 conference, 33
   1873 conference, 36–37, 39
   1884 conference, 124–26
   Abraham Unger, 17, 33
   adopt practices learned from German Baptist, 34
   Annual Meetings, 158
   Baedeker's contact with, 113
   Baptists and, 32–36
   baptism by immersion, 34, 49
   blocks Wieler's attempt to invite Baptists, to meetings 121
   confession, 266
   division within, 33
   Gerhard Wieler, 30, 33
   invitation to Russian Baptists blocked, 121
   Johann Wieler, 30, 33
   Kargel's ministry to, 155–58
   meeting in Rückenau, 119
   ministry to, 155–58
   Molotschna Settlement conference, 3
   Oncken works among, 32–33
   origins of, 49
   Paul I rights given by, 32
   persecution of, 237
   Russian Evangelical Alliance and, 200–201
   Russian Orthodox baptized into, 17
   St. Petersburg and, 71
   training program, 151, 156–57, 176
   Ukrainian roots of, 6
   Zionsbote, 208
Meyer, F. B., 283
"Minutes of the Mennonite Brethren-Baptist Convention in/Rückenau, May 21–23, 1882," 34
"The Mission School." *See* Hamburg Mission School
Missionsblatt, 3–4, 24, 42, 296
   Kargel on Russian Baptist love of Jesus, 61
   often sent reports to, 61
Missionsschule. *See* Hamburg Mission School
Molokans, 14, 113
   education and 159
   foot washing, 127
   Russian Evangelical Alliance 122,
   Novo Molokans, 129, 201–2, 306
Molotschna Colony, 3, 116–17, 130
   excludes Baptists, 25
   Kargel and, 33, 155–57
   preaches to, 109,
   Russian Baptist and, 38
   influenced by, 14–15
   visits, 112, 149
   Wieler settles in, 33
Molotschna River, Mennonite villages on, 32
Moody, Dwight L., 137, 144, 187, 304
Morgunov, suspicions of, 290–91
Moscow
   Kargel and Baedeker travel through, 112
   Orlov becomes leader of ECU churches in, 196

Moscow (cont.)
Pashkov
Kargel and family rest at estate near, 237
owns land near, 66
uses fairs near to distribute literature, 68
prison camps visited by Kargel, 166
Russian Baptist Union starts Bible school in, 264
ten day congress held in, 203
youth meetings held in, 194
Moscow Evangelical Christian, registration of, 196
Motorin, I, 304

Mott, John, 109
visits Kargel and Nicolay, 110, 193
Müller, George, 109
Pashkov baptized by, 120
visit to St. Petersburg, 61
visits Kargel in St. Petersburg, 110
Murray, Andrew, 192, 187, 288
Abide in Christ, 229
on obedience, 272
"My Friend in the Garden," 208

Neudorf German Baptist Church, 49
Karl Ondra pastor at, 36
Nicholas II
abdicates throne, 254
exiles and, 169
Nicolay, Paul Nikolayevich (Baron), 109
elected vice-chair of Russian Evangelical Alliance, 200
signatory of Russian Evangelical Alliance, 200
visits Kargel in St. Petersburg, 110
visit to Siberia with Kargel, 193

Nikolaevka
Kargel visits, 163
welcomes the Kargels, 260
Nishni Novgorod, Kargel visits, 163
Nishni Udinsk, Kargel visits, 163
Novo-Grigorivka, Kargel and Baedeker travel to, 112
Novorossiia, villagers resettled to, 15–16
Novo-Vasilievka, 119, 149
conference, 124–28
outcome of, 128–33
Kargel, Johann G. and, 124–28
outcome of, 128–33
Nukki, Kargel visits, 141

October Manifesto, 254
October Revolution, 254
Odessa Baptist Church, 49
Odessa German Baptist, Johann Kargel and, 97
Offenberg, V. X., signatory of Russian Evangelical Alliance, 200
"Old Testament Prototypes," 213
Oncken, Johann, 3
banished to Poland, 64
baptism of, 26–27
crafted German Baptist confession of faith, 31
defends German evangelicals before Count Sievers, 48, 50
disbands Hamburg church deacons, 41
early history of, 26–27
encourages a Calvinist position, 43–44
friendship with Johann Wieler, 35
letter from Kalweit to, 24
report on Russian Mennonites/Lutherans, 33–35
Russian Mennonite brethren and, 32

Oncken, Johann (*cont.*)
   statement of faith, 265
   view on Calvinism and Arminianism, 286
Oncken, Sarah, baptism of, 28
Ondra, Karl, 36
   asks Kargel to visit St. Petersburg, 52
   baptizes believers in St. Petersburg, 52
   letter delivered by J. Schultz, 49–50
   St. Petersburg visit and, 50–52
   Volhynia trip, 37
Ordination, 127
   of ECU members, 199
   of Mixail Akimovich, 199
   of Prokhanov, 199
   of Yakov Nikitich Xodyush, 199
Orthodox Church
   anti-Orthodox organizations, registration of, 195
   to monitor religious teachings, 69
   national culture and, 12–13
   Patriarch Tikhon, arrested, 256
   view of peasant activism, 13
   See also Russian Orthodox Church
Osnova, meeting in Rückenau attended by Christians from, 119
Ottoman Empire, puts down Bulgarian rebellion, 82
The Outpouring of the Holy Spirit and the Pentecostal Movement, 186

Pacifism, 257
Palmer, Phoebe, 9
Pashkov, Vasily Alexandrovich, 2, 13, 25, 65–70
   Anna Semenova and, 72
   Baedeker works with, 111
   Balta humanitarian aid and, 91
   baptism of, 120–21
   ministry to lower classes, 67
   called "soul of the Christian movement," 65
   Council of Educational Affairs formed by, 204
   desired Kargel be co-pastor in St. Petersburg, 98
   the Evangelical Alliance and, 121–24
   evangelical unity and, 243
   exiled, 102, 123
   friends with Alexander II, 67
   Kargel
      assists at ordination of, 113
      reports to on Bulgarian work, 89
   Lord Radstock and, 66–67
   meets with evangelicals in S. Russia, 119
   premillennialism and, 241
   teacher at St. Petersburg Bible College, 207
Pashkov Papers, 306
Pashkovites, 2
   in St. Petersburg, 6
   Kargel and, 66–70
   Lord's Supper and, 71
   pacifism and, 257
Pastors, authority over deacons question, 41
Pavlov, Vasily G., 13, 161, 190, 295
   baptized, 15
   at BWA inaugural meeting, 198
   elected president of Russian Baptist Union, 162
Peace, internal sense of, 230–32
Penn-Lewis, Jessie, 109
   visits Kargel in St. Petersburg, 110
Pentecost, Kargel's view of, 245–46
Pentecostalism, Keswick and, 186
Perm, Kargel visits, 163
Persecution
   during wedding in Russia and, 63

Persecution (*cont.*)
  of Baptist by Lutherans, 38
  of evangelicals by, 139–40, 197
Pia Desideria, 7
Pietistic movement
  new ideas from, 7–9
  within Lutheranism, 143
Pilli, Toivo, 290
Plonus, C., began Bible studies in St. Petersburg, 49
Pobedonostsev, Konstantin, 113
  alarmed at Pashkov's meetings, 67
  influence of on Alexander III's *ukase*, 69–70
  orders cleansing of Russia of non-Orthodox, 131
  persecution of evangelicals by, 139–40
  on Russian nationalism, 12–13
Poland
  Banishment to, 67
  Ivanov visits, 37
  Kargel and, 109, 114, 131, 166
  Volhynia and, 39
Poysti, N. J., 185–86
Prague, Prokhanov ordained in, 199
Prayer life, Kargel's view of, 232
Premillennialism, 238, 239–43
  Keswick Convention on, 11
Presbyters, elected or appointed, 108
Prison ministry, Johann G. Kargel and, 162–66
Privilegium, 32
Prokhanov, Ivan Stepanovich, 13
  connections of, 191–93
  ECU chair, 262
  elected
    BWA vice-president, 198
    chairman of All-Russian Congress of Evangelical Christians, 196
  evangelical unity and, 200–204
  forced to retract statement on pacifism, 258
  The Gospel Call and, 256
  letter to State Duma on legal status of the Evangelical Christians, 197
  ordained in Prague, 199
  organizing ability, 194
  pacifism and, 257
  participates in *Vetograd*, 152
  post-millennial view, 240
  premillennialism and, 241
  served within the BWA, 199
  signatory of Russian Evangelical Alliance, 200
  signs registration documents, 195
  spread of Evangelical Christian movement and, 300
  statement of faith, 265
  support of British Union and Evangelical Christian Union of Russia uniting, 191
  Tenth All-Russian Evangelical Christian Conference and, 264
  work in St. Petersburg, 151–52
  St. Petersburg College and, 204–8
Protestants, Bulgarians view of, 91–92
Puchtin, 119

Quarterly Reporter of the German Baptist Mission, 3–4, 61, 84, 144
  Drumnidov's letter published in, 83
  on his spiritual need, 90
  Kargel described his trip to Bulgaria in, 85

Radcliffe, Reginald, 109
  visits Kargel in St. Petersburg, 110

Radstock (Lord), 109, 298
  influence of, 57–61
  Orthodox curtail activities of, 69
  Pashkov and, 66–67
  peaches in,
    Copenhagen, 67
    Helsinki, 146
  premillennialism and, 241
Randall, Ian, on the Keswick Convention, 10
Ratushnyi, Mikhail, 14, 16–17, 97
  attends meeting in Rückenau attended, 119
Red Army, 254
Redemption, three features of, 273–74
Registration of
  All-Russian Evangelical Christian Union, 196
  German Baptist
    births and deaths of, 73
    congregation, 64–65
  non-Orthodox organizations, 195
Reimer, A. A., teacher at St. Petersburg Bible College, 207
Reimer, Jakob, 157
Repentance, 179–80
Repressionism, 232–34
Rest, internal sense of, 230–32
Resurrection, Kargel's view of, 242, 282
Revelation (NT Book)
  Kargel
    teaches class on 205, 260, 263, 301
    writes commentary on, 183, 210
Riaboshapka, Ivan, 14, 97, 148
  attends meeting in Rückenau attended, 119
  baptizes believers, 17
  expresses thanks for gifts, 115
  Kargel and, 115, 125
Riess, M., graduate of Hamburg Mission School, 42
Riga, Kargel and, 109
Rodionov, S. G., Kargel assists at ordination of, 113
Romania
  lack of evangelists in, 158
  Wieler becomes pastor in Tultscha, 121
Romans (NT book)
  Kargel on, 183, 215, 233, 253, 269–76
  chapter 6, 272–76
Romanticism, 234–39
Rostov, Baedeker and Kargel visit, 114
Rückenau
  Kargel's and, 98
  meeting held in, 119–20
  Minutes of the Mennonite Brethren-Baptist Convention in, 34
  Sängerfest held in, 155
Rumberg, J. A., 42, 133
Rushbrooke, J. H., on spiritual awakening in Russia, 256
Russia
  emigration assistance plan, 158–62
  German Baptists church with government registers with, 64–65
  new freedom, 65
  spiritual awakening in, 256–57
Russian Baptists
  Confession of Faith, 298
  disassociate from German Baptist, 131
  Kargel and, 1–7, 15
  as an interdenominational organization, 198
  leaders from Tiflis, 295
  Mazaev dominant figure among, 131
  Molokans influence on, 14–15
  poetry and, 235

Russian Baptists (*cont.*)
  in Tiflis, 24
  persecution of leaders, 97
  report by the Ministry of Internal Affairs on number of Baptists, 255–56
  Voronin acknowledged as first, 15
  Wielers home meeting place for, 124
  See also Baptist
Russian Baptist Union, 138
  annual conference, 194
  Berlin conference 1908 and, 189
  Bible College in St. Petersburg and, 263
  Bible School in Moscow and, 264
  BWA and, 198
  ECU, 198
  forges identity of, 197
  expansion of, 256
  Kargel
    influence of, 290, 298
    representative in Berlin of, 188
  merged with Evangelical Christian Union, 265
  origin of, 124, 130
  pacifism and, 257–58, 260
  Pavlov elected president of, 162
  tripled their numbers in seven years, 256
  view on Calvinism and Arminianism, 290
Russian Christian Youth Movement, 193
Russian Evangelical Alliance, 129, 203
  Prokhanov's intention to start, 200
  signatories of, 200
"Russian Evangelical Church in Finland," 146–47
"Russian Fellowship of Evangelical Christians in Finland," 145–46
Russian nationalism, Konstantin Pobedonostsev on, 12
Russian Orthodox Church
  Bolsheviks and, 256
  Johann G. Kargel, and, 12–17
  national culture and, 12–13
  view of salvation, 12
  See also Orthodox Church
Russian Revolution, 254
Russia's Lost Reformation, 16
Russo-Turkish War, 82
Rustchuk
  baptisms in, 92
  described, 85
  Kargel's work in, 84, 87, 89–92
Rustchuk Baptist church, Baptist Union of Bulgaria established in, 116
Ruth the Moabitess, 182–83, 209

Sagradovka, meeting in Rückenau attended by Christians from, 119
Saint Petersburg
  Bible College, 178, 204–8
    receives funding from BWA, 264
  first Baptist church in, 49
  George Müller's visit to, 61
  Kargels and
    1875–1880, 47–79
    1884–1887, 105–38
    1898–1909, 178–217
    assists work in, 40
    breaks with German Baptist, 105–6
    German Baptist life in, 48–53
    Lord Radstock's influence, 57–61
    ministry in, 106–10
    publishing efforts, 208–17

Saint Petersburg (*cont.*)
  members added to the church, 63–64
  Ondra baptizes believers in, 52
  Pashkov and the Evangelical Alliance, 121–24
  Pashkovite movement in, 6
  problems
    in church, 98–99
    with government in, 106–7
"Saint Petersburg Community of Evangelical Christians," registration of, 195
Saint Petersburg Evangelicals, 147
  Kargel's expanded contacts through, 109
  pacifism and, 257
  split among, 107–9
  tensions among, 191
Sakharov brothers, 126, 129
Salvation
  Kargel and, 8–9, 288
  Orthodox view of, 12
  three features of, 273–74
Salvation Army, 110
Sanctification, 96
  experience of by Kargel's, 94–96
  follows justification, 272
  Kargel's view of, 230, 246, 268
  Keswick Convention and, 11, 136, 271
  necessity of, 246
  repressionism and, 232–34
Sanctified life, 218–52
  element of crisis and, 223–26
  evangelical unity and, 243–45
  exaltation of faith and, 226–29
  Kargel's emphasis on, 219–23
  premillennialism and, 239–43
  repressionism and, 232–34
  romantic affinities and, 234–39
  sense of internal peace and rest and, 230–32
  suffering and, 249–52

  work of the Holy Spirit and, 245–49
Sängerfest, 155
Sankey, Ira, 137
Saratov, 148
  Kargel visits, 114
Schemacha, Kargel visits, 168–69
Schiewe, Adam Reinhold, 42
  banished to Poland, 64
  becomes pastor at Sorotschin German Baptist Church, 40
  Erik Jansson meets, 144–45
  Kargel and, 98–99
  questioned about Kargel's income, 109
  raises money in America, 115
  studies at Hamburg Mission School, 42
Schulz, J., St. Petersburg and, 49–50
Schwan, J., Ondra and, 51–52
Schwegler, D., officiated opening of Bucharest Baptist Church, 98
Scroggie, Graham, 231
Sears, Barnas, Johann Oncken baptized by, 28
Second Advent of Christ, 185–86
  Keswick Convention on, 11
  premillennialism and, 239–43
Second Evangelical Christian congregation, 196
Semenova, Anna Alexandrovna
  Kargel and, 71–72
  marriage of, 72–73, 296
SESER (Society for the Encouragement of Spiritual and Ethical Reading), 68
Sevastopol, Kargel and Baedeker travel to, 112
Sheldrake, Philip, *Spirituality and History*, 20
Shunning, 126
Shusha, Kargel visits, 162, 168–69

Sievers, Jacob (Count), Oncken defends German evangelicals to, 48, 50
Signatory of Russian Evangelical Alliance, 200
Simpson, A. B., 216
Sin
  Christ redeemed humanity from, 136, 180–81
  Godet's view of, 271
  Kargel's view of, 9, 180–82, 227–28, 233–34, 271–78, 287
  Keswick theology and, 11
  rules over or enslaved to, 276
Sin and salvation, Baedeker lectures on, 113
Sin and Sanctification, course taught by Kargel, 205–6, 301
Sin, the Evil of All Evils in this World, 211
Singapore, Kargel visits, 163
Skopina, Irina N., 2, 3, 195
Smirnova, Maria Maksimovna, 146
Smith, Hannah Whitall, 10
Smith, Robert Pearsall, 10
  presents Holiness message to St. Petersburg Germans, 111
Society for the Encouragement of Spiritual and Ethical Reading (SESER), 68
Soltau, Henry W., 183, 187
Sonship, 283–84
Sorotschin German Baptist Church, 49
  establishes preaching stations, 40
  Kargel's first pastorate, 36–41
  persecuted by Lutherans, 38
Southern Baptist Convention, St. Petersburg Bible College and, 264

Soviet Socialist Republics (USSR), 254
  military service as litmus test, 258
Speaking in tongues, 186
Spener, Philip, 7–8
Spirituality, Kargel disappointed with Baptist, 133–35
Spirituality and History, 20
Spurgeon, Charles, 44, 187, 304
  on Baptism and salvation, 57
Spurgeon's College, 42
  V. A. Felter studied at, 201
Stalin, Joseph
  gains control of the government, 254–55
  spiritual awakening cut short by, 257
Statement of faith
  Friesen's, 266
  German Baptist, 31
  Hamburg, 266
    Kargel and, 268
    view on Calvinism and Arminianism, 286
  importance of AUCEC-B, 265
  Kargel's, 9, 183–84, 265–67, 286
  mentioned in *The History of Evangelical Christians-Baptists in the USSR*, 265–66
  Oncken's, 265
  Prokhanov's, 265
  Russian, 268, 298
Sternberg (Baron), 142
Stockholm, Lord Radstock preaches in, 67
Stockmayer, Otto, 109, 187
  visits Kargel in St. Petersburg, 110
Studism, in the Ukraine, 6
"Studobaptist," 34
Stundo-baptist movement, 17, 34, 125, 266

Suffering
  God's will and, 270
  sanctified life and, 249–52
Sumy Province
  Kargel
    invited to come to, 260
    returns to, 290
    travels to, 253
    work in, 262
Svensson, Johannes, 202

Tabernacle, Kargel's view of, 180–83, 209
Tabolsk, Kargel visits, 163
Taurida Province, Kargel's and, 98, 109
Ternovenko, Victor Mikhailovich, opposes Kargel family, 261
Theosis, Orthodox view of, 12
Tiege, Kargel's and, 98
Tiflis Baptist Church,
  begun by Kalweit, 295
  compared to Russian Baptists, 37–38
  emigration assistance plan and, 161
  greetings sent to Odessa, 36
  Kargel
    baptized by, 23
    helps found, 112
    officiated at founding of, 112
    writes letter about, 113
  Kargel and Baedeker work in, 112–14
  Karl Kalweit baptized by, 26
  meeting in Rückenau attended by Christians from, 119
  sent "mite" to Onchen, 25
Timashev, A. E., supports Pashkov, 67
Tjirmen, Kargel visits, 163
To the Ends of the Earth: Among the Brothers in Chains, 22

Tokara
  Kargel returns to, 290
  Kargels life in, 261–62
Tokyo, Kargel visits, 163
Tomsk, Kargel visits, 163
Torrey, R. A., 192
Trepov, Fydor (General), supports Pashkov, 67
Tschita, Kargel visits, 163
Tsymbal, Efim, 17
"Tuesday Meetings for the Promotion of Holiness," 9
Tultscha, Romania
  Baptist Church, 73
  emigration assistance plan and, 161
  Wieler becomes pastor in, 121
Turchaninov, Dimitry, 2, 3, 70

Uklein, Simon, 14
Ukraine
  Studism in, 6
  villagers resettled to, 16
Unconditional election, 288
Unger, Abraham, 17
  Khortitsa settlement and, 33
  Oncken's influence on, 30–31
  ordained by Oncken, 31
Üxküll, Woldemar (Baron), 189, 190
  advocated local training of ministers, 205–6, 204–5

Vertograd, 152
Vladikavkaz
  Baedeker and Kargel visit, 114
  meeting in Rückenau attended by Christians from, 119
Vogel, Julius
  graduate of Hamburg Mission School, 42
  studies at Hamburg Mission School, 42
Volhynia Province, Kargel and, 98, 109, 157

Voronin, Nikita Isaevich, 14
   encourages Molokans to be baptized, 15
   Yakov Deliakovich Deliakov and, 25
Vyborg, Finland, Kargel moves to, 140, 143–47

Wahrheitszeuge, 3–4, 64
   Drumnidov's letter published in, 83
Ward, W. R., *The Protestant Evangelical Awakening*, 7
Wartemjagi, Anna Kargel takes daughters to, 172
Weist, Wihelm, Adamov German Baptist church and, 30
Wesleyan Holiness, 96
What is Your Relationship to the Holy Spirit?, 186–87, 245, 268, 301
   conversion discussed, 179
   Elisha and Elijah discussed, 248–49
   fruit of the Spirit discussed, 238
   republished, 185
   translated into Bulgarian, 212
Where are the Dead according to the Scriptures, 214–15, 241
White Army, 254
Whitefield, George, 8
Wieler, Gehard, 30
   Khortitsa settlement and, 33
Wieler, Johann, 13, 30, 119, 190
   death of, 130
   embraced idea of open Table, 117
   evangelical unity and, 243
   flees Russia, 121
   friendship with Kargel, 35–36
   Khortitsa settlement and, 33
   meeting in Rückenau and, 119–20
   in Molotschna Settlement, 3

Nove-Vasilevka conference and, 124–28
   outcome of, 128–33
Oncken's friendship with, 35
pastor in Tultscha, Romania, 121
Tiege and, 98 Johann Wieler settles3
Windolf, Emil, 40
World Congress of Baptist, first, 190
World Missionary Conference in Edinburgh, John Mott presides at, 193
Worms, Kargel visits, 141
Woterdorff, Ernest G., 187
Wuest, Eduard, Russian Mennonite brethren and, 32–33

Xodyush, Yakov Nikitich, 199–200
Xristianin, 192
   Christ—Our Sanctification published in, 215

Zhidkov, Yakov Ivanovich, 188
   Baptist Congress report by, 190
   becomes leader of Evangelical Christian Union, 191
   elected BWA vice-president, 198–99
   letter from Kargel on military service, 258–59
   Prokhanov's assistant in St. Petersburg, 195
Zhitomir, Kargel and, 97–98,
Zhuk, Sergei I., *Russia's Lost Reformation*, 16
Zinzendorf, Nicolas Von, 8
Zionsbote, 4, 208
   Kargel article on Ruth published in, 209
Zwischen den Enden der Erde: Unter Bruedern in Ketten, 22, 214

www.ingramcontent.com/pod-product-compliance
Lightning Source LLC
Chambersburg PA
CBHW071231290426
44108CB00013B/1374